Advance Praise for *Over Work*

"A bold vision for transforming work from a burden that takes over our lives into an activity that enriches them. Brigid Schulte is a vital voice on the future of work, and her carefully researched book lights the way to fewer hours, less stress, and more meaning." —**Adam Grant**, #1 *New York Times* bestselling author of *Think Again* and *Hidden Potential* and host of the podcast *WorkLife*

"*Over Work* illuminates diverse change agents driven by visions of a fairer, more fulfilling work-life paradigm. Brigid Schulte weaves captivating storytelling with essential data to expose the roots and ramifications of our overworked society, while spotlighting innovative solutions. Through tales of resilience and resistance, from advocating for better labor laws to fostering individual agency, *Over Work* urges readers to challenge entrenched myths, embrace meaningful change, and envision a future where work truly works for all."

—**Heather McGhee**, bestselling author of *The Sum of Us: What Racism Costs Everyone and How We Can Prosper Together*

"Revelatory and inspiring, *Over Work* delivers the hopeful news that real change is possible. While we've all been tied to the grind, workers of every kind—from domestic workers to CEOs—have been building a movement, refusing to accept that our punishing, perilous way of work is the only way to organize our lives. The stories captured in Schulte's book point to the possibility of an economy where we move beyond winners and losers to shared opportunity and true progress." —**Ai-jen Poo**, president of the National Domestic Workers Alliance and author of *The Age of Dignity*

"As with her first book, *Overwhelmed*, Brigid Schulte has once again captured the zeitgeist and brought it home to us with a mix of unforgettable people and unacceptable facts. The American workplace needs the same kind of dramatic transformation that Henry Ford created a century ago. *Over Work* shows us how." —**Anne-Marie Slaughter**, CEO of New America and author of *Unfinished Business: Women Men Work Family*

"In her fantastic new book, Brigid Schulte combines meticulous research with compelling profiles to argue that the exhausting way we work is a choice. More sustainable and equitable options are possible, but only if we're willing to engage at the societal level in the hard but necessary work of making needed change." —**Cal Newport**, *New York Times* bestselling author of *Slow Productivity*

"Brigid Schulte is one of America's foremost caretakers of the idea of care. In *Over Work*, she argues that care work *must* be respected and economically supported. The book's data is striking, as are its stories of workers who have made awful sacrifices on the altar of success, including a lawyer whose heart actually wore out from stressful labor. But Schulte also presents surprising, happy experiments, as in Scotland, where care labor is properly remunerated. *Over Work* will stick with you."

—**Alissa Quart**, author of *Bootstrapped* and *Squeezed*

"*Over Work* is a powerful, hard-hitting critique of the shabby, callous way that many American corporations treat their workers, whether at fast-food companies or fancy law firms. Well researched and well argued, the book proposes changes and examines companies and countries with innovative policies that ensure workers are treated humanely and with respect."

—**Steven Greenhouse**, author of *Beaten Down, Worked Up*

"*Over Work* tells the story of a dystopian society in which humans are inputs into just-in-time delivery work shifts controlled by algorithms and mothers are forced to choose between working to feed their children or staying home to care for them. It would make for good sci-fi if it weren't real—but it is. Fortunately, Brigid Schulte delves into solutions—public policy and private sector strategies—that point us in a new direction. *Over Work* is a must-read for anyone who cares about the strength of the American economy and the people who propel it."

—**Heather McCulloch**, senior fellow, Aspen Institute Financial Security Program

"For anyone who has ever felt overwhelmed or burnt out due to work, it is not your fault. Work systems were designed to keep us devoted to our jobs at the expense of our families and personal lives. *Over Work* is a call to action for work cultures that allow everyone to have meaningful lives and be more productive employees. A must-read!"

—**Amy Diehl**, author of *Glass Walls: Shattering the Six Gender Bias Barriers Still Holding Women Back at Work*

Over Work

ALSO BY BRIGID SCHULTE

Overwhelmed: How to Work, Love,

and Play When No One Has the Time

Over Work

Transforming the Daily Grind in the Quest for a Better Life

BRIGID SCHULTE

HENRY HOLT AND COMPANY
NEW YORK

Henry Holt and Company
Publishers since 1866
120 Broadway
New York, New York 10271
www.henryholt.com

Henry Holt® and Ⓗ® are registered trademarks of
Macmillan Publishing Group, LLC.

Distributed in Canada by Raincoast Book Distribution Limited

Library of Congress Cataloging-in-Publication Data

Names: Schulte, Brigid, 1962– author.
Title: Over work : transforming the daily grind in the quest for a better life / Brigid Schulte.
Description: First edition. | New York, NY : Henry Holt and Company, [2024] | Includes bibliographical references and index.
Identifiers: LCCN 2024014061 | ISBN 9781250801722 (hardcover) | ISBN 9781250801739 (ebook)
Subjects: LCSH: Quality of life. | Work-life balance.
Classification: LCC HN25 .S37 2024 | DDC 306—dc23/eng/20240425
LC record available at https://lccn.loc.gov/2024014061

First Edition 2024

Designed by Omar Chapa

Printed in the United States of America

1 2 3 4 5 6 7 8 9 10

To April Kimbrough, Kiarica Schields, Kari McCracken, Brittany and Danielle Williams, and all those who work so hard and sacrifice so much to care for others

CONTENTS

PROLOGUE

Meaning, Fairness, Cooperation

> All human beings, irrespective of race, creed or sex, have the right to pursue both their material wellbeing and their spiritual development in conditions of freedom and dignity, of economic security and equal opportunity.
>
> —*International Labor Organization, Declaration of Philadelphia, 1944*[1]

I love my work. Perhaps too much. Work shapes my days and gives me a sense of meaning and purpose. But what I mean by work is not only the reporting, research, and writing that I do for my paid job (and as paid jobs become more complex, the managing, fundraising, brainstorming, organizing, speechmaking, going to meetings, and answering the emails that demand more time and attention than I will ever have). I also mean the unpaid work I do at home to make it a home, that connects me with family, community, and people I care for and who care for me—everything ordinary and extraordinary that makes life joyful, rich, surprising, complicated, and truly worth living. The soup I cooked yesterday. The job application I talked through with my son and the school essay I helped a friend's son with. The tuition bill I paid for my daughter. The cough medicine I ran out to buy for my husband. The laundry I folded, the dishes I washed, and the plumber I called. The leaves I raked from our enormous pin oak so they wouldn't keep blowing into our neighbors' yards. All the years spent raising children, preparing meals, searching for the right gifts, planning family events, volunteering in classrooms and my community, and cleaning out and organizing what amounted to 351 years of artifacts of various family members crammed into boxes in my ninety-two-year-old mother's attic. It is all the work of my life.

In his masterful book *The Story of Work*, which traces our relationship with work from the earliest humans to the modern day, Dutch historian Jan Lucassen defines work broadly as "all human pursuits apart from free time or leisure." That expansive definition encompasses all the unpaid labor of home and care that has traditionally fallen mostly on the shoulders of women. It is enormously valuable work. In economic terms alone, including that unpaid labor in our gross domestic product would, according to feminist economist Nancy Folbre, boost it by 25 to 40 percent.[2] So the first of the three main arguments of this book, then, is that when we talk about work, it is time to think of it more comprehensively to encompass both what we do for pay and our unpaid labors of care and home.

The second argument: All of that work, paid and unpaid, needs to be good work.

Good work, Lucassen argues, depends on three principles: cooperation, meaning, and fairness.

Much as we Americans are enamored of the myth of individual striving and making it on our own, humans have only been able to stay alive and evolve from early hunter-gatherer societies to our modern, complex way of life by cooperating, working together, and caring for each other.

That work has also been, in the best of times, a source of meaning, pleasure, identity, purpose. It has furnished us with our daily bread for survival, as well as served as a way to show that we belong in the world, that we matter. In Studs Terkel's book *Working*, featuring interviews with more than one hundred workers of all types, readers were surprised by the sense of meaning that people derived from their work. It wasn't just the high-profile Hollywood agent, professional jockey, and CEO, who had the kinds of jobs people tend to think of as exciting. It was also the telephone switchboard operator, cop, and autoworker, who often toiled in obscurity.[3] In my interviews, too, with workers of all types over the years, I've heard the same feelings of pride and meaning in work, whether among exhausted doctors and nurses sacrificing their own health to save lives, or the home care workers who know exactly what music to play, food to cook, or hairstyle to give an elderly client. It is the same with the shelf stocker who lines up merchandise just so and cares far more about the big-box store where he works than that store will ever care for him. Or the restaurant waitstaff—the majority of whom are women[4]—who deliver service with a smile, both because they want to and because they won't be able to pay their bills on their unlivable $2.13-an-hour federal tipped minimum wage unless happy customers leave them a little extra with the check.[5]

When it comes to fairness, in the worst of times, when work is exploitative, a way for the powerful to coerce others and take more of the fruits of their labor, then workers have banded together and acted to balance the scales, motivated by the deep human drive for fairness. Union workers strike for better conditions, better pay, and time in their lives for both bread and roses, as the old protest song goes. Even unpaid workers have joined together in pursuit of fairness. The women and mothers in Iceland, for instance, fed up with persistent gender pay, wealth, and opportunity gaps, famously organized a "day off" in the 1970s, refusing to do either paid or unpaid work. That left men scrambling to buy hot dogs for dinner and effectively shut the country down.[6] The International Wages for Housework campaign, Black Women for Wages for Housework, and Global Women's Strike groups have been fighting since the 1970s for recognition of the value of the unpaid labor in the home done primarily by women.[7] And overburdened women and mothers who've had it with the unfair and often unspoken expectation that they'll just do it all at home, regardless of whether they work for pay or are the family breadwinner,[8] are more likely to seek a divorce or sever a relationship,[9] even if that leaves them in a more financially precarious position.[10]

Finally, I argue that now is the time to change the way we work, that this change is entirely possible, and it's up to us to make it happen.

As grueling as the Covid-19 pandemic was, the global disruption showed us just how much work and care could change, for better and for worse, literally overnight. After years of resisting flexible and remote work, insisting it was incompatible with productivity, managers were abruptly forced to make it happen. People who were able to do their work from home began seeing colleagues' laundry rooms, bedrooms, children, and dogs—the invisible side of our lives and unpaid work—through a virtual connection. There was an explosion of digital nomads who worked from wherever they liked.[11] Disabled employees[12] and people of color[13] working from home reported feeling less stress and that their managers and colleagues focused more on the quality of their work and performance rather than on their identity.

Though burnout, shapeless workdays, and screen fatigue ran rampant, more people reported feeling more autonomy over their lives.[14] Hours shifted and became more flexible. Americans spent sixty million fewer hours commuting to their jobs every day.[15] They filled their time instead with more productive, concentrated work[16] and, with seventy-two additional minutes a day,[17] relished things like having regular family meals. Some even found or rediscovered hobbies[18]—a word that a writer once confessed to me she had actually forgotten in the rush of modern life.

Millions retired early.[19] Hundreds of thousands, the majority of them women, started working for themselves.[20] Tens of millions quit jobs at astronomical rates[21] in search of something better or more meaningful.

The changes didn't go far enough. Millions of mothers were forced out of the workforce to care for children, with mothers of color hit the hardest.[22] Millions more had to reduce hours or quit jobs to care for ailing spouses, siblings, aging parents, and grandchildren.[23] We temporarily rewarded the millions of low-wage delivery drivers, warehouse workers, caregivers, and grocery store clerks whom we called "essential" and "heroes" with evenings of applause and a few extra dollars per hour. Congress then showed them how disposable they are by cutting as many as one hundred million off from temporary legislation granting workers emergency paid sick and child-care leave.[24]

Despite the evidence that giving workers more control and flexibility over their work lives enabled them to be more productive, skeptical managers snapped up surveillance software to track keystrokes, take random screenshots, and otherwise spy on employees,[25] convinced they must be slacking off.

It may take years, if not a generation or more, for the pandemic disruptions to settle into a new normal of work. But the direction must point forward toward something better. "The idea that we're ever going to go back to work like we did in 2019 is a myth," Dr. John Howard, director of the National Institute for Occupational Safety and Health, has said. "Flexibility is here to stay."[26]

In our modern world of work and in the technologically driven labor of the future, nothing is preordained. As writer and economist Heather McGhee put it, "everything we believe comes from a story we've been told."[27] We are limited only by the horizon of our imaginations and the stories we tell ourselves about the way things ought to be. Our modern story of work is divorced from reality, and an astoundingly myopic failure of vision, one that has led to an exhausting daily grind. We are over work. Done. It is time for a better story. That's where this book begins.

Because work has not been working for far too many people for far too long.

In the United States, you must work for pay to survive. There are few protections for workers, regardless how unfair the circumstances, compared to other advanced countries, and little support for working families. If you lose your job or you can't work, there is no real safety net to catch you. And if a low-wage service job is all you can find, rather than being a starter job or a placeholder until you find something better, as many policymakers think, you may just end up stuck there.[28]

No longer is paid work a vehicle for moving families closer to lives of independence, freedom, and security, nor does it advance the nation toward greater shared prosperity. Work has instead become a source of both inequality and insecurity.

There is much handwringing in the press about how higher wages lead to inflation. But this simplistic story ignores the fact that productivity soared by nearly 65 percent between 1979 and 2021, while wages nudged up only by about 17 percent. Compare that to 1945 to 1979: productivity rose 118 percent; wages rose 107 percent. For nearly the past half century, it is the owners and shareholders who have been benefiting from workers' labor.[29] Today CEOs earn orders of magnitudes more than workers[30] and profits flow to the top 1 percent, at the cost of increasing precarity and instability for everyone else.[31] Business practices that in recent decades have steered profits to shareholders rather than to workers[32] have contributed to grotesquely unfair inequality across race, class, gender, and ability: the United States now registers the highest income inequality of all G7 countries.[33]

"If we had the same relationship that existed in 1965 between productivity and wages, the world would be a very, very different place," Dave Regan, president of one of the largest hospital unions in the western United States, told me. Indeed, one 2020 study by the Rand Corporation estimated that, between 1975 and 2018, nearly *$50 trillion* shifted from the bottom 90 percent to the top 1 percent of Americans.[34] "That is so gargantuan it's obscene," Regan said. The American Dream, which held that each generation surpasses the one before it and enjoys more economic security, is fading: In the 1940s, 90 percent of children could expect to do better financially than their parents. Now, about half will, and the odds are much lower for Black and Native American children.[35]

Despite a media that obsesses over every release of new jobs numbers to predict the health of the economy, nowhere is there a discussion of whether the jobs being created are actually big enough to sustain human life. Of all advanced economies, the United States, the wealthiest country on Earth, ranks *fifth*, behind Israel, Bulgaria, Croatia, and Latvia, for having the largest share of low-wage workers.[36] These workers are more than twice as likely to live in poverty as those in the general workforce.[37] They also suffer disproportionate job losses, financial strain, sickness, and—during the pandemic—death.[38] Which raises the question: wealthiest country for whom?

People find themselves working harder and harder and feeling as if they're falling farther and farther behind.[39] Overwork has become a fact of life in the United States. Most of us spend about one-third of our waking lives at work. But Americans spend among the longest hours engaged in paid work of any advanced economy—save South Korea.[40] Americans also put in more time working "strange" evening and weekend hours than workers in European countries.[41] But what the data doesn't capture is all the free labor workers do in a 24/7 economy: late nights and weekends spent finishing work tasks, catching up on emails, or getting a jump on the week ahead. It doesn't account for how work seeps into the pores—the mental bandwidth taken up with thinking about work—such a common phenomenon that it's called "work-related rumination"[42]—or the anxious energy expended worrying about getting unexpected messages from the boss or waiting for the week's schedule to drop at the last minute, and agonizing over whether it will include enough hours to pay the rent.[43]

As in so much of our unequal society, how you experience overwork depends on your position on the socioeconomic ladder.

A professional or knowledge worker may overwork in one job. In a number of professions, intensive paid work—bordering on self-sacrificing workaholism—has become expected, especially in billable hour cultures where more hours mean more money, and as firms consistently have cut their workforces without reducing workloads, expecting fewer people to do more.[44] As work has become more demanding—some economists call it "greedy"[45]—

knowledge workers often end up tying their identity and meaning almost entirely to their jobs. Writer Derek Thompson dubs it the new religion of "workism."[46] Yet as I watched another wave of massive layoffs in Silicon Valley, the media, and other sectors in early 2024,[47] I would argue that workism may be less a conscious choice than an imperative driven by fear to survive in what's become an unforgiving world of paid work.

For the fifty-three million people in America with a low-wage job—an astonishing 44 percent of the workforce[48]—the overwork story is different. Rather than overwork in one job, many must string together a series of poorly paid jobs, gigs, or part-time side hustles just to make ends meet, often with no benefits like health care or retirement savings.

The cashier who speedily checked me out at the grocery store the other day works there on the weekends because her full-time job at a nonprofit service organization doesn't pay enough to cover her rent. A full-time minimum-wage job is no longer sufficient to rent a two-bedroom apartment in any city, county, or state in the United States.[49] The Uber driver in her seventies who picked me up one day explained that she spends hours on the road so she can pay for her heart medication. And when a low-wage worker isn't juggling two or three jobs, struggling to manage unpredictable schedules while figuring out child or elder care, or working long past retirement age, they are expending precious time and attention jumping through the often-convoluted administrative hurdles that it takes to apply for public benefits to help them survive.

Despite all the angry rhetoric about how people just need to work harder, or how those who rely on public benefits are lazy, 70 percent of those who receive federal Medicaid and food assistance actually work full-time in poorly paying jobs.[50] The problem isn't with the workers. It's with the quality of work corporate America chooses to offer and that U.S. policymakers enable. We often hear that low-wage workers just need more education or better training to get better jobs. Yet that begs the question: what better jobs?

In 2023, companies complained that they just couldn't find

workers to fill job openings. They blamed what they called this labor shortage on the fact that workers must not want to work. The truth, however, was that companies and sectors that were offering stable jobs with good wages and benefits were able to find plenty of willing workers.[51]

But rather than offer life-sustaining work, with decent pay, livable hours, time off work, access to health care, and benefits like help with child care, some companies and states sought instead to weaken child labor laws. The effort was orchestrated in part by a conservative anti-regulation campaign[52] and was pushed in states where the hourly minimum wage hasn't changed, or changed much, since Congress raised it to $7.25 an hour in 2009. (For restaurant workers, the federal tipped minimum wage is $2.19 an hour. For disabled workers, the subminimum wage is as little as 25 cents an hour.)[53] A Hyundai supplier in Alabama employed workers as young as twelve. And in Nebraska, the Department of Labor cited a meat producer for "oppressive child labor,"[54] which has been against the law since 1938.[55]

Work is also becoming increasingly precarious. Company leaders, taught in business school that labor is a wasteful liability to be cut out of the budget rather than an asset to be cultivated, regularly slash jobs to "right size" or outsource them either overseas or to a myriad of subcontractors or temporary employment agencies. Now, independent, contract, and gig workers in unstable jobs, once a rarity, comprise 36 percent of the workforce.[56]

Yet even white-collar jobs that were once considered prestigious and secure have also become more precarious since the 1970s.[57] Taken in by buzzy trends like "lean" efficiency, companies adopted high-stakes, high-stress "tournament" up-or-out promotion structures that drive overwork and pit workers against each other, gladiator style, in the hopes that they'll be the one left standing.[58]

Frequent brutal layoffs have become standard business practice for workers of all types so business leaders can make their short-term balance sheets look better to Wall Street investors. Layoffs are bad for workers. They cause extraordinary stress and, research shows, increase mortality by as much as 20 percent in subsequent years.[59] But layoffs are bad for business, too. They do more damage to companies in the long run.[60]

Yet the practice continues. Research shows that the proliferation of managers with MBAs indoctrinated with this "labor as waste" belief is not only behind layoffs but a big reason why workers' wages have fallen in recent decades.[61] Many of these same leaders are also responsible for creating toxic work cultures that demand total work devotion—often signaled by long work hours—and drive burnout and high quit rates.[62] A toxic work culture is ten times more likely to lead someone to leave than low pay,[63] which Gallup estimates winds up costing shortsighted U.S. businesses an unnecessary $1 trillion a year.[64]

All this overwork and uncertainty robs people of time and energy for leisure, love, and friendship. It keeps us from getting to know our neighbors, volunteering, becoming active in civic life or voting. And it makes it close to impossible to combine paid work and the unpaid work of care, family, and home.

As the scholar Adia Harvey Wingfield told me, "Most of us are not people who can live off investments. Most need to work to pay for housing and actually eat. There's got to be a way that allows us to do those things, contribute to the economy, and not suffer so much."

For workers with caregiving responsibilities, paid work has never been fair.

Avni Malik, a young medical student, eagerly went to a special lunch lecture on family planning for women in the medical field. Malik had wanted to be a doctor from the time she was five. She worked diligently through high school and college, taking a heavy load of tough classes—she studied premed *and* got a degree in computer science with a minor in Spanish—and volunteering as an emergency medical technician, performing research, and getting a master's degree in data science. She wanted both a meaningful paid career—a calling—helping to heal people and a full and happy family life. She had visions of picking her children up from school, sharing regular meals with her family, and having time to sleep and take care of her own health. But after the hour-long lecture, she emerged depressed, stressed, and questioning her life choices. The message? "Freeze your eggs," Malik said. Put off having children as long as possible, then prepare to rarely see them. "They advised us to find a residency program with insurance that covers fertility preservation. It was pretty disappointing."

That's the best advice we give to aspiring women doctors? Either you devote yourself to your job in the public sphere and postpone or forgo a rich home life, *or* you choose to have a family to love and care for in the private sphere and limit your expectations for what you contribute to the world. Young male medical students aren't faced with the same impossible dilemma. Their total focus on the job is assumed. In American overwork culture, such single-minded dedication to work is expected of an "ideal worker." They aren't supposed to have caregiving distractions or family demands. Someone else—usually a woman—is expected to tend to that. That has made paid work a masculine domain,[65] where men are far more likely to rise into leadership roles and earn more money and where gender bias and sexual harassment are as commonplace as wallpaper.[66]

A majority of women and mothers have participated in the paid workforce for decades.[67] Seventy percent can expect to be their family's top breadwinner at some point during the first eighteen years of motherhood.[68] A majority of the nation's children are being raised in families where all available parents work.[69] Yet the prevailing story that work is a man's world has meant paid work hasn't changed to make room for care: it is still difficult for most people to do both without penalty.

We're still wedded to the idea that paid work is what is valuable. Paid work, not the time spent on unpaid labor, is what we factor into GDP—an equation developed in the Depression-era 1930s to determine the monetary value of goods and services produced and bought or sold on the market in any given country. Even though the equation's creator, economist Simon Kuznets, cautioned against adopting GDP as a measure of a nation's health, wellbeing, or its success, that's exactly what's happened.[70] The paid care work done as a job for others counts as valuable. The unpaid care that primarily women and mothers do for their own families doesn't.[71] That, our national story goes, is a sacred labor of love.[72]

Though we talk about the importance of care in this nation of "family values," all you have to do is look at paid care work, most of which is done by women, and women of color, to see that we don't prize it highly at all. The median hourly income for child-care workers in the United States was $13.71 in 2022.[73] Nearly half earn so little that they qualify for public benefits.[74] Home care jobs are predicted to be not just one of the fastest-growing fields but *the largest occupation in the economy by 2032*[75] as the population ages and we all live longer with more chronic illnesses that will require more intensive support. In 2022, the median income for home health and personal care aides was $12.15 an hour, with no benefits and irregular hours.

In truth, there are few ideal workers. One Harvard Business School survey found that three out of every four workers of all genders have some kind of caregiving duties.[76] Men striving to live up to the ideal worker norm may be able to keep their caregiving duties quiet and under the radar, successfully playing the role of the fully enlisted ideal worker.[77] Women with care responsibilities cannot play the same game, and they pay a steep penalty in pay and opportunity as a result.[78] But men suffer, too. Prevented from participating fully in both the day-to-day drudgery and the moments of pure, inspired joy that come with the care of home and family, or time for oneself, many look back on their lives with regret.[79]

For workers with care responsibilities, the pandemic crucible was more of a Great Push.[80] Some economists argued the unprecedented quit rates of what they dubbed the Great Resignation were due to workers looking for something better or reassessing what was important in life as we all confronted the nearness of mortality. But I'd argue that for women, who took on the majority of the care work as schools and child and elder care facilities shut down, the pandemic left them yearning for a yet-to-come Great Reimagining of work and care.

I met both Kari McCracken, a former district sales manager and operations supervisor for Coca-Cola in Kentucky, and Kiarica Schields, a former hospice nurse in Georgia, early in the pandemic and began to follow their stories. Both are mothers and love caring for their families. But they also loved their paid work, needed the income to support their families, and took pride in their jobs, which helped shape their identities. Both were forced out of paid work when they lost their child-care arrangements in pandemic closures. Both suffered. In the fall of 2023, more than three and a half years after the start of the pandemic, neither woman had managed to find the kind of flexible work arrangement and affordable child care that would have enabled them to return to paid work. One had even been living in a homeless shelter and shuffling between hotels with her four children for several months.

When she was a teen growing up outside of Atlanta, Georgia, Kiarica Schields's brother died of HIV complications. She was inspired by the hospice nurses who eased his pain and soothed his spirit and decided to do the same with her life. "I wanted to show people love, like those nurses had for my brother, and make their way out of life better, if I could," she told me. She received her RN degree from Columbus State University, juggling care for a newborn daughter, school, and working at a Waffle House. In 2011, she began working in home hospice care. She felt it was a calling, her mission in life.

By the time the pandemic broke out, she'd left an abusive marriage and taken her growing family of four children to live in a small town, where she earned $28 an hour as a hospice nurse. But with schools and child care closed down, no family nearby, and no paid leave available, she had no option other than to quit her paid job to care for her children. Millions of mothers and workers with care responsibilities were in the same position. Child care was difficult to find and afford long before the pandemic. But the crisis forced an estimated sixteen thousand child-care providers to shut down,[81] put tens of thousands of child-care workers out of work, and left countless families floundering.[82]

Without a paying job, Schields burned through her savings, racked up credit card debt, and scrambled to pay the rent. Her unemployment ran out in December 2020 and her appeal to be reinstated was denied, though she never understood why. She'd been taking on various odd jobs to try to make ends meet. She worked an overnight shift at UPS but worried about neighbors calling Child Protective Services if she left her children on their own with her then twelve-year-old daughter in charge. She lost that job and the family was evicted in March 2021, though Georgia's pandemic eviction moratorium didn't end until that summer. She doesn't understand this, either.

The family moved. She delivered for DoorDash, with the two-year-old strapped into his car seat in the back, but she netted only $5 an hour. She cooked meals to earn money as a caterer. She took in laundry. She tried hospice nursing again. But she began missing shifts because the school repeatedly called for her to pick up her son, who had begun acting out with all the instability. Considered unreliable, Schields lost that job. Schields's car was repossessed. The family was evicted again in September 2022. They moved in with Schields's mother, living with her brother and a niece—eight people in a two-bedroom apartment.

Schields sank into a deep depression. If her purpose was to care for others, who was she if she wasn't able to do that anymore? "It was ugly. I had suicidal thoughts," she told me at one point, weeping. "The only thing that saved me was thinking, 'Who the heck is going to raise my kids if I do something crazy?'"

Schields directed her despair toward activism, becoming an advocate for Unemployed Action, a group working to improve the unemployment insurance system. Still unable to find affordable child care that matched the ten- to twelve-hour shifts most jobs required, she'd taken a job as a volunteer coordinator for a homeless shelter, earning $20 an hour. It was enough to move her family into their own apartment, though she had to borrow her mother's car to get around. She tried to stay positive, she told me, playing upbeat music, singing and praying with her children, and reciting positive affirmations. "But I am not my best," she admitted. "To everyone else, they probably see me as doing good. But once I get home some nights, I cry."

She lost the shelter job after her health broke down, then worked in a prison and again took on odd jobs. Unable to pay bills or afford a rent increase on the new apartment, she once again lost her home. The family spent the summer and fall of 2023 in a homeless shelter and bouncing around cheap hotels. Deeply in debt, her credit shot, Schields wondered how she would ever recover, although she had high expectations for a new job lined up at a call center starting at $18 an hour. "I really hope I can get back to nursing, eventually," she said. "Maybe when my kids are older."

Kari McCracken is a mother of five and lives outside Louisville, Kentucky. She'd never finished college but worked at Coca-Cola in a job that she loved and was regularly promoted. Traveling in the field as district sales manager gave her flexibility over her schedule and location, which allowed her to manage both her paid work and caring for her family. "I really took pride in my work and what I was able to accomplish," she said. "I worked in a male-dominated industry, and I was able to be successful and be on top and just kick butt and not have people look down on me and think, 'She's a girl, she can't do anything.' I was able to show 'Yes, I can.'" When she shared her ten-year career plan with coworkers, they told her she could do it in five.

Like so many others, she was furloughed in April 2020 as the pandemic shut schools and businesses down. On June 8, she was told to report back to work. But with no child care, schools, or summer camp, with no family available to help her care for the children and a husband struggling to keep his own job, McCracken instead asked for personal leave. She didn't qualify for the emergency paid child-care leave Congress had passed that spring because Republican lawmakers in Congress pushed to exempt both small businesses and those with more than five hundred employees, like Coca-Cola. So McCracken, like millions of other workers, received nothing.[83]

Still, the company gave her leave until June 29 to figure out child care. When McCracken was unable to do so, she asked to extend her leave until September, hoping that schools and child-care facilities might open up again at the start of the school year. On June 30, her company denied the leave request. Unless she returned to work that week, the company would assume she had left voluntarily.[84] McCracken had no choice but to leave. Her male coworkers, whose spouses had primary responsibility for caregiving, all were able to return to work. "It tells a story," she said. "I never felt I was treated any differently because I was a woman, or that I was less than. And this was one point in my career where I felt less than."

McCracken reached out to lawyers at A Better Balance, a non-profit organization that runs a caregiver discrimination helpline. But she had no case. "Kentucky is a right-to-work state," McCracken explained. "So the company can let me go for any reason, basically. What they did was perfectly legal. But it wasn't moral."

In the years since, McCracken has applied for hundreds of jobs, but none offer her the flexible schedule she had in her previous position at the same pay and benefits. She received unemployment for a few months, relied on savings, and cut back on household expenses to manage the loss of her good middle-class salary. Though she was busy with homeschooling and care, she sank into a severe depression and had difficulty sleeping. Even the sleeping pills her doctor prescribed didn't make a dent in her insomnia. She had always loved showing her daughters how it was possible to combine good paid work and time for family and care. They were so proud of her. "My daughters are under the assumption that I lost my job because I was a mom," she said. "And that breaks my heart, because they blame themselves for it."

McCracken's former male coworkers shrugged at her story and told her she probably should have been home with her children anyway. "That hurt," she said. "My career was very important to me. It defined me in many ways. I feel like I've lost a lot of who I am."

The stories of Kiarica Schields and Kari McCracken and millions of others are common in the United States.

Virtually alone among advanced nations, the United States doesn't guarantee workers any paid time off.[85] There is no national paid family and medical leave policy, no paid sick days, no paid annual leave. What is considered a human right in other countries is instead consigned solely to the discretion of private employers (though a few states and cities have stepped in with regional paid leave or paid sick days policies). In the overworked United States, paid time off work is considered either a grudging perk, a privilege to attract high-wage "talent," or an unnecessary expense for just about everyone else.

Think of the rail workers who were willing to strike at the end of 2022, with potentially devastating consequences of $2 billion a day for the economy,[86] calling for paid time off work to care for themselves or their families when sick. The issue had become acute since, in the name of efficiency, the major railroads had cut their workforce by 30 percent over the previous decade. The move nearly doubled railway company profits, the bulk of which went to shareholders and stock buybacks. But it meant that fewer workers were available to cover all the shifts. So those who remained had to work more hours and with grueling and unpredictable schedules.[87] "Quality of life and time are our two goals," one union representative explained during tense negotiations.[88] With rail companies refusing to budge and the Biden administration worried that a strike could devastate the economy,[89] Congress passed legislation forcing the workers to accept a deal granting them one paid personal day a year.[90] The unions kept fighting, and by the summer of 2023 the majority of unionized rail workers at major railroads had won between four and five days of paid sick leave every year, with a provision to turn two or three paid personal days into paid sick days.[91]

Workers need paid family leave to recover from giving birth, to care for a new child, or to take care of their own health or that of a disabled, ill, or elderly loved one. Just 27 percent of private-sector workers received this benefit through their employers in March 2023. High-wage workers were eight times more likely to have paid family and medical leave than low-wage workers.[92] But even so, fewer than half of the highest-paid white-collar professional and managerial employees had access to it. One analysis found that, with no paid leave, one in four new mothers return to work within two weeks of giving birth,[93] a statistic as hard to believe as it is cruel.

That lack of paid time off is punishing, and not just for new mothers. The story of April Kimbrough continues to haunt me. Kimbrough lived in Colorado, working at a hospice triage call center and studying to be a nurse. As the pandemic shuttered businesses, she began working from home and received high marks for her performance. When her only child, Da'Corey, was diagnosed with a rare cancer that typically afflicts young adults of African descent and is nearly always fatal, she jumped on a plane to be with him in Atlanta. Doctors gave him four months to live. She continued working virtually and was able to spend time with her son and coordinate care for him. Then her office ordered all staff back to the worksite. Because Kimbrough had no paid time off, her only choices were to leave Da'Corey or lose her job.

Desperate to find help, it was then that Kimbrough was shocked to learn that she wasn't alone, that there is no federal law that guarantees paid time off for anyone in the country. She joined Colorado Families First, an advocacy organization campaigning to pass a statewide paid family and medical leave policy through a ballot measure, and shot an ad for them sharing her dilemma. A few weeks later, Kimbrough was fired.

In November 2020, Kimbrough celebrated when voters of all political persuasions overwhelmingly passed the new law mandating paid leave. But without her job, she was unable to pay her rent. She lost her apartment and for a time lived in her car. Kimbrough picked up waitressing gigs and delivered groceries for Instacart to pay for flights between nursing school in Colorado and caring for her son in Georgia. She graduated in 2021; Da'Corey died in 2022. He was twenty-five. "I felt sure there would be compassion for me," Kimbrough told me.[94] There was none.

Paid leave is designed to cover a short, acute period of time needed for caregiving. But caregiving lasts a lifetime, and in the United States, there is an utter lack of support for any of it. Unlike peer competitive nations that subsidize child care so it's affordable for families and pay living wages to child-care workers, the U.S. government doesn't. It invests among the least of any advanced nation.[95] New parents pay for expensive tuition out of pocket that can run up to as much as 20 percent of the family's income per child.[96] That tuition still doesn't cover the cost of care. So child-care workers earn poverty wages, and the small business and family providers who make up the majority of care facilities barely eke by, effectively subsidizing the entire system. Government subsidies for the very poor cover only a fraction of those eligible and come nowhere close to reimbursing providers what they actually need.[97]

Child care is so expensive because it takes a lot of people—teachers, child-care workers—to provide high-quality care. One child-care teacher is able to care for only a few infants or toddlers, while a kindergarten teacher might handle classes as large as twenty to thirty, depending on state law. K–12 public education is seen as a public good that benefits everyone, like libraries, parks, and national defense. So policymakers are willing to cover the estimated $16,000 per pupil cost every year.[98] But care and education for children birth to five is considered a private matter for families to figure out on their own—despite the long-lasting benefits of quality child care to society, like better school performance that leads to higher paying jobs and a happier, healthier workforce. For these reasons, U.S. Treasury Secretary Janet Yellen has called child care a "textbook example of a broken market."[99]

Germans, in contrast to Americans, have a legal right to child care for children ages one to three—most parents care for their infants in their first year through a robust universal paid leave policy.[100] Canada is committed to investing in universal child care infrastructure that costs families no more than $10 a day.[101]

Many families in the United States can't even *find* child care: more than half live in child-care deserts. As a result, one in four parents reported being fired from their jobs in 2022 because of child care breakdowns, which cost an estimated $122 billion in lost wages, productivity, and tax revenue.[102]

Strapped families are the nation's default for providing, organizing, and paying for the care of loved ones,[103] leading many to cut back their hours or leave paid work entirely, creating financial precarity.[104] In our national story, care is women's work. So, instead of investing in supportive policies to benefit everyone, individual families are forced to pay for their health, wellbeing, and survival out of their own pockets, which creates a perverse incentive to keep home care worker wages low in order for the broken care system to limp along. It's a policy choice that also keeps families working long hours to pay for it all.

The way we work and fail to make room for care comes at a significant cost. Rising work stress is associated with the rising incidence of chronic illness—high rates of cardiovascular disease, high blood pressure, diabetes, depression, anxiety, obesity, and insomnia, to name a few conditions. And the unpredictable scheduling so common in low-wage work leads to increased psychological distress for adults and harms the healthy development and wellbeing of children.[105] One 2015 study found that work stress alone is associated with $190 billion in health-care costs and up to 120,000 premature deaths in the United States every year, more than those caused by diabetes or Alzheimer's, and comparable to deaths from heart disease and accidents—the fourth- and fifth-leading causes of death in the country.[106]

We're unhappier, too. The U.S. Surgeon General reported that in 2021, nearly 76 percent of employees were struggling with at least one symptom related to a mental health condition like anxiety or depression, and 84 percent blamed at least one workplace factor, like emotionally draining work, lack of recognition, or challenges with work-life balance.[107] In their survey of workers in the United States, UK, Canada, and Australia, Deloitte's 2023 Well-Being at Work report found that 60 percent of employees—and even three-fourths of powerful C-suite executives—say they're considering quitting to find other paid jobs that would better support their wellbeing.[108] Around the globe, nearly 77 percent of workers say they're disengaged at work and more than half of the workers Gallup surveyed for its 2023 State of the Workplace said they're looking for the kind of work that would give them better quality of life.[109]

Overwork, impossible work-family conflict, and precarity are features of what I've come to think of as the "crappification" of paid work. In the past fifty years, the blue- and pink-collar jobs that were an entrée to the middle class and a stable quality of life have evaporated for a host of reasons: the clerks and secretaries were automated out of existence by answering machines, Microsoft Word, email, and Google docs; the factory workers were let go as the plants moved overseas, where labor is cheaper, or shut down entirely as taste or demand changed in an increasingly global market.

The Ronald Reagan era ushered in a new national story: that slashing regulations, laissez-faire small government, and giving tax cuts to businesses and the wealthy would not just engorge their coffers but unleash the "magic of the marketplace," enlarge the economic pie, and trickle down to make life better for everyone.[110]

Free market economists such as Milton Friedman preached as gospel in business schools and the halls of power that the purpose of a corporation is to benefit its shareholders, not its people or society. Driven by this pro-business free market ideology, business leaders and policymakers in Washington have weakened labor union power and severed the New Deal–era social contract. That contract between business, government, and labor was based on the assumption that good jobs that support families lead to better businesses *and* a healthy society and democracy.

The result? The U.S. standard of living has dropped.[111] Trust in institutions has fallen.[112] And Americans are living shorter, sicker lives. In a twist on New Hampshire's Revolutionary War–era call to arms state motto, Live Free or Die, authors of a 2023 groundbreaking National Academies of Sciences report on falling American life expectancy wanted to title it "Live Free and Die."[113] MIT economist David Autor describes our corporate profit-driven free market free-for-all as extreme "cowboy capitalism." In contrast, he calls systems that come together to support worker and human health, care, and wellbeing, as in Scandinavian countries, "cuddly capitalism." "If I were to be really rich, I would want to be in the U.S., probably," he told me. "If I didn't think I was going to be so affluent, I would probably want to be somewhere else."

We've now made it so impossible for workers and working families to live decent lives that a 2019 bid to restrict immigration is instructive. At the time, Republican president Donald Trump proposed denying green cards or a path to citizenship to new arrivals who used public benefits like health care and nutrition or housing assistance. One economist calculated that a significant share of the existing *American* workforce is paid so poorly and relies on those same public benefits to survive that they wouldn't be able to meet the tough new guidelines.[114] In effect, U.S. taxpayers are subsidizing companies' predilection for creating bad jobs and keeping profits for themselves and their shareholders.

Even beloved early care and education teacher Rashondah Anderson wouldn't have qualified for citizenship under Trump's proposed self-sufficiency standards. In 2019, when I first met her, Anderson, like other child-care workers, earned poverty wages and had to rely on public supports like Medicaid and food nutrition assistance[115] for her and her daughter to survive. After she was furloughed when the pandemic forced her upstate New York child-care center to close, she wound up leaving the profession she loved to become a dental hygienist, going further into debt to pay for her training and education, in the hope of making enough money to get by.[116]

Where will all this lead in the future? Technology, automation, robotics, globalization, and artificial intelligence are set to destroy thousands of jobs but perhaps create untold thousands more that we can't yet fathom. An MIT report on the future of work found that 63 percent of the jobs in 2018 didn't exist in 1940 and couldn't even have been imagined:[117] solar or wind power engineer, life coach, content moderator, TikTok influencer, mental health counselor, even the invisible "ghost workers," most of them poorly paid contractors, who keep the internet economy going.[118] Who knows what the jobs of 2094 will be? But the report cautions that left to its own devices, the market is creating two types of jobs—high-paying knowledge and professional jobs that require specialization and education, and poorly paid jobs in service and care. The middle class—what former labor secretary Robert Reich calls the true job creators[119] and the key to a stable democracy[120]—continues to hollow out.

Joe Liebman's story is just one of millions of that cratering middle. If we don't do things differently, it could be the story of millions more. As a young man, Liebman expected to work like his father, a chemist at the Anheuser-Busch Brewery headquarters in St. Louis for forty-three years who retired with a pension that paid 85 percent of his wage. When his father's division was sold off in 1986 just months before Liebman graduated from college, that door closed. He found a white-collar job in newspaper distribution at the *St. Louis Post-Dispatch* in Missouri. Over the years, he married and had six children. They lived in a pretty house in a good school district with a big oak tree in the yard and surrounded by a white picket fence. Liebman thought he was living the American dream.

Then came the 2008 global financial collapse. The newspaper, already struggling to survive, shed workers, including Liebman. He collected unemployment, but it was never enough to pay the bills. When it ran out and when his savings dried up, he worked odd jobs in construction or moving, but he never found anything like his former job. He fell into a depression and lost the house—it was bought on the courthouse steps. His marriage broke up. By 2021, at age fifty-eight, he was working as a picker in a warehouse, following a robot and putting items ordered off the internet into a big shopping cart, making $17.50 an hour after five years with the company, and living alone in an eight-hundred-square-foot apartment. He's had to work faster and faster as his bosses, guided by algorithms they don't explain, set higher and higher quotas. Liebman holds out hope that his children, all of whom have college degrees, will fare better. But he has no illusions for himself. Though he got involved in a local worker center to advocate for better conditions, he surmised that in the not too distant future engineers will have designed arms and hands for the robots and the warehouse won't need human ones any longer. "My job's gone in less than 10 years."[121]

The way we work is a choice. Throughout our history, humans have organized the way they work "in infinite variations,"[122] as historian Jan Lucassen writes. So why not shape paid work so that it sustains human life and ensures that there is time to share the unpaid work of care and connection[123]—and for the leisure and joy that feed the soul?

For 98 percent of human history, we lived and worked in egalitarian hunter-gatherer societies. We shared toil and reward relatively fairly. Only after we moved into agricultural societies, Lucassen writes, and started building up surpluses, did the "aggrandizers" enter the picture. In early societies, those aggrandizers were the priests and elites, who made claim to a larger share of the rewards of work, and thus inequality was born.

Anthropologists have long wondered, as Lucassen notes, why once-equal peoples agreed to relinquish the rewards of their labor to benefit the few. The answer, in essence, is that the elites were able to concoct a good story about why they deserved more. Perhaps enforced with the persuasive power of swords, and status, the elites were able to convince everyone else to believe it.[124]

In our day, one of the most powerful stories we've been told is that people are inherently lazy and don't really want to work, an inheritance from Adam Smith, the Scottish economist known as the father of capitalism. In Smith's view, the only way to get people to work was either through the incentive of money, the carrot, or the discipline of control, the stick. That story is untrue. Americans routinely rank "important work" that gives them a "feeling of accomplishment" as significantly more valuable than pay.[125] Nearly 40 percent say work is extremely or very important to their identities.[126] And an astonishing *70 percent* agree or strongly agree that they'd enjoy working, even if they didn't need the money.[127]

Yet we have shaped work and organizations based on the false story that humans would rather loaf than work, are transactional rather than moral, and are motivated by money, which, in turn, have become self-fulfilling prophecies, the social psychologist Barry Schwartz argues in *Why We Work*. "If we want to help design a human nature that seeks and finds challenge, engagement, meaning and satisfaction from work," he writes, "we have to start building our way out of a deep hole that almost three centuries of misconceptions about human motivation and human nature have put us in, and help foster workplaces in which challenge, engagement, meaning, and satisfaction are possible."[128]

In my decade of reporting on paid work and the unpaid work of care for this book, I've been struck by how simple some of the changes can be to design better work: research shows that when people have choice, challenge, a sense of purpose, and connection to a larger mission, when they are well supported, trusted, and feel respected, then workers are happy, businesses are profitable, and society flourishes.[129]

There are already good examples, role models, and evidence-based ideas. Far from radical, they would unleash the creative dynamism of a new kind of capitalism, one that aims for the broad, shared wellbeing and prosperity of all stakeholders—people, families, workers, communities, business and the economy, and the planet.

We can choose to change our system, to remake the economy, and reinvigorate a democracy that has come to feel bought and paid for by those with power and wealth. Transforming paid work and embracing the value of care are how we begin to create the more just, egalitarian, and inclusive world of human freedom and possibility I sought in my first book, *Overwhelmed: Work, Love, and Play When No One Has the Time.*[130] Once I finished writing it, I became convinced that so much of the time scarcity, stress, busyness, and damaging overwhelm of modern life that I explored, which falls most heavily on women, originates in and is driven by our dysfunctional and gendered culture of overwork. So I set out to understand what drives this culture and its consequences, and to look for the people and movements working to change it, often in the face of fierce resistance—for good. More importantly, I wanted to see how they were doing so and what we could learn from their efforts, large and small, the successes as well as the failures.

In this book, I tell the stories of change agents. These are visionaries imagining, wondering, playing with ideas, and contemplating a world of better work. They are leaders and believers, people who are willing to take risks and have the power to set change in motion. There are those who try the change on for size—the designers, pilots, activators, and implementers who figure out the how of change and show that it's possible. Validators use data to track why this change is better than the old way as well as how it could be improved. Agitators, organizers, and "persuaders," as author Anand Giridharadas calls them, keep a spotlight on the need for change and bring others along. Evangelizers have done the research, seen the light, or experienced something different, and they share the stories that get people excited and willing to believe and act differently, which makes it more likely that the change will actually stick. The stage can be set for change by a catalyzing event, however unrelated. And time and persistence are key, as is the recognition that deliberate change is often slow, hard, and never linear.

By no means comprehensive, this is a work of journalism and a journey to find hope in the change agents who are driven by dreams of a different way of working and living, and acting to make them real. I found people who are no longer satisfied with fiddling at the margins, with adding a few wellness programs such as lunchtime yoga or meditation apps to reduce stress, promises of flexibility to a handful of lucky individual white-collar workers, another employee resource group, or a few more dollars per hour. The piecemeal approaches are certainly easier. They are aimed at both blaming and "fixing" individual workers, as if we just needed to breathe our way out of overwork or our poorly paid jobs and all would be well.

These visionaries are aiming bigger, targeting individual, organizational, and societal change, and seeking to transform the very way work is organized and the assumptions we make about why it has to be done in a certain way.

This book is intended for all of us humans in all of the ways that we work to know that we are not alone in our yearning for something better. It is for business leaders and managers and skeptics to see that there is a better way. It is for policymakers, to call them to be wiser and braver. Ultimately, this is a hopeful book about how we have the power to begin telling a different story and making better choices that will shape the future of our work, care, and life. It is about why we must do this—and how to start.

CHAPTER 1

AMERICAN KAROSHI

John Henry hammered in the mountains
His hammer was striking fire
But he worked so hard, he broke his poor heart
He laid down his hammer and he died.

—*American folk song*

From the moment Cate Lindemann's mother set up a visit to a neonatal intensive care unit for a "Take Your Daughter to Work" day as a preteen, Lindemann knew she wanted two things out of life: to make her own way, earning her own living and not being dependent on someone else, and to make a mark on the world.

She decided early on that she'd be a lawyer. Her father, a lawyer for a bank, warned her against it. But she was determined to prove him wrong, just as she made it her mission to prove that she could be a great lawyer with a successful career and have time for the children and family she had always wanted. She graduated with a political science degree from the prestigious liberal arts college of Haverford, then obtained a master's degree from the London School of Economics and a law degree from the University of Wisconsin, where she met and married her husband. With an internship followed by a high-paying job with a prominent law firm in Chicago in 2007, she was on her way.

Most women at her firm, if they had children, waited until

they had made partner in their forties, but again Lindemann was out to prove everyone wrong, push herself, start her family in her thirties, and still make partner. She moved to a progressive firm to do employment litigation. Her husband, also a litigator, stepped back at one point and took a government position so that Lindemann could focus on having the big career—the "ideal worker" always available to the needs of her clients and coworkers and the vagaries of court schedules.

They sought to share the unpaid work of home. Lindemann's husband cooked. He made the children's health appointments. They split grocery shopping and laundry. Though she suffered frequent bouts of depression, she was determined not to let anyone at her office know, fearing the stigma of being seen as weak in the hard-charging, male-dominated environment of so many American law firms. Lindemann regularly worked to the point of exhaustion. To prove her devotion to work even though she was a mother with children, Lindemann felt as if she could never say no to work without suffering a penalty. When the full scope of her commitments seemed impossible, Lindemann forced herself on with a mantra: "I will just do it. I will just be better. I will just be stronger. I will work harder."

And she did work hard. Like most big law firms, hers required lawyers to bill at least two thousand hours a year to clients.[1] But given all the work that can't be charged to clients—emails, consulting with colleagues—Lindemann figured that for every eight billable hours, she was really working ten to twelve hours a day. There was always work to be done on Saturdays, on Sundays, and on every family vacation, always things to check late at night or email first thing in the morning. "It was grueling," she told me. "But I just got used to it." She also tried to get used to men referring to their female colleagues as "girls," commenting on their hair, their dress, their bodies, or grabbing them inappropriately. She stayed silent when female colleagues without children were promoted ahead of her. She kept working. "People see these things as innocuous, but they're designed to put you in your place. To remind you that you really don't belong there," she said. "I would complain to my husband, but you just kind of dealt with it."

It wasn't until the birth of her second child in 2015 that things began to fall apart. As with her first pregnancy, Lindemann was expected to work full steam until the day she delivered. She had to get special permission for each child to take about six months of partially paid leave to recover and bond with her newborns. (The firm's expectation was that women would take only the twelve weeks of unpaid leave guaranteed by the federal Family Medical Leave Act.) The end of her maternity leave in March that year coincided with glowing performance evaluations for the previous year from Lindemann's direct managers. At the same time, the firm gave her the lowest performance ranking she'd ever received and her compensation suffered. Why? She had missed her annual billable hour target by twenty-five hours. "I remember being very surprised and upset," she said. But Lindemann knew she was violating the firm's unspoken overwork culture. After the birth of her first child, she had negotiated an 85 percent schedule. She was told by a partner that no other attorney in their office had ever been successful on a reduced schedule, saying, "This isn't a part-time job."

After returning to work in 2015, Lindemann began being passed over for big assignments because partners assumed she wouldn't want to do them. Still, she kept trying to prove herself. When she was pregnant with her third child, she worked through debilitating morning sickness, calling clients from bed some mornings. In her ninth month, the head of her office pressured her to go to court and argue a motion. "When I told her I was having pain, she made it clear that I either went out on leave or I go and argue the motion," Lindemann recalled. Still hoping to make partner, she went to court, asking the judge for permission to deliver the argument seated because she was in so much pain. Lindemann wound up going into labor three days later, delivering her third child two weeks early in mid-2018. "You don't stop to say, 'This is so wrong, I'm not going to do it,'" she said. "You just do it. And I think that goes for a lot of people in a lot of jobs. They just suck it up and do it."

Lindemann finally did make partner, but it cost her. She was struggling with depression, which affected her billable hours. She was then warned that unless she took on more work and put in longer hours, she could hurt other women's chances of making partner. Lindemann's depression deepened. She took a mental health disability leave in January 2020. Panicking about her career, she returned to work a few months later, just as the pandemic left her family without school or child care. Lindemann found she could no longer just suck it up and do it. By the end of June, she quit.

On the morning of July 5, a few days after quitting, she took her dogs for a walk and spent time at the garden center, which was always her happy place. Back at home, Lindemann started feeling intense pressure in her chest. She wondered if her sports bra was too tight and tore it off. Her jaw started to hurt, maybe, she thought, from clenching her teeth for more than a decade. She downed some Advil. She felt exhausted, and though she rarely napped, that was all she wanted to do. She tried to meditate and calm down. When that didn't help, she searched her symptoms online. Perhaps she was having an anxiety attack. Google told her they were signs of a heart attack. She didn't believe it, but the pain was unbearable. So Lindemann's husband loaded her and their three children in the car and dropped her off at the ER. Because of Covid-19 distancing protocols, they couldn't come in with her. Leaving her distraught husband and three frightened children in the car, she walked in, alone.

Lindemann's EKG was fine. So were the ultrasound and X-ray. She was in great physical shape, having run a marathon in recent years and from working out throughout the pandemic with a Peloton. Her cholesterol had always been normal. A vegetarian since her teenage years, she never ate red meat. She had the occasional glass of wine. She was just thirty-nine years old. The doctors were puzzled—there were none of the typical risk factors for cardiovascular disease. Was she drinking any weight-loss teas? No. Was she on any drugs? An antidepressant and a multivitamin. She had been living with intense stress for years, she told them, and had just resigned from her job as a partner in a law firm where she worked long hours and that still wasn't enough. She had three little kids and, despite years of trying to prove otherwise, she felt like a failure at both. One avuncular older male doctor nodded in sympathy. It was a good thing that she'd quit her job, he said. "Women can't really have big careers and be good mothers to small children at the same time."

The doctors then measured the enzyme troponin, found in the muscles of the heart. When the heart becomes damaged, troponin shows up in the bloodstream. Lindemann's blood showed elevated levels and she was immediately admitted. Despite the normal EKG, she was in fact having a heart attack. More precisely, Lindemann was having a spontaneous coronary artery dissection, or SCAD—a type of heart attack caused by a tear inside a coronary artery that carries blood to the heart. SCAD affects primarily women, who have 90 percent of the cases, most commonly between the ages of thirty and sixty.[2] They can be fatal if not treated promptly. Doctors aren't sure what causes a SCAD, but some researchers say the most common factor is extreme physical or emotional stress,[3] in Lindemann's case, the stress from trying to combine her paid and unpaid work of care and home. A few weeks later, when she shared her ordeal with her longtime primary care physician, the doctor's comment to Lindemann was, "Your job really made you sick."

Once a hard-charging litigator who was ferocious in the courtroom, Lindemann now speaks softly but with quiet resolve. She gestures with her hands to emphasize her collision with the unfairness of her work situation, the lack of support or cooperation she felt, and how it ultimately robbed her of the meaning and sense of purpose she once hoped it would bring—the key elements required for good work. But her gestures are, like her voice, muted. Not too emphatic. She's careful not to get too riled up. The SCAD heart attack completely changed Lindemann's life. She had yet to return to paid work when I spoke to her in the spring of 2023, too afraid to resume a high-pressure law career, recognizing her privilege in that her lawyer husband earns enough to support the family. The doctors don't want her heart rate elevated above 130 to 140 beats per minute. She can't shovel snow or lift anything heavy. Lindemann had to get an electric mower to keep from overexertion when she mows the lawn. In February 2023, doctors implanted a pacemaker to keep her alive. "This has definitely changed my mindset as an employment attorney," she said. "Legally, a corporation is a person and has an identity, but we don't prioritize humans at all. This isn't something we can just self-care our way out of."

Dr. Sharonne N. Hayes, a cardiologist at Mayo Clinic who researches SCAD heart attacks, said Lindemann's case is not at all unusual. The majority of those who have SCAD heart attacks have none of the typical cardiovascular risk factors, such as high cholesterol, high blood pressure, or a family history of heart disease. SCAD, Hayes said, is kind of a "virgin victim" disease—meaning that most sufferers haven't engaged in unhealthy behavior or done anything to bring it on. In other words, they did not "deserve" to get sick. And, because they don't "look the part," younger women with few or no cardiovascular risk factors, like Lindemann, who show classic heart attack symptoms are often not evaluated appropriately. So SCAD heart attacks can be missed or diagnosed late. While much rarer, men who've had SCAD attacks are more likely to report recent physical exertion, like running a marathon or strenuous body building. "Among women, heart attacks like SCADs are associated more with toxic emotional than physical stress," Hayes explained. "It's more, 'I had a heartbreaking experience,' like heightened stress from interpersonal relationships, or overwork. It's usually something that's been going on for weeks or months. It builds up. Then it breaks."

Though most sufferers are found to have abnormalities in other arteries that may make them more vulnerable to an emotional or physical trigger, Lindemann's case may represent an example of someone who is stressed to the breaking point by trying to keep up with external expectations, like a workplace that rewards overwork, a culture that expects women to put family first, and the impossibility of being pulled hard in opposite directions simultaneously by two demanding institutions.[4] Said Hayes, "All those norms feed into the outcome of cardiovascular disease."

■

Dr. Peter Schnall, a social epidemiologist and professor emeritus of medicine at the University of California, Irvine, has spent his entire career trying to get people to understand that work stress is as pernicious as it is widespread, that it not only makes people sick but can kill them. Trying to get people to care, much less convince them to do something about it, is hard. Most of the time, he feels like a prophet in the wilderness—he has seen the light and is seeking valiantly to convert a public that is as skeptical as it is stuck in the status quo. The ignorance, apathy, and resistance he meets can be galling. But he remains passionate, undeterred, and, like any true believing evangelist that most people are ignoring, slightly pissed off.

Schnall has started up and contributed to multiple new research projects to add weight to the more than forty years of evidence on the harms of work stress and the benefits of good work cultures based on historian Jan Lucassen's three pillars of fairness, cooperation, and meaning. He's constantly reviewing research, compiling data, writing articles and books, and designing tool kits to show how creating such work cultures is possible. He's designed work stress surveys for workers and workplaces. He asks uncomfortable questions at conferences. He's largely self-funded a nonprofit organization, the Center for Social Epidemiology; coleads the Healthy Work Campaign; produced a documentary called *Working on Empty*; and is trying to goad businesses into signing the campaign's Healthy Work Pledge. Schnall does all this because lives, like Cate Lindemann's, are at stake and because their suffering and misery are, as his data shows, completely unnecessary. "We're trying to raise people's consciousness," he said. "All this illness is preventable."

The only way to prevent it is to change work itself, Schnall argues. Some companies and some countries are already adopting what he proposes: fair pay, decent work hours and workloads, control over one's schedule, supportive policies, and cultures that enable people to combine paid work with the unpaid work of home and care. In overworked America, however, what Schnall is asking for can seem impossible, even though his mission shows that his proposals would improve lives and make businesses more profitable and sustainable in the long run. But Schnall is asking the very people who've risen to power in the current system and who view labor costs as a liability to cut for short-term gain, to radically shift their approach to work. That's hard. "Businesses in general have an economic motive to deny that work is causing illness," he said.

I first met Peter Schnall in 2018 at his condo, which is stacked with academic journals, papers, and medical books and overlooks the Pacific Ocean in Marina del Rey just outside Los Angeles. Like any change evangelist who sees the world differently from most people, he dresses the part, in Teva sandals, blue jeans, and a checked shirt, his thinning white hair mussed as if he has more important things to do than grooming. I had come to see him and his colleague, Marnie Dobson, a sociologist who studies work, stress, and gender and codirects the Healthy Work Campaign, because I was stunned by the research they and so many other change evangelists have done showing that work stress can be life threatening. I knew people burned out and had come close myself. But work killing you? I was skeptical. As I continued to talk with them and other experts over the years, read more research, and absorbed the weight of their evidence, I was then equally stunned that people weren't screaming in the streets and demanding change.

Schnall smiled wryly when I asked why the studies surface occasionally in news headlines but quickly disappear. His argument, he explained, goes against the ethos of individualism in the United States. So it's easy for those entrenched in the status quo to ignore him or dismiss him as an academic crank. In our U.S. hustle culture, work stress, like so much else, is seen as the individual failure of someone who just can't hack the pressure, and it's the individual's responsibility to fix. Cate Lindemann's colleagues, for instance, thought of her as weak, a liability, a "complainer," she said, once she no longer wanted to suck it up and take whatever her workplace threw at her at all hours of the day or night. So instead of looking to their work practices, executives who have long proclaimed that overwhelmed, stressed-out employees are one of their top concerns offer the burned-out "talent" they seek to retain individual "wellness" programs, such as lunchtime yoga, weight loss or smoking cessation guidance, or meditation apps.[5] (A 2024 study of more than forty-six thousand workers in the UK found no benefit whatsoever to workplace wellbeing from these wellness programs.)[6] Workers in low-wage or precarious jobs are often supposed to be grateful they have a job at all.

In Japan, where long work hours are commonplace, there's a word for dying from the stress of overwork: *karoshi*. The government collects and publishes data on karoshi-related illnesses, depression, suicides, and deaths. Victim families, unions, and labor lawyers can sue companies for recompense and lobby the government for worker protections and better laws. In the United States, there is no such word. There is no such government system to track how work stress may be tied to illness and death. But that doesn't mean it isn't happening. "We have widespread karoshi. We simply don't call it that. We basically are in denial about the work environment," Schnall told me. "We carry in the United States a complete belief that disease is the responsibility of individual behavior, and that somehow or other, whether or not you have depression, or you have high blood pressure, or you have a heart attack, it's because you didn't take good care of your body—eating improperly, not exercising, being overweight. And those are definitely factors. But we don't examine the way in which society organizes itself, or organizes work, as potential contributors to those outcomes."

Social and individual factors are linked, of course. The work environment often shapes individual choices, Schnall said, noting that acute work stress—meeting an unreasonable deadline, or the shock of receiving an unexpectedly negative performance review—can have a direct biochemical impact on the body and lead to heart attacks and strokes. But being exposed to chronic work stress day after day may lead to life changes that have a creeping negative impact on health and wellbeing. That chronic stress elevates stress hormones such as cortisol in the bloodstream, which can make people feel tired and sluggish. If a person is fatigued, they may not have the energy to exercise or eat well. They may be so overworked that they have no time to cook healthy meals and rely on high-fat fast food or seek comfort in sugary junk food. Or they may be so stressed by their toxic boss and consistently unreasonable deadlines or feel so angry about a situation they can do nothing to change, that they can't sleep well at night. All of this can lead to illness over time. Chronic work stress is associated with high blood pressure, diabetes, and up to 20 percent of all causes of cardiovascular deaths among those of working age in industrialized countries.[7] It is also the cause of so much misery—such as depression, anxiety, insomnia, and a 76 percent higher risk of missing work because of a diagnosed mental health disorder.[8] Work stress is so pernicious and pervasive that research shows that the way we work is now the fifth leading cause of death in the United States.[9]

The link between work stress and health surprised even Schnall early in his career. In the 1970s, high blood pressure was thought to be a chronic condition—once a patient received the diagnosis, they were stuck with it. Working as an internist in the South Bronx, he found that the blood pressure of about half of his patients who stopped taking their medications dropped. Could something else in their lives—their work, their living circumstances—be playing a role? "That was the moment that started me on this forty-year crusade," Schnall told me.

His research soon led him to a startling conclusion: a key factor driving high blood pressure is chronic exposure to what he calls noxious negative job conditions and job strain.[10] He began studying the psychological and social factors that can harm or kill workers such as Cate Lindemann—what he and others call "psychosocial" work stress. "You can teach people 'resilience,' help them to reduce stress, all of which have some beneficial impacts," he said. "But will they remove the negative effects of a hostile psychosocial environment? A bad boss? A job where you don't have a say in what happens to you?"

Far from an individual problem, Schnall's research and that of others in the United States and around the world shows that work stress is the result of work systems, work practices, and the work environment.[11] Taking a bubble bath or a few deep breaths may help individuals cope with stress in the moment, but it won't address the cause. Popular media is littered with self-help articles about coping with burnout. But the foremost expert on burnout, social psychologist Christina Maslach, and a number of other researchers[12] maintain that burnout is not an individual's problem and the responsibility to fix it lies with organizations.[13]

Those long slogging hours at work? That low-wage or precarious job with no benefits? The unpredictable retail work schedule that makes it impossible to organize child care or a doctor's appointment? The $2.13-an-hour-plus-tips minimum wage for restaurant workers that forces them to smile at rude customers just to earn enough for the gas to get home? The work-care conflict that pulls women and caregivers in opposite directions? These are not individual choices.

Nor is the fact that the public safety net is full of holes, where there is no guarantee of paid family leave, no paid sick days, no paid vacation time, and low investment in care infrastructure. In recent years, some states, particularly red states, have slashed funding for their unemployment insurance programs or deliberately made them difficult to navigate—a result of America's culture bias that people out of a job must be lazy and what Georgetown University economist Harry Holzer calls an "unholy alliance between right-wing ideologues who are just against government in general and people with these implicit or explicit racial biases."[14] So barely one-third of unemployed workers have received unemployment insurance, and in some states the number is less than 10 percent.[15] *That's* what's responsible for so many workers' chronic stress, Schnall argues. Just the thought of losing one's job causes stress. And actually losing a job more than doubles the risk of heart attack and stroke among older workers;[16] it increases the chance of developing stress-related diabetes, arthritis, or mental health issues by 83 percent;[17] it even shortens life expectancy.[18] In the United States, losing a job also often means losing access to health care and is linked to a higher risk of suicide.[19]

Precarious work also creates stress. Cherri Murphy became a rideshare driver in San Francisco because she needed a job flexible enough to enable her to pursue her doctorate in theology. What at first seemed like the perfect situation, however, soon sent her blood pressure spiking. With no company-provided health or car insurance, she was on her own if she were to have an accident. If she turned down rides—which she did when, as a Black woman, she thought the situation might make her unsafe—the algorithm seemed to punish her with fewer lucrative rides to bid on. She found herself working longer hours and earning less. Murphy felt trapped and powerless, and the stress and uncertainty of how much she'd make, the risks she alone was shouldering—car maintenance and repair, insurance, and gas—and sitting for hours on end all began to take a toll on her health. Like so many gig workers with precarious work, she found herself working constantly, anxious, unable to sleep, and exhausted.[20] "I gained tons of weight. My body atrophied significantly. My health deteriorated significantly," she said. Driving in the heavy smoke from California wildfires left her with asthma. "It's a system designed for distress," she added, which ratcheted up during the pandemic, when sharing a closed space with a stranger became a potential matter of life and death.

As Cate Lindemann's experience shows, professional and knowledge workers are not protected from this degree of stress. At one time, the higher one's status at work, the less stress a person experienced along with an easier and healthier life. The famous Whitehall study of civil servants in the United Kingdom, begun in 1967, found that the lower the employment grade, the higher the mortality rate, specifically for cardiovascular disease, compared to those of more senior rank who had more control over their work.[21] But more recent research shows that high-status jobs are stressful now, too, and getting worse. One researcher has dubbed the phenomenon the "stress of higher status."[22] Other researchers have found that women in higher-status professional and managerial positions have higher breast cancer rates than women in lower-status positions or women who don't work for pay outside the home.[23]

Knowledge workers are often expected to conform to increasingly greedy work demands, or they risk being sidelined or let go. Yet people who put in long hours are two and a half times more likely to experience depression and have a nearly 60 percent increased risk of coronary heart disease than those who stop after an eight-hour day.[24] In medicine, where, like law, the jobs may pay well and come with benefits, the expectation of total devotion is known as the "Iron Man" culture. It is also well known that this culture leads to stress, depression, substance abuse, and suicide rates that are shockingly high.[25] It also causes more mistakes, which can be fatal in medicine.[26]

The American Psychological Association's annual "Stress in America Report" typically finds that work is the second-highest source of stress in the United States, just after money.[27] Gallup has consistently found that workers in the United States and Canada are the most stressed out in the world, with 57 percent saying they were stressed every single day in 2020.[28] (That year, far more women, 62 percent, than men, 52 percent, reported high daily stress at work, which was hardly a surprise in the middle of a devastating pandemic as women were more likely to be shouldering the lion's share of child care, homeschooling, and other care responsibilities, in addition to paid work.)

The root cause of work stress, researchers like Schnall and Dobson say, is a lack of fairness. It's all about who has the power. Stress can arise when the demands of work exceed one's resources, support, or ability to cope, when the effort exceeds the reward received, or when one has little control over one's workload or schedule.[29] High blood pressure,[30] heart disease,[31] and depressive symptoms often follow.[32]

For Black workers and other people of color, regardless of the job or status, the daily stresses they face can be even higher, sociologist and Washington University professor Adia Harvey Wingfield told me. Harvey Wingfield wrote about her research on the experience of Black doctors and nurses in her book, *Flatlining: Race, Work, and Health Care in the New Economy.* Many face differential treatment and daily microaggressions, both intentional and unintentional. "All of this leads to higher stress, hypertension, obesity, and other illnesses," she said. "You might think with higher-status workers, it would be a different picture, but research has shown that's not the case." Black professionals or other professionals of color are often expected to educate their white peers about equity and creating inclusive cultures, which can extend already long workdays and produce feelings of alienation, frustration, and increased distance from coworkers.

Nahsis Davis is a single foster mother of three in Chicago and one of the very few Black registered nurses—about 14 percent—in the country.[33] At times in her career, she said, she's put up with crummier shifts, heavier patient loads, and less flexibility than her white colleagues. "It really makes you kind of angry. It makes you not want to even work with them or work around them or even put your all into it."[34]

Similarly, LeRon Barton, a Black tech worker, said he's been the subject of racist jokes—when his coworkers heard police sirens, they would call out, "Hey, LeRon, they're coming for you!" He has had his credentials questioned when entering buildings. The strain of keeping his head down, staying silent, trying not to be labeled a troublemaker, and just focusing on work got to be so stressful that Barton quit. He began speaking out and writing about the toll of racism at work. "You hear about how Black and brown kids have to have grit to be able to make it through these situations," he told me. "How about we create an environment where you don't have to endure it? There's a huge difference between grit and stick-to-itiveness and this endurance of an absolutely unbearable culture. Every time you accept bad behavior, every time you look the other way, that kind of chips away at you."

When the World Health Organization declared burnout from chronic workplace stress a serious problem in 2019, Schnall and Dobson were hopeful that it would spark change in the overworked United States. However, it's complicated. The WHO classified burnout as an "occupational phenomenon," not a "medical condition."[35] "That's a good thing," Dobson explained. "It puts the onus for dealing with burnout on the workplace, rather than expecting individuals to get medical treatment." But without burnout being classified as a medical condition, Schnall and Dobson said, it, along with general stress or psychosocial work stress, isn't listed as a diagnosable condition in the *Diagnostic and Statistical Manual of Mental Disorders*. That means workers have no basis to file workers' compensation claims, to be paid for by companies.

If it were a diagnosable condition with companies being held liable, that would increase the likelihood of employers changing organizational practices to address it, such as increasing staffing, reducing workloads, adopting flexible schedules, and creating cultures of trust. They would be on the hook to pay for any medical treatment burnout might require. Financial consequences for companies, hitting them in the bottom line, could force more employers not to just take notice but to take action.

So in the United States we're stuck somewhere in the middle: more people are finally beginning to realize that work stress is a systems problem that requires solutions at the organizational level. Yet the solutions offered still largely rest on the classic American notion that work stress is the fault of the individual, who needs to buck up and get a little resilience training or lunchtime yoga. In April 2023, for instance, Mayo Clinic noted on its website that more people were reporting feeling burned out at work than at the height of the pandemic. While acknowledging that the problem is caused by organizations and is therefore theirs to resolve,[36] the "workplace tips" offered on the website advised stressed-out workers to—yes—take a yoga class or cut back on their to-do list.[37]

There are no laws or regulations to prevent or mitigate work stress in the United States or much recourse for any related illness, even as reports and articles about the harm it causes[38] and "alarming" rates of burnout[39] become increasingly visible.[40]

Although Cate Lindemann had a heart attack, the way many state workers' compensation regulations are written makes it close to impossible for her to prove that the cause was work-related. "Not unless she were clutching her chest" as she keeled over in the office, Schnall explained. Even then, in some states, she'd likely have to prove that her illness was due to "unusual exertion," which typically refers to physical strain.[41]

Part of the reason for this, Schnall and Dobson maintain, is that rather than putting a premium on worker wellbeing and stress reduction, as in Scandinavia, the European Union, and other countries, the United States focuses instead on worker efficiency and productivity. In 1970, President Richard M. Nixon signed the law that created the U.S. Occupational Health and Safety Administration—OSHA—after decades of battles between workers and employers.[42] But its scope has been limited to tracking and regulating physical workplace hazards, such as industrial accidents, chemical spills on the job, breathing in coal dust or asbestos, or falling off ladders on construction sites. What U.S. OSHA doesn't track or regulate is psychosocial work stress,[43] while other advanced economies have long made it a priority.[44]

"The lack of attention to the psychosocial stress of workers is just part of unfettered capitalism in the United States—you work until you drop, or put work above all else," Dobson said. "Business and management have more power than workers. Squeezing labor is seen as a means to unfettered growth." This is the cowboy capitalism that MIT economist David Autor describes. "There's a lot of overload, stress, and burnout among public-sector employees, like teachers or county workers, too," Dobson added. "There are severe staffing shortages. That's led to heavy workloads. And there's inadequate public funds to solve the problem."

In the European Union, an EU-OSHA survey found that half of workers consider psychosocial work stress commonplace, brought on by job insecurity, reorganization, long working hours, excessive workload or harassment, and violence at work. There is yet no such comparable government survey in the United States. The statistic used on U.S. OSHA's website—that 80 percent of U.S. workers have experienced work stress at some point—comes from a 2013 survey by Everest College, not U.S. OSHA.[45] To EU-OSHA, "managing stress is not just a moral obligation and a good investment for employers, it is a legal imperative."[46] And though work stress hasn't disappeared, governments are seeking to address it by passing laws limiting work hours and guaranteeing paid leave and rest, among other efforts. EU-OSHA supplies employers with tool kits and fact sheets requiring them to offer workers such remedies as reasonable or shorter work hours, control over their workloads, adequate staffing levels, and support and resources to do their jobs, stable schedules, adequate rest periods, civil harassment-free cultures, performance-based management training, paid leave, and the like to counter work stress[47]—in other words, systems-level protections for workers and laws and regulations designed to change work practices, not yoga sessions.

By contrast, the U.S. OSHA website gently suggests that employers be "aware," "show empathy," and provide access to mental health resources to workers struggling with stress. At most, it feebly nudges them to "identify factors" that make it harder for workers to get their jobs done "and determine if adjustments can be made."[48]

This hardly seems like a sufficient response to an alarming and entirely preventable phenomenon, which, according to one meta-analysis of more than two hundred work, stress, and health studies, is associated with so much illness in the United States that it takes 120,000 lives prematurely every year,[49] shortens life spans,[50] and costs employers as much as $300 billion annually in absenteeism, turnover, diminished productivity, and increased medical and legal costs.[51] In recent years, for instance, GM has spent more on health care than on steel. The case for tracking and regulating work stress is a strong one.[52] The meta-analysis determined that the negative impact of workplace stress is about equal to that of secondhand tobacco smoke, a known and regulated carcinogen.[53] And all because of management practices and the way work is organized. "In Europe, it's illegal—you can't have jobs with high demands and low control," Schnall said emphatically. "Why can't we do that here?"

To Jeffrey Pfeffer, a Stanford business professor and author of *Dying for a Paycheck*, the answer is obvious: the absence of U.S. law, regulation, or policy addressing workplace practices. Pfeffer, who coauthored the sweeping meta-analysis of the devastating consequences of psychosocial stress, argues that absent legislation, nothing is going to change. In 2019, French courts found several executives from France Télécom (now called Orange) guilty of creating a work culture that, as one inspector put it, "endangered human life." They were sentenced to jail terms and ordered to pay millions of euros to the victims' families in damages. The court noted that deep and aggressively enforced layoffs designed to boost company profits left those who remained with more work to do than was humanly possible. At least nineteen workers killed themselves and twelve others attempted suicide, blaming the company's overwork culture.[54] "All it would take," Pfeffer said, "is one DA to arrest one hospital CEO where a doctor has committed suicide and things would change in a hurry."

Pfeffer had hoped that his research and book, published in 2018, would shake things up and prompt the kinds of laws and regulations that could change work culture. But that didn't happen. "Fundamentally, this is a story about power. You have a system that's running along. There's enormous amounts of inertia. And in order to overcome inertia, you need a force that is larger than the inertia. When you ask, 'Why don't things change?' I would ask you, 'Why would you expect them to?' Where is the force with sufficient power to cause this inert system to actually change? I don't see it," he continued. "There's lots of talk. Lots of reports. Lots of articles. But almost no action. The analogy I make is to environmental pollution. That didn't stop because companies figured out that it was actually costing them money—though, by the way, it was. It didn't stop because suddenly companies got a conscience. It stopped when there was legislation, litigation, and regulation. And there has been no legislation, litigation, or regulation to speak of with respect to workplace health" and the effect of stress in the United States.

It boils down to the fact that it is easier and cheaper for businesses to offer the equivalent of lunchtime yoga, a mindfulness app, a basket of healthy snacks, or a sympathetic employee assistance program and be done with it. Rather than, say, hire sufficient staff to manage the workload, pay them well, and streamline processes to focus on getting the most important work done. Rather than on the hours spent at the office or worksite. This despite the research showing that failing to address the real problem of work stress leads to moral injury, feelings of betrayal, and burnout, all of which sap a business's purported aim of productivity.[55] It's easier for policymakers to look the other way and avoid confronting the powerful businesses and business leaders who contribute to their campaigns and keep them in office. To applaud the monthly job numbers without being honest about how many of those jobs are decent, with fair wages and benefits that could support a human life, much less a family. And it's easier for exhausted, often isolated workers, worried about paying their bills and proving their worth, to resign themselves to thinking that this is just the way it is and go back to work. "Talking about toxic work cultures is like the bad uncle at Thanksgiving dinner," Pfeffer said. "Everybody knows it's a problem, but nobody wants to confront it. So they all avert their gaze."

Peter Schnall is impatient with such inertia and apathy. Though his crusade is still very much David to the Goliath of corporate America, he no longer feels quite so alone. Some workers are at least beginning to speak out. Rideshare driver Cherri Murphy has spent the last few years organizing rideshare drivers with Gig

Workers Rising and lobbying policymakers for better conditions for gig workers. Lawyer Cate Lindemann, after years of staying silent and feeling ashamed, has begun sharing her story and finding she's not alone, first with a group of SCAD survivors who had also nearly died as a result of work stress, and now more broadly to the media, urging workers to demand better from their employers and policymakers.

A handful of employers are reevaluating work practices to put a value on humans, exploring four-day workweeks and shorter hours and other innovative redesign pilots born of the pandemic. Some federal officials, too, are paying attention. From its inception in the 1970s, the National Institute for Occupational Safety and Health, an arm of the federal Centers for Disease Control and Prevention, has been charged with carrying out research and proposing means to prevent work-related injury and illness. Though NIOSH early on recognized that stress at work was a "leading safety and health problem" and sponsored conferences and research, a groundbreaking paper that NIOSH published in 2002 called on the agency and federal government to do more. "The revolutionary changes occurring in today's workplace have far outpaced our understanding of their implications for work life quality and safety and health on the job," the authors wrote.[56]

As a result, NIOSH's Total Worker Health program funds ten academic Centers of Excellence across the country to carry out surveillance and research on psychosocial work stress and what to do about it. Instead of focusing on individual resilience strategies, as many traditional interventions have in the past, the centers research the impact of workplace organizational design and other structural factors on health and wellbeing. They also explore the systemic changes that could reduce such stress, such as reducing workloads, supporting workers with care responsibilities, and ensuring economic security. "The ways we've tried to improve work in the past I don't think are adequate for the modern way that we actually work," L. Casey Chosewood, director of NIOSH's Total Worker Health program,[57] told me.

"In order for a nation to thrive, to sustain a strong economy, create good jobs, and maintain a quality of life for workers, the work experience has to be continually renewed and optimized . . . All those traditional risks like chemical, physical, biological hazards at work, they're still there. But they're not the most critical challenges that organizations are facing today. There's a lot more risk around the unrelenting change workers experience, increasing pace and greater work demands, and stressors—like the stress arising from technology, and the new types of work arrangements that are oftentimes far more insecure." The program's goal, Chosewood continued, is to change mindsets, laws, policies, and practices to ensure that workers are both physically and psychologically safe. "To actually create something good from the work experience itself."

Dr. Christian Rathke is the director of Total Worker Health within the National Oceanic and Atmospheric Administration. "We're wanting something much more than a wellness program that focuses on individual resiliency, where we're monitoring diabetes and blood pressure. I have zero interest in that," he said. Rathke fielded a survey on employee burnout that he found particularly revelatory. "The biggest problems we're facing are chronic," he said. The sobering survey identified heavy workloads as a key problem. So he has focused on redesigning work, starting at the executive level, helping managers make what he calls a "paradigm shift" and encouraging them to remake budgets and change operating procedures, like matching workers to workloads, for instance, and tracking and discouraging after-hours work—like all those late-night emails—to counter overwork. He seeks changes recognizing that lack of flexibility and child care has an enormous impact on retaining workers with care responsibilities and that an organization has a responsibility to address that.

Rathke was inspired to think big, in part, by U.S. Surgeon General Vivek Murthy's 2022 advisory statement on health worker burnout. The report recognized that health work itself needed change, involving reduction of the administrative burden on doctors and nurses to give them more time with patients, and ensuring hospitals have adequate staffing levels, rather than the standard practice of skimping on labor to boost profits.[58] "The problems of society are the problems of the workforce. They're systemic and complicated. And they're deep," Rathke said.

NIOSH's Chosewood acknowledged that the success of Total Worker Health will require legislation and regulation, and that the U.S. has a long way to go. Some U.S. companies have chosen voluntarily to follow some international standards to reduce work stress and promote worker wellbeing,[59] he said. "Oftentimes, the voluntary approach is the first step to mandating something more dramatic. So, we're hopeful. Workers deserve this. Their lives literally depend on it."

▬

From his twenty years as a lawyer and executive working with physicians and hospitals inside the U.S. health-care system, Corey Feist was no stranger to the medical "Iron Man" work culture, where long hours and sacrificing personal lives and health for the profession is not only expected but celebrated as a mark of heroic dedication to a higher calling.[60] Feist had read the endless reports, seen the statistics, and heard the years of handwringing statements and lip service of concern about the consequences of that culture. One in every two physicians shows at least one symptom of burnout[61] (higher since the pandemic[62]). Doctors have the highest suicide rate of any profession in the country—as many as four hundred annually. The suicide rate for physicians[63] and female nurses[64] is more than twice that of the general population.[65] One study estimated the rate for female physicians is 250 to 400 percent higher.[66]

When that tough-as-nails, work-'til-you-drop culture took the life of Lorna Breen, his sister-in-law, in April 2020, Feist decided to dedicate himself to changing that work culture. Breen, an avid snowboarder, athlete, salsa dancer, and devout Christian, was the director of the emergency department at New York-Presbyterian Allen Hospital, which serves a largely low-income community in northern Manhattan. In March 2020, Breen had been on a ski trip in Montana with Feist and his wife, Jennifer, Breen's younger sister. Breen abruptly left to return to her hospital on March 14, when New York began to shut down in response to a new and deadly virus.

Throwing herself into work, Breen contracted the then-mysterious Covid-19 virus four days later. She became intensely sick. Forced to quarantine at home, just the effort of walking from her bedroom to her kitchen so exhausted her that she had to lie down and sleep. She lost weight. Even so, she felt compelled to work. Breen had rarely taken a sick day in her career. She worried she was letting her short-staffed colleagues down, as well as the patients who needed her help. She spent hours searching online for the potentially lifesaving oxygen tanks, goggles, and protective gear that were in such short supply.

As soon as her fever broke, on April 1, she returned to the hospital, with homemade care packages of personal protective equipment.

By this time, the hospital was overrun with sick and dying patients. She worked twelve-, fourteen-, fifteen-hour days, and still patients were dying on stretchers in the hallway, in the waiting room, in hospital beds as the staff held up smartphones so they could say their final farewells to their families. In New York City, ground zero of the pandemic at the time, the daily death toll would soon rise above two thousand. "It was Armageddon," Feist told me. Breen was having a hard time keeping up. "But she was concerned that her inability would be seen as a sign of weakness by her colleagues and hurt her reputation," Feist said. "So instead of heeding our requests that she rest and recover, she pushed on."

Breen, frazzled, overwhelmed, and still suffering from the effects of Covid-19, told a friend on April 5 that she felt like she was drowning.[67] On April 9, when the typically unflappable Breen called her sister and said she could not get out of her chair, Jennifer arranged for a chain of friends to drive a nearly catatonic Breen south from New York to Virginia, where she and other family members lived. Once there, Breen was admitted to the University of Virginia inpatient psychiatric unit.

Almost immediately after being admitted, Breen began to worry that receiving mental health treatment would cost her her medical license, Corey Feist recalled. In the overwork and burnout culture of medicine, where doctors and nurses are supposed to be superhuman, asking for help, much less help for mental health, is seen as a sign of weakness or failure.[68] She feared that the career she'd carefully mapped out all her life, which shaped her identity and gave her life meaning, would be over. After eleven days, Breen was released from the hospital and went to stay with her mother. On April 26, she took her own life. She was forty-nine. "She tried to do her job, and it killed her," her father, a surgeon, said.[69]

Shaken, Corey and Jennifer Feist decided to share her full story, not just of Breen's death, but the factors that drove her to it, and the loss of "this amazing physician, this amazing human." The two gave an interview on NBC's *Today* show. Within hours, Feist said, the letters and emails began pouring in—from health-care professionals sharing similar stories of burnout, depression, and despair, and from health-care organizations wanting to find solutions and asking for help. That June, in response to what Feist called a "tsunami," the family found themselves channeling their grief into setting up the Dr. Lorna Breen Heroes' Foundation,[70] with a mission to end the burnout culture in health care. "We're focused on the wellbeing of the entire health-care workforce," he said. "And, more importantly, envisioning this world where seeking mental health care is viewed as a sign of strength."

I spoke with Feist in the sunny living room of his white brick home in Charlottesville, where he takes on the health-care industry's burnout culture from his home office. The Feists have been speaking out about how the causes are systemic, not personal, and so must the solutions be, too. They have made that case in pieces for national publications, in countless media interviews, in talks to tens of thousands of health-care workers and leaders, and in recorded videos on suicide, burnout, and mental health.

They've forged partnerships across the health field and, in coalition with several health-care organizations, lead a research-based nationwide education and training program, All In: Caring for Caregivers. "Organizations are starved for solutions," Feist said. "So we're bringing them a starter kit." A top priority for the foundation and a key focus of the training program is pushing states, hospitals, and health organizations to audit their licensing, credentialing, hiring, and promotion practices and remove any intrusive questions about mental health history. The questions stigmatize mental health diagnoses or disorders, Feist said, and create cultures where health professionals won't seek mental health care when they need it, fearing, like Lorna Breen, that they'll lose their medical licenses. So, they soldier on, sometimes to the breaking point. The American Hospital Association lists the fear that mental health treatment will cost licenses and end careers as one of the three drivers of physician suicide, along with lack of access to mental health services and work stress.[71] By the fall of 2023, twenty-five state medical boards had audited their licensure applications and dropped the intrusive language, with more states in the process of doing so. Twelve health systems had similarly removed language that stigmatized mental health treatment from their credentialing applications, with more underway.[72]

The foundation recognizes hospitals that complete their three-step process—audit, change, communicate—with a "Wellbeing First Champion for Credentialing" badge. One of the foundation's biggest wins, so far, Feist said, is a new law aimed at improving the health and wellbeing of the health-care workforce. In 2020, just after Lorna Breen died, when Virginia senator Tim Kaine called the family to offer his condolences and ask what he could do to help, the Feists presented him with an action plan. Most laws can take years, if not decades, to build support and wind their way through Congress. However, the Dr. Lorna Breen Health Care Provider Protection Act passed with bipartisan support, as well as that of more than seventy organizations, and was signed into law by President Joe Biden in March 2022, just over twelve months after first being introduced.[73] The law requires the U.S. Department of Health and Human Services to identify and share best practices to improve mental health and prevent suicides in the health-care sector and funds a national education campaign, Impact Wellbeing, aimed at removing the stigma and encouraging health-care professionals to seek mental health and substance abuse treatment. The law also authorized $135 million over three years to train health-care providers on suicide prevention and behavioral health.[74] The goal, Feist said, is to help health-care students and professionals recognize the signs of burnout or mental health struggles in themselves or colleagues and educate them on how to intervene. By the winter of 2024, forty-four organizations had received grants and were actively setting up wellbeing programs, including a peer support program at the University of Utah's Resiliency Center, the Thrive Program to teach graduate students about wellbeing at Kansas City University and help them create supportive networks, and a wellbeing curriculum that Duke University turned into bite-sized interventions for continuing education credits.

Some worry that the law is just another wellness pat on the back, like the bottle of water and a mini can of Pringles one hospital gave out in a sorry attempt to reward health workers' herculean efforts during the pandemic.[75] But Feist and others say it's at least a promising start.[76]

To really transform the dysfunctional work culture will require addressing the root causes of work stress, overload, and burnout. Feist is working with others to push the health field to "get radical to shore up staffing" and recognize that burnout is driven by staff shortages, which Covid-19 made worse.[77]

The foundation is also working with partners to address the crushing amount of paper and administrative work that keeps the professionals from actually providing health care. So crushing is the burden—about fifteen hours a week[78]—that in the 2023 Medscape survey on burnout and depression in health care, "I Cry but No One Cares," physicians rated bureaucratic tasks and paperwork as the number one cause (61 percent), followed by lack of respect from colleagues and long work hours.[79] (Working on paperwork late into the night is so common for doctors it's called "pajama time.") Some promising initiatives to change include hiring medical scribes or creating support positions to manage electronic records, ensuring proper training, offering 24/7 support, and eliminating duplicative, time-wasting, or unnecessary administrative work. The American Medical Association offers a training that includes a lesson on "Getting Rid of the Stupid Stuff."[80]

To Feist, Lorna Breen and other burned-out health professionals are like the proverbial canaries in a coal mine. "What we don't need are stronger canaries," he told me. "We need a new coal mine."[81]

CHAPTER 2

YEARNING FOR A GREAT REIMAGINATION

> If the feminist program goes to pieces on the arrival of the first baby, it is false and useless.
>
> —*Crystal Eastman, "Now We Can Begin," 1920*[1]

Down a lush, winding country lane in rural Virginia, in a pretty white farmhouse on two acres of land not far from what remains of a string of Confederate earthwork forts and the farms where her enslaved ancestors once toiled, attorney Jessica Lee climbs the stairs to her office. It's a desk against the wall, really, in a second-floor loft strewn with children's toys and the guitars and keyboards of her husband's instrument repair business. There she spends her days diligently striving to change the greedy culture of paid work to make room for the unpaid work of care.

Lee is an attorney and codirector of the Center for WorkLife Law at the University of California College of the Law, San Francisco. She specializes in caregiver discrimination law. Lee is always busy. But during the pandemic, it was nonstop. She was one of a handful of attorneys fielding an unending flood of helpline calls from workers with care responsibilities who were pushed out of paid work as schools and care facilities shut down and were desperate for help. It was Lee's job to fight to get them back in. She uses the legal system to help people, to push for better laws and policies to prevent family caregiving discrimination in the first place, and to educate business leaders to change the way they think about and treat employees with care responsibilities. Lee has to be creative, because she and attorneys like her don't have much to work with. In 2024 there are no U.S. federal laws and just a scattering of state laws that explicitly protect such workers, despite the fact that a majority of employees of all genders juggle care duties. There are only a few imperfect policies designed to help families combine work and care. Even though a great boss or a good company here and there can create systems and cultures that embrace workers with care responsibilities, individual solutions for the few come nowhere near addressing the needs of the many. Long before the Covid-19 pandemic unleashed a raging crisis of care, U.S. workers with families to care for were regularly squeezed by an unforgiving overwork culture. The pandemic only increased the sheer volume of her caseload of mothers, fathers, and family caregivers on the verge of catastrophe or those already ensnared in its depths.

Josh Sprague, a machinist in Texas, took intermittent paid leave under the temporary emergency paid sick and child-care leave that Congress authorized in the early days of the pandemic. He took two days off a week for two months, switching duties with his wife in order to care for their young children and monitor homeschooling. He returned to work full-time at the end of May 2020 and was fired two days later.[2] He sued, claiming his employer retaliated against him for using emergency paid leave.

Carly Stephens, a content creator for a social media management services company in Miami, was twenty-one weeks pregnant, working from home four days a week and self-isolating on her doctor's orders while awaiting the results of a Covid-19 test. When she refused to return to in-person work, she was fired. Her coworkers, who also refused to return in person, were not fired. Stephens sued, citing the Pregnancy Discrimination Act that prohibits employers from treating pregnant workers differently from others. The case was eventually settled.

Yiyu Lin, a fifty-five-year-old engineer in Massachusetts, had worked for his company since 2005. When his office closed in the early days of the pandemic, Lin began working from home and, he said, was able to perform well. His company ordered everyone back into the office, but Lin requested to continue working remotely, citing his high blood pressure and his eighty-one-year-old disabled mother, who he lived with and who had health issues. He worried about exposing her to the still potentially deadly virus. His bosses refused and fired him, claiming "job abandonment."[3] The court dismissed his caregiver discrimination claim. While the Americans with Disabilities Act requires employers to make reasonable accommodations for disabled workers, it does not require the same for workers who care for the disabled. The Equal Employment Opportunity Commission, early in the pandemic, left workers like Lin facing difficult choices when they made clear that employers didn't have to provide accommodations like telework or flexible schedules under the ADA to those who were worried about exposing disabled or high-risk family members to Covid-19.[4]

Yaritzianne Figueroa-Collazo was an administrative assistant at a construction company in Puerto Rico. When she received notice in August 2020 that her nine-year-old child's school would be virtual that fall, she requested a hybrid work schedule. Her managers granted the hybrid request but fired her eleven days later. Collazo's case was dismissed.[5] Kristen Jarry in Rhode Island was in a similar situation. Though she worked from home for most of the spring and summer of 2020, she was fired in the fall after requesting telework on the days her son with learning disabilities would be in virtual school.[6] The court agreed to hear her case, then dismissed it, ruling that while the Family Medical Leave Act gives people the right to request leave without retaliation, there is no protection to work from home. "That is a fair interpretation of the law," Lee said, "but a reminder that the law is unhelpful."

These are just some of the cases that have made it to court.

Discrimination cases against people with care responsibilities were already on the rise before the pandemic—by 269 percent in the previous decade, according to Jessica Lee and her colleagues at the Center for WorkLife Law.[7] During the pandemic, the number of cases rose. But the reasons for filing—lack of legal protection and an unforgiving overwork culture—hadn't changed. Alaina Harwood, on a fellowship at the Center, tracked forty-three caregiver discrimination lawsuits filed between March 2020 and February 2021. The majority involved disputes over requesting or taking leave from paid work because of a care emergency. The plaintiffs were variously denied leave, approved for leave but then terminated, or suffered retaliation, unfair treatment, demotion, or harassment for even making the request. In half the cases, workers requested flexible hours, a change of schedule, or the ability to work from home because of care responsibilities.

One construction worker requested either a temporary leave or a temporary move to a job site closer to home so he could care for his five-year-old daughter and sick family who had all tested positive for Covid-19. Though he had worked for the company for sixteen years, he was fired just for asking. Nine cases cited sex discrimination. One pregnant worker, worried about having another miscarriage, was furloughed after asking for a flexible workload and schedule. She later learned she was the only employee furloughed. While women brought the majority of cases, twenty-six, it's important to note that seventeen were filed by men. Harwood wrote: "It is evident . . . that many employers do not believe workers can successfully work with accommodations while having caregiving responsibilities."[8]

Long after the pandemic eased, the calls kept coming. "It's constant," Lee said. "It's every state. It's every class of worker, from people who are working hourly jobs all the way up to the folks with the nice, fancy office. Everyone is facing these dilemmas." Before the pandemic, many had set up the complicated web of informal networks that the lack of policy forces households to create on their own, weaving together some child care or after care, with families, friends, and neighbors who can help in a pinch, which enabled people to limp along. But once all those fragile, patchwork arrangements fell apart, it became clear, as the sociologist Jessica Calarco wrote, that while other countries have safety nets, the United States has mothers and caregivers.[9]

For a time during the worst days of the pandemic, Lee was hopeful that things would change for the better. With temporary emergency paid sick and child-care leave, stimulus checks, monthly child tax credit payments, and enhanced unemployment payments, Lee and her colleagues on the helpline spent their time guiding families through these new laws and their rights and navigating a myriad of confusing systems to get the benefits they needed. The temporary measures helped, though they were far from perfect. After a last-minute push by Republican lawmakers, the emergency paid sick and child-care leave law exempted companies with more than five hundred employees, as well as small businesses. That meant the largest employers in the country, such as Walmart, Amazon, and Coca-Cola, didn't have to offer any paid time off. Unless those companies chose to do so, as many as an estimated one hundred million private-sector employees—more than half the entire private workforce, among them the essential frontline workers who stocked shelves, cared for children or the elderly, or made deliveries—were forced to choose between working while sick or staying home without pay. Or they could quit their jobs to care for their families and risk financial ruin.[10] But Lee's hope soured as lawmakers failed to act to permanently support families. By the beginning of 2021, the emergency measures that kept struggling families afloat expired. By September 2023, Congress let a $24 billion Child Care Stabilization Fund expire. The money had enabled more than two hundred thousand child-care providers across the country to pay rent, lower the tuition they charge families, and raise wages for poorly paid child-care workers, which helped stanch the loss to other, higher-paying sectors and kept programs open.[11] Without that support, one survey predicted as many as one in four child-care programs would shutter.[12]

Lawmakers did come closer than ever before to passing universal family-supportive policies that are common in virtually every other advanced nation. But that effort died in late 2021. Congress failed to pass—by one vote—the Biden administration's Build Back Better legislation, which would have provided hundreds of millions of dollars to raise the poverty wages for child and home care workers and capped the cost of child care at 7 percent of a family's income.[13] A provision to give workers four weeks of paid family and medical leave also failed, leaving the United States alone, along with Papua New Guinea and a few Pacific Island nations, as the only countries on Earth that fail to guarantee paid maternity leave to new mothers, and one of a handful with no paid paternity leave for fathers.[14] Build Back Better was eventually resurrected and passed in 2022 as the Inflation Reduction Act, but every mention of support for families and workers with care responsibilities had been erased.[15]

Congress has helped some working families who work for the federal government. Lawmakers have passed bipartisan legislation that makes the federal government and the U.S. military, the largest employers in the country, among the most progressive workplaces in the nation. In 2019, a bipartisan Congress agreed to grant 2.1 million civil servants in the federal workforce twelve weeks of paid parental leave after the birth, adoption, or foster placement of a child.[16] Then in 2023, Congress extended that guarantee to active-duty and reserve members on active duty in the military.[17] Those who give birth in the military now have up to six weeks of consecutive paid maternity convalescent leave to recover from birth,[18] and both parents have twelve weeks each of paid caregiver or parental leave to bond and provide care that they may use intermittently for up to one year.[19] The military also operates the largest employer-sponsored high-quality child-care program in the United States, paying teachers well and charging families on a sliding scale to make it affordable. Military leaders view investing in family-supportive policies as essential to resiliency and mission readiness, recruitment, and retention.[20] The United States is also one of only a handful of countries without a national guarantee that sick workers or those who need to care for someone who's sick may stay home without penalty. (The others are India, South Korea, Sri Lanka, Somalia, and a handful of small Pacific islands.)[21] A few states and local jurisdictions have adopted paid sick leave laws, which have been shown to stabilize the workforce[22] and slow the spread of colds, flu,[23] and the Covid-19 virus.[24] The U.S. system allows employers to choose voluntarily to offer paid sick leave or not. Perhaps not surprisingly, only 6 percent of the lowest-wage employees have access to employer-provided paid leave, compared to 43 percent of employees with the highest wages.[25] That's the difference between viewing paid workers as essential but expendable or as talent.

The pain is acute. "We've had calls from folks who were still in the hospital saying, 'My boss is telling me I have to come back to work. What can I do? Am I going to lose my job? Am I entitled to days off? Can I get paid for any of that?'" Lee recounted. "For a lot of these folks, we just had to tell them no. It's heartbreaking. There's just nothing there for folks."

The general assumption is that only women need work to change to make room for care. But that's not true, not anymore. People with family responsibilities make up nearly three-fourths of the entire U.S. workforce.[26] Let's not forget the millions with chosen families or families of one. People are not machines. Everyone needs time to care for themselves as well. That need to care can be costly to workers.

Women, who are still primarily responsible for providing care, are most likely to be passed over for jobs or promotions or forced out of the workforce. Researchers have puzzled over why U.S. women's labor force participation soared in the 1970s and '80s but then stalled in the early 1990s, even as rates continued to climb and surpass the United States elsewhere. They concluded that the lack of family-supportive laws, policies, and workplace practices in the United States is a big reason why.[27]

The pandemic provided striking evidence: millions of women were missing from the workforce,[28] largely because of care duties. Women made up 60 percent of the first wave of pandemic layoffs, the Kansas City Federal Reserve Bank reported.[29] More mothers lost jobs than fathers. Latina mothers and mothers of young children experienced the steepest initial job losses. Black mothers and mothers with high school educations remained unemployed longer than other mothers.[30] In 2000, the United States ranked seventh of all high-income countries in the share of women in the labor force. By 2022, the United States ranked twenty-fifth.[31] In contrast to the United States, Covid-19 did not force as many women out of paid work in many other countries with more robust support for workers with care duties, including the United Kingdom, Germany, France, and Canada.[32]

The pandemic disruptions and lackluster response to the ensuing care crisis reinforced that workers with care responsibilities didn't need a Great Resignation but a Great Reimagination of paid and unpaid work.

That includes men, too. Masculine "ideal worker" norms at paid work make it difficult to impossible for men who want to be engaged in care and the unpaid work of home. Women around the world perform 265 minutes of unpaid work a day, far outstripping the 83 minutes that men do.[33] In truth, we're caught in a Catch-22. Until there's gender equality in the unpaid work of care that gives women more time and opportunity outside the home, there can never be gender equality in the world of paid work, civic engagement, and political leadership. And there will never be gender equality in the home until men are able to more fairly share the labor there, which will require greedy and exploitive overwork cultures to be transformed.

The World Economic Forum estimates that after the pandemic and its disproportionate harm to workers with care responsibilities, primarily women, reaching full economic gender parity will likely take 268 years.[34] In her book *Equality Within Our Lifetimes*, Jody Heymann, founding director of the WORLD Policy Analysis Center at UCLA, and her coauthors argue that the huge gaps in gender equality are directly linked to laws. Or rather, the lack of them. In their analysis of 193 countries, they found that more than 90 percent have some legal protections against gender discrimination. But only half protect mothers from discrimination, and even fewer protect fathers. "A lot of times gender discrimination actually comes in the form of caregiving discrimination," Heymann said. "The big pay gap is not between men and women. That pay gap exists. But the much bigger pay gap is what happens once a woman has a child or other caregiving responsibilities."[35]

Researchers call this the "maternal wall"—a term popularized by Joan C. Williams, a law professor and founder of the Center for WorkLife Law—to describe the hit in paid work that mothers take after having a child. In ideal worker cultures, the expectation is that women will become the primary caregivers and will thus be less committed or available to the job. Fathers, on the other hand, receive a documented "fatherhood bonus."[36] The expectation is that, once they become fathers, they'll take their paid work even more seriously to provide for their families as breadwinners. Yet the truth, according to an analysis of 2018 data by the Institute for Women's Policy Research, *Holding Up Half the Sky*, is that "one in two of more than 30 million families in the U.S. with children under 18 have a breadwinning *mother* who contributes at least 40 percent of the earnings to the household." Nearly 80 percent of Black married and single mothers are breadwinners, as are about two-thirds of Native American mothers, 56 percent of multiracial mothers, 43 percent of Asian and Pacific Islander mothers, nearly half of Hispanic mothers, and about half, 48 percent, of all married and single white mothers.[37] The share of breadwinning-mother families ranges from a high of 71 percent in Washington, D.C., and 60 percent in Mississippi to a low of 34 percent in Utah, where the Mormon Church espouses traditional gender roles and teaches that men are heads of household tasked with breadwinning while women provide care at home.[38] Over the first eighteen years of motherhood, longitudinal research has found that 70 percent of mothers can expect to be their family's breadwinner at some point.[39] From the time women entered the workforce en masse in the 1970s, they've played a critical role in their family's economic stability and wellbeing. Economist Heather Boushey has shown that one of the key factors driving mothers into the paid workforce was the declining and stagnating wages for men and the beginning of the end of good-paying full-time blue-collar jobs, which have since been replaced by temporary, part-time, low-wage service and precarious contract jobs. Gone was the family wage with benefits that policymakers, business leaders, and unions worked together to craft in the two decades following World War II. It was mothers' additional hours and income, Boushey's research shows, that kept many families afloat, clinging to their middle-class status or staying out of the depths of poverty.[40]

That story has gotten buried under a false narrative that selfish mothers are "choosing" to abandon their families to work outside the home.[41] Far from pin money for extras, as many still think,[42] mothers' earnings are vital to their families' ability to survive, much less thrive.

Yet only about one-third of the workforce is covered by laws that make it illegal to discriminate on the basis of care,[43] Lee explained, and these are state and local laws and often only protect parents.[44] To win cases, attorneys like Lee have to figure out how a caregiver discrimination suit might work under this patchwork of state and local laws or existing federal laws that are designed for other things. When they filed their first brief on gender discrimination before the U.S. Supreme Court,[45] Ruth Bader Ginsburg and civil rights activist Pauli Murray used the Fourteenth Amendment to the Constitution, which guarantees equal protection under the law to all citizens. Similarly, Lee and others have been forced to use Title VII of the Civil Rights Act, which prohibits sex discrimination, or the Family Medical Leave Act, which guarantees some full-time workers—about 60 percent of the workforce—twelve weeks of unpaid family leave, or the Americans with Disabilities Act, the Pregnancy Discrimination Act, the Equal Pay Act, or a handful of others.

During the pandemic, when workers with care duties were denied or unable to telework or weren't eligible for paid leave, Lee and other attorneys had to resort to helping them file mental health claims for severe depression or anxiety in order to qualify for ADA disability accommodations.[46] In late 2022, a bipartisan Congress passed the Pregnant Workers Fairness Act. That law, for which advocates lobbied for ten years, requires employers to make reasonable accommodations for pregnant workers when medically necessary to keep them on the job, such as offering a stool to pregnant cashiers, appropriate body armor for pregnant police officers, or lighter duties rather than heavy lifting for pregnant delivery drivers or warehouse workers—all scenarios that employers have refused to accommodate in the past.

Sometimes the law works. Lee was able to use the law to help Lindsey Smith. Smith was a top-rated nurse practitioner working for a private home visiting company in Minnesota. She had begun to have complications with her pregnancy. After her daughter was born in 2021 and Smith returned from a partially paid four-month maternity leave, the baby struggled to breastfeed, couldn't tolerate formula, and began to lose a significant amount of body weight.

Worried, Smith, a single mother, asked for one of the company's open telework positions so she could help her baby eat between calls. Her company refused. She then put together a plan for a flexible schedule that would enable her to meet her client load and return home to pump or breastfeed between house calls. Instead, the firm told her to pump breast milk in her car twice a day for twenty minutes between appointments. It was winter. Smith worked in areas where carjackings were on the rise and police warned people not to sit idly in their cars. "I'm imagining myself with my scrub top off, my boobs out in these big suction cups," she said. The company told her to buy curtains for her car. "I kept being told, 'This is what others do and no one complains.'"

Smith had spent years working as a nurse practitioner on the Syrian border, running refugee clinics and advocating for better health and conditions for women and children throughout the Middle East. She decided to do the same for herself in the United States. She *would* complain. Especially after her employer began scheduling appointments that made it difficult even to pump during the promised two times a day. Smith reached out to Lee and her colleagues, who wrote letters informing the company that they were violating both state and federal law. In 1998, Minnesota became the first state in the country to require employers to provide reasonable accommodations for nursing mothers.[47] And in 2010, the Affordable Care Act, known as Obamacare, included a requirement for employers with more than fifty employees to provide breastfeeding mothers with reasonable break time and a shielded place other than a bathroom to be able to pump breast milk for one year after a child's birth.[48] But the law had inadvertently excluded about nine million workers, including teachers and nurses. So in the waning days of 2022, a bipartisan Congress passed the PUMP Act to rectify that. The act also protected mothers against retaliation and gave them the right to sue their employers.[49]

Shortly after Jessica Lee and her colleagues sent the warning letter to Smith's employer, Smith was terminated, just five weeks after returning from maternity leave. In a panic, Smith applied for public benefits and unemployment. She borrowed from family to pay her rent. And she reached out again to Lee, who connected her to an attorney who helped Smith sue the company for caregiver discrimination. Her case was settled out of court. Smith has now partnered with another nurse practitioner and they've started their own clinic and telemedicine company. "Part of the reason for me starting my own business is never wanting anyone to have the power to take away my own livelihood again," she told me.

In cases where there's no legal recourse, Lee and her colleagues can write letters citing workers' legal rights that employers might have been violating or try to negotiate for accommodations to keep workers on the job. Sometimes, they offer to coach workers through the process of standing up to their employers. But it can be arduous, with no guarantees. "People either stop answering their phones or they say they're just going to move on."

Lee can tick off these anguished stories like a well-worn litany: The retail worker who needed vacation time to care for her aging parent and was denied, even when her coworkers were allowed to schedule vacation time. No reason given. The grocery store assistant who asked to keep her part-time schedule so she could care for her family and was then ghosted by her manager; though technically still on the payroll, she was cut to zero hours of guaranteed work. The men needing to care for loved ones who were denied schedule changes because their bosses said that their wives should be the ones giving care. The low-wage workers without child care who worried that if they left their children unsupervised at home, they'd be reported to Child Protective Services. The workers with care duties who are forced to stop teleworking, regardless of how productive they've been, and summoned back to their offices with no recourse other than to quit. The people who are denied the right to work from home or have a flexible schedule, even as coworkers are granted the same requests, unless they can prove they have regular child care.

It shouldn't be so ridiculously impossible, Lee said, to combine good paid work and time for good care. Employers act with impunity because they can, since there are so few laws or policies that prohibit caregiver discrimination. Many offer no explanation for why they refuse reasonable requests that would keep people working, which Lee finds "infuriating." In her calendar, Lee schedules regular times to cry or rage at the unnecessary suffering and what she calls the absurdity of it all, before moving on to the next case.

What keeps Lee coming back to her desk on the second floor of her Virginia farmhouse is a deep and profound belief that changing paid work and care is possible. Her own history is proof of change. "Most of my ancestors had no choice but to work for someone else who literally owned them," she said.

Her last name, Lee, came to her from her ancestors' enslavers: the family of Confederate general Robert E. Lee. Her grandfather integrated his profession and boasted about being the first Black electrician in western Connecticut. He lived in Connecticut because he returned from fighting for the air force in Europe in World War II with a white German wife and it was illegal for an interracial married couple to live in his home state of Virginia at the time. "Just knowing exactly how far we have come, the mountain doesn't feel quite as high."

Caregiver discrimination has been around as long as there have been workers with care responsibilities in the workplace. One attorney calls the period just after a parental leave the "danger zone." "That's a very dangerous time for our clients," Susan Crumiller, an attorney in New York, told me. But the cases are difficult to litigate. In addition to the patchwork laws and lack of case law that sets clear precedents, half of U.S. workers are subject to pay secrecy cultures or policies—although they have been illegal since the 1930s. So it can be difficult to find and prove pay gaps or discrimination compared to coworkers without care responsibilities.[50]

The kind of caregiver discrimination Jessica Lee specializes in is discrimination against pregnant and breastfeeding workers. In the past decade, she found prevalent lactation discrimination and hardship. In three-fourths of breastfeeding discrimination lawsuits filed, families experienced economic losses and two-thirds of plaintiffs wound up losing their jobs.[51] That doesn't include those women who never filed a complaint to begin with—typically people with fewer resources or who are isolated and not attached to a union. (It's not surprising, perhaps, that employment attorney Tom Spiggle's book is titled *You're Pregnant? You're Fired!*[52])

Galen Sherwin, an attorney formerly with the ACLU, says she has seen the most egregious examples of caregiver bias in male-dominated professions. In 2016, Sherwin began filing a series of lawsuits against Frontier Airlines on behalf of flight attendants and pilots who said they were forced to choose either their job or breastfeeding, which both the American Academy of Pediatrics and the World Health Organization recommend be done exclusively for the first six months of an infant's life and continued as long as mutually desired, along with appropriate nutritious food, for two years or longer.[53] The airline settled with the flight attendants in 2022, promising that they could pump breastmilk during flights and that they would no longer be disciplined for a pregnancy-related absence. Frontier agreed to provide a list of airport lactation facilities as well as alternate work assignments for flight attendants unable to fly because of pregnancy or lactation, rather than force them to take unpaid leave, as had been the practice.[54]

Frontier settled with the pilots in December 2023. Frontier will now be one of the first airlines to allow pilots to pump breastmilk in the cockpit during noncritical phases of the flight, the ACLU reported.[55] To Sherwin, the difficult yearslong battle for the breastfeeding pilots is a clear example of how the way in which some businesses organize work can close a field off to those with care responsibilities or force them out of their jobs at a time when they most need economic security, while starting or growing a family. "The decks are really stacked against them," Sherwin told me. "That's perhaps why only 6 percent of airline pilots are women. It's not coincidental."

It's also not coincidental that women, particularly those with young children, are leaving the unforgiving workforce to start their own businesses. That way, they can have the kind of flexible paid jobs they need to make their family lives work. Like Lindsey Smith, the nurse practitioner who started her own business when she was fired after demanding breastfeeding accommodations. Attorney Susan Crumiller also started her own law firm in 2016 after her employer reneged on an agreed five-month paid maternity leave. Instead, he asked her to return to work seven weeks after delivery. "I built this law firm myself, starting with just me in my bathrobe and my baby, sitting at the dining room table," she said. Her team is primarily female. The attorneys all have flexible schedules and work virtually. "Everyone works super hard, everyone is committed. And I give as much paid maternity leave as I can," she said. "I just gave one of my associates five months. Oh my God, that makes me so happy."

In 2022, an estimated six hundred thousand more workers than in 2019 opened their own businesses or started working for themselves; the majority of them women. The increase was much larger among women with children under the age of six,[56] women such as Michelle Sunder. A mother of two small children, she had been working flat out as an events director for a nonprofit in Chicago before the pandemic. Once everything went into lockdown, she frantically tried to figure out how to convert in-person gatherings to meaningful virtual events while also managing the care and education of her children without school, child care, or much structure in their lives. What had been a complicated and often frazzled life became even more so. "It was really hard. Hard to be a good parent and a good employee," she said. Sunder needed more flexibility than she felt her organization could allow.

"I kept telling myself that I wanted something to be different," she said. She began having conversations with her husband, wondering if she could turn her hobby as a wedding planner into a full-time profession. His full-time job would provide the family with health-care coverage. "The answer we kept coming back to was, 'If I was doing my own business, I would have a lot more flexibility during the week when he didn't. Then he could really pick things up on the weekends or in the evenings when I needed to be on for my clients. We saw that as just a win for us." So she made the leap and opened Bustle and Lace. "No regrets," she said.

While conservatives and neoliberals have hailed self-employment as an answer to work and care conflicts,[57] it is no panacea. For people with education, resources, and status—and a high-earning partner certainly helps—self-employment *can* give workers with care responsibilities more control over their schedules and the flexibility they need. But for low- and moderate-income workers and single mothers or caregivers, self-employment is risky and often comes with more precarity.[58] Caitlyn Collins, a professor of sociology at Washington University in St. Louis and author of *Making Motherhood Work: How Women Manage Careers and Caregiving,* calls the push for women to become entrepreneurs a "neoliberal solution to a structural failing." "I have so many women talk to me about entrepreneurialism as the solution to their work-family conflict, and I'm like, 'Yeah, that's a highly individualized decision you've made to find a way to manage your own stress better, absent the sort of robust structural changes that would enable more flexibility for all workers,'" Collins told me.

"You don't hear folks in Sweden talking about needing to become entrepreneurs to resolve their stress," she said. That's because they have policy structures such as paid family leave and affordable child care and the right to request flexible work, which make it easier to combine paid work and care. Collins understands that self-employment is a logical choice for many Americans with care responsibilities in the face of impossible circumstances. "U.S. culture really prides itself on individualism, so of course we applaud people for pulling themselves up by their entrepreneurial bootstraps," she says. But applauding them obfuscates the larger problem, "which is that it is impossible for most people to combine work and family in ways that feel just and humane to them. So six hundred thousand more people choosing that route doesn't surprise me. But it's also a Band-Aid on a bullet hole."

Why is it so difficult to combine work and care? Why are there no real laws, policies, or regulations to support working families, and why is work organized to so easily discriminate against those with care responsibilities, when the majority of workers have them?

It all comes down to the stories we choose to believe. Most Americans still believe that it's better for young children to be raised at home by a parent—in heterosexual couples that means the mother—and for the family to be supported by the father's work, like in the imagined 1950s white middle-class breadwinner-homemaker households. In a 2018 Pew Research Center survey, 44 percent of Americans said this was the ideal family style. Thirty-six percent favored one full-time and one part-time working parent. Four in ten thought the mother should be the one to stay home or work part-time. Only 18 percent thought both parents working was ideal. (Just 21 percent of men and 16 percent of women preferred dual working-parent families.) Among those over sixty-five—about the age of many lawmakers in Congress,[59] CEOs, and business leaders[60]—nearly 60 percent favored traditional families. Just 8 percent considered both parents working an ideal situation.[61]

This is hardly surprising. Why would anyone choose a family arrangement that a lack of policy and rigid overwork cultures make so impossible?

Another Pew Research Center survey asked Americans which traits society most values for men and women. "Caring" and "compassionate" were chosen nearly unanimously as the most valuable traits for women and were seen more negatively for men. For men, participants chose "provider" as a key valuable trait. No one chose that for women.[62]

There are other arguments that get thrown around explaining the status quo in America. Some will fret that child care is bad for children and snap up deeply flawed studies produced by conservative think tanks.[63] Conservatives will say family is a private matter and the government should play no role in providing child care, paid leave, or requiring flexible work schedules. That was the argument President Richard Nixon used to veto a bipartisan bill that would have created a universal child-care system in the 1970s. He likened child care to Soviet communism.[64]

These same lawmakers, however, have no problem violating the most private part of family life: one's bodily autonomy, personal liberty, and right to control one's own reproduction and decisions about when and how to start a family. They've been pushing restrictive and dangerous policies after the Supreme Court overturned the fifty-year-old *Roe v. Wade* legal precedent guaranteeing access to abortion care as part of a constitutional right to privacy.

Lawmakers in both parties will balk at the cost of family-supportive policies or say that the market should fix the problem. That view conveniently ignores the fact, as we've seen, that child care is a broken market: parents pay too much, child-care workers earn too little, and most providers barely scrape by.

But these are all distractions. The real issue is the still unsettled norm around gender roles and the queasiness we have about mothers of young children working outside the home. This queasiness has harmful consequences. The Idaho state legislature, for instance, prohibited some pandemic-era federal funds it received from being spent on child care for children ages one to four.[65] They voted to return millions of dollars to the federal government rather than spend it on child care, despite the protests of local parents and child-care providers. Republican representative Charlie Shepherd said that he wanted to stop any effort "that makes it easier or more convenient for mothers to come out of the home and let others raise their child."[66]

This discomfort about mothers working outside the home, however, has extended only to white mothers. Black mothers and mothers of color have been expected to work to support their families or struggle to survive on a miserly public safety net when they can't.[67] American policymakers had no trouble supporting women staying home to raise their children with public dollars when they thought the beneficiaries were white widows in the 1930s. That changed in the 1960s when they, falsely, believed Black "welfare queens" were scamming the system. Benefit levels dropped and were replaced with intrusive policies and stringent work requirements.[68] In 2019, poverty researcher Zach Parolin found that the higher proportion of Black people there are in a state, the more likely those states are to redirect welfare funds to programs like marriage promotion or abstinence-only sex education, "to try to change the way poor families run their lives, rather than simply help them with basic expenses."[69]

Views like these are why the child-care system is so starved in the United States. They've made having a child prohibitively expensive. The first seventeen years of a child's life costs the average middle-class family about $300,000, according to one estimate, and that's before the cost of often outrageously expensive college tuition or help transitioning to adulthood.[70] The Build Back Better goal to cap child-care costs at 7 percent of family income is so out of reach to most parents, who instead pay between 8 and nearly 20 percent of their income *per child*, according to a detailed database of child-care prices by county compiled by the Women's Bureau at the Department of Labor. For single parents, infant care can eat up anywhere from 24 to 75 percent of family income. Annual child-care costs in 2018 ranged from more than $4,810 to $15,417 per child, depending on the type of care, a child's age, and the population size of a county. The Women's Bureau analysis found that the cost of child care exceeds 7 percent of family income in *more than 90 percent* of U.S. counties.[71] That cost continues to climb: average household child-care costs have spiked more than 30 percent from 2019 to 2023.[72] As one researcher told me, "Child care is not affordable anywhere."

Far from furthering traditional families, as conservatives hope, one survey found that the high cost of child care is discouraging family formation in the first place. Many young people are choosing not to have children, or not as many as they had hoped.[73] This is contributing to the aging of the population and the concern that there won't be enough young workers in succeeding generations to pay for the Social Security and Medicare promised to the top-heavy aging population. Yet caring for adult loved ones at the other end of life is costly, as well as physically and emotionally draining. Nearly fifty million people—one in five Americans—care for an adult. The majority, around 60 percent, are women. But in recent years, more men are spending time as caregivers.[74] With the high cost of paid care for the aging, most try to juggle their own paid work with about thirty billion hours a year of unpaid family caregiving, one RAND study found,[75] which often comes at a steep price, particularly for women, in lost jobs, reduced hours and pay, and financial instability.[76]

The argument against investing public dollars in supporting families with child care, family care, paid leave, or flexible work ignores the fact that these policies typically end up paying for themselves. Instead of a slew of lawsuits, complaints to the U.S. Equal Employment Opportunity Commission (EEOC), pain and suffering, lost morale, toxic work environments, disrupted workplaces, employee turnover, and steep training and replacement costs, workers with care responsibilities could actually *keep doing their jobs* and supporting their families.

California's state paid leave policy, for instance, enacted in 2004 and the first in the country, led to fewer hourly workers being forced off the job after having a child and kept them out of poverty and off public benefits.[77] Quebec's subsidized universal child-care program, which raised caregiver wages in the public nonprofit sector[78] and held the cost of child care to $7 a day, wound up paying for itself. With stable child care, more mothers and parents were able to keep doing their paid jobs. That produced greater family economic stability and higher returns to the government: more workers with jobs meant more people could pay income taxes and fewer would need to rely on public services. With a steady paycheck, workers also increased their purchasing power, so businesses expanded and the government reaped the benefit of increased consumption, investment, and corporate taxes.[79]

The benefits of high-quality care can last a lifetime. Nobel economist James Heckman's research showed that comprehensive, high-quality child care can deliver a 13 percent return on investment every year, from the near-term benefit of keeping parents employed to the long-term benefits to children. In his studies, children in high-quality child care did better in school and graduated from high school at higher rates. These factors led to better jobs with higher incomes, better health, and lower spending on public benefits.[80]

The deeply held belief that children will suffer if their mothers work in the labor market is a clear example of what researchers call the pervasive and persistent motherhood myth.[81] That false notion stymies public policy and organizational change at work and slams many mothers into the maternal wall,[82] in Joan C. Williams's phrase. Williams is a visionary who pioneered the legal theory behind caregiver discrimination. Research shows how employers see mothers and workers with care responsibilities as less competent, committed, and ambitious.[83] This makes it easier to pass them up for jobs, promotions, and pay raises. They're often the first to be fired, furloughed, or laid off. Daphne Delvaux, an attorney who focuses on caregiver discrimination cases, noted that she has seen job offers rescinded once employers discover that a woman is pregnant or finds out they have children. "I'm seeing a lot of caregiver discrimination on the front end now," she said.

This steadfast belief that those with care responsibilities are lesser workers has meant that none of the evidence showing how they are instead highly productive, creative, and capable contributors, despite often working in unforgiving circumstances, has made much of a dent. Nor have the statistics confirming that gender equity and family-supportive policies create a happier, healthier, and engaged workforce and lead to greater business efficiency, performance, and profits. The organization and culture of work hasn't changed much. It is also why the same workers suffered disproportionately during the pandemic and received so little support.[84] "The problem is not really about efficiency or productivity," Williams said. "It's about identity." In U.S. culture, paid work and overwork define the status and measure of a man, and care is what women are expected to do. Mothers are tolerated at paid work as long as they prioritize providing or managing unpaid care at home. The fact of mothers working outside the home has been so threatening to those deeply held notions of traditional gender roles that they've been blamed for a host of ills, from the high cost of housing to unemployment, divorce, child rowdyism, crime, increased mental illness, economic woes, and more.[85]

"Advocating change in the way work is done and life is lived meets resistance because it places these cherished identities at risk," Williams once wrote. "Resistance to these identity threats keeps current workplace norms in place."[86] For this reason, men who hold babies on their laps during virtual meetings or have children pop up in the background are often seen as endearing or adorable—*Look! He's helping out. What a great guy!*—while mothers such as Drisana Rios get fired—*How can she get her work done with her kids running around?* Rios's employer said her children were too noisy.[87] Rios sued, citing gender discrimination and disparate treatment compared to her male coworkers, who also worked on calls with children's noise in the background but were *not* fired. Rios's company settled with her out of court.[88]

The treatment Rios suffered was not at all surprising to Jill Yavorsky, a sociologist at the University of North Carolina at Charlotte, who researches the interplay between work and gender. Yavorsky and her colleagues, Yue Qian and Rebecca Glauber, found that when care responsibilities encroached on workers' productivity, mothers suffered more. In a survey of 280 managers, Yavorsky and her colleagues found that managers were much more likely to penalize mothers during the pandemic if their productivity dropped due to care responsibilities, writing them off as less ambitious or less committed to their jobs. When fathers experienced the same productivity drop for the same reason, managers were still more likely to promote and reward them, seeing the caregiving duties as a short-term anomaly warranting a little slack and support of an otherwise dedicated worker.[89]

These gendered beliefs are powerful and sticky. Sarah Thébaud, a sociologist at the University of Santa Barbara, along with other researchers, surveyed a representative sample of the U.S. population to determine just how powerful and sticky. They found some signs of progress: men and women were viewed as similarly knowledgeable, persuasive, hardworking, successful, brave, well connected, and logical. Respondents in fact perceived women to be, on average, *more* competent, even brilliant, intelligent, unconventional, and visionary than men. But they saw those traits as significantly more *desirable* in men than in women. In a hopeful sign, respondents viewed traits that have long been associated with women, such as being caring, supportive, family-oriented, kind, and affectionate, to be highly desirable traits for both men and women, particularly for mothers and fathers. But holding a breadwinner/provider status, they found, was "extremely durable" as one of the most desirable traits for a man and far less so for a woman. Being seen as submissive and deferential were considered somewhat desirable traits for women, whereas they were intensely undesirable for men.

Just as our gendered cultural norms tolerate women in the paid workforce as long as their care duties come first, the norms are beginning to tolerate men who take on more care duties. But only if they don't get in the way of their paid work.[90] "What the research shows is that men cannot *not* be breadwinners," Thébaud told me.

This gendered notion that the ideal worker/breadwinner is or *should* be a man with no caregiving duties and women *should* shoulder the responsibility for the unpaid work of care and home is a big part of the reason for the gender wage and wealth gap. Jobs men tend to do pay more than jobs women do. All but four of the thirty highest-paying jobs in the United States are male-dominated. Of the thirty that pay the lowest, all but seven are female-dominated[91] (think computer programmers vs. health-care workers). Even in lower-wage work, men are paid more (think higher-paid male-dominated janitors vs. poorly paid female-dominated house cleaners).[92] Women in the U.S. labor market tend to work in lower-paying female-dominated professions[93] and make up two-thirds of the low-wage workforce.[94] Beyond that, men in female-dominated professions tend to make more than women in the same roles.[95] And when more women enter what had been male-dominated fields, the pay drops.[96] The bottom line is that our society values men and the work they do, whatever that work is, more. And the time women spend caring for others and making homes, caring for families, and enhancing everyone's quality of life remains invisible, unvalued, and taken for granted, even though advocate Ai-jen Poo calls it "the work that makes all other work possible."[97]

■

Though the pandemic led to increased caregiver discrimination, it also, in some cases, opened up opportunities for people who don't fit the ideal worker mold. In some companies, leaders and managers are finally willing to think differently and experiment creatively, weaning themselves from the notion that being always available is a mark of the best workers or that work is best done in one rigid way. At the Kawasaki plant in Lincoln, Nebraska, for example, managers couldn't find enough candidates to meet demand. They approached the community to ask what would bring people in to fill the jobs. Those with care responsibilities said that Kawasaki's set shift schedules didn't work for them. So the company created a new part-time 9:00 a.m. to 2:00 p.m. shift, paying $19 an hour. This allowed people to pick up or drop off children at school or spend afternoons caring for family members. "We started something new here . . . that's helping people be successful with their families," one Kawasaki manager told CNN.[98]

Many workers who in 2019 might have been afraid to ask for flexible hours now either expect them or are willing to walk away if they don't get them. Some desk workers with care responsibilities have thrived as firms switched from focusing on physical presence and hours to output, deliverables, and performance. At one point during the pandemic, Jenna Jordan, a senior manager in the Dallas office of BDO, a large accounting, tax, and advisory services firm, thought she'd have to step back or out of the workforce entirely. Without child care, and with a husband who had an equally demanding career in IT, it became close to impossible to combine work and caring for their two small children. But BDO had a history of embracing flexible work, judging workers by performance, not face time or hours logged. Jordan's managers encouraged her to focus on her job's key priorities and attend to them at times when it made most sense for her family. She and her husband also committed to sharing the unpaid care responsibilities at home, trading off by working in shifts. Instead of leaving the workforce, Jordan was promoted. "It's very easy for me to demonstrate what I'm doing from a remote perspective, where you don't need to see me day to day. And I don't need to see that from the people I manage, either," she said. "We do truly try to judge by the work product, as opposed to when, where, and how it's done."

For essential workers, labor shortages resulting from the pandemic led many companies to raise wages, by 20 percent in the low-wage retail sector and by about one-third in the low-wage food and accommodation sector.[99] That benefited the women and women of color who are overrepresented in these jobs.[100]

The pandemic changed some men, too. Many who were forced to work at home for the first time saw the once-invisible unpaid labor that goes into caring for a family and making a home. "I could no longer keep stepping over the basket of unfolded laundry thinking that wasn't my job," Stephen Dypiangco told me.[101] Or not noticing it at all. Some men began sharing care and housework more fairly. In some cases, partners of nurses and other female essential workers became the primary caregivers for their families, and they have remained so. In the early days of the pandemic, when Melissa Head, a nurse in Salt Lake City, began working long shifts, sometimes up to eighty hours a week, her husband, Richard, a sales rep for a large food distributor, shifted to at-home work and became the primary caregiver for their two young children. In 2023, he was still filling that role. "I do the brunt of the housework. She does help out for sure, when she's home on her days off," he said, sounding like many women describing their male partners helping out. "But I'm the sole child-care provider for my kids."[102]

Most men reverted to their more traditional breadwinner role once schools reopened, one survey found. But a not insignificant share of fathers, one in five, continued to do more child care than before the pandemic, and one-quarter continued to do more of the housework.[103] Some men came to love the time they spent with their families and refused to return to full-time, inflexible in-person work, cutting back hours or quitting and changing jobs to maintain a flexible schedule.

That's the story of Mark Attico, a single father, one small bright spot that shows how changing policy and work can make life better for people with care responsibilities. Attico had worked for fifteen years booking corporate travel in Arizona. An acrimonious separation, a twenty-mile commute to his ex's house, and a hectic fixed work schedule left him with little time for his son. After having been a hands-on father when his son was little, he rarely saw his preteen more than a few times a month. He worried that they were growing apart and that he wasn't the kind of father he'd hoped to be. "I'm a Black man. There's this whole societal trope of how Black men don't want to be fathers or participate with their kids. I'd tried to get away from that. When my son was a baby, I made sure I made it to all the pediatrician appointments. I was signing him up for activities, looking for summer camps. Really trying to go over the top in terms of participating and being part of his life, and not doing just the standard Stoic Dad stuff," Attico told me. Things started to go sideways when his son reached middle school. "He had his room at my apartment. But it was like a ghost town for all those years."

Attico couldn't shake thinking about the pernicious stereotype of the absent Black father. "I knew that's not what I wanted," he said, but he felt that he didn't have much choice. Still, "it gets into your head," he said. "It was devastating for my sense of identity, my mental health."

Not surprisingly, in the early days of the pandemic, there was little demand for booking business trips as the travel industry shut down. After a few months, Attico's company turned his furlough into a layoff, and he applied for unemployment. In the first bright spot of Attico's story, the system worked. The unemployment insurance system in the United States often doesn't, which can hit people with care responsibilities who depend on regular earnings the hardest.[104] In 2019, less than one-third of unemployed workers who needed insurance payments received them, and their experiences differed wildly depending on where they lived. Other high-income countries, such as Denmark, Iceland, Belgium, Japan, and South Korea, provide the unemployed with as much as 70 to nearly 90 percent of their lost wages,[105] and some for as long as two years or more. Some, like Germany,[106] also provide education and retraining opportunities to help people find not only new jobs but better jobs.[107] In contrast, the U.S. system has grown increasingly less effective since it was created in 1935.[108] To get the legislation through Congress in the first place, lawmakers were forced to appease legislators from the South, who, some argue, were intent on preventing Black workers from receiving benefits. Although the program is funded through federal and state taxes collected from employers, Congress failed to set national standards, granting states the authority to run their unemployment insurance programs virtually any way they like, limiting who is eligible, the amount they receive, and for how long.[109]

Some states reimburse 50 percent of a worker's wages. Others provide only 30 percent.[110] In some states, like New Jersey, 59 percent of unemployed workers received benefits in 2019. That same year in Florida, only 11 percent did.[111] Some states provide unemployment insurance for only twelve weeks. The amount workers receive ranges from decent to punishingly stingy. With payments averaging $236 a week, Arizona, where Attico lives, was ranked at the very bottom of *Forbes*'s 2023 list.[112] Instead of an unemployment insurance system that helps workers bounce back or climb farther up the socioeconomic ladder, it can send them spiraling into poverty.[113]

The experience of being unemployed in the United States is so fraught that people out of work are 83 percent more likely to develop a stress-related condition, such as stroke or cardiovascular disease.[114] They experience higher rates of depression[115] and face a higher risk of suicide.[116] The reason why the system doesn't work is due to another story many in power in our ideal worker overwork culture choose to believe: that people who aren't working are lazy. They fear a functioning unemployment insurance would make it easy for people to avoid getting back to work.[117]

Sarah Damaske, a professor of sociology and labor at Penn State who researches unemployment and is the author of *The Tolls of Uncertainty: How Privilege and the Guilt Gap Shape Unemployment in America*, said such views and a parsimonious system can create intense stigma and guilt for those out of work, and for women and mothers in particular. She has found that women and mothers, who have been taught to think of themselves first as caregivers, will devote whatever means they have to their families, often sacrificing their own health. Because losing a job typically means losing employer-provided health care, Damaske found that unemployed women were more likely to stop taking medication to make sure the family got fed. Damaske even interviewed women who shared asthma inhalers because, without health insurance, they were too expensive. "The image of having to call your neighbor while you're gasping for breath, I just couldn't get over that," she said.

But when Attico was forced to apply for unemployment, twenty-two million people in the United States were similarly out of paid work because of the pandemic lockdown.[118] In response, Congress temporarily increased unemployment insurance payments by $600 a week, expanded eligibility, and enabled part-time workers, gig workers, and the self-employed to apply for benefits for the first time. They also extended the time that people could receive benefits. The understaffed and antiquated state systems were overwhelmed, and desperate people reported being kept on hold for hours, erroneously denied benefits, or forced to wait for them for months. But Attico sent in his paperwork and within a month began receiving regular deposits.

The sum was enough to cover his rent and bills, sparing him, a man in his forties, from losing his apartment and moving in with his mother, as he'd feared. Congress and the states also expanded Medicaid eligibility, so when Attico lost his employer-provided health insurance along with his job, he still had access to health care. Because he had these supports, he could survive. He also had the time and psychological ease he needed to look for a stable yet flexible job with good pay and benefits, rather than panicking and taking the first one that came along at a time when there were few. "Back then, you could maybe get a job as a clerk at a grocery store making twelve or thirteen dollars an hour," Attico recalled.

In a few months, he found a position as a customer service rep for a health insurance company with pay and benefits on par with his previous job. It offered a flexible schedule and the ability to work from home. So when Attico's son began struggling with online schooling, the boy's mother, who worked on-site in a doctor's office, suggested he spend his days with his father. Attico was able to organize his time around his son and patiently helped him with schoolwork, poking his head out of his home office to check on him. "Need anything? Doing okay?" he'd ask at various points throughout the day. The two began taking long walks with the dog, since there wasn't much else that people could do at the time. They cooked together and watched TV. Attico taught him to drive. Slowly they rebuilt their relationship. "It has been such a blessing," Attico said.

In the second bright spot of Attico's story, he would have been unlikely, before the pandemic, to find a flexible work arrangement. If he had one, research shows, as a man he would most probably have been stigmatized and seen as a lesser worker for violating the masculine ideal worker norm. In one study, senior managers mocked a man with caregiving responsibilities who wanted a flexible schedule and thought of him as "a bit of a wuss."[119]

In an ideal worker work culture, real men aren't supposed to *want* to give care. Some men don't, but I wondered for years how true the assumption was. When I became director of the Better Life Lab at New America, a nonpartisan think tank, we had the chance to find out. Through a nationally representative quantitative survey, qualitative focus groups, and extensive reporting, we found that more than 80 percent of men believe that unpaid care work is as valuable to society as paid work *and* that men should share those responsibilities equally. But most felt that they couldn't, expecting to be punished at work if they did.[120] That's a chance that many men weren't willing to take. In most different-sex partnerships, men tend to be older, farther along in their careers, and make more money. Because the United States' lack of family supportive policies leaves people to pay for everything out of pocket, it's not surprising that couples tend to prioritize the man's job, with women taking on paid work that is more flexible and less time intensive. And this only cements traditional gender roles further.[121] When Attico's new company, like so many others, started calling employees back to the office, saying they worked "better together," Attico began looking for another job. He was no longer willing to give up the flexibility he needed to be the kind of father he wanted to be. His son had begun to stay with him regularly and text him when they weren't together. After his son's grandfather died, Attico had the time to sit with him and help him sort through his grief. A few months later, Attico quit and took a fully telework position with good pay and benefits. His story isn't of sweeping workplace change, but it is a small light of hope in the dark. That the unemployment system worked for him shows that the government *can* work to make people's lives better when it wants to. That he was able to find good, fully flexible digital work, something that would have been much harder to do before the pandemic, shows that there are at least more options than before. And the fact that he can be open about caregiving as a man without penalty is a big step forward.

"My passion has always really been wanting to have a relationship with my son. It's by far the most important thing," Attico said. "This is just pure quality of life."

CHAPTER 3

THE WICKED PROBLEM OF REDESIGNING WORK

> You can't depend on your eyes when your imagination is out of focus.
>
> —*Mark Twain*[1]

In late 2013, Richard Taylor, then a senior vice president and director of human relations at Intel, came up with a novel idea with his team. They wondered how far they could go to change work, people's experience of it, and the perceived norms that shape workplace cultures. They wanted to test pilots of "very, very different" models to redesign work in a way that would help the company's goals *and* create the kinds of jobs that would enable employees to feel fulfilled and give them time for their lives and care responsibilities. The small group of dreamers, the Work Practice Innovations team, began to test "wild and wacky ideas and see which ones get some life," he told me.

Freelance Nation was one of those ideas. The daring brilliance of the idea, its execution, and ultimately its fate serves as both an inspiration and a cautionary tale at a time of potential transformation after the disruptions and innovations of the Covid-19 era. The story of Freelance Nation shows how powerful and fast-moving businesses can be when legislation, litigation, regulation, or worker risings can take years to compel change. It proves that taking a risk and pioneering new and better ways to work can benefit companies as well as employees, especially those with care responsibilities. By showing the contours of the possible and building from the principles of fairness, cooperation, and meaning, a single company's work redesign can inspire others to follow suit. But the story demonstrates how hard it is, despite solid evidence of success, to make change stick.

At Intel, one of the world's largest manufacturers of central processing units and semiconductors, the Work Practice Innovations team, true to the radical vision of doing things differently, wasn't your typical HR team. It included a social scientist, an electrical engineer, a veteran manager, a user experience design expert, a leader of the Great Places to Work team, a content strategist, a manufacturing expert, and one "not quite-HR HR person."[2] Once assembled, they sat on bouncy balls. They papered the walls with colorful Post-it notes from design thinking sessions. They dug into work redesign research. Perhaps most important, they fanned out to talk to employees across the company to listen to their pain points, their sense of unfairness, and their ideas for how to work better. They used what they called a "blue sky" approach. Everything was on the table. There were no limits. They joked that they were "poking the bear"—the inertia of the status quo—looking for big ideas as well as smaller tweaks that could make day-to-day work better for everyone.

For Taylor, the redesigns had to work for the company. He'd have to justify whatever the team came up with to the top brass. But they also had to work for people. In the tech world, Taylor explained, the key to a company's success is hiring and retaining the right people, the talent. The biggest challenge in doing so is competing with rivals to attract and keep that in-demand talent. At the time, Taylor said, the company was losing many of its best women, especially those with care responsibilities, and workers of color. "One of the key reasons they would cite is the lack of fulfilling jobs," Taylor said, "as well as a lack of understanding how to develop themselves, a lack of understanding where to go next, and a lack of flexibility."

In their conversations across the company, the Work Practice Innovations team quickly hit upon two trends. On the worker side, the gig economy was taking off. A lot of tired employees they talked to spoke wistfully of having the kind of autonomy over their schedules and workloads that gig work promised and more control over when, where, and how they worked. They loved the idea that gigging would expose them to variable, creative, and challenging job tasks. Some had skills that were of use to the entire company, but they were siloed into departments that couldn't utilize them. While some people were considering jumping into independent gig work, most needed the stability of a regular paycheck and, in particular, benefits, such as health insurance.

In other advanced economies, universal health-care systems enable workers to move more freely from job to job without losing access to medical care. Without universal health care, workers in the United States can get stuck in jobs they hate just to keep their health insurance, a phenomenon known as job lock.[3] This is hardly a recipe for inspiring a loyal, innovative, and motivated workforce, nor for unleashing creativity and innovation.

Looking at Intel as an employer, the Work Practice Innovations team found that siloed business departments not only kept workers from focusing on the skills they loved (and that the company needed) but that the departments often operated in isolation. One part of the company would lay a worker off and another part would hire someone with the very same skills. Sometimes workers were rehired who had just been fired, an innovation team member told me. The layoffs were often devastating for those let go and demoralizing and demotivating for those who remained.

Layoffs have been a common practice in U.S. corporate culture since the "lean and mean" efficiency and deregulation heyday of the early 1980s, and they have come to be seen as the sad human price to pay for a dynamic economy, for a "rightsized" company, and for a short-term boost in profits that makes the company books look better in Wall Street quarterly earnings reports.[4] But the truth is that layoffs cause human suffering and can create more problems for companies in the long run. Research shows that they prompt some survivors to quit, and the resulting loss of expertise and unexpected staff shortages hinder the very productivity and efficiency the company sought to create in the first place.[5]

At Intel, the company was expanding into new areas, such as data centers and the Internet of Things, and closing down others. It was both hiring and shedding workers at an astonishing rate. "In a company of our size, we were getting thousands of employees going back and forth, in and out of the company all the time," an innovation team member told me. "You start to multiply those numbers, you get into the tens to hundreds of millions of dollars. We thought, holy cow, look at all the money we're spending doing this. It's not great for employees and it's hurting the company." Some of the same workers were hired and fired three or four times.

The team mulled over the two pain points: workers wanting more freedom and autonomy to choose and do the work they loved and control their schedules, and the company needing a more agile workforce with the skills these workers had. In January 2014, they launched their first work innovation pilot: Freelance Nation.

The idea was elegant. The group wanted to take the very best elements of the gig economy, with its flexible work, varied assignments, and often surprising opportunities that fostered creativity, and couple them with the best of what Intel had to offer: stable employment, benefits and wages, and the chance to work across the company with some of the most interesting teams on cutting-edge projects. The program would create a cadre of W2 workers within the company who *act* like freelance gig workers. They would focus on a variety of short-term projects for a variety of departments, all while staying on Intel's payroll, with Intel security clearances and benefits. Siloed departments would no longer have to spend precious time and money hiring and firing so frequently. Instead, they could fill a short-term need with an already vetted Intel worker from Freelance Nation. The idea and the process of developing it were all about fairness and cooperation among employers and employees and restoring a sense of meaning to people who, as many said, "used to love" their jobs.

The Workplace Practice Innovation team put out an ad for freelancers to try a new model of work. Control your own hours! Control the mix of jobs you want! Make your work life more fulfilling! They hosted open houses and gave flash presentations to get the word out and drum up visibility and interest. More than two hundred people applied, a number that quickly swelled to eight hundred as word began to spread. The team chose twenty to start and soon expanded to about sixty-five.

The workers chosen to join Freelance Nation posted their skills and availability on an internal Intel database or "marketplace." Intel teams and managers posted the projects, job tasks, and activities for which they needed short-term help. Freelance Nation Talent Champions then helped match the freelancers with the Intel project managers. The Talent Champion would manage the workers' professional growth and career trajectories, acting more like career coaches than placement supervisors. And the freelancers were free to pick and choose the projects that most interested them and fit their desired schedules and workloads. They were to think of the Intel project managers as their clients and to build relationships and deliver high-quality customer service. But there were no nine-to-five or forty-hour workweek requirements. Salaries would scale—if a person worked a 75 percent schedule, they were paid 75 percent of their salary.

Freelance Nation was wildly popular. Department managers saved the time, hassle, bandwidth, and emotional toll of hiring and firing as well as saving money, while getting excellent work done in a timely manner. Productivity soared.

"People were freakishly happy," Taylor told me, happier, in surveys, than traditional Intel employees. "And the quality of work was very, very high. We've seen people pushing themselves and developing themselves in a way that I didn't envision, pushing themselves in the tasks they take on. Expanding their skills. Just happy." A big part of what made Freelance Nation work was that freelancers were being judged on their performance, their output, and not on corporate America's traditional "management by input" method, tracking the hours spent in the office or logged on a computer. Their jobs were all about clear tasks and achieving high-quality deliverables.

As long as they met their deliverables, freelancers controlled the time, manner, and place of their work. One freelancer, a principal engineer whose wife had a demanding, time-intensive "greedy"[6] job, joined the project to have the flexibility to drive his daughters to school, be home with them in the afternoons, and work a lighter schedule in the summer. Others organized their schedules around competitive bowling or training for fencing competitions.

Sarah Moyle, who worked in HR, was fascinated by white board animation, the creative explanatory graphics that facilitators use to capture key themes during speeches or presentations. But the opportunities to master that in her current job were few and far between. She also needed both a stable income and a flexible schedule to manage the care responsibilities of her young and growing family. Moyle joined Freelance Nation and was soon doing exactly what she wanted on a short-term basis for teams across the company, which no longer needed to search for and hire a contract graphic facilitator. She put in about thirty-two hours a week and controlled her schedule.[7] Eric Chin, who started out as a chip designer, was able to try different projects outside the career path he had originally envisioned for himself, from health care to robotics, marketing, and competitive analysis. Before joining Freelance Nation, Cyrene Domogalla, a digital artist, had been demoralized after a trying and sometimes hostile experience with multiple managers, some of whom were steeped in an aggressive management style fomented by former Intel chairman and chief executive Andrew Grove, which one colleague described as "hit you over the head with a two-by-four."[8] Domogalla became reenergized by working on different projects for different teams, and working at times when she felt most creative and productive. "It forced me to get really good at communication, time management, and just doing my work, which led to more challenging and interesting work," she told me. "Freelance Nation was a critical experience for me."

Herman D'Hooge, nearing retirement, who only worked six months on and six months off, found that Freelance Nation, because of its focus on deliverables, cut out one of the most common drivers of overwork and burnout, as well as inefficient, low-value work: busyness. In input cultures, where long hours are equated with dedication and commitment, managers tend to reward most those who appear to be busy, rushing around and answering email. "People equate busyness with productivity," he said. "It's the biggest mistake people can make."

Freelance Nation began winning awards and accolades as an innovative way to redesign work. The Workplace Practice Innovation team thought they'd hit on a way to create the "agile" workforce that CEOs and managers were always talking about, but without the human pain that often comes with that agility in the form of layoffs. "All firms talk about having engaged, happy, committed employees," Taylor told me at the height of Freelance Nation's popularity. "We're showing that maybe there's more than the traditional way to get workers engaged, motivated, and proud to work for the company. What Freelance Nation has taught me is that sometimes the wildest ideas are spot on."

But it didn't last. In 2016, Intel laid off fifteen thousand workers, the largest mass layoff in the company's history at that point.[9] Richard Taylor retired. A new head of HR killed the program. She didn't give a reason why. Freelance Nation died a quiet death in July 2017, after just three years. Some freelancers, like Chin and Domogalla, left the company as a result. As did Talent Champion Vikki Mueller Espinosa, who later retired. "I'm still ridiculously proud of what we achieved," she told me. "I have to say Freelance Nation was the highest high of my career. I loved the program and the happiness and fulfillment the program brought to the freelancers. They still tell me it was the best work they did." Jennifer Monnig, who ran the Workplace Practice Innovation team, said simply, "We were ahead of the curve." Monnig, too, has since left the company.

▬

The fate of Freelance Nation was most on my mind as I watched the Covid-19 pandemic force companies to experiment with and struggle to adapt to new ways of working, at least for the 40-some percent of the workforce who can work digitally from anywhere.[10]

In 2020, almost overnight, the share of knowledge workers employed exclusively digitally leaped from 6 to 65 percent.[11] Author Anne-Marie Slaughter called the pandemic disruptions a "time machine to the future," speeding up the pace of change from decades to weeks or months.[12] Over the ensuing years, some companies have embraced change and completely redesigned their work cultures, giving employees more control and flexibility while finding surprising benefits to workers and their business as a result.

The pandemic forced Blackbaud, a global cloud software company, to reevaluate and then completely redesign their work culture. The company had always thought of itself as an in-person culture. As in so many organizations, the path to top leadership had required a stint working in one of its brick-and-mortar locations, such as its headquarters in Charleston, South Carolina, or other large offices in Texas, Minnesota, New Hampshire, or London. This limited the pool to employees who could move themselves and their families, which research shows tend to be men. As we know, women tend to take more flexible or lower-paying jobs than their higher-earning spouses,[13] or are simply paid less because of the gender pay gap, and thus are more likely to upend their own careers and follow along as the "trailing spouse."[14]

In 2020, Blackbaud instantly moved to a digital-first culture to continue supporting their global customers while also prioritizing the health and wellbeing of their employees. The entire organization was forced to rethink the way it worked. Rather than dictating policies from on high, the company engaged employees from the start, which research shows is key to crafting a successful work redesign.[15] Managers asked them about challenges, particularly for workers with care responsibilities, and created teams like Together Anywhere, dedicated to providing the right tools for everyone to succeed in a digital environment. These and other efforts provided people with a sense of belonging and the feeling that they were all involved in figuring out the work transformation experiment. "We built it on a premise of trust and wellbeing, which is key," Maggie Driscoll, chief people and culture officer, explained.

CEO Mike Gianoni embraced the spirit of experimentation. He held weekly thirty-minute Monday meetings with about two hundred of the company's global leaders to share updates and answer any questions. The company instituted virtual quarterly all-hands meetings for everyone to come together and participate in what it called a "global by design" approach. Managers saw that the virtual gatherings enhanced transparency and improved coordination, so they kept them up, even as the company planned to transition to a hybrid model of work. As the pandemic dragged on, however, and as leaders continued to ask about employee preferences and research best practices, they decided instead to transition to a flexible, remote, or digital-first environment.[16]

Blackbaud still believes in the effectiveness of in-person gatherings, but the company is more creative about how they take place. Employees are encouraged to use a workday to volunteer with their communities. Those who live in the same region often coordinate their volunteer schedules, meeting people from across the organization. Teams organize in-person events as necessary, Driscoll said. Meanwhile, the organization has developed a rich digital culture, hosting virtual parties, including wedding and baby showers, and coordinating online projects and meetings to help support getting work done. Blackbaud has been recognized as one of the best companies in the United States for digital-first work.[17] "One of the learnings of the last few years is that it's okay to say you don't know the answers," Driscoll told me. "To stop, pivot, and change, and let your people know why."

Its redesigned work culture has also enabled Blackbaud to tap into and promote wider and broader talent pools, offering more opportunity to diverse workers who no longer have to be located in one physical place. "No longer do we look at a role based on location and geography. We look at a role based on experience, skills, and execution," Driscoll said. Both employees and the company have reaped the benefits. Applications shot up, with an increase in diverse candidates. By eliminating the promotion requirement of being present in a brick-and-mortar office, Blackbaud management, too, has become more diverse. The global leadership team promoted several candidates, including women, who had never worked at a headquarters location. Military spouses, who once may have had to leave the company when their partner was transferred, are no longer forced to do so, so the firm is able to retain their skills and expertise.

Driscoll's direct reports, who had previously been required to live in Charleston, now work in Pennsylvania, Kentucky, and Michigan to better manage their work and care responsibilities and live the kinds of lives they want. On the day we spoke, Driscoll herself was working in Massachusetts so she could be near family for a few weeks. Company surveys show workers are happier and value the increased equity and inclusion. "Our employees are really seeing the impact. And so is the company," Driscoll said. "We're everywhere now. And productivity has remained high."

Across much of the globe, a new flexible work norm has taken hold. Research released in March 2023 found that listings for hybrid or fully digital job openings rose more than threefold from 2019 to 2023 in the United States and by a factor of five in Australia, Canada, New Zealand, and the UK.[18] In its January 2024 report on work trends, Mercer, a global consulting firm, noted that 92 percent of the firms they'd interviewed had adopted hybrid work practices, and office occupancy rates continued to hover around 50 percent.[19]

Even though the business case for flexible work—how it benefits workers and companies—was been made[20] and made[21] and made[22] for years, before the pandemic it was stigmatized as part of a lesser "Mommy Track." It was often only grudgingly offered, and then only to select mothers and workers with care responsibilities who happened to have won the "boss lottery," reporting to an understanding manager willing to give it a try. Flexible workers often wound up overworking, a paradox researchers call the "gift exchange theory."[23]

Heejung Chung, professor of sociology and social policy at the University of Kent, explained that in overwork work cultures, anything deviating from the norm is seen as a perk or a privilege that can be taken away on a whim. So employees double down and work harder to prove they still fit in and to repay their employers.

I understand this paradox because I lived it. When I nervously asked for and was granted a four-day workweek after the birth of my second child, I was so grateful—even though my supervisors said it would destroy my career—and so fearful it would be taken away that I wound up working far more than a thirty-two-hour week. But because I could fit the hours around my family schedule and I had a dedicated Monday to spend with my children, the time was a gift to my employer that I was willing to give.

Pandemic-era shifts might lead to an end to the gift exchange theory, fairer workplaces, and the advancement of mothers and workers with care responsibilities, workers of color, workers with disabilities, and those who simply prefer flexible and digital work. Although mothers were forced out of the workforce in droves during the pandemic, the Hamilton Project, for instance, reported that by February 2023, they were back at work. The labor force participation of women between the ages of twenty-five and fifty-four—particularly mothers with young children—not only rebounded from pandemic lows but reached an all-time high of 77.8 percent. Much of the reason for this, economists surmise, is that work has become more flexible, not just with digital telework but because more jobs give people more options to control when, where, and how they work.[24]

Many people of color who began working digitally during the pandemic also reported being happier at work, free from the stress of daily microaggressions; additionally, managers had to focus more on work product and performance than identity, stereotypes, or ideal worker assumptions. More than 80 percent of the Black, Latinx, and Asian respondents in one of Slack's Future Forum pulse global surveys of ten thousand knowledge workers reported a desire to continue working digitally, and the share of these workers who said they felt a sense of belonging at work and that their workplace was fair increased dramatically.[25]

Natalie Orozco used to put in what felt like 24/7 in a high-level policy job at a tech firm in Silicon Valley, sleeping next to her phone to answer late-night calls from colleagues in time zones across the globe. She burned out within one year. "I saw people sleeping under their desks," she said. But she and others put up with the ideal worker overwork expectations in what she described as "trauma bonding." She also felt isolated. Most of the other Latinx people she saw were secretaries, janitors, or cooks, she said. She dreaded taking a seat at the conference table at meetings, where, as the only Latina in the room, she was often asked, "Are you here to take notes?" and expected to move to the back of the room. This happened even when she was on the agenda as the main presenter.

Orozco became ill, unable to get out of bed for days with fevers, chills, sweats, and what was later diagnosed as lupus and fibromyalgia. "I couldn't go into what honestly felt like the knowledge work version of a war zone." She took six months to recover and reconnect with her heritage and what she calls the wisdom of her ancestors. The way work shifted during the pandemic opened possibilities that could never have been imagined. She began working as a coach and consultant for a fully digital company, Artemis Connection, focused on diversity, equity, inclusion, and belonging. She slowed down and took more control of her life, with time to cook the Ayurvedic recipes that helped reduce her inflammation, go on morning walks near the lake, volunteer for local boards, and spend time caring for her grandparents. She stopped straightening and dying her naturally curly, graying hair. She began wearing clothes that felt comfortable and made her feel true to herself, rather than an idealized notion of a good American worker. With a gentler pace of life, less stress, good paid work, and time for care, Orozco was finally able to become pregnant and delivered a healthy baby girl. She had the time and mental and emotional capacity to breastfeed her daughter and hug her anytime she wanted and enjoy both her paid work and the unpaid work of care and home. "I found a way not just to survive but to thrive."

Orozco also found that working digitally helped her assert her voice. Unlike her experience in conference rooms, there is no head of the table in digital meetings and no jockeying for who sits next to whom. There is no status signaling through power suits or designer clothes. No one sees or cares about the shoes someone is wearing, or not. Orozco found that teleconferencing leveled the playing field for workers of color. "If I didn't have a face in the conference room, I have a face now on Zoom." She still sees plenty of mansplaining and airtime hogging, but now it's her job to call out unequal power dynamics. Her role is to help others see them and reflect on how they damage relationships, morale, and the quality of work. Being in a digital-only environment, she said, helps people "just let go of a lot of the petty crappy stuff that wasn't working anyway."

In the past, people laboring digitally or flexibly, outside of the traditionalist face-time office culture—namely mothers—might have been doing excellent work, but they were more likely to be passed over for promotions, research has found, as well as plum assignments. Those are sometimes handed out when someone walks by the boss's office—what researchers call "Hey, you" tasking.[26] They were casualties of presence or "proximity" bias.[27] That bias, coupled with confirmation bias—we tend to favor people who remind us of ourselves—creates and reinforces an old boy network. So strong are these biases that one study of a large financial institution published by the National Bureau of Economic Research found that men who worked on-site with male managers, especially if they took smoke breaks together, were promoted at a faster rate than men with female managers, men whose bosses didn't smoke, and women. The differences in promotion rates had nothing to do with performance, the researchers concluded, yet contributed to about one-third of the gender gap in promotions at the firm.[28]

Knowing that, some companies that have adopted a mix of hybrid in-person and digital work are taking active steps to counter the potential for proximity bias. Some have adopted a "Zoom One, Zoom All" meeting strategy, in which everyone—on-site and off—participates virtually, and they encourage managers to stay online after meetings end to ensure that digital employees, too, have the opportunity for more informal connecting and virtual "water cooler" moments.[29] Deloitte, the global audit, consulting, tax, and advisory professional services network, for instance, drew on key lessons from its consulting work with other companies and saw the challenges presented by the crisis of the pandemic as an opportunity to rethink equity and work redesign for the long term. They give teams autonomy to figure out when they need to move projects forward in person and when and where it's better for them to have time for concentrated work on their own. It's a philosophy they call Together When It Matters, Denise Shepherd, Deloitte's US Workforce Strategy and Solutions leader, told me. The company is also using data to watch for and manage proximity bias and ensure leaders are promoting and rewarding people based on performance. "We're trying to drive this equitable experience," Shepherd said, "so we can both serve our clients effectively and people feel included regardless of whether they're in the room or not."[30]

▬

The new, more equitable flexible work norm taking hold is a huge advancement.

But effecting a transformation is a far from certain outcome. In the finance industry in particular, flexible ways of working have been deemed an "aberration"[31] to be tolerated only in an emergency. Some who work digitally for greedy companies and industries where overwork is the norm have had to appear on Slack and email at all hours, a digital avatar of the ideal worker, which has fostered high rates of burnout.

Some leaders sought to jettison any work style that didn't resemble 2019, regardless of the data on productivity, like a body's immune system swiftly rejecting a foreign organ. They've mandated in-person return-to-office policies from on high and count badge swipes to make sure everyone is following orders.[32] In April 2023, leaders at JPMorgan Chase, for example, obliged all managing directors to return to the office five days a week to "strengthen" culture,[33] similar to the new leadership at Intel that quickly abandoned Freelance Nation to return to old ways, despite the evidence of success. A three-year Boston Consulting Group study showed sales grew faster at companies that had adopted flexible work practices compared to those that didn't. But that didn't stop organizations like Goldman Sachs, Google, and others from mandating employees return to the office in 2023 and use their compliance in performance evaluations. Executives at Wayfair and other companies have targeted or say they will target digital employees in 2024 layoffs.[34] The *Wall Street Journal* reported that digital workers were 35 percent more likely to be laid off in 2023 than those working in person or hybrid schedules.[35]

Many companies have been a little lost, stuck somewhere between the old and the new, making pronouncements, then walking them back, announcing hybrid policies but executing them badly, the way forward clear as mud. Three years into the vast work redesign experiment, in the spring of 2023, nearly one-third of executives said they still judged worker productivity by what they could see, number of work hours being a key metric. For their part, workers said they were spending about one-third of their hours on time-wasting garbage work just to appear productive to their managers.[36]

Most workplaces continue to use the word "remote" to describe work that isn't done in an office, as if that's where the real and important business gets done. I've come to describe it as digital, distributed, or networked work, which is what it is. Using those terms signals that the work is just as valuable as anything done in a headquarters office or physical location, that the *what* of the work matters more than *where* it's done.

Some leaders want to change, but they're not sure how to make it happen. In a 2023 survey of ten thousand business leaders, 87 percent said that finding the right model of flexible work is important to their organization's success. But only 24 percent felt that they knew what to do.[37] Flexible work strategist Cali Yost calls this an enormous "knowing-doing gap."[38] It's similar to the long-running "knowing-doing" gap that exists among the majority of employers who worry their employees are stressed and overwhelmed and call it an "urgent" trend, and those who say they're ready to deal with the problem.[39] Many have no idea what to do about it.[40]

So they fall back on what they know, fostering ideal worker corporate cultures that researchers liken to masculinity contests.[41] In this dominant overwork culture, senior executives say that work-life balance is "at best an elusive ideal and at worst a complete myth."[42]

The controversial billionaire Elon Musk, owner, founder and chief executive of Tesla, SpaceX, X, and other ventures, is an extreme example of this pervasive overwork culture. He boasts of working seven days and as many as 120 hours a week—that's 17 hours a day—taking a handful of days off a year and sometimes sleeping at his desk.[43] He's warned his employees to work long hours at high intensity or be let go[44] and has called digital work "morally wrong."[45] People who work for him have reported sleeping on factory floors, fainting from dehydration, being fired in a fit of Musk's capricious rage, exposed to unsafe working conditions, and enduring alleged racist or sexist behavior.[46] Musk likes to say that revolutionizing industries is not for the faint of heart and takes "excruciating effort." But his hard-core ethos has led to instability and turmoil that's been criticized as ill-advised and unnecessary at best and incompetent at worst.[47]

In all this confusion, one thing is clear: the pandemic triggered a power struggle over work that will likely take years to resolve.

This power struggle began soon after the shutdowns in March 2020. At a time when proximity to other humans meant risking contact with a potentially fatal disease, "return to office" stories began popping up in the media. Some leaders began demanding all hands on deck in the office and workers began resisting. Blanket demands to return in person, especially when schools and child-care centers were still shuttered, resulted in workers with care responsibilities quitting in droves, or in lawsuits, such as the one the American Civil Liberties Union filed against the state of South Carolina. The ACLU voluntarily dismissed the lawsuit after the state agreed to change the policy to allow workers to request reasonable digital work accommodations.[48] Survey after survey has captured the disconnect between bosses who want everyone back where they can see them, and workers unwilling to give up the flexibility and control over when, where, and how they work that they finally got to taste during the pandemic. In early 2024 SAP, Europe's largest software company, ordered people back to the office for at least three days a week—still a hybrid schedule. But within two weeks, five thousand employees signed a letter of protest, deeming the policy "unreasonable."[49]

It's not as if everyone wants to stay home all the time, working digitally in their pajamas. Young people in particular yearn for camaraderie, mentoring, observing coworkers and learning skills by osmosis,[50] and feeling that they are part of a larger culture. Just not all the time.[51] In fact, the majority of desk workers repeatedly say they prefer a hybrid work arrangement, with a few days in the office to collaborate and meet up with colleagues in person and a few days a week working digitally to better concentrate on bigger projects. Mercer's 2023–2024 "Inside Employees' Minds Study" of more than forty-five hundred U.S. workers reported that 52 percent had a hybrid or digital work arrangement but that nearly 90 percent wanted one.[52]

Ipsos Karian and Box, an employee engagement firm, reported in 2022 that nearly 70 percent of desk workers around the world want flexible hybrid schedules. For desk workers of color, and those with care responsibilities or disability challenges, surveys have found the share is even higher. Only 8 percent wanted to be present full-time in an office.

Compare that to bosses: around the world, 90 percent of senior leaders preferred hybrid or in-office work and were more likely to believe collaboration was more effective in the office than more junior staff.[53]

Doing hybrid paid work well is a skill, and it requires training people how to coordinate, set communication protocols and boundaries, better define their work, and focus on what they actually produce. "The people doing it best are data driven," said Christy Johnson, founder of the strategic consulting firm Artemis Connection. The best firms, she said, use, review, and adapt practices based on metrics like analyzing who speaks in meetings and how often. They also develop structured mentoring, sponsorship, and networking opportunities. They track promotions and growth assignments to ensure they're being distributed on a fair basis, and offer management training. "Good managers set smart goals based on outcomes," she said, "and it doesn't matter where people are." But management training is "highly variable" and often falls into what Johnson calls motivational, feel-good "edutainment" that may boost spirits for a day but doesn't leave managers with concrete skills like motivating teams, navigating proximity, confirmation, and other biases, or giving good feedback in hybrid settings. "Management training isn't exciting. And there isn't a quick fix," she said. "But we should be equipping more managers with the skills to manage this new way of work."

Doing hybrid work well also requires intentional planning at the team and organizational levels. No one wants to schlep into an office to sit on Zoom meetings all day. (That was me on my first day back in the office under my organization's new hybrid policy.) No one wants to miss out on opportunities to meaningfully connect with colleagues in person, either. Both these things have happened. "It's going to take time," Johnson said. Learning how to make the most of hybrid work is still very much a study in progress in many organizations as they feel their way forward. Hybrid work has become the new normal for so many, Harvard Business professor Tsedal Neeley writes, workers, managers, and companies need to learn to be "awesome at both in person and distance arrangements."[54]

But some senior leaders have pointed to poorly planned hybrid policies that leave everyone frustrated as one more reason to give up and come back to the office full-time. Others have even charged that resistant leaders design hybrid policies poorly to ensure that they will fail.[55] Some managers have vowed to just wait workers out.[56] "I've heard so many male executives say, 'All we need is a good recession and that will get everybody back in the office,'" Johnson told me.

Both sides of the employer-employee divide have dug in. But if companies are truly interested in productivity, motivated workers, and getting the job done well, the evidence is on the side of hybrid jobs. Stanford economist Nick Bloom, who found digital workers were more productive than in-person staff long before the pandemic,[57] has consistently put out meticulous research over the past few years. He and his colleagues have found that digital and hybrid employees are happier and less likely to quit than those in traditional settings. Along with the other benefits—eliminating commutes, the ability to better manage care responsibilities, being able to attract and retain a diverse workforce—hybrid work can also save space. Bloom estimates that it boosts a firm's profits by 10 to 20 percent over traditional "full return" workplaces.[58] Flexible, digital work has kept more women in the workforce, some economists have found, and closed gender gaps in once notoriously family-*un*friendly sectors like finance and marketing.[59] Other research has found that well-designed hybrid work gives workers more autonomy, which reduces worker fatigue and boosts performance,[60] improves work-life balance,[61] and, in addition to productivity, enhances job satisfaction and engagement.[62] One study of return to office directives between 2020 and 2023 found that they were more common in firms with poor stock performance, for which they blamed employees' digital or hybrid arrangements as a "scapegoat." Forcing everyone back to in-person work led to considerable declines in employee satisfaction, work-life balance, and trust in senior management. Perhaps most importantly, the study found no significant improvement to firm performance after everyone was back in the office.[63]

Part of the power struggle is over perceptions of productivity. Rates began to drop in 2022.[64] Traditionalist leaders were quick to blame hybrid and digital work or the viral phenomenon of quiet quitting—what some would call just doing your job, rather than going above and beyond. CEOs such as BlackRock's Larry Fink blamed the productivity drop on people refusing to return full-time to the office.[65] Congress even jumped into the fray in February 2023 with a newly elected Republican House majority passing the SHOW-UP Act: Stopping Home Office Work's Unproductive Problems Act of 2023.[66] (It died in the Senate.) But in fact productivity began to drop in 2022 when CEOs issued back-to-office mandates, author and workplace consultant Gleb Tsipursky argued in *Fortune*.[67] "Disengaged workers aren't productive," he wrote. "That's especially the case if they're looking for a new job."

Slack's 2023 Future Forum Pulse survey found that workers with rigid schedules are more stressed and anxious, report worse work-life balance, and are two and a half times more likely to say they'll "definitely" look for a new job in the coming year.[68]

Many leaders insist company culture can only be created in person and that innovation is fostered by serendipitous and accidental "hallway moments." But research shows that this is only true if leaders fail to adapt new ways of brainstorming and creating culture in digital and hybrid settings, and instead impose old practices on new work styles.[69] A 2023 Pulse survey found that about a quarter of executives say offering employees flexibility has a negative effect on company culture. Yet flexible workers are equally or *more* likely than in-office-only workers to feel connected to their teams, their direct manager, and their company's values.

Ironically, many of the same leaders who want employees back in the office full-time have been working flexibly themselves from wherever they want, and not surprisingly show lower levels of stress and work-life conflict than their employees.[70] Executives, one survey found, were four times more likely than individual contributors to have zero schedule constraints.[71]

To better understand this disconnect and what it could mean for the long term, I turned to Brian Elliott, Future Forum's executive leader, and forum vice president Sheela Subramanian, who have consolidated their research into strategies for successful flexible work in their book, *How the Future Works.* The root of resistance to flexible hours is pretty simple to understand, they say, and helps explain why it's so thorny to change. Blame it on corporate leadership monoculture. Many leaders want people to return to work like 2019 because it's what they know and how they succeeded. The reason for the disconnect with employees is that most leaders *don't look like them and don't have the same life experiences.* The majority of senior leaders have had at-home spouses managing the family responsibilities so they could devote themselves entirely to the job,[72] unlike nearly three-fourths of employees, who have to juggle the job with care at home.[73]

In 2023, the majority of executives and board members listed in the Fortune 500 were white men.[74] "There's a leadership and management monoculture in the corporate world, and they're the ones who are making the decisions," Subramanian said. And unless corporate leaders allow for more flexibility for all workers to succeed, "that monoculture is only going to get perpetuated."

"It's not a cabal. It's an echo chamber," Elliott added. "I've had people say to me, 'I can show our CEO that my [flexible] team was actually more productive, not just in terms of hours worked, but literally in output over the past few years. And I can't get them to listen, because instead they're listening to their fellow CEOs and board members, who are ex-CEOs'"—all of whom rose to power in heavily male-dominated, white, often pre-digital corporate cultures. "I also see the 'it worked for me' attitude with fifty-plus-year-old female executives who felt like they needed to make sacrifices to get where they are," Subramanian added. So they think others should as well. "It's assimilation rather than inclusion," she said, "if you want to survive as a female leader."

Their Future Forum data shows that younger leaders tend to be more sympathetic to their employees' care responsibilities and desire for flexible work. "If you're under fifty, it's actually one of your top concerns," Elliott said. "If you're over fifty, it's literally the last thing on your list."

At heart, the future of work redesign comes down to a conflict between power and trust: how much power leaders can cede to workers, how much the two sides can trust each other, and what each group believes to be true about work. "So much of work culture has been premised on the command-and-control model. That's a conversation about power. And the future of work needs to be about trust. That shift has been difficult for many leaders to make," Subramanian said.

At the height of the pandemic, the power conflict came into stark relief. Many leaders who had relied on managing and judging workers by sight were at a loss. Instead of retraining managers or figuring out how to judge performance and deliverables, companies invested in surveillance bossware to spy on workers by counting keystrokes, tracking mouse activity, and taking random screen shots of their computers.[75] Warehouse and other low-wage workers who have long operated under the watchful eye of video cameras also saw increased surveillance over their every move. Along with the proliferation of bossware came a rash of clever tweaks to circumvent it, devices that would regularly jiggle a mouse to give the appearance of constant work, for example.

The combination of technology and mistrust also led to a new and growing kind of work stress—"technostress." Ashley Nixon, a management professor at Willamette University who studies technostress, said surveillance software is perhaps one of the worst ways to manage staff. Research shows that workers who have discretion and control over their work are more engaged and generate more ideas, while workers who are oppressively monitored are distressed.[76] "We have a ton of empirical evidence that shows that surveillance of employees leads to bad health-care outcomes," she told me. "It leads to emotional disengagement from work. It leads to creative and knowledge workers being occupied with the monitoring, which leaves them with far less mental capacity to actually do the work. So this is basically our employers kneecapping us and then expecting us to still perform well." The stress and distrust are worse for low-wage workers, Nixon said, who often don't know what their employers are watching for, nor how the data collected will be used.

Madi Swenson, a digital copywriting specialist and strategist who was based in Utah, became so stressed about her firm's constant digital monitoring that she began having panic attacks and ultimately quit her job. "Just last night, I had a nightmare that I had forgotten to press play on the time tracking app and got fired as a result of it," she told me. Nixon said such monitoring is a violation of trust. "What we know is that trust and justice within organizations is a huge predictor of satisfaction, commitment, and motivation," she said. "People stay in organizations that trust them, that they feel they are treated fairly in." But they leave organizations if they don't feel trusted.

Along with trust, Slack Future Forum's Elliott and Subramanian say that transparency is key to creating successful work redesign policies. Engaging *with* employees, really listening to their needs and ideas, instead of issuing edicts from on high, are core tenets of both fairness and cooperation at work. That involves giving workers the skills to master flexible and hybrid work rather than expecting them to pick it up on their own. It means coaching managers to stop being gatekeepers, overseeing by sight, monitoring the input of long hours of butts in chairs, and instead giving them the tools to define the real value of the work: breaking it into tasks, helping employees set priorities and deadlines, and managing for performance and measuring outcomes. It also requires doing the hard and often emotional labor to make organizations diverse and inclusive rather than expecting diverse workers to assimilate into a white male corporate monoculture. "Ultimately," Subramanian said, "this requires a new kind of leadership."

■

Changing entrenched work culture is hard. I had a front-row seat to a project that tried. Directed by ideas42, a firm that uses behavioral science to help solve real-world problems, the project sought to better understand what drives people to overwork and to test interventions that would improve individual work-life conflict and wellbeing. Ideally, the goal was to help change work culture.

Pretty quickly I discovered why my behavioral science colleagues called our search for solutions a "wicked problem." It's hard to alter individual behavior in an overwork culture, no matter how dysfunctional and unproductive it might be, when leaders celebrate it. Like the solutions to work stress, the real transformation comes not from changing the individual but in redesigning the system. Behavioral science principles stem from acknowledging that the environment, not individuals, can be more powerful in shaping individual attitudes, choices, and behaviors. The discipline recognizes that humans can find it tough to make decisions now that will benefit them in the long run. This is called present bias.[77] It's easier to choose to eat the doughnut because it's right in front of us rather than resist to achieve the future goal of better nutrition for a healthier and longer life. We put off studying for the big test or we procrastinate on a work deadline in the present moment because we imagine that we will be more motivated or prepared in the future. (We aren't.) We spend money now to have a bright shiny object in our hands rather than save for retirement in a theoretical far future. The present moment is the most powerful influence in our often flawed human decision-making.

Behavioral science interventions are based on creating choice architecture that makes it easier for people to opt for the harder choice for the future. If you want to eat more fruits and vegetables, cut them up and store them in the fridge at eye level, where you can easily see and grab them, rather than in a solid drawer at the bottom where they're more likely to wilt and rot, uneaten. In one famous intervention, new employees were automatically signed up for a company's retirement plan, instead of giving them the choice of opting in or out, which requires filling out complicated paperwork that people often avoid. The simple change boosted individual retirement savings by nearly $30 billion in a few years and won the intervention's designer a Nobel Prize in Economics.[78]

In our project, we wanted to see if we could design similar interventions to create the organizational choice architecture that would reduce individual work-life conflict. We began with the understanding that busyness culture and overwork are key factors driving that conflict. My colleagues at ideas42 set out to talk to employees at all the participating organizations—all nonprofits. Nonprofits are often classic overwork and burnout cultures. People work "hero hours" because they're passionate about the issues and see the work as mission-driven.[79] Nonprofits also tend to be woefully understaffed and under-resourced, so people aren't paid much and don't have a lot of support, which intensifies the workload. And if the work, barring radical change, likely won't be done in a lifetime, it's difficult to know when to call it a day.

One thing struck me immediately. In conversation after conversation, workers said they spent their days being super busy, rushing from one meeting to the next, jumping on and off the phone, and plowing through their email. It was only at what should have been the end of the paid workday that they realized they hadn't gotten to the one big thing they really needed to do. Their work hours were constantly interrupted and filled with busywork. Researchers have found that desk workers in an office setting tend to be interrupted about every three minutes. And after that colleague has dropped by or we've switched screens to check email, texts, social media, or a pinging notification, it can take, on average, twenty-three minutes and fifteen seconds to get back to where we were.[80] Over and over and over throughout the day.

Then there are the meetings. One survey found that executives spend, on average, twenty-five hours a week in meetings, half of which could disappear without any negative impact. Those lower down the corporate ladder spend about ten hours a week in meetings and say 43 percent are a waste of time. But they go because they have to, or they fear they'll miss out, or they want to show their managers how busy and committed they are.[81] This means huge swaths of the workweek are a huge waste of time and money. One Bain and Company study found that after accounting for meetings, excessive emails, office chitchat, or unproductive conversations and low-value administrative tasks—all unproductive busywork—the typical middle manager has only *six and a half uninterrupted hours a week* to do their actual work.[82] As behavioral economist Dan Ariely once told me, "We've created a work environment that gives us a lot of empty calories."[83]

While many workers we spoke to were clearly frustrated by how work encroached on their lives, they were also conflicted by the strong norm to brag about their overwork as a sign of their dedication, like wearing a badge of honor.[84] Some reported that though they saw the benefit of work-life balance, they routinely overworked to the point of exhaustion. "If we all hated our jobs, it would be much easier to create work-life balance," one participant told us. At one organization, workers said that no one should work more than forty-five hours a week. Yet the typical employee worked more than fifty-two. Leaders at many of the organizations had the best of intentions. They expressed a desire for better work-life balance, if not for themselves then at least for their staff.

But they, too, were caught up in the prevailing busyness culture. Some were among the worst offenders, texting at 9:00 p.m., emailing over the weekend, even in the middle of the night, and rarely taking vacation. Many leaders knew they weren't walking the talk: "We do a poor job modeling" work-life balance, they would say. Yet they appeared powerless to change themselves or their busyness cultures. "One of the things I found odd is that people were acutely aware of how bad they are with work-life balance and they wanted to be better, but they've almost accepted it, like it is what it is," Antonia Violante, then an ideas42 colleague, told me. "It seemed unachievable to a lot of people."

I came to think of work in three ways. There's the "real" work—the tasks and outcomes that create value for the organization and give employees a sense of meaning and pride. There's the "work around the work"—all the emails and meetings, some necessary, many not, that can consume entire days. And then there's what I call the "performance of work": sending late-night emails or Slack messages, showing up at the office or online early and staying late, shaming those who take lunch breaks, giving the appearance of super productive busyness when you're really wrapped up in low-value tasks or focusing on email rather than making progress on a big project. Authors Anne Helen Petersen and Charlie Warzel call the phenomenon "live action role playing" the job. In overwork work cultures, those who *appear* to perform well are often the ones who are rewarded.

Yet when we're busy and have that high-octane, panicked feeling that time is scarce—what one participant called the "sustained moment of hecticness" through the workday—our attention and ability to focus narrow. Behavioral science researchers call this phenomenon "tunneling." And like being in a tunnel, in that heightened state of time scarcity and busyness, we're only able to concentrate on the most immediate and often low-value tasks right in front of us. (Research has found we lose about 13 IQ points in this situation.[85]) "If you're in this firefighting state of time pressure and tunneling, you're not making time to meet long-term goals. You're not dealing with any of the root causes that led to the firefighting in the first place," said Matthew Darling, then ideas42 vice president and project lead. "The tendency is to do the stuff that's easy to check off. That's all you have the bandwidth for."[86] So the high-value work spills into what should be time off. We also found that this busyness style is sticky, even though it clearly doesn't result in better output, nor better individual health and wellbeing, because work has become more complicated and most organizations haven't figured out how to measure performance based on outcome.

After hearing from workers about being caught up in busyness culture, my ideas42 colleagues started thinking about interventions to improve flexibility, collaboration, and autonomy. To do this, they had to construct a new "mental model" of an ideal worker. To paint this new picture, ideas42 designers at the time Dan Connolly and Uyhun Ung worked with participants to imagine a workplace that valued work-life balance and how that would change the social signals people sent. At work, all people see are others working.

When they see late-night emails or texts, they often assume that their coworker or boss has been working all day and night without interruption, when in fact they might have been walking the dog or having dinner with their families. That life outside work doesn't register because they don't see it. (Often people don't want to share their lives outside work with coworkers and bosses to preserve the busyness myth that they're always working.[87]) "You end up miscalibrating," Darling explained, thinking that people are working more than they actually are, so you automatically think you have to do the same to keep up. For an ideal work-life balance workplace, designers imagined leaders who were open about taking lunch breaks, working flexibly, going on vacation, and sharing more about their lives and families outside of work.[88]

Having envisaged this new type of leader, my colleagues then designed, implemented, and tested practical interventions focused on four key pain points: long hours, endless and often pointless meetings, the guilt people felt about vacations (which they often didn't take), and email.

Humans also have a tough time estimating how much time and effort are needed to accomplish things. We tend to overestimate the to-do list and underestimate the time needed to get it all done. Behavioral scientists call this the planning fallacy.[89] The busyness imperative only exacerbates the tendency to underestimate and overpromise. So one intervention asked workers to schedule big blocks in their calendars for their most important uninterrupted work, rather than, as many of us do, expecting it to just happen at some point during the workweek. Then the designers encouraged workers to create open space or slack in their calendars every week so that, instead of getting to the end of the day or week without having done that big project, they had a built-in cushion in case they had underestimated the time or an unanticipated emergency cropped up. "You almost always need a lot more slack than you think you will," Darling explained, "and it is actually markedly important for doing good work."

Intentional scheduling that you share with coworkers makes

it much more apparent that calling a meeting involves a trade-off. What are you not doing because you're being asked to go to a meeting? And is the meeting the better use of time? The intervention also called for organizations to design and enforce better "meeting hygiene." Meetings account for about 15 percent of an organization's time, a share that has increased steadily in recent years. Many are not run well and are a waste of productive time that adds to the busy overwork culture. In the intervention, an agenda would be circulated before every meeting listing clear goals to keep things short and focused on discussion, debate, and decisions. Those calling the meeting were encouraged to be judicious about who needed to be in the room or on the call rather than putting out a blanket invitation, which can wind up being a time suck and an impediment to getting the most important work done. One study, for instance, found that one organization's routine weekly executive meeting cost a total of three hundred thousand hours a year.[90]

To encourage time for rest and vacation, some organizations experimented with nudging workers to put their summer breaks on their calendars as early as January or February, when the summer months were likely to be clear, rather than a few weeks beforehand, when calendars are cluttered with meetings and obligations. Planning early would force teams to map out how to meet deadlines and delegate tasks so people would no longer feel compelled to work on vacation. My colleagues helped design vacation prep checklists, an activity that recognizes the work involved in planning time off and gives team members the tools to prepare so that they can all successfully unplug. They encouraged organizations to experiment with allocating two vacation "transition days"—one before vacation and the other the first day back in the office, with the only expectation being that they use the time to disconnect and reconnect with work.

One organization adopted a "vacation roulette" intervention. The HR team found every person who hadn't used their vacation days over a ninety-day period and sent them a note reminding them of their vacation balance and copying their manager. They then sent them an invitation to take a random Monday or Friday off and signed the note, "From your vacation fairy godmother." Oftentimes, the managers would encourage workers to take a break. Another organization experimented with closing down between Christmas and New Year's. That changed the conversation, one participant told me, from the usual snarky "Going on vacation? Must be nice for some" to a more welcoming "Tell me about your break and I'll tell you about mine." Research in Sweden found that when everyone takes vacation at the same time like that, there's less guilt, a big boost to mental health, and the entire organization—or in Sweden's case, the entire country—benefits from "collective restoration."[91]

Some interventions worked well, at least during the experiment. But interventions to ease the pain of email were, perhaps not surprisingly, among the least successful. My ideas42 colleagues designed a tool to enable workers to pause their email inboxes in an It Can Wait campaign. They sent reminders to people at the end of each workday asking whether they had paused their inboxes. They sought to amplify the effort with a campaign to affirm people's identities outside of work, sharing postcards showing happy people running, cooking, painting, reading a book to a child, and so on. But very few people clicked on the tool to pause their inboxes.

Violante reflected on why some interventions had caught hold and others had not. The ones that didn't work were those aimed at individuals taking individual action to improve their personal work-life balance. Those that were more successful involved a change to the entire system.[92] "You can't design a work redesign intervention aimed at one person," Violante concluded. "For it to stick, people have to have the assurance that it's aimed at the whole culture."

▬

How *can* whole cultures change?

Erin Kelly, who researches and directs work redesign projects as a professor of work and organization studies at MIT, has devoted her life to this question. As a child, Kelly saw her aunt, then in her first year of law school, become a single mother after the unexpected death of her spouse. Kelly watched as her aunt sought to navigate that time with virtually no support other than her family. There were no public policies to help, Kelly recalled, and no institutions willing to accommodate the complicated work, life, and care responsibilities of a newly widowed single mother. Kelly saw how her aunt's ambitions shifted and how her family's survival rested solely on her shoulders. By ninth grade, Kelly was writing school papers on how universal child care could positively boost women's labor force participation.

Once in college and graduate school, Kelly began to focus on work, care, and wellbeing dynamics and how workplaces could be more supportive of those with care responsibilities. The deeper she got into the subject, the more she saw how work could be redesigned through public policy, worker movements, and cultural shifts. But in the United States, any kind of positive change would also require shifting policies and practices in private business. "The United States is a place where we look to employers to solve the challenges that many other industrial countries solve with public policy," she said. "Policies and culture shifts are still important, but they're not the only avenue for providing these key family supports."

She began working with Phyllis Moen, a leading scholar on work-family issues. They decided to apply the rigorous approach of academic research to work redesign experiments, running control groups and randomized trials with the aim of capturing the kind of data that might persuade business leaders to change the way organizations work. Kelly and Moen began collaborating with a group of interdisciplinary scholars in the Work Family and Health Network. They devised innovative experiments that sought to both improve individual wellbeing and make work itself more effective. By broadening the scope to target worker wellbeing, Kelly thought, more employers might buy into changes that would ultimately benefit employees with care responsibilities, too. "Redesign research that's about organizational change is so exciting to me," she said, "because it appeals to this sense of hope."

They tracked the results-only work environment, or ROWE, at the corporate headquarters of Best Buy. They led or were part of redesign studies in the IT department of a Fortune 500 company and in several nursing homes. Over time, they began to understand *how* successful redesign works, which they recount in their book, *Overload: How Good Jobs Went Bad and What We Can Do About It*. Kelly and Moen and their colleagues developed and tested a methodology aimed at changing the workplace, not the worker, called STAR—Support. Transform. Achieve. Results.[93] Like Freelance Nation, STAR builds on the good work principles of fairness, cooperation, and meaning.

To start, it's fairly simple: Leaders have to take a leap of faith. They have to believe that work can not only be done differently but that the change can make work better. Then, they have to turn the reins over to their teams and workers and listen to what *they* say is and isn't effective. Leaders need to create the space and provide the prompts and expert facilitators to help their staff come up with ideas for what could work better. Experiment, learn, gather data, adapt, repeat. The redesigns Kelly and her colleagues help teams come up with are intended to increase employees' control over when and where they do their work, promote social support for personal and family lives—including time off—and manage high work demands by reducing low-value tasks and focusing on results. "Sitting in on the workshops," Kelly said, "you see this sense of relief, like, 'I'm not the only one frustrated by the daily meeting that came in the middle of my most productive time.'" Some of the changes proposed are small, but Kelly has found that just going through the process alone can be powerful because it gives people a voice and enhances the sense of fairness and cooperation. "It really signals respect for workers' whole lives and for them having a say in how they put their days together."

Work redesign efforts typically focus on three goals: reducing work demands, increasing worker control, and increasing worker support. Reducing demands is the heaviest lift because it requires system-wide change, such as Freelance Nation or the STAR interventions Kelly tracks. Increasing worker control can provide helpful tools, strategies, and tips, but, as my ideas42 colleagues and I saw in our behavioral science–focused redesign efforts, they may not stick unless they are aimed at the entire company culture. So, many organizations wind up concentrating on the third goal, increasing support, spending billions of dollars every year on wellness programs and employee resource groups[94] because it's easier to do.

Still, increasing support, done right, can have a far-reaching impact. WFHN's Leslie Hammer, a psychology professor and co-director of the Oregon Healthy Workforce Center, has helped design an intervention to teach middle managers how to better support people with families with care responsibilities. It's called family-supportive supervisor training.[95] Experience shows that middle managers are key to ensuring the success of any redesign effort. In this one, managers are trained how to help resolve work and family scheduling conflicts, and how to model healthy behavior. This might involve being open about taking time off to attend a parent-teacher conference or to accompany an aging parent to an appointment. Managers are also taught how to work across departments and with others at their level on cross-training and similar initiatives to increase coverage options when people are away because of care duties. "Just training managers in these basic yet critical behaviors leads to improvements in sleep, improvements in cardiovascular disease, and less physical pain," Hammer told me. "We now have a one-hour computer training, and we've been able to see positive effects on workers three, six, nine months down the line. It's low-demand and high-yield training. I continue to be completely blown away."

In fact, the results for flexible pilots like Hammer's manager training and Kelly's STAR interventions have been remarkable.[96] Compared to control groups, participants in the experiments reported higher job satisfaction, reduced burnout, better sleep, better work-life balance with families, less work-family conflict, better mental and cardiometabolic health, and less stress and psychological distress, particularly for women. Even workers' children benefited. Parents noted that having more time at home meant their children had better sleep patterns and emotional health, compared to those of workers not in the redesign pilots. In many WFHN studies, workers were just as productive, if not more, than those in control groups. They were less likely to want to quit. All of which provided firms with a significant return on investment for every dollar spent on the redesign.

Just as with Freelance Nation, though, even some of the most successful redesigns didn't last. A new CEO at Best Buy put an end to the ROWE experiment. The Fortune 500 IT company was bought out and the new management didn't like the flexible team practices. The corporate monoculture snapped back. "We had watched the organizational cultures shift over time," and they changed to such an extent that "it felt like, 'This is the way we work here.' It was settling in as the new normal," Kelly told me. "But it's not the new normal in the broader corporate world. Those who are at the very top of an organization want to go with what feels right to them, what they're comfortable with, and what they've seen and believe to be efficient and effective. So a work redesign process that's flourishing and working pretty well can still get squashed by top leadership."

The forced pandemic-era changes are different. As Kelly said, there are more than a handful of teams in a handful of organizations trying something new. *Everyone* had to reimagine work and figure out together how to do it in some other way. "That's changed expectations on a larger scale. It's harder to put the cat back in the bag," she said. "Going back to the old ways doesn't seem feasible for so many more people."

▬

The sheer scope, scale, and duration of the way workplaces were forced to change during the pandemic have opened the door to a new and growing four-day workweek movement. I met movement leaders Andrew Barnes and Charlotte Lockhart for the first time in early 2020, just after they presented the idea to business leaders at the U.S. Chamber of Commerce, the citadel of corporate overwork monoculture. The first thing Barnes noticed, he said, was that just about everyone there sought to find the one example where a four-day week wouldn't work, just to prove him wrong. But then they began to listen. "They certainly recognize that there is change afoot," he said at the time. "They're just not sure how to react to it." By 2023, after the upheavals of the pandemic, they know they must, Lockhart said when I spoke with her again.

Barnes, a former investment banker, is a product of that corporate culture, so he understands how hard it is to wrap one's head around changing it, especially when you're at the top of it. "My life was all about work. It cost me a marriage," he said. "And later on in life, you start to wonder, 'Was that success?'" Then on one of his many long flights between the United Kingdom and New Zealand, where he'd founded the trust company Perpetual Guardian, Barnes read an article in the *Economist* on two studies that found desk workers in the UK and Canada were productive for only one and a half to two and a half hours on a typical day.[97] "I was gobsmacked." But the more he thought about it, the more it made sense. Once you accounted for the busywork—the endless meetings and emails, the administrative tasks, the chatting and interruptions, a little internet and social media surfing, and the calls to arrange a plumber or a child's appointment that can only be made during work hours—he could see how that was true.

Barnes was immediately seized with an idea: What if he paid his organization of 250 workers their full five-day week salary and asked them to work only four days? The caveat was that on those four days, they'd give 100 percent of their time and attention. They'd have an entire day to themselves to manage plumbers and children's schedules and take care of their lives, families, and care duties. Barnes's idea to try a four-day-week experiment at his firm was first met with a mix of excitement and disbelief or resistance. Some already felt overloaded and busy, so they couldn't imagine being able to get the same amount of work done in less time. But as with the best STAR and other redesign interventions, Barnes told teams to talk to each other and try to figure it out on their own. "I basically said, 'Look, we have absolutely no idea how to deliver this. So we're going to ask *you* how *you're* going to do it. It's your responsibility." That led to intensive discussions and brainstorming within teams. There were, of course, familiar individual time management and productivity hacks—DO NOT DISTURB flags to signify concentration and ward off interruptions, for instance. But the pilot forced teams to radically change the entire system. Each had to rethink *what* their work was, what was most important, and how to change processes to prioritize that. "Our whole organization had to go through a process of understanding. 'What are we really doing here? What does productivity *mean* at Perpetual Guardian?'" Lockhart said. "So everybody had a really good look at what they did in the day, what their teams did, what other teams did, and came to understand better how the business functions and makes money. So a lot of miscellaneous things that don't feed into that were dropped," Lockhart went on.

Some teams cut meetings from sixty minutes to thirty and circulated agendas beforehand. Others cut some meetings altogether. They devised creative ways to streamline tasks. Some teams came up with a system to alternate rest days so someone would always be available to clients. Teams set clear performance expectations that helped people prioritize important projects, keep them accountable, and reduce time spent on multitasking or low-value tasks, like being obsessed with getting to inbox zero. That, they realized, was ensuring that everyone *else's* priorities got time and attention. Not necessarily theirs. "When you understand better why you're there" and how "you contribute to the greater whole, you feel a whole lot better about what you're doing," Lockhart said. "People just knew why they were there."

At the end of the pilot phase, the results turned Barnes and Lockhart into evangelists bent on creating a global movement. Productivity remained just as high in four days as in five. The firm also saw big improvements in engagement, empowerment, and loyalty. Stress levels dropped.[98] "The most surprising thing to come out of the experiment was that more people said they were better able to do their job working four days rather than five," Barnes said. "Now that was a shock."

The shorter work hour movement is challenging deeply flawed yet deeply held notions that long work hours lead to better work. One researcher said Perpetual Guardian's pilot proved Parkinson's law, that work will indeed expand—or shrink—to fill the time allotted to it.[99]

The pilot data only confirmed what other research has found over the years: that the more hours we put in and as stress levels and poor health rise, the work itself suffers. Long hours can lead to unnecessary errors,[100] accidents, fuzzy thinking, revising shoddy work done in an exhausted state, and more busywork.

The story of software engineer Bill Brice is a case in point. Brice worked in his field for thirty years. One Fortune 500 company where he had been employed was obsessed with overwork, what Brice called "the Death March." The company, he said, routinely made unrealistic bids for contracts "and mostly, they failed spectacularly. Mid- and low-level managers were rewarded for failed projects—because their people had put in 55-hour weeks for months on end; results just didn't matter." This was an attribute "the company extolled as leadership, one they could put an easy score on," he wrote me. "Unfortunately for them, it was a metric that was, at best, detached altogether from work results—and, at worst, that directly detracted from results."

For a while, Brice had worked on a contract in Germany, and the company was subject to European regulations that limit overtime. "What a difference! They put great stress on producing realistic estimates based on forty-hour workweeks. If your estimate showed that the desired deadline couldn't be met, then solutions were to renegotiate the deadlines," he continued. "The American solution (non-solution) was just 'do whatever it takes'—and, never mind how bad the result." That Fortune 500 company no longer exists.

In international comparisons of productivity, dividing a country's GDP by total hours worked, the relationship is as clear as it is damning: the longer the work hours, the lower the productivity.[101]

In the course of my reporting, I visited the cramped, book-lined office of Stanford economist John Pencavel, author of *Diminishing Returns at Work: The Consequences of Long Working Hours*, who studies the relationship between hours and productivity. He famously found in one of his studies of munitions workers in World War I that long hours led to more errors and lower quality. Productivity drops steeply after fifty hours a week, he found, and drops even more after fifty-five hours. He calls it the "productivity cliff."[102] "What my research suggests," he told me, "is that it may be in the *firm's* best interest for workers to work less." But the responsibility for that change can't simply rest on workers' shoulders, he insisted. "If everyone in your social circle" is overworking, "it's difficult to break out of it," he said. "That's why the employer has to take the lead."

That's something Henry Ford learned through his own experience on his factory floor. For most of the nineteenth century, sixty- to seventy-hour workweeks, at least six days a week, were common in manufacturing and other sectors.[103] After he introduced a moving assembly line, Ford found that longer hours didn't yield more productivity and led to costly errors or accidents. So he shortened shifts to eight hours.[104] Beginning in 1914, at a time when unions had been calling for shorter days and weeks for decades, Ford became an early adopter[105]—because it was good for business. He instituted three eight-hour shifts that wound up keeping worker wellbeing and productivity levels high. He cut the workweek to five days from six and raised wages so that employees would have the money to buy his automobiles and the leisure time to enjoy them—creating a ready market for his new product.[106] Today, with technology layering new work processes (email, online collaboration tools, and other messaging platforms, for example) on top of old systems (in-person meetings, phone calls) without much thought, all manner of work has become more complicated, intense, and demanding. Researchers have identified not just work-family conflict creating stress but *work-work* conflict, when too many competing job tasks pull people in too many directions at once.[107] So how many hours should firms push modern employees to work?

It's an open question. Research shows that high-performing athletes, musicians, and creatives appear to be able to engage in concentrated work, or "deliberate practice," for no more than about four or five hours a day.[108] In a 2019 pilot program of a thirty-two-hour, four-day workweek tested by Microsoft in Japan, the company found that the shorter hours boosted productivity by 40 percent.[109]

I spoke with Lockhart and Barnes again in late 2023. At that point, the pandemic disruptions had jump-started their movement and they were running four-day workweek pilots in the United States and the UK and around the globe. The governments of Spain and Scotland were exploring four-day workweek pilots, and bills were being introduced in the U.S. Congress, as well as the states of Maryland, California, and New York.[110] "A lot of what I'm talking about now is really the *why*. Why do we need to work shorter hours? Why do we need our time back?" Lockhart said. "It's not just the fact that we're overworked. Our lack of time has led us to being under-engaged in our communities and personal lives." A generation ago, people belonged to service and volunteer organizations such as the Rotary Club and played pivotal roles in solving community problems. Rotary was instrumental in the global fight to eradicate polio,[111] Lockhart pointed out. Now, few have time. The hours Americans spend volunteering continue to decline.[112] "People want to solve problems in their local communities," she said. "But that's not possible when there's no time to be part of the community."

Lockhart and Barnes understand that a big reason why companies are finally listening to them is the benefits of better effectiveness at work and profitability. "We make the argument from a business perspective," Barnes said. "If we come from a social perspective, it will go nowhere." Their pilots show workers' mental and physical health improve, along with their wellbeing and work-life balance, making them better able to manage care responsibilities and enjoy a social life. At the same time, company revenue and productivity rise, while turnover drops significantly.[113] Most of the companies that have participated in their pilots intend to retain a four-day workweek. CEOs told researchers that the pandemic had taught them to trust their employees about *where* they work, so managers felt confident they could also trust them on how many hours they needed to do their jobs.[114]

"The four-day workweek has the potential to make a significant difference to society," Barnes said. "Equally, the research indicates that it will have a positive impact on GDP.[115] So you'll work less, but you'll create more and you'll generate more. To me, that's a win win win."

CHAPTER 4

WORKERS RISING: MORE THAN CLAPPING FOR ESSENTIAL WORK

> Capital is the fruit of labor, and could never have existed if labor had not first existed—labor can exist without capital, but capital could never have existed without labor. Hence labor is the superior—greatly the superior of capital.
>
> —*Abraham Lincoln*[1]

Adrian Ugalde knows what it feels like to be invisible. For twenty years, almost every day of his adult life, people have walked by without noticing him, as if he's part of the store's scenery as he stocks shelves, runs to the storeroom, checks inventory, arranges merchandise, and returns items to their place after shoppers pick them up and haphazardly discard them. Sometimes he comes into focus, emerging from a shopper's hazy peripheral vision when the customer can't find something. Or during the pandemic, when he would remind them to wear a mask. Then they let him have it.

Ashley Worthen and Onie Patrick know that feeling, too, standing at their cashier stations year after year, ringing up groceries piled on the checkout conveyor belt, as does Sam Hughes, slicing meat and serving up salads behind the deli counter.

It's not just their paid work that is invisible. So are their struggles in the rest of their lives, the low pay, the lack of benefits, and the wildly unpredictable schedules that come with the work. There is scarcely time for care and home, much less anything else. That's the situation for millions of people in retail, restaurant, service, care, and other low-wage jobs—an astonishing 44 percent of the U.S. workforce[2]—and independent, contract, and gig workers.[3]

During the pandemic, everyone called them "essential workers" and clapped as they marched to their jobs every day, facing the risk of a deadly virus. The country cheered, even though it was a forced march, as millions were excluded from temporary federal emergency paid child care and sick leave[4] and had no choice if they wanted to feed their families. Then, just as quickly, these workers fell from view, and most people forgot about them as the pandemic began to ease. Even the news makes low-wage workers invisible, erasing their lives and their stories from the picture. Much coverage goes to the ups and downs of the stock market, even though half of all people in the United States, including most low-wage workers, don't have a penny invested, and 84 percent of the stocks are owned by the wealthiest 10 percent of families.[5] While there's been a slight uptick in news about the plight of these workers in recent years, most media outlets dropped their dedicated labor reporters back in the 1970s.[6]

Politicians routinely forget low-wage workers.[7] Each month, when the economic media report the job numbers released by the Bureau of Labor Statistics, the story they tell is typically simple: Jobs up = good, a political win; numbers down or lower than expected = bad, a worrying sign of slowing growth or a weakening economy. This story misses the real question: How many of these new positions are good jobs? Do they pay enough to live on—to own or rent a home, eat, pay bills, and support a family? Can one even contemplate having a family with these jobs? Will there be time for love, care, leisure, and joy, or will the job eat up all of a person's time? Do these jobs provide a predictable schedule and the stability that offers peace of mind, keeps stress levels low, and makes the future seem hopeful?

Take the November 2022 jobs report. Employers added 263,000 jobs. "Another month of strong job growth!" "Women gain more jobs than men!" enthused the headlines.[8] But a closer look revealed that one-third of those jobs were in the low-wage leisure and hospitality industry,[9] in which nonsupervisory workers earn an average of about $18 an hour[10] and work an average of about 24.5 hours a week, well below the 30-hour-week cutoff that may entitle them to employer-provided benefits. Just 15 percent in these professions have retirement benefits and only about one-third have health care, and their erratic schedules are all over the map.[11] Women of color, immigrant women, and women with disabilities are overrepresented in this sector. This is essential and important work, but these are crummy jobs.

If people don't know about lousy conditions, then they won't care and nothing will change. Not unless the workers themselves make change happen. That's a lesson Ugalde, Worthen, Patrick, and Hughes learned the hard way. When the unfairness of their paid work became untenable and their lives barely livable, they all joined worker movements or unions. Once they spoke up, they realized they weren't the only ones suffering in silence. Once they became visible to each other, they began to strive together for something better, no longer accepting, as they had, that this is the way it has to be. As historian Jan Lucassen wrote of the aggrandizers who were able to justify inequality with a good story, today's aggrandizers have been selling the story that labor is expendable, and these workers began to realize that they didn't have to buy it anymore.

Let's start with Adrian Ugalde. Though many policymakers and business leaders would have us believe that the terms of part-time and low-wage work are justifiable because these jobs are done by teens earning extra cash on summer break or after school, this is not the case. Ugalde has worked most of his adult life in such a job, stocking retail shelves. The average age of a low-wage worker is thirty-six. In 2023, Ugalde was forty-one. And far from a part-time gig, more than half of such workers do this full-time.[12] Another argument made by some conservatives over the years is that the low wage is justifiable because the job is just entry-level and workers quickly move up.[13] This might have been true at one point but now it is simply false. One Harvard Business School study found that 60 percent of people starting in low-wage jobs in 2012 were still stuck there five years later.[14] A study by the Federal Reserve Bank of New York found that just 5 percent of low-wage workers found better jobs in a given year in that same time period.[15] Ugalde has worked in retail for two decades.

When Ugalde is asked why he hasn't moved on or moved up, the answer in part is because the big-box companies where he worked never offered training, cross-training, or a pathway to advancement, which the Harvard Business School study found was a common failure in most companies, despite the PR lip service they pay to the importance of offering opportunity. The rest of the answer is that his managers routinely gave him a schedule that was so chaotic, he never knew when he'd be working or for how many hours. The random schedules make it impossible to find time to go to school or develop new skills or plan for, well, virtually anything, even though many workers like Ugalde know that automation will likely change or destroy jobs like theirs.[16] "I never imagined, growing up, that this is what I'm going to do for the rest of my life," Ugalde told me. "And it's, it's kind of a sad feeling. Like overwhelming, like 'Whoa, how am I in this mess?'"

When I first met him in 2018, Ugalde described his impossible schedule. Sometimes, during the holiday rush of Christmas or back-to-school time when Ugalde's Los Angeles Target store would be packed with shoppers, he'd be given the full-time hours he was promised when he was hired in 2008 as a backroom team member for $10 an hour. But otherwise, his hours bounced around, sometimes wildly. One week, he'd have twenty hours and the next just twelve. He'd be called in suddenly or, just as unexpectedly, sent home mid-shift.

To keep his health insurance, Ugalde had to scavenge for shifts, begging coworkers to give up their slots so he could cobble together the thirty hours each week that would allow him to stay eligible for health insurance benefits. "I hit up the employees I know live with their parents first," he said. "Not that everyone doesn't want their money. But I go after the people who don't have the same responsibilities of living on their own and paying bills." At the time, Ugalde was living in a one-bedroom apartment with his now husband, his sister, her partner, and their two children. His father built bunk beds in the living room so that everyone could fit. Even Ugalde's daily schedule was all over the map: the morning shift one day, the midday shift the next. Sometimes he's been on the closing shift until 12:30 a.m., taken an hour-long bus ride or expensive rideshare home, only to be back on the job the following morning at 7:00 a.m., a "clopening," as it's called in the retail and service sectors. It was as if his life were hostage to the whims of the store and its schedulers. That was just business as usual. "It's very rare for anyone to have a set schedule," he said.

He learned quickly not to ask for one. Ugalde had seen managers not hire people who were in school or who requested specific hours. In low-wage jobs, the expectation is that workers will always be accessible when the boss calls. In low-wage work, an ideal worker has "open availability," and must be willing to be "on call" to come in at the drop of a hat or go home when the boss no longer needs them. Ugalde did once ask for a set schedule so he could go back to school. His managers warned him he probably wouldn't get it, and they'd likely cut his hours, too. "And that was it. That made me decide like, 'Well, I need to live. Even if I do go to school, I've still got to pay rent. I've still got to pay for the car.' I wouldn't be able to do it. So, of course, at that point you decide to give up on moving up, and you stay stuck where you're at."

These chaotic schedules may be invisible to many in the United States, but they are standard for millions of low-wage and service workers. The pandemic put a spotlight on these essential workers, and the severe labor shortage in the service industry could have led to better working conditions, but it didn't. Though still inadequate after a forty-year slump, wages did rise somewhat during the pandemic for the lowest earners.[17] But the Shift Project at Harvard, which has been tracking erratic service worker schedules since 2017, reports that unstable and unpredictable hours continue to be the norm, especially for workers of color, such as Ugalde, and women of color. About two-thirds of service workers receive their upcoming shifts with less than two weeks' notice. One-third get one week's notice, and about a quarter only find out seventy-two hours before their shifts are due to begin. Shift times also swing erratically for nearly 60 percent of low-wage workers and the majority experience last-minute changes. More than one-third work "clopenings." And though the majority wish they had more stable schedules and some one-third of all part-time workers want to work more hours, 42 percent have no say in how many hours they'll get on their schedule or when.[18] Businesses like to say that these jobs offer workers the "flexibility" they want to meet family and care responsibilities. But this isn't flexibility—it's instability.

These workers also tend to be among the most powerless. Research in Oregon found that low-wage workers who are disproportionately more likely to have nonstandard hours are women, people of color, the young, and those with children.[19] Another analysis of schedule volatility showed that workers who are "black, young and without a college degree appear to be at highest risk."[20] The Shift Project pointed out that non-white workers are as much as 30 percent more likely to have precarious work schedules as white people.[21]

The problem of unstable schedules was for many years largely absent from the national conversation and even from research agendas. In 2014, sociologists Daniel Schneider, then with the University of California, Berkeley, and Kristen Harknett, at the University of California, San Francisco, were studying how the 2008 recession had affected families. Much had been written about plummeting birth rates, higher divorce rates, and lower marital quality. Many attributed this family instability to the loss of jobs and the devastation of unemployment.

But Schneider and Harknett began to find lasting negative effects beyond job loss. Even among those who kept their jobs or found new ones, there was an enormous and enormously debilitating sense of everyday uncertainty. Many workers reported they didn't know when or how much they would work, if they'd be asked to stay late, or called in at all. Were these erratic schedules a new phenomenon? they wondered. Were they tied to the lower quality of life people assumed had been brought on by the recession? They quickly realized there was no data about what was going on. They founded the Shift Project to find out. "We're so focused on wages in our labor force surveys in the United States," Schneider said. "This is different. This is about time."

The story of modern erratic scheduling begins in the 1970s. To boost profits, companies began to move away from full-time workers and rely on a contract or a part-time workforce with open availability.[22] By the late 1980s, these companies had turned to Big Data to cut labor costs as close to the bone as possible. They started to use "smart" software algorithms to crunch data to predict when stores would be busy or slower to better match customer demand with labor supply, an idea borrowed from Toyota and their "just in time" management practice. Except instead of ordering auto parts as needed rather than storing them in warehouses, service-sector business owners sought to do the same with human lives. "Technology isn't creating this, it's exacerbating existing underlying social problems," said Aiha Nguyen, who heads the Labor Futures Initiative at the Data and Society Research Institute and has chaired a labor conference panel titled "When Your Boss Is an Algorithm." "Unpredictable schedules are another form of precarity of work, which we've been seeing for a while."

The idea behind algorithmic scheduling, to increase efficiency, sounds laudable. Brilliant, even. Many brick-and-mortar stores have been struggling to survive as more consumers turn to online retail. Stores need to be as efficient as possible just to keep their doors open. Analysts who've tracked retail chains, such as Forever 21, Payless, Toys"R"Us, and Sears filing for bankruptcy,[23] say we're in an era of "Retail Apocalypse."[24] Pandemic closures and supply chain woes have driven even more consumers into the arms of Amazon and other e-commerce giants, which can deliver contactless cheap stuff to our doorsteps, often within hours of ordering.[25] The cost of labor is the single largest controllable expense for employers in the retail, restaurant, and service industries, so it's usually the first place they look to cut.

To better match labor supply with customer demand, a software program crunches complex and fine-grained analyses of previous years' sales patterns, by the month, day, and hour. Some stores have begun to use sensors and video cameras to track foot traffic, shopper movements, and their "dwell time" in front of certain products. There are scheduling software programs that even track weather patterns, local and regional events like football games and concerts, as well as social media traffic, upcoming deliveries, or sales promotions to make real-time adjustments to their demand projections in fifteen-minute increments.[26] More rain predicted; more customers likely to dash indoors to buy things or take shelter in cafés and restaurants and order food and drink. That means last-minute calls to workers to come in. Or if the rain doesn't bring in the expected rush, sending those workers home, frequently without pay. Managers are under often intense pressure from corporate headquarters to stay within the algorithm's bare-bones "labor budget."[27]

While the algorithms have become sophisticated at tracking fluctuating customer demand, they aren't perfect. They can often be wrong. They have been programmed to treat human beings as interchangeable widgets. As a result, algorithmic scheduling has wreaked utter havoc in the lives, health, financial stability, and future prospects of millions of workers, trapping them and their families in a cycle of precarious and unpredictable low-wage work. "A computer has decided when I work and how much I work and whether I work," Ugalde said. "It's just trying to fit me in like a puzzle piece. A computer doesn't know your life."

Bob Clements, CEO of Axsium, a global workforce management consultancy, has helped companies implement scheduling technology all over the globe since the 1990s. The erratic schedules that plague workers in the United States, he said, are a peculiarly American problem. That's because other countries have laws and regulations governing work time and scheduling, while the United

States doesn't. Given the industry's reliance on worker availability, the snazzy new technology, instead of leading to business efficiency and productivity, has myopically driven high turnover and workforce instability. The technology, Clements said, has turned workers' lives into a "game of fifty-two-card pickup."[28]

Try finding any child care, much less quality care, with a schedule that looks like the mayhem of a scattered deck of cards. Try scheduling pediatrician appointments, or making any kind of plan at all, even for family dinner. Ashley Worthen, a thirty-four-year-old single mother, started working as a cashier at Albertson's in Eugene, Oregon, at seventeen, just weeks after finishing high school. The store offered her part-time hours to start and never promised how many she'd get. Her schedule each week was erratic. Some weeks, she'd be asked to work one day only. Other weeks, when more senior cashiers were out or had called in sick, Worthen would get called in unexpectedly, and she'd sometimes wind up working thirty-eight or forty hours. As with Ugalde, her daily schedule was always different. Sometimes she'd be called in to work the 3:30 p.m.–to–12:30 a.m. shift and would then come back to do the 10:00 a.m.–to–7:00 p.m. shift the following day. "That was really hard on my son," Worthen told me. "I was never home."

Because the weekly schedules were posted on Friday afternoon for weeks that started on Sunday, Worthen could never plan in advance or she would have to cancel appointments for herself or her son, Brantley. She felt as if she was constantly bracing herself. "It's a very uneasy, very unsure feeling," she said. "I didn't like it. But at the time, there really wasn't an option. That's just how it was. I didn't know better. Though I kept thinking, 'I don't know why this is so hard.'"

With such an erratic timetable and an equally erratic paycheck, Worthen was forced to live with her mother and brother for a while in a small apartment. Worthen's mother, Ruth, had to step in again and again to care for Brantley when Worthen's shifts didn't line up with her child care, which they often didn't. Because Ashley, and later her younger sister, had to keep "open availability" and be on call, Ruth Worthen wound up quitting her own job as a dishwasher so that she, too, could be on call to care for both their children. That meant she was also held hostage to her daughters' unpredictable schedules and couldn't get her own job, which kept the family struggling financially.

How are people to pay their bills when they have no idea how many hours they'll work each week? Or care for their health when they have only a day or two's notice for their hours? This leaves workers scrambling to swap shifts, fearing that if they ask their manager for time off, they'll find their hours cut even further the following week because they dared to ask. When Sam Hughes got a job at a Fred Meyer's Deli in Salem, Oregon, in 2018 and was promised twenty hours of work a week, Hughes, who identifies as non-binary, made it clear that they needed four hours a week for doctor appointments. They wouldn't have "open availability" and couldn't be on call for twenty erratic hours. When Hughes asked for two additional hours off for an unexpected doctor appointment one week, their hours were cut to fourteen. Even if they worked a full schedule, Hughes was making so little money—$12 an hour—that they qualified for public benefits like food stamps and Medicaid. So the cut in hours sent them into a panic. And because they never knew when or for how long they'd be working the deli job, they weren't able to get a second job. Desperate, Hughes did whatever they could to pay their bills, working odd jobs for their landlord to pay their rent. They held out their arm to show me scars. "I was selling my plasma."[29]

Erratic schedule algorithms, data scientist Cathy O'Neil writes in her book, *Weapons of Math Destruction*, are the dark underside of the future of work. "It's almost as if the software were designed expressly to punish low-wage workers and to keep them down," she writes, calling them the ultimate "captive workforce."[30] One retail consultant likened the scheduling practices to modern-day "sharecropping."[31] Instead of cotton, low-wage workers are forced to sharecrop their time.

Onie Patrick, a cashier at an Aldi in Illinois, is the sole breadwinner for her family of four children with her $16.50-an-hour paycheck. Because child care is so expensive, she and her fiancé—they can't afford to get married—decided that it made the most sense for him to stay home to provide child care. When her hours are cut, Patrick is tied in knots. She does her taxes early, hoping for a refund; she makes more trips to the food pantry and takes on after-hours cleaning and shifts through the weekend. But it eats at her. She thinks of her grandfather's dying regret that he was always working and hadn't had more time for his family. Or how her mother worked days at a gas station while her father worked afternoons and evenings at a factory. At least they had regular schedules and could make ends meet. But she rarely saw her father growing up.

"You want to have memories with your children. Children who grow up without having that bond with their parents feel like they've really missed out on something," Patrick said. "I don't have a lot of memories with my dad, except for on the weekends sometimes. But I wish I did. Being on call is very stressful on a parent, especially a mother, because I want to do everything I can for my children. I want to teach them responsibility and independence. But there are times where I just—I'm breaking, and it's hard to stay strong in front of them," she said. "I need to be home with them. I need that time with them. I need to be that mom, that moral figure, that person they look at and find laughter and happiness, the one who helps them with issues and helps them with homework. But I need to work, too. So what am I supposed to do?"

For years, Patrick blamed herself for not having a better job, a steadier schedule, or a bigger paycheck. Why hasn't she moved on? She has a Certified Nursing Assistant degree from a community college, but when her boss wouldn't give her lighter duties during a difficult pregnancy, she was forced out of the job—something that the 2022 Pregnant Workers Fairness Act has since made illegal. Things kept falling apart once she had a family. With no paid leave, no paid sick time, and her savings burned through while she healed after difficult births, she was nearly evicted twice from the home she owns, which makes her feel ashamed. Patrick didn't want anyone to know how much her family was struggling. "It hurts your pride to speak out," she said. "It's scary and embarrassing to think I can't take care of my children." She'd love to do something else, but she can't afford to go back to school, and her sharecropping work schedule doesn't allow her the time.

Workers like Patrick have begun to fight back, finding strength in numbers. A few years ago, as she was being laid off after nearly nine years at Kmart, she found an online petition protesting working conditions very much like hers. It was a revelation to discover she wasn't alone. What could she do? Certainly not fix her work by herself. So when she learned about the workers' movement United for Respect, Patrick joined up. Ugalde followed the same path, joining other people in his situation in the Los Angeles Alliance for a New Economy, or LAANE. In Oregon, Worthen and Hughes joined the United Food and Commercial Workers Union 555. And as part of a slowly reemerging labor movement across the country, they've been having some successes.

Labor organizer Carrie Gleason began organizing retail workers back in 2005 when she founded the Retail Action Project[32] in New York. Back then, she said, you could walk into a JCPenney and find workers with stable jobs, full-time hours, health insurance, and commissions. Initially, she had focused on helping retail workers fight for better wages. But by 2008, spurred by the Great Recession, the JCPenney workforce had become almost entirely part-time, and across the retail industry the new expectation of worker open availability had taken hold, with no commitment of set schedules or hours from employers. With algorithmic scheduling and workers whipsawed by unpredictable hours and low wages, the fabric of the workforce changed, Gleason said.

Workers were isolated, rarely sharing shifts or schedules. As they saw more jobs go to part-time or temp workers, people who had once cared deeply about their companies became detached and more likely to quit and move on. People no longer knew coworkers' names, much less their stories. "There was a real change in workers' attitudes and their connection to each other," Gleason told me. She went on to found the Fair Workweek Initiative and, based on the experiences and demands of retail employees, began to build a coalition to drive new federal, state, and city labor standards and better business practices around scheduling.

Worker isolation may be one reason why chaotic scheduling practices stubbornly persist, and why workers, thinking they're alone, are more likely to blame themselves or their financial instability, as Onie Patrick once did. Gleason and other advocates began bringing workers together. "A lot of it is about organizing workers to *believe* that they deserve stable, predictable income and hours," said Francisco Diez, senior policy strategist at the Center for Popular Democracy, a progressive advocacy group. The center houses the Fair Workweek Initiative in partnership with United for Respect and has been instrumental, along with other organizations, in helping to organize the fair workweek movement.

Working with individual stores, restaurants, chains, and companies, the stable schedules campaign began racking up wins. Some companies dropped on-call scheduling, Gleason said. Others committed to providing schedules with three weeks' notice or guaranteeing consistent hours. But the efforts didn't make much of a dent across the industry. Some states do require companies to pay workers when they're asked to report for work and then sent home; the law is called "reporting time pay." But many don't.[33] "I knew it was time we needed to promote better standards more broadly," Gleason said. "It was out of control."

The movement began pushing for legislation and regulation. Workers began coming together and organizing on the local level to push for better working conditions like paid sick days, a living wage, and fair workweeks. In 2014, the city of San Francisco passed the first fair scheduling law, led by Jobs with Justice, a nonprofit labor rights organization with a grassroots network of coalitions and leaders. A host of local unions and coalitions built on that moment—Working Washington, Worthen and Hughes's UFCW 555 Oregon, and UFCW 881 Chicago. Ugalde's LAANE was a driver[34] behind the fair workweek ordinance that the Los Angeles City Council passed in November 2022,[35] following similar wins in San Francisco, Philadelphia, New York, Seattle, and a handful of other local jurisdictions. A key strategy, advocates said, is to have workers share their stories to show how unfair practices make life impossible.

Worker organizing spurred a coalition of nine state attorneys general to begin an inquiry into on-call scheduling in 2016. They called on fifteen big retailers to put an end to it. Six of them, including Disney and Aéropostale, agreed.[36] In 2019, workers scored a win when the California Court of Appeals held that "on call" scheduling amounted to abusive wage theft.[37]

In what was a common practice at retail outlets at the time, Tilly's, a clothing store, required employees to be on call and phone in to a manager two hours prior to an on-call shift to see if they'd be needed. Workers could be disciplined if they didn't call in, called in late, or refused to work the on-call shift. California law requires payment for workers who show up to work but are sent home. Tilly's argued that if workers didn't report to work in person, the company didn't have to pay them.

But lawyers for Skylar Ward, a sales clerk there, argued that the practice held employees hostage. Workers like Ward had to keep their time open just in case they would be called in to work. They couldn't get other jobs, go to school, arrange child care, or make any plans. They argued that Ward didn't have to show up in person to get reporting time pay. Putting her life on hold in order to be available to work was enough to qualify for it. The court agreed.

By 2023, advocates estimated that local stable schedule laws had improved life for more than two million people, as well as countless more who benefited when some companies voluntarily adopted stable scheduling practices.

Emboldened by these legal, state, and local wins, national advocates began pushing to bring the campaign to the federal government. In 2013, the National Women's Law Center, the National Partnership for Women and Families, the Center for Law and Social

Policy, and other organizations lobbied for the introduction of the Schedules That Work Act in Congress. Democratic lawmakers in Washington backed the stable scheduling legislation that year, and Sen. Elizabeth Warren and Rep. Rosa DeLauro have pushed for it in every legislative session since. Although the act has not yet passed, the national attention that comes from holding congressional hearings has placed the issue in the media spotlight. Workers and advocates continue to urge companies to voluntarily pledge to fair workweeks[38] and have been pushing legislation city by city and state by state ever since.

Jeff Anderson led UFCW 555's campaign for a fair workweek law in Oregon using the same strategy workers in the state had used to fight for a statewide paid sick leave law: go jurisdiction by jurisdiction until employers themselves ask for one statewide standard that is easier for them to comply with. "When I heard employers complain about not wanting to have a patchwork of laws, I set out to create the patchwork they didn't want as leverage for a statewide law," he told me. Another key strategy, said Anderson, who retired as the local's secretary-treasurer in 2021 after more than forty years in the union, was to ensure bipartisan support. "To me, that's a point of pride," he said. "We never made it about Democrats or Republicans. We made it about what was good for people and their families."

Those strategies helped raise the standard of living for all workers in the state. Oregon voters had raised the state's minimum wage by ballot initiative in 2002 and required an annual increase indexed to inflation and based on the Consumer Price Index.[39] In 2015, the state legislature passed a statewide paid sick leave law,[40] followed, in 2017, by the state's fair workweek law.[41] In 2019, Oregon's governor also signed into law one of the most generous paid family and medical leave policies among the handful of states with such policies.[42]

Worthen and Hughes took part in the Oregon campaign to enact stable schedules legislation.[43] In 2024, Oregon was the only state with a law that guarantees workers in large companies at least two weeks' advance notice of their schedules in writing and additional pay for last-minute employer changes; the right to rest between shifts or to receive additional pay; the right to have input into the schedule; and a good faith estimate in writing at the time of hiring of how many hours a worker can expect to work each week, and if or how they'll be expected to work on-call shifts.[44] "I definitely saw people happier," Worthen told me. "And it was so exciting to be part of the union because everyone who was involved was really passionate about making things better. It was really empowering." Both Hughes and Worthen eventually moved on. Hughes was hired by the union itself, and by 2023 Worthen was working as a medical receptionist with a more livable $20-per-hour pay and a consistent schedule.

Still, even with those wins, life remains hard for retail and service workers. After nearly nine years of unpredictable schedules at Target, Ugalde couldn't take it anymore. He moved to stock shelves at Walgreens in 2019. Though others were scheduled "like Ping-Pong balls," he advocated for and won his own stable schedule. He was laid off in 2023 during a round of trimming to boost company profits.[45] It happened just days after returning from his brother's funeral. Ugalde was unsure of his next move. "I'm lost," he told me. "I just don't want to go back to a life in retail," he said, although it's all he knows.

In Chicago, Patrick has been campaigning to expand the citywide fair workweek ordinance to cover the state, along with advocating for fair pay and fair working conditions. "Workers do feel alone. But when you become part of something as large and amazing as United for Respect, you realize you're not," she said. "We all have to work. We all have to make money. But we all don't have to suffer in silence. We're human. Not robots. We have family. We need to be treated with respect in our work lives and home lives, not just be a ghost of who you are because you have to work."

Living with an unstable, chaotic paid work schedule is hard for people, and terrible for children. Harvard's Shift Project research has found that workers with unpredictable schedules tend to experience higher levels of depression and psychological distress—feelings of nervousness, hopelessness, and being overwhelmed—than low-wage workers with stable schedules. The more variability, the higher the distress. Workers with unstable schedules are also more likely to experience hunger and rely on free food from soup kitchens or food pantries than those with stable schedules. One in six have trouble with housing and end up staying with others, living in a shelter, or sleeping in their car or an abandoned building.[46] Nearly three-fourths of workers with erratic schedules report fair or poor sleep.[47] It's not hard to imagine the stress, anxiety, and sleepless nights—on top of the financial hardship—when your income swings by as much as 32 percent but your bills don't.

Researchers also tested what would make a bigger difference in the lives of low-wage workers: higher wages or more predictable schedules. Decent wages are clearly desirable and key to a stable life. But time strain, the researchers found, had twice the negative impact.[48] "Wages are not the end of the story, they're just a piece of it," said Kristen Harknett of the Shift Project. "The number of hours that you get, the regularity of the number of hours, and the timing and predictability of those hours. They're huge. It doesn't just determine what's in your paycheck but it shapes your entire life." Shift Project codirector Daniel Schneider, who now teaches public policy at Harvard's Kennedy School, added: "It's really stressful to have no control over disorganized time."

There are considerable numbers of people who earn so little or are scheduled to work so few hours that they qualify for public benefits like Medicaid and the Supplemental Nutrition Assistance Program. Relying on Medicaid and SNAP benefits is the only way Onie Patrick and her family or Sam Hughes can survive. In fact, in a review of eleven states, one 2020 U.S. General Accounting Office study found that *70 percent* of those receiving Medicaid and food stamps actually work full-time.[49] A 2015 study found that the United States spends nearly $153 billion every year on public benefits for people, many employed full-time, who work for wealthy corporations "that do not pay a living wage."[50] Nor do they offer sufficient or stable paid work hours. To Schneider, business leaders and policymakers have enabled this system of volatile, low-wage work, which relies on taxpayers to subsidize the earnings and benefits that companies won't provide. These leaders have also enabled the chaotic scheduling practices that hold not just workers but their extended families hostage, the way Ruth Worthen was unable to work, for example, so she could care for her daughters' children. "In order for workers to work these crazy schedules, so many other people have to put their lives on hold," Schneider said. "It's a hidden subsidy to companies—all these broader networks it takes to make these unpredictable schedules work."

Children whose parents have erratic hours, Schneider and Harknett found, are more likely to have school absences, behavioral problems in school, disrupted sleep, higher levels of anxiety, and worsening health.[51] At a time of rapid brain, cognitive, and social-emotional development, very young children most need stability and attachment to a warm, responsive caregiver. Unpredictable schedules for parents make that close to impossible to provide. Schneider and Harknett found that many children in their research had multiple caregivers, had constantly changing schedules, and were more often in informal, makeshift care settings with family, friends, or neighbors rather than in high-quality or accredited care. Most formal child-care centers or family homes cannot accommodate wildly shifting schedules.[52] Children in unstable care arrangements exhibit more behavior problems and lower wellbeing, which puts them at a further disadvantage to children in families that have more control over their time and schedules. This only serves to exacerbate existing trends that reinforce grotesque inequality.[53] "The intergenerational costs of this kind of scheduling" expose "the lie that all kids have an equal chance at the starting gate," Schneider said.

When Schneider asked one young single mother what kind of schedule she'd prefer, she said it would be "amazing" if she could work a predictable night shift and have someone she trusted stay with her child at night. That way, she wouldn't have to frantically call around for help or park her child in front of the TV of whichever relative, friend, or neighbor might be available at the last minute. "I thought it was really sad that a stable night shift was her big dream," Schneider said. "It shows how limited workers see the realm of possibility."

What began in 2016 as Schneider and Harknett's informal interviews with hourly retail and service-sector workers in the San Francisco Bay area has grown into the Shift Project,[54] now based at Harvard. It is the largest source of data on work scheduling for low-wage workers, with reports from over two hundred thousand employees in the retail and fast-food sectors. The data includes schedules, economic security, and the health and wellbeing of workers and families.

As the labor movement has picked up and more stable scheduling laws or pilot programs have improved work conditions, the Shift Project and other researchers have been able to track real benefits—to workers, their families, and, in what may come as a surprise to company owners, to productivity and business success, too.

In a study of nearly one hundred hourly workers in Emeryville, California—another jurisdiction that passed a stable schedule law—researchers found that when last-minute schedule changes and surprise shifts dropped, more stable hours reduced work-family conflict and stress. Working parents reported major improvements in wellbeing for the entire family.[55] When Seattle passed its fair workweek law, research showed that material hardship like hunger and housing instability dropped, good-quality sleep increased, and workers reported feeling much happier.[56]

Unpredictable worker schedules are not the cost-saving efficiency boon that many businesses expected—in fact, they are quite the opposite. A randomized controlled trial at select Gap Inc. stores found that predictable schedules not only improved worker health, sleep, and stress levels but actually increased productivity and sales.[57] Previous studies at the Gap found that, rather than wild fluctuations, there is quite a lot of stability in consumer demand. That should, in theory, translate into stable schedules. Yet the Gap's scheduling algorithms weren't configured to assign people to regular or consistent shifts. So researchers tested an intervention that was hardly rocket science. "We told managers to take the schedule from the week before and start with that," said Susan Lambert, a professor at the University of Chicago and one of the Gap study coauthors. They trained managers to take worker preferences for the upcoming week into account. "Some managers told us it was so much easier," Lambert said. "And it got people more stable schedules."[58]

So much of what drives schedule instability, Lambert and her coauthors found, are poorly executed operations systems—shipments that come in unexpectedly, new promotions handed down from headquarters at the last minute, a surprise visit from an executive. That, and what Lambert calls "management by fright." Algorithm or no, managers are driven both to meet strict sales targets, based on Big Data's forecasts, and to keep to tight labor budgets. "So what ends up happening," Lambert explained, "is a manager will say, 'We were supposed to sell sixty sweaters by now, and we've only sold thirty! Someone has to go home!'"

David Sciaudone found himself repeatedly in that situation as the manager of a Sears automotive center in Waterbury, Connecticut. His supervisors told him to tightly align his staff with demand, he said, so when the center slowed down, he had to send people home. "It was really horrible," he said. "But if you didn't get under budget, you'd get a phone call, screaming . . . They'd say, 'You have forty-five seconds, or you're going to be on the unemployment line.'"[59]

The algorithms, rather than creating efficiency, can actually create more problems, more stressed, unhealthy, and dissatisfied workers, costly higher turnover rates, and an unknown amount of lost sales. Eighty percent of consumers say an important factor in deciding where to shop is whether they get personalized service from a sales associate.[60] Yet research from MIT's Sloan School of Management shows that large shares of shoppers can't find anyone to help them. They're put off by jumbled piles of unfolded clothes or misplaced items.[61] And many walk out the door without dropping a dime, costing, in one estimate, between 5 and 15 percent in lost sales, potentially more if people are frustrated enough to broadcast their annoyance. Good workers, researchers say, are the service industry's "most potent weapon."[62] Saravanan Kesavan, a business professor at the University of North Carolina and coauthor of the Gap study, told me that understaffing can be far more costly to a business than overstaffing. Poor customer service or disorganized merchandise could lead to a lost sale and the potential loss of a lifetime customer, and, if they're angry enough, their networks. It's called "future lost sales."

Frustrated shoppers like Kelly Donaldson are "future lost sales." She was so angry at the lines snaking around a big-box retail store with only two cashiers open that she walked away from a full cart and took to ripping the store on social media. "If I hadn't been angry AF that they wouldn't put more people on the registers," she posted, "I'd never have left that cart. I still needed a lot of that stuff and had to go elsewhere."

Unlike labor costs, future lost sales are invisible on corporate balance sheets, so businesses tend to overlook them. "Understaffing costs are potentially large but can't be measured easily. On the other hand, overstaffing may be a smaller cost, but it's highly visible," Kesavan explained. So shortsighted supervisors create perverse incentives for managers to do more and more with fewer and fewer workers. Said Kesavan, "It creates a race to the bottom."

As it turns out, the algorithms are fairly easy to reprogram with a different set of values instead of cutting labor to the bone.

Derek Jones, a vice president of Deputy, a scheduling software company headquartered in Australia, said stability, or what he calls "recipes for balanced schedules," can be easily programmed into newer systems. "We have at least twelve additional fields for employee preferences," he said. When American companies wind up with erratic schedules, he and his team have done "root cause analyses" and have found that human error, AI error, and inflexible labor-cutting mindsets are to blame.

So if predictable schedules can be easily programmed into algorithms, even for part-time labor, and that's better for employees and for business, why is it taking worker-driven legislation to force businesses to do that? It defies logic. Wharton School professor Marshall Fisher blames businesses' cognitive bias that unstable schedules are necessary, which can lead to "self-delusion"—the same delusions of corporate monoculture that believe long work hours and a physical presence are necessary for maximum productivity.[63] What's not so easy, it appears, is convincing businesses that their labor practices are the problem. "It's so strange," Axsium's Bob Clements said. "It's almost like cutting off our nose to spite our face."

Labor inspectors who enforce the stable schedules ordinances see this understaffing self-delusion all the time. "What surprised me," said one, "is how much deference there is to internal HR policies, even when they conflict with local law." Indeed, some state legislatures, including Arkansas, Georgia, Iowa, and Tennessee, have bought into the false narrative that volatile schedules are just the cost of doing business, and they have passed laws *prohibiting* fair workweek legislation.[64] So if change isn't coming from the top, it has to be demanded by the bottom.

■

The fair workweek campaign is only one effort underway in a slow renewal of the U.S. labor movement. The Fight for $15 campaign, for example, sparked by a walkout of two hundred fed-up fast-food workers in New York in 2012 and supported by New York Communities for Change and the Service Employees International Union (SEIU), has led to higher wages and higher minimum wage laws in several states for tens of millions of workers, many of them women and workers of color.[65] That and the successful Justice for Janitors[66] and other campaigns, have also brought wider attention to a once obscure argument among economists.

The conventional economic wisdom has long held that when you raise wages, employers will respond by cutting jobs, so workers will actually suffer. The argument has, not surprisingly, benefited employers and kept wages shockingly low. But, by observing what actually happens when one state chooses to raise wages when a neighboring state doesn't, a new generation of economists have proved just how flawed the conventional thinking is: raising wages lifts families and children out of poverty and financial precarity. It boosts worker productivity and loyalty, reduces turnover, and is a boon to business. One study found that employment didn't fall—because the jobs were better jobs, more people were willing to take them.[67]

Throughout the pandemic, the media was filled with stories of workers of all kinds voting to organize unions—Starbucks baristas, Amazon warehouse workers, adjunct professors, medical residents, and workers at tech companies, media outlets, and think tanks.[68] Workers were also willing to strike to protest unfair wages and working conditions, like those at one McDonald's who were provided with dog diapers instead of protective masks.[69] With the appearance of story after story of poor working conditions and the high sickness and death rates of essential workers often as a result,[70] the reality of invisible low-wage work came into sharper relief. "Essential. Not Disposable" became a rallying cry. Amid all the suffering, and the guilt of those able to work safely from home, more people began to realize their terms of employment had to change.

For decades, as media outlets dropped labor reporters, workers and worker movements received little coverage. So instead of monitoring the decades-long slide into unfair working conditions and the everyday struggle of people laboring harder and harder for less, the media tended to focus only on the latest strike, which made workers look greedy and disruptive.[71] Some of the unions' bad press[72] was self-inflicted through corruption scandals, and some was influenced by pro-business coverage that painted union members as lazy and a drag on innovation and productivity.[73] I'm not proud to admit that, as a young reporter in an already shrinking newspaper industry, full of self-doubt and raised in a pro-business, conservative family, I was too afraid to join my union—afraid that I couldn't afford the dues and I'd be seen as a troublemaker instead of the compliant, hardworking, people-pleasing woman I'd been raised to be, just grateful for the job. It was years before I was able to overcome the fear that I'd be jeopardizing my livelihood and my family's economic security, and finally join the Washington–Baltimore News Guild, part of the Communications Workers of America union.

But in 2022, after the pandemic had made it impossible to ignore abysmal working conditions and the powerlessness of workers, public approval of union membership soared to 71 percent, the highest it's been since 1965.[74] Majorities agreed that unions have a positive impact on the United States and that the decline in membership has been bad for everyone.[75] Emboldened, unionized workers negotiated a five-year contract in 2023 with UPS that includes pay raises up to 55 percent for certain employees and bars managers from forcing drivers to work on scheduled days off.[76] Hollywood writers and actors went on strike demanding a fair share of streaming profits and protection from the use of artificial intelligence.[77] United Auto Workers launched strikes at selected plants run by the three big automakers,[78] demanding a four-day workweek and the restoration of the wage cuts and concessions made during the Great Recession, which, they argued, the companies could readily afford after years of record profits.[79]

With the reality of workers' lives coming into clearer focus, politicians and business leaders could no longer tout the myth that training and educating workers would lead them to get better jobs. The country—all countries—had to find a way to make all jobs good and decent now, not in some hazy future of work.[80] Given outsize CEO salaries,[81] low corporate taxes,[82] and record profits,[83] more people realized that corporations could afford to make their lousy jobs good jobs. They also knew that given past history, businesses were unlikely to do so on their own. It would require business leaders, along with worker power and government muscle, bringing together the three traditional players in a social contract to make paid work good work.

The increased media attention, the surge of union activity, and a stubborn labor shortage led to speculation that worker power and the labor movement were finally "having a moment."[84] While that is true, it's also important to keep the big picture in mind and realize just how much ground workers have to make up. In the 1950s, one in three workers claimed union membership. Through the years, unions have ensured higher wages, benefits, and standards of living and have reduced income, gender, and racial inequality for their workers.[85] Their presence has raised standards for nonunion workers, too.[86] Researchers have also found that unionized workers in states with higher union membership have more stable schedules than nonunion workers.[87]

But in 2022, just 10 percent of all workers belonged to a union. In the private workforce, the share is 6 percent. And even after the reports of a pandemic "union boom," the share of unionized workers actually *dropped* in 2022 because more nonunion jobs were created.[88] In 2023, the trend accelerated, bringing union membership to record lows.[89]

"The power relationship between workers and employers, and now including professional workers and their employers, is more skewed than it's ever been. The power of corporate America is ascendant," Dave Regan, president of one of the largest hospital workers unions, told me. "It's nice when someone wins a union election at Amazon or Starbucks. But the truth is, these are blips." In 2022, unions won a record increase in elections, but that yielded just 75,000 new union members[90]—in a labor force of about 160 million,[91] Regan said. In 2023, 139,000 more workers joined unions, a fraction of the 2.7 million new jobs created.[92] Half of those new members, he said, will never get a first contract. "The difference between where we are and where we need to go is just enormous."

Still, if the numbers are modest, the conversation has been on the upswing. During the pandemic, a wave of "good jobs" initiatives and discussions began sweeping the country, from the Department of Labor[93] using the power of federal contracts to guarantee good jobs, to a group of more than one hundred business, labor, and policy leaders who hammered out the definition of a good job as part of the Good Jobs Champions Group. Central to a good job, they wrote, is not only equity, respect, a voice, economic mobility, and stability, but a fair and reliable schedule.[94]

The labor movement's slow and arduous patchwork progress—city by city, state by state, employer by employer, worksite by worksite—that keeps workers down and hard-won gains small is a feature, not a bug, in the U.S. labor law system. It's happening entirely by design.

The United States was once a world leader in the creation of good work and good conditions. The National Labor Relations Act of 1935 guaranteed workers the right to organize and bargain with employers for better conditions. The Social Security Act of 1935 guaranteed that older or disabled workers would not be left starving and penniless. The Fair Labor Standards Act of 1938 abolished child labor and established a minimum wage, overtime protections for hourly workers, and a forty-hour workweek. None of the laws were perfect: to appease Southern lawmakers intent on keeping racist Jim Crow laws in place, these labor laws excluded domestic and farm laborers, many of whom were Black and brown workers who have been trapped in low-wage positions ever since. (Both groups were included in Social Security benefits in the 1950s. In 2013, domestic workers, save for live-in caregivers, were finally covered by fair wage and overtime laws.)[95]

Still, the 1930s-era laws were pioneering for their time. They were due to the free market failures of the Great Depression as well as the vision and fierce determination of then labor secretary

Frances Perkins. A New Yorker, Perkins had toured factories packed with child workers and even witnessed young people jumping to their deaths to escape the horrific 1911 Triangle Shirtwaist Factory fire that left 146 dead and more injured—all because the owner, fearing worker theft, kept the factory doors locked from the outside.[96]

That worker-centered era is long past now. Unlike a number of peer competitive economies, U.S. labor law makes it tough for workers to organize. More than twenty states have enacted "right-to-work" laws that weaken unions. According to these laws, workers don't have to join a union or pay the dues that keep unions alive, even though all workers benefit from collective agreements. Research shows that states with right-to-work laws tend to have lower workplace safety and political participation and greater inequality.[97] Federal labor law also requires workers to organize worksite by worksite rather than allowing them to organize and bargain by sector, as an innovative law in New Zealand does[98] and a European directive encourages.[99] Workers must also convince more than 50 percent of their coworkers to join. If that weren't time-consuming and costly enough, organizing must be done *outside* of work hours, while employers are given license to thwart union efforts, calling workers to anti-union meetings or delaying elections. They suffer little consequence for their sabotage or retaliation against those who try to organize.[100] Unlike labor laws in Germany, U.S. companies are not required to put workers on decision-making boards and councils, a practice that research indicates has led to stronger protections for workers and higher company profits.[101]

"Workers basically have to be like a little Navy SEAL team in order to successfully unionize under the radar of an employer," economist Suresh Naidu told NPR's *Planet Money.* Employers have forced an estimated sixty million workers in recent decades to sign mandatory arbitration agreements waiving their right to collective or class-action litigation.[102] Employers have also begun to classify more low-wage workers as "managers" rather than hourly employees, so they won't qualify for overtime pay. They then cut staff levels to the bone and force these managers to cover for absences, saving on overtime. Arbitration clauses make it difficult for workers to fight back.[103] It should come as no surprise, then, that the United States is ranked low when it comes to workers' rights and laws, on par with Saudi Arabia, Romania, Uganda, and Venezuela, with companies and governments "engaged in serious efforts to crush the collective voice of workers."[104]

With the law so firmly arrayed against workers, those intent on finding each other, banding together, and leveraging their numbers to demand better conditions are forced to be creative. Increasingly, that's what they've become. Family home child-care providers in California found that after paying teachers' salaries and covering the cost of supplies, equipment, curriculum, training, cleaning, and other expenses, many were earning barely $5 an hour. The majority made so little, they qualified for public benefits and few received health care through the job.[105] But because each of these family child-care centers is its own private, independent business, usually run out of the owner's home, providers are often isolated and it's difficult to band together. Many such small family child-care businesses look after children whose parents earn such low wages that they qualify for public child-care subsidies: there's no possibility of making up their costs by charging parents higher tuition.

The federal government sends about $8 billion a year to states for subsidies to help low-income families afford child care. That's among the lowest levels of support for child care of any peer competitive economy. It means that just 16 percent of children eligible for a subsidy actually receive one.[106] It also means that the rates state governments set to reimburse providers who accept subsidies are laughably low and come nowhere close to covering what it actually costs to provide care.[107] One Texas study found that the true cost of infant care is twice that of the state's average subsidy reimbursement.[108] And since most parents are already paying more than they can afford,[109] teachers and providers are forced to essentially subsidize the U.S. child-care infrastructure by accepting poverty wages.

Once they began coming together, it occurred to family child-care home providers that maybe they *could* band together and demand better subsidy reimbursement rates and other benefits from the state. After more than a decade of diligent outreach and organizing, in 2019, California passed legislation giving family child-care home providers who receive public care subsidies the right to collectively bargain. The providers, the majority of them women of color, voted to form the Childcare Providers United union in 2020 and by 2024 were about forty thousand strong.[110] As a host of small businesses, there was no "employer of record" to negotiate with. In 2021, the state of California agreed to be that employer of record and bargain with the union, joining about a half dozen other states where family child-care home providers have secured collective bargaining agreements.[111] In July 2020, the new California union signed its first contract with the state, which increased reimbursement rates by at least 15 percent, set aside $40 million for professional development, and created a "rate reform workgroup" to recommend future changes.[112]

In what organizers hope will be another move to shift the balance of power away from employers, fast-food workers in California won the right to bargain as a sector. After years of strikes and hundreds of safety and wage violations, the state passed legislation in 2022 to allow fast-food workers to bargain collectively for wages—the U.S. labor movement's first foray into sectoral organizing. Now, a first-of-its-kind ten-person statewide Fast Food Council, composed of workers, corporate representatives, franchisees, and state officials, will have the power to set minimum standards for wages, working hours, health, safety, and training that will affect not just one worksite but the entire fast-food industry in the state.[113] Though business groups mobilized quickly to fight the law, its survival could mean better pay and conditions for workers of color and women, who make up 80 and about 66 percent of the state's fast-food workforce, respectively.[114]

Some gig workers, too, are getting creative. Gig workers are classified as independent contractors, not employees, despite efforts by workers in California to change that.[115] Labor law prohibits them from organizing and bargaining for better contracts and conditions. When rideshare drivers began hanging out together waiting for rides at airports, they realized they were all struggling with the same unfair issues. They formed organizations such as Gig Workers Rising to increase awareness and advocate for themselves.[116]

Because it can be so difficult to form a union, a wealth of local and national worker and community organizations have sprung up to play an instrumental role in raising awareness, forging partnerships with academics for better research, and lobbying policymakers. These include not just Ugalde's LAANE in Los Angeles and Patrick's United for Respect but worker centers such as the Restaurant Opportunities Centers United (ROC) and the National Domestic Workers Alliance.[117] The nonprofit Jobs With Justice has spent three decades building a broad coalition of workers, community organizations, faith groups, and student activists in several states to fight for a decent standard of living.[118] And as companies ratchet up tactics such as surveillance of employee communication to crush organizing,[119] more activists are becoming "salts"—getting jobs at the companies to organize workers from the inside.[120]

Shareholder activism is another creative strategy being employed to achieve better conditions for workers. Arjuna Capital, an impact investment firm, for example, has forced many companies to track their racial and gender pay equity and demographics and share the information more transparently.[121] There are also efforts to harness the enormous power of consumer spending—which accounts for two-thirds of U.S. GDP—to push companies to create fair work conditions.[122] Research is finding that consumers prefer to spend their dollars on items that have been made under certified good working conditions. And one hospital workers union in California is taking an entirely novel approach to creating better jobs. The AlliedUP Cooperative, a partnership with SEIU–United Healthcare Workers West, one of the largest unions of hospital workers in the western United States, operates much like a for-profit healthcare staffing agency. The goal is to create good-paying union jobs, whether someone works in a union-organized workplace or not. It works like this: The union provides training for in-demand health positions, such as medical assistant. Upon graduation, the newly qualified assistant joins the cooperative. The co-op executes contracts with nonunion employers to place its members and ensure they're given union-scale wages and benefits. Instead of a private agency charging employers fees for recruitment and placement, that money goes directly to the co-op workers' higher wages. "The idea is that you create a vehicle where not only are the individuals employed union members but they also have an equity position in the co-op itself," explained union president Dave Regan. "It's a way for them to build wealth if we succeed."

The goal, if the co-op catches on, is to go national and operate at a scale of potentially hundreds of thousands of hospital workers. "We're using the levers of capitalism, but we're also trying to evade a real problem: it's just too hard these days to organize enough people to be able to move the needle on the standard of living. The ugly truth is, unions are not raising the standard of living for union members in America anymore," Regan said. "So step one is, admit you have a problem. The majority of American workers are experiencing a real decline in their standard of living. And we need efforts and organizations and institutions that are operating on a scale that can make a meaningful difference."

■

The story of home care worker Brittany Williams offers one of the best and most hopeful accounts of transforming paid work at scale, showing how it benefits everyone and can renew our broken social contract. Williams is a third-generation home care worker. Her mother, Danielle Williams, also cares for elderly and disabled clients. Mother and daughter both love the work they do, although both acknowledge that the "job can be a burnout." It's important, dignified work. "I do it from my heart," Danielle told me. Though both are home care workers, the quality of their jobs—and the lives those jobs enable—are vastly different. Brittany makes nearly twice what her mother does. Brittany has health insurance, dental care, retirement savings, paid vacation, mileage reimbursement, and mental health support. She gets free training and a pair of non-skid shoes every year. Danielle has none of that. Brittany has access to the state's public paid family and medical leave, public paid sick days, and the first-in-the-nation public long-term care program. Danielle doesn't. It is all because Brittany lives in Washington State and belongs to a union. Danielle lives in Arkansas, a right-to-work state, where there is no home care union.

Brittany Williams said that while doctors and nurses may save lives, she, her mother, and other home care workers like them "are the ones maintaining life." She said, "We need to be recognized for the professionals we are."

But in most states, these workers are not. A little context: because the largely female home care workforce was excluded from protections and labor laws during the New Deal in the 1930s, it is one of the most poorly paid of all professions. Home care workers earn about $14.15 an hour, few have benefits, and the hours are often erratic or irregular.[123] As the population ages and lives longer with more chronic illnesses requiring more intensive care, home care work is predicted to be the fastest-growing job in the future of work and the largest occupation in the economy by 2031.[124] Home care workers enable millions to receive the care they need so they can stay in their own homes and out of more expensive nursing homes. Their work also allows family members to continue working to keep their families stable. Without the help of home care workers, the nearly 10 million people caring for their aging parents, often women, are forced to cut back or quit work, which amounts to a staggering $3 trillion in lost wages, pensions, and retirement benefits over their lifetimes, research has found.[125]

Rather than being distracted by frankly ridiculous conversations about developing robot caregivers,[126] we should be learning from Brittany Williams and her union about how to make these jobs good jobs.

In Washington State, where Brittany Williams lives, leaders became alarmed in the 1990s by the increasing aging population and the ballooning costs associated with caring for those on low incomes who qualified for Medicaid in expensive skilled nursing facilities and nursing homes. At the same time, more of the disabled and aging populations wanted to live independently, stay in their own homes "aging in place," and receive care that would enable them to do so. So the state needed to recruit, hire, and retain a *lot* more home care workers. They realized that the only way to do that was to make the jobs better. At that point, most home care workers were independent, working in isolation, with no employer of record to bargain for improved conditions. In the early 2000s, the SEIU Local 775 union began to organize home care workers and won the right to collectively bargain for the entire sector. Washington State created a Home Care Quality Authority that became the employer of record, and in 2003 the workers negotiated their first contract and have successfully renegotiated several times since.

In 2024, more than forty-five thousand home care workers in Washington State earn among the best wages and have the best benefits of their sector in the country. In 2022, they made more than $18 an hour, up from $7.68 before the involvement of the union.[127] By 2025, the starting wage will be $21 an hour, the result of successful negotiations in 2023.[128] The 2023 contract includes health care for care workers' children. Every home care worker also receives seventy-five hours of free training and becomes a certified home care aide—the highest training and certification requirement of any state. Workers can continue with other free trainings to increase their skills and their wages. During the pandemic, the union also won $3 an hour hazard pay, personal protective equipment, and the ability to do paperwork and other distance tasks digitally.

Better jobs, the union argues, leads to a more stable workforce—turnover in the home care profession was 77 *percent* in 2022.[129] A more stable, well-trained workforce improves the quality of care. Over time, state leaders have found that, even when care wages increase, the state is saving money when more people are cared for at home. "It's a fraction of the cost of nursing homes," said Peter Nazzal, director of long-term care at Catholic Community Services of Western Washington. "The taxpayers like it." When the pandemic arrived, home care workers were ready, since they receive infection control training as part of their certification. "We simply sent a memo to all of our staff saying, 'Remember what you're doing? Keep on doing it.' Because it was almost exactly word for word what the CDC was saying we should do."[130]

"I really do like my job," Williams told me. With the union, "they give us that sense of stability." She added, "We are truly blessed here. It's heartbreaking to hear people doing the same work in other states are not being respected on the same level."

Her mother, Danielle Williams, moved from Washington State to Arkansas to look after her aging grandmother. She makes about half Brittany's salary, although Danielle has more certifications and training. In 2023, she earned about $12 an hour, and that's only because voters in the state passed a ballot measure raising the minimum wage from $9 to $11 an hour in 2021. When I asked Danielle about benefits, she just laughed. She earns so little that she qualifies for Medicaid for health insurance, though she was dropped from the rolls in 2023, along with an estimated eight to twenty-four million others, when pandemic provisions expired.[131] After paying for rent, her phone, and her monthly car loan—there's no bus service to get to and from clients—Danielle has hardly any money left. She put off necessary dental work, she said, because, without insurance, it's not affordable. She works seven days a week. In her little spare time, she likes to volunteer to care for hospice patients. Moving to live and work in Arkansas was like "diving into the deep end of a swimming pool when you can't swim," she said. "You try to save yourself, but at the same time, you're hurting yourself."

Danielle Williams can't imagine ever being able to retire. "I wish there was a union here. I was involved in the union in Washington and I miss that. You have your sister and brother caregivers and if something wasn't going right, you could always depend on them," she told me. "But this isn't a union state. You have to fend for yourself. You work all these hours, but you don't have nothing to show for it. It's almost like working for free, so I might as well be doing it just from my heart. But somebody's got to take care of the baby boomers."[132]

Had Danielle stayed in Washington, she figures she'd be making close to $30 an hour. "This just gives me even more drive to continue to fight for caregivers' rights," her daughter, Brittany, interjected. "I believe that you truly can't cry victory until everyone's made it."

CHAPTER 5

UNLIKELY ALLIES AND THE BUSINESS CASE FOR RESPONSIBLE CAPITALISM

> The culture of corporate America needs to change . . . When we finally start focusing on stakeholder value as well as shareholder value, our companies will be more successful, our communities will be more equal, our societies will be more just and our planet will be healthier.
>
> —*Marc Benioff, CEO of Salesforce,*
> *"We Need a New Capitalism"*[1]

The afternoon sun sparkles over the deep blue of Maine's Casco Bay and filters into the modern, airy glass-and-wood waterfront offices where Warren Valdmanis, a private equity investor, is proving himself a surprising ally of low-wage workers and their drive to create good, life-sustaining jobs.

Sitting in the conference room, his yellow Lab, Cricket, snoozing happily at his feet, Valdmanis is dressed for casual Friday. Far from the button-down business look of his popular TED Talk, "What Makes a 'Good' Job—and the Case for Investing in People,"[2] he seems like he's just stepped out of the Maine-headquartered L.L.Bean catalog. He runs his hand through his graying hair and explains how investing in people is not just good for humans. It also benefits business, society, and democracy. This is at the heart of a new kind of responsible capitalism, which, he says, "does well by doing good."

Valdmanis is a partner at Two Sigma Impact, a small social impact investing firm whose mission, he said, is to use data and science to invest in companies committed to creating good jobs and furthering the wellbeing of the workforce—and making money while doing so. It's an approach that challenges the accepted gospel in boardrooms and business schools, which considers workers an expense to be cut and that the purpose of a corporation is to make short-term profits for a small group of shareholders. Two Sigma Impact turns this dogma completely on its head. With the data to back him up, workers, Valdmanis insists, are an asset to be cultivated. And not just the highly educated "talent" that the business press and management consultants concern themselves with, but all workers. Especially low-wage retail employees like Adrian Ugalde, Onie Patrick, Ashley Worthen, and Sam Hughes, and caregivers like Brittany and Danielle Williams. Investing for the long term with a broader group of stakeholders in mind has lasting benefits.

Valdmanis argues that the standard business model when it comes to labor—cutting the workforce, overworking staff, outsourcing or contracting out, paying as poorly as one can get away with, and offering no benefits—has immiserated the lives of millions of workers and their families, frayed communities, fostered mistrust and discontent, *and* been bad for business. (By some estimates, corporations now spend about a third of their labor budgets on nonemployee outsourced and contract workers.[3])

Lousy jobs, he argues, lead to high turnover and disaffected workers who don't care about doing a good job for companies that are so clearly exploiting them. That can result in subpar products and services and untapped potential. For business leaders, he said, so much comes down to what you believe. "When you talk about workers, a lot of times what you see is what you get. The belief that workers are lazy and you should try to pay them as little as possible and you see them as automatons? That's often what you're going to get back. Because when you're treated that way, it's hard to be motivated," Valdmanis argues. "And when you tell workers your chief goal is to drive value for a bunch of shareholders" they've never met, "that's not a very motivating idea, either."

So what *does* motivate workers? Why treat them well? How does that benefit business? And what *is* a "good" job?

Valdmanis realized that before Two Sigma Impact could begin investing in companies committed to good jobs, they had to define what that is. He was struck by data showing that "half of Americans don't feel a sense of connection to their company's mission or get a sense of meaning or significance from their work." Research also confirmed that good pay alone isn't enough—it can often lead to solely transactional relationships[4]—and a toxic work culture is ten times more important than pay in predicting worker attrition.[5] So Valdmanis and his team came up with four key drivers that make for a good job. More, they developed metrics to measure a company's progress on each one. He ticks through the list:

- Fair treatment—good pay and benefits, fair scheduling, and a good corporate culture.
- A promising future—a path forward with the chance to grow, progress, develop new skills, and an opportunity to make more money over time as you do so.
- Psychological safety—the ability to share your ideas and feel heard, especially when it comes to how to make your job and your company better.
- A sense of mission and purpose—the view that what you're doing actually has some value.[6]

As other change agents seeking to remake work have found, leadership is key. The companies Two Sigma invests in are ones whose leaders are committed to this vision of good jobs and to creating a worker-supportive culture of trust. These companies take pains to define their mission and purpose, make sure everyone's on board, and provide the training to help middle managers set up systems to show that they value workers. "When those things exist, people not only describe themselves as having a good job, they also perform better on the job. The company is more innovative, grows faster, and is more profitable," Valdmanis says. "When we create those conditions inside companies, we see great results. When we fail to, we often find ourselves paying the price." Treating workers well "drives alignment internally and leads to higher retention and productivity," Valdmanis argues. "These are all things companies should want."

In theory, yes. I wondered how fellow capitalists, still married to the idea that labor is a cost to be squeezed to serve the goal of shareholder profits, were taking to his approach.

I first heard Valdmanis speak at a business conference on the future of work in the middle of the pandemic. Most of the speakers spouted the usual platitudes about the wonders of technology along with the same old lip service to wellbeing for burned-out high-skill workers. But the thinking was very much of the narrow, lunchtime yoga variety. I was tuning out when Valdmanis began to speak. The reason for the Great Resignation during the pandemic, he said, "is because most jobs suck. That's got to change, not only for the well-being of workers, but the wellbeing of businesses."[7]

A private equity investor concerned about the wellbeing of workers? Isn't this the industry that controls $6 trillion in assets with the rapacious reputation for gobbling up firms, "finding efficiencies" by firing workers, slashing pay, then selling off the remains and making gobs of fast money in the process?[8] Curious, I sat up and began to take notes.

Valdmanis listed many of the arguments for transforming work that I'd heard in my reporting:[9] how we've unleashed a brutal system, generating such obscene profits for the few and grotesque inequality that it has destabilized communities and faith in democracy and soured hope for the future. "We've been heading for a reckoning in the labor market for some time," he warned.[10]

I was blown away. Here was someone inside the church of corporate monoculture who embraced the dynamism of capitalism but said we were doing it all wrong. The purpose of a corporation is not to enrich a handful of shareholders—the prevailing "fiduciary absolutism" since the 1970s. Business, he argued, had a *responsibility* for taking the longer, bigger view and creating jobs that lead to better lives. In his book, *Accountable: The Rise of Citizen Capitalism,* this unabashed capitalist argues that if businesses can get this new "responsible capitalism" right, everyone will profit. "Our society has suffered the reign of fiduciary absolutism for nearly 50 years," Valdmanis and his coauthor Michael O'Leary write. "When will we recognize that our economy is capable of so much more?"[11]

I sought out Valdmanis and began a series of conversations with him that brought me to his Portland, Maine, office. I wanted to understand his journey from success in private equity to responsible capitalism. If he could change, could others?

For Valdmanis, the seeds of his evolution were sown early. The son of Eastern European immigrants, he started working at a young age, and in the very kinds of jobs he wants to make better: he's worked in restaurants as a busboy and waiter, in bakeries, on farms, and in the blueberry fields of Maine. "That helped me to see different perspectives," he says. He worked in a fancy hotel restaurant to supplement his scholarship to Dartmouth and remembers waiting on students' families who could afford to stay where his family couldn't. That allowed him to see them not only as fellow students and strivers but "through the eyes of the people who served them. That shaped me."

He studied economics at Dartmouth and was taught the dogma of Adam Smith and the market's "invisible hand," according to which people acting in their own economic self-interest do good for themselves and for the world. Nineteenth-century philosopher John Stuart Mill cemented Smith's view, describing humans narrowly as *homo economicus*—rational actors who make rational choices based on furthering their own self-interest.[12]

Valdmanis, like most economics students at the time, accepted these theories as received truth. "I didn't really inquire much beyond that," Valdmanis says. He had a lot of college debt, and the concept of an invisible hand securing a high-paying consulting job that would enrich his life and in some vague way somehow do good for the world seemed like a fine idea, and a convenient one.

Later, at Harvard Business School and working in consulting and private equity, Valdmanis came face-to-face with the consequences of the freewheeling free market approach let loose in the 1970s by the influential libertarian economist Milton Friedman. Friedman took Smith's "invisible hand" approach and amplified it: Rather than participating in a social contract in which business, government, and labor cooperated to ensure shared prosperity—the doctrine that had guided post–World War II economics and created a strong middle class, Friedman maintained that the first responsibility of business was to maximize profits and increase returns to a handful of shareholders. While he also advocated shrinking government oversight of the market—though not eliminating it, as many modern acolytes assume—corporations responded by spending billions on campaigns and lobbyists to ensure that the rules in place favored unfettered, short-term profit making.[13] In keeping with Friedman's view, business students and future leaders were taught to revere the management approach of executives such as GE's Jack Welch and the "GE Way." This involved a system of ranking employees and firing the bottom 10 percent every year—a brutal "tournament style" practice that has driven insecurity, stress, and long hours in high-wage knowledge jobs.[14] Rather than focusing on the core business, Welch also popularized dealmaking and sexy mergers and acquisitions that shredded employees' lives but made vast profits for shareholders and those at the top.[15] Political philosopher Michael J. Sandel writes in his book *What Money Can't Buy* that in this era of uncritical "market triumphalism," the United States has gone from *having* a market economy to *being* a market society. Everything now has a price. Money is what matters. Relationships have become transactional. And when everything becomes a commodity to be bought and sold—including the price of labor and workers' lives—human values like fairness, meaning, and cooperation get crowded out. "Putting a price on the good things in life can corrupt them."[16]

Valdmanis began to see the dark side of American cowboy capitalism. "I felt like something isn't going according to plan," he explained. "That there's room for the people who've been fortunate—where the systems worked for them—to find ways to make the system more responsive to the broader population." And to solving instead of exacerbating the "big issues" like inequality, climate change, and the political instability and cynicism that come from working harder and harder and falling farther and farther behind and feeling the system is rigged.

He was drawn to social impact investing, first with former Massachusetts governor Deval Patrick, and then with Two Sigma Impact, a twenty-six-person firm with offices in New York and Portland, and investments in a handful of companies around the country committed to creating and maintaining good jobs and investing in workers. He began writing and speaking out about capitalism and work. "*Homo economicus* doesn't exist any more than the invisible hand," he wrote in his book, calling them "simplifying" and "dehumanizing constructs."[17] Instead, he urges corporations to commit to the longer term and a deeper purpose than profit. He argues that markets should be driven not by fear and greed but by hope, purpose, and a shared belief in a common project—the common good.[18] A crucial part of that vision is the kind of dignified paid work that can support and sustain human life and offers time and support for the unpaid work of care and home.

"When it comes to what's happened to the workforce over the past, frankly, forty or fifty years, we have seen a long-term trend in America toward trying to slow down the workforce: Companies cutting jobs. Companies cutting benefits. Companies outsourcing jobs. And I think that this all came from a view in the seventies that American companies were in some way fat, that they needed to trim down. I fear that we've done our job too well," Valdmanis says of the prevailing "lean efficiency" business doctrine.[19] "Now, the biggest problem is not that companies have too many workers. The biggest problem that almost every company that we talk to has is they don't have enough motivated, skilled workers to grow."

Valdmanis points out there's nothing inherently wrong with seeking efficiencies, or even "creative destruction"—another business fad of doing whatever it takes to make companies profitable. But both approaches can encourage shortsightedness, short-termism, and shortcuts. "It's always profitable to cut workers today. You will almost always have higher earnings tomorrow," Valdmanis says. "But that doesn't mean you have a better or more valuable company." This approach is destructive, he argues, and obscures real opportunities.

In 2021, when Two Sigma acquired Circle of Care, a home- and clinic-based pediatric therapy provider offering physical, occupational, and speech therapy largely to families living on low incomes, Two Sigma wanted the company to invest in human capital as a way to attract workers and close a severe labor shortage in one of the country's largest growth industries.[20] Using their jobs assessment tool, Two Sigma made leadership changes and promoted a new CEO willing to commit to that vision. Since seeking worker input is a key metric to good jobs, they discovered that therapists wanted to learn new skills and take on more complicated cases that could lead to higher pay. So Circle of Care began to offer training.[21] "The challenging thing about that industry is that there are many more children who need this service than there are therapists out there to provide it," he said. "Our strategy with that company is: How do we become the employer of choice? And how do we become better at going out and finding the right people for our company, developing those people, and retaining those people? And that's the way you build a great business. So yes, the natural by-product of that is good jobs and happier workers, but it's also just good business."[22]

Valdmanis faces an uphill battle. Although responsible capitalism has gained more mainstream support in recent years, many in the business community remain skeptical of investing with environmental, social, and governance goals (ESG) in mind.[23] Some Republican lawmakers in Congress and in state capitals have led efforts to bar and even criminalize ESG investing with public funds,[24] opening a new front in the culture wars by condemning it as left-wing "woke" capitalism.[25] Valdmanis does sometimes get frustrated, less by the business community's resistance than by its inertia. "There's a belief that somehow it's too good to be true, that you can really make as much money or more money by investing in things that also do good. They think there's got to be some catch somewhere," Valdmanis says. "There are a lot of things in business that are done certain ways, and it's just hard to change them."

For one thing, Two Sigma's investment strategy is at total odds with what Wall Street typically rewards. Wall Street loves good quarterly earnings reports and layoffs when times are tough. It measures success in profits, and its time horizon is myopically limited to weeks or months. When firms take a longer view, thinking in years or even decades, and *try* to invest in workers by raising wages or providing training, Wall Street pummels them. Many firms see their stock values drop sharply after announcing wage increases.[26]

That's what happened to Walmart, the nation's largest private employer. After a decade of pressure from groups like Our Walmart, which later changed its name to United for Respect, Walmart executives agreed to raise wages for their poorly paid retail workers. They had seen how costly and inefficient their high turnover rates were. So, in 2015, Walmart executives began changing operations systems, saving money through better inventory management, and investing what would amount to $6 billion in higher wages, benefits, more full-time positions, more stable schedules and training, and pathways for advancement. Wall Street quickly signaled its displeasure. Walmart's stock price tumbled, shaving millions off the company's value.[27]

Valdmanis describes this as Wall Street "savagely punishing" firms trying to do right by workers based on the false "zero sum" belief that investing in workers means "taking money from investors."[28] Thus the way corporate America currently works, the odds are stacked against his mission. For that reason, Valdmanis felt his sole option to practice responsible capitalism would be through private equity, which isn't beholden to Wall Street's addiction to the short term. Rather than needing to prove that his investments will pay off in the next quarter, as do most publicly held companies with shareholder primacy in mind, Valdmanis can take a longer view, with investments that might take many years to pay off. "Long-term owners now are beginning to see the light that, not just for society but for our companies, investing in people is part of the way to get to a better future."

The only way to convince more business leaders, he maintains, is to *prove* it works. "The social stuff is obvious: when people have good jobs, they have much better lives and society functions better," he says. "But the commercial story needs to be told—that there's so much that would begin to get unlocked if people realized that some of these social considerations are also commercial considerations." And that's just going to take time.

Valdmanis isn't a lone voice in the business world calling for good jobs and a new responsible capitalism, however. Social impact investing, even as it's under attack, is expected to soar from $18 trillion in 2022 to $33 trillion in assets by 2026.[29] Nearly two hundred CEOs in the Business Roundtable, a lobbying group of the CEOs of the top companies in the United States, have, at least in public statements, repudiated Milton Friedmanomics and embraced the idea that the purpose of a corporation is to promote "an economy that serves all Americans."[30] Friedman's intellectual legacy, economist Jeffrey Sachs now argues, "has proven to be a disastrous misdirection for the world's economies."[31]

Other business voices are also making the case for good jobs. Wharton business professor Peter Cappelli has argued for shifts in the financial accounting system—to value humans as assets, not liabilities. This would allow companies that share data on their investments in helping workers do their jobs better—from providing decent pay and benefits to offering training and professional development—to look more valuable to investors.[32] Harvard Business

School professor Joseph B. Fuller claims that companies will reduce their costs and increase productivity with better policies, such as paid leave and flexible schedule control that help workers with care responsibilities, which, he found, includes nearly three-fourths of the workforce.[33] Others are noting research that shows that the U.S. tax code is accelerating the trend to automation and reinforcing the notion that human labor is a liability: investments in human capital, in people, are taxed at between 25 and 33 percent. Investments in capital, such as equipment, machinery, and software, are taxed at 0 to 5 percent.

Other experts and researchers, like Zeynep Ton, an operations management specialist and professor at MIT's Sloan School of Management, are helping companies and investors like Valdmanis figure out how to transform organizations and create good jobs. Ton runs the Good Jobs Institute and is the author of the books *The Case for Good Jobs* and *The Good Jobs Strategy*. She and her team analyzed a restaurant for Valdmanis. Most of the workers had erratic, part-time schedules and were poorly paid with few to no benefits. Internal promotion rates were low. Customer service had fallen off and food costs were soaring. Ton estimated that if the company began to treat workers better and could retain them, the restaurant's productivity rates would go up, bringing the investment it needed to grow and address its shoddy customer service. In turn, that would draw more customers and boost income. Ton calculated that providing good jobs would amount to a $20 million opportunity for the company, which had a roughly $13 million cash flow. It was missing out on its potential with crummy jobs and business as usual.[34]

Ton and her colleagues at the Good Jobs Institute have a proven track record of helping a host of companies to improve the crummiest of crummy jobs for frontline workers—the typically poorly paid service workers at places like retail stores, call centers, restaurants, and care facilities. Ton and her team work with company leaders to reduce turnover and improve performance and guide them to "make new choices that can set up their employees to succeed," Ton said. Along the way, she and her colleagues have compiled convincing business cases showing why it's better for companies, not just workers, when jobs are good. Ton said it takes a systems approach—providing livable wages, benefits, and schedules, staffing adequately, getting worker input, streamlining operations throughout the organization, and offering career paths, new skills, and varied experiences through cross-training.

Like Valdmanis, Ton thinks that often what leaders *believe* gets in the way. "Theory X managers believe that workers are lazy. They only work for money and don't want to have responsibility. Theory Y managers are those who believe people go to work wanting to do a good job,"[35] Ton told me. "Whatever your assumption about workers is, you're right. You end up designing a whole system that proves you right." If workers don't make enough to survive, if they have unstable schedules, which harms their physical and mental health and cognitive ability, she said, then of course they can't do a good job. Ton sees that a lot of executives look at that and say, "These workers aren't capable. They're not motivated." So then the conversation turns to "upskilling" workers so *then* they can get better jobs, which is also problematic.

There are fifty-three million people in low-wage jobs, some of which are expected to be in the fastest-growing sectors in the coming years. There aren't enough positions for upskilled workers. "Where would the fifty-three million people go?" Ton asked. Some of these jobs are critical and help make the economy run, such as those in child care and home care. There is no upskilling solution. Someone will always have to do this work. "There's no reason for these to be bad jobs," Ton maintained. Costco, for instance, pays workers well, provides benefits and stable schedules, promotes from within, offers customers some of the lowest prices, and turns a healthy profit. Seventy cents of every dollar spent to run the company, Costco cofounder Jim Sinegal once said, goes to people.[36]

"I haven't met an executive who would rather offer a worse job than a better job. I haven't met a frontline employee who would rather not do a good job. Most people have the right intentions," Ton said. "But the way we've taught business leaders for decades is that it's appropriate to cut labor costs, and that the best way to manage is to maximize profits for the short term. People get trapped in the system and they don't know how to get out of it."

Still, Ton is hopeful. "When people see good jobs working, I'm hoping it will give courage to more leaders."

▬

Some companies are figuring out themselves how to create good jobs for frontline and service workers. As restaurant after restaurant went out of business in the pandemic, Zazie, a French bistro in San Francisco's Cole Valley neighborhood, survived and thrived due to its philosophy that doing right by workers is good business. Zazie owners had paid living wages and offered stable schedules before the pandemic, along with a host of benefits, such as giving a 60 percent discount to their employees to encourage them to come to the bistro with their families. The restaurant industry is notorious for its low wages. In 2024, only seven states, including California, required employers to pay the full state minimum wage before tips, ranging from $4 an hour for small employers in Montana to $16.28 an hour in Washington. Fifteen states and several U.S. territories require employers to pay only the federal tipped minimum wage of $2.13 an hour. The rest are somewhere in between. Servers are expected to make up the difference in tips to get to the federal minimum wage—which has been stuck at an abysmal $7.25 an hour since 2009.

When San Francisco voters approved a ballot measure to raise the minimum wage in 2015, Zazie owners worried that the increase along with tips would benefit only servers, not the cooks and back-of-the-house staff, who typically don't receive tips, owner Megan Cornelius explained. So the restaurant decided to raise menu prices by 25 percent and share the proceeds with all the workers: servers get 12 percent of their day's orders and kitchen workers get 12 percent of all the orders. On the menu, a note proclaims, "Zazie is Proud to be Tip Free! All of our menu prices include a living wage, revenue share, paid family leave, fully funded health & dental insurance, paid time off, and a 401(k) with employer match for all of our hardworking employees. No Tips Expected." This policy and the restaurant's transparency won great support and loyalty from Zazie customers.

During the pandemic, Zazie was forced to close, but the owners continued paying 75 percent of salaries until unemployment insurance payments came in. They also kept workers on the company's health and dental insurance plans and offered free groceries from the restaurant. They were transparent about the financial impact of the pandemic, so workers readily agreed to share reduced shifts until the restaurant found its financial footing with outdoor seating. Some staff even came in to help refinish tables or with cleaning projects. "Investing in employees is one of the best investments you can make. It can be expensive. But turnover is expensive. It costs a lot of money to retrain people constantly. And we don't have to do that," Cornelius told me. She is a prime example of what can happen when you treat workers well. A server at the restaurant for twelve years, she and two others, the general manager and the chef, became co-owners in early 2020. "So many companies say, 'I could never do this.' Well, we're doing it. I get that small businesses feel stretched. But these corporations . . . They make money hand over fist," Cornelius added. "It's about reprioritizing, and a lot of people don't do that because the industry has been the same for so long. People say that we're so innovative. But treating people well shouldn't be innovative."[37]

Businesses like Zazie, Costco, and the companies Ton and Valdmanis work with can do a lot on their own to create good, stable paid jobs. But individual companies acting alone isn't enough. In his sobering book *Still Broke,* author Rick Wartzman recounts how, even after Walmart began raising wages for its poorly paid workforce between 2015 and 2021, it wasn't enough. Workers at Walmart, the country's largest private employer, make less than $29,000 a year on average. "The company's transformation has been real," Wartzman writes. "But this is also real: if you work at Walmart, even after everything it has done to improve your job, there's more than a fair chance that you'll still be poor. Just because things are better doesn't mean they're good."[38]

Zeynep Ton and others argue that it will also take government and public policies, unions, customers, investors, boards, and business schools to do their part to create better jobs.[39] What we need now, Valdmanis said, is "cathedral thinking"—the kind where generations of people with a shared vision for a hopeful future work together for hundreds of years to build something magnificent that will enrich the common good. Today, he said, that means moving from the short-termism of Wall Street and cowboy capitalism and creating a new approach that builds a healthy economy and society now and with future generations in mind, based on the values of protecting the planet and respecting the dignity of all human life. "We can build something that would make our forebears proud and posterity forever grateful," Valdmanis writes. "We are accountable to no one but one another, to no one but those to whom we will leave this world. And so we face our final charge: whether we also in our day and generation may not perform something worthy to be remembered."[40]

CHAPTER 6

WORKAHOLICS IN AN OVERWORKED WORLD

> Work addiction, "the pain that others applaud," is the only addiction that is both socially sanctioned and financially rewarded.
>
> —*Workaholics Anonymous*[1]

It's easy to miss the weekly meeting spot for Workaholics Anonymous in downtown Washington, D.C., home to some of the most overachieving disciples of overwork culture in the world. The neon sign above the unobtrusive glass door wedged between a high-end cosmetics shop and a nail salon in the trendy Dupont Circle neighborhood advertises "Psychic Readings." Hiding in plain sight is a small square sign emblazoned with a *D* in a bright orange square for the innocuous Dupont Circle Club. The worn, creaking stairs lead to a warren of small, bare rooms where all manner of people come week after week to sit in a circle of wooden chairs and, in the fellowship of others in pain, share their secrets and shame, unburden themselves of suffering, and hope to heal. The club's website lists AA for alcoholics, GA for gamblers, NA for narcotics users, SLAA for sex and love addicts, and a host of others. At the bottom of the list lies WA—Workaholics Anonymous.

I wanted to understand more about workaholism and work addiction. In so many cultures, people talk with pride about being dedicated to their work and the importance of hard work and doing a good job. So many believe that the longer they toil, the better work they produce, and that overwork is simply the price of admission if you want to be excellent at what you do. Many talk ruefully of health problems, stress, failed marriages, estrangement from loved ones, or even loneliness because work leaves them no time for the rest of their lives. In a culture that celebrates and rewards overwork, where do we draw the line between good, healthy work, overwork, and unhealthy addiction? I was wondering where to draw that line in my own life.

On the Monday evening I visited WA, a woman named Christine was running the D.C. meeting. She had invited me to attend. As long as I respected the group's anonymity and understood that no one there spoke for the organization, only for themselves, then any self-identified workaholic in attendance was free to speak with me and share their story. I agreed to use first names only. There were only two people present that night. "You would think in D.C. there would be a lot of people looking for help. But a lot of people don't know they're suffering. Plus, it's game night," Christine explained with a shrug as she put the board game Ticket to Ride on a table in the middle of the room. "People don't think it's important enough to come"—leisure, play, and fun being things workaholics struggle to make time for. Many saw game night—which fell on the rare fifth Monday of the month—as an unproductive waste of time.

"Hi, my name is Christine and I'm a workaholic," the meeting began.

"Hi, my name is Jeff and I'm a workaholic and a procrastinator."

They turned to me.

"Uh, hi. My name is Brigid. I'm a reporter interested in learning about workaholism in overwork culture." I hesitated, the curious yet impersonal veil of my reporter persona lifting. "I work too much. And I guess I'm wondering if I might be a workaholic, too."

Christine had spent most of her life in the nonprofit world and felt her work was a calling. Throughout her career, she'd always achieved and achieved and achieved. She got kudos for the long hours she put in. She received rewards and promotions for always being the dependable, go-to person. "But I was always in pain," she said. "No matter what kind of performance reviews I got. It didn't matter how people were saying what I was doing was great. It was never enough. And every single day at work, I mean, really, my whole career, I have been in pain that I'm not doing enough. That I'm not enough."

One Friday night, she recalled, she had been at a rare party making small talk when she described herself as a workaholic. "I realized they thought I was boasting." Back at home, she broke down. "I was freaking out and desperate," she shared. She googled Workaholics Anonymous just out of curiosity, wondering if such a thing even existed. "Lo and behold, there it was." She ordered the *Book of Recovery* and the *Book of Discovery* workbook that night and joined a phone meeting the next day. People from all over the world were sharing stories that sounded exactly like hers. "I just started crying."

Jeff faced a similar breaking point. He'd always thought of himself as a dedicated, hard worker who perhaps struggled to use his time effectively. But wasn't being a hard worker something good? A hard worker provided for his family. A hard worker was a respected member of society.

One night, he'd overbooked his social calendar as well as his work calendar and was running late to a party. An older coworker took him aside and said, "'Most people would look at your job and think of it as just a job. You think of it as a crusade,'" Jeff recalled. Not long after, a younger colleague Jeff had considered a protégé sent him a note: "'I appreciate all the time you've ever spent with me, but I think you need to go find a mentor to help you spend less time at work.'" That got him thinking. One Sunday, he and his wife returned from a long vacation and he finally felt relaxed. Is there a way I could be like this all the time? he wondered. His wife showed him a Dear Abby advice column about an organization named Workaholics Anonymous. Jeff showed up for his first meeting the next night. "I was hoping it would be like *The Matrix*. That there'd be a magic blue pill I could take and suddenly be better," he said. "But I learned there's a whole process you go through. And I learned I wasn't alone."

Jeff began to reflect. The first WA steps require you to take an inventory of your work history.

He had always been so wrapped up in getting things done, or just getting one more thing done and then one more, that he often cut people off. He never took time to get to know colleagues or listen to different points of view. He began to realize that he hadn't been the best colleague. "In the past, I've been at times pretty horrible to people." He started to see that just as people who aren't alcoholics have no problem leaving half a drink on the table, there were people he worked with "that are very effective and work very hard, and they *can* just put it down." He was not one of them. While he strove to find meaning and identity in long work hours and hustle-harder culture—a phenomenon the writer Derek Thompson called the new Sabbath-less religion of "workism"—it came with a high price.[2]

Christine and Jeff both started attending WA meetings regularly. The organization was founded in the early 1980s as people around the country recognized they were struggling with what felt like an addiction to work, among them a corporate financial planner, a schoolteacher in New York, and a nurse in California. Informal groups started meeting, inspired by the twelve-step practical and spiritual approach of Alcoholics Anonymous. By 1990, the original groups joined together to form the Workaholics World Service Organization. They created their own twelve steps, compiled readings into a book, developed a workbook, set up meeting formats, and, over the years, expanded to add phone and Zoom meetings, a website, and an annual conference. The spouses and partners of workaholics formed a separate, though allied, group, Work-Anon, modeled on Al-Anon.[3]

Jeff and Christine began to work with WA sponsors who were, just like them, flawed and struggling workaholics, but they had been traveling the road to recovery a little longer. They read. They worked the twelve steps. They learned what distinguishes a hard worker from a workaholic and the factors that drive long hours of work. "It's fear," Jeff said. "And, to some extent, trying to fix the hole in you by thinking, 'Well, if I just do this one more thing . . .'" That one more thing will make everything well and bring ease. But it never does. They learned that workaholics get "adrenalized" by overwork, thrilled with the swirl of busyness and extreme multitasking. Though they're weighed down by guilt and shame and burdened either by endless work or endlessly thinking about it, overworking also gives them a charge.

Christine found she fit a classic workaholic profile. Well behaved as a child, a "good girl" terrified of getting anything less than 100 percent on a test, always seeking to please others and ward off even a hint of criticism. Her father, clearly influenced by the culture's embrace of the Protestant work ethic—that one's devotion to work and economic success were signs of God's favor[4]—repeatedly told the family that work itself was the highest virtue. He was never happy unless he was working. Christine felt she had to not just achieve but excel. Be perfect, special—better than everyone else.

Over the years, she found it increasingly difficult to relax. She'd finish all the tasks on her to-do list, then find a few more, then a few more, always feeling frantic, compulsive, and powerless to control the drive always to be doing something. She worked late into the night and then would lie in bed feeling anxious and worrying about work. In the mornings she'd wake up with a feeling of dread in the pit of her stomach. She always overscheduled, almost as if she were bingeing on being busy, compelled to meet impossible expectations and beat the clock that seemed to be threatening to run out. Her former husband wouldn't let her work on weekends, but she couldn't sit still and would jump up to water plants or pay bills instead of watching a baseball game on TV. "He wanted me to be present with him, and that was really hard for me."

Christine hated unstructured time. "Workaholics are uncomfortable on vacations," she said. "They make us unhappy. We cannot sit down and just be. Work is a means of finding identity, gaining approval, and justifying our existence. Some people can work really hard but not be workaholics. The difference is the emptiness inside that you're trying to fill by work." Vacations made her feel that emptiness acutely.

In WA, to begin to tackle her perfectionism, Christine was given a recovery assignment by her sponsor: she had to turn in work that she knew was half-assed. Christine almost couldn't do it, but she forced herself. "Then my boss came back and said, 'Well, this needs some work, and could you change that and add this?' I discovered that that wasn't terrible," she said. "And in fact, it saved me a whole lot of time." Her sponsor called it a "recovery success." Christine wasn't perfect. Her work wasn't perfect. But she survived.

For both Christine and Jeff, connecting to peers has been a powerful way out of their workaholism and into recovery. "What makes WA work is being in a group of people who have a shared understanding of what the problems are and are committed to supporting you," Christine explained. Jeff has learned how to make changes in his life when people share what has helped them. He's strived to set his own "bottom lines" that he will not cross, such as pledging to limit his work hours or not taking on a new commitment without giving up an old one. He also has hopeful "top lines" to help him make room for what's truly important, including time with his family, rest, learning to relax, and even enjoying WA game nights. He swears by using a daily action plan that helps him prioritize his work and know when to stop for the day. "There's so much societal pressure to overwork. But here, we have peer support. We have role models. We have sponsors. It's really all about the power of community," he said.

At the meeting, they turned to me. To find out if I fit the workaholic profile, they told me to look at page 2 in the *Book of Recovery* and take a twenty-question quiz. "Three or more positive answers indicates that there may be a problem with workaholism." I circled thirteen. "Are there times when you're motivated and push through tasks when you do not even want to, and other times when you procrastinate and avoid them when you would prefer to get things done?" Check. "Do you regularly underestimate how long something will take and then rush to complete it?" Check. "Have your long hours caused injury to your health or relationships?"

At the height of the pandemic, I was producing a weekly live podcast on *Slate*, "Crisis Conversations," trying to understand in real time how Covid-19 was disrupting work, family, gender equity, and care, while being down two staff members *and* on a tight deadline to write and edit a series of major reports. And I was writing a magazine story, running the Better Life Lab, reporting for this book, *and* trying to navigate the bitter waters of helping my sisters and mother get her will, advanced health directive, and all the paperwork together to prepare for the end of her life. At 3:00 a.m. one night, an empty container of mint chocolate chip ice cream sat by my computer mouse, my shoulder ached, my butt was asleep from sitting for so long, and I began to feel dizzy. I became short of breath. My chest felt like it was on fire.

A few days later, I was in a cardiologist's office. My chest still hurt and I was easily winded. The doctor ran tests and delivered the diagnosis: Costochondritis. An inflammation of the soft connective tissue between the ribs, likely brought on by acute stress. I wasn't having a heart attack, but it felt like I was, all the time. I would come to call this period of intensive overwork my crucible of nails and shattered glass.

So, yes, I've let my long work hours cause injury to my health. And while I'm so grateful for my family and friends, I know I've let them down and they've sometimes felt they come a distant second to my paid work life. (My disappointed husband just set off to hike alone on a beautiful Sunday afternoon while I was writing this chapter, saying over his shoulder, "Aren't you the one who says how important it is to play?") But was I a workaholic?

I began, as Christine suggested, to reflect on my work story. My faults are many. I was certainly a driven overachiever in school. I am plagued by perfectionist tendencies, which have led to the pain of constant worry, procrastination, and pulling all-nighters at the last minute because I never feel ready or smart enough to tackle big things. I have that restless, guilty drive that is so common in the United States to do more, be more, accomplish more—the very American drive to "self-improvement," instilled in our national culture from the earliest days of Benjamin Franklin's "Project for Moral Perfection,"[5] and the compulsion to be the very best you can be, though I'm often bewildered and unsure just exactly who or what that is.

Starting my paid work career in the 1980s only a decade after women began entering the paid workforce en masse, I was definitely caught up in overworking to prove to my male colleagues and bosses that I belonged, that I wasn't just a "skirt," as someone once called me. I quickly bought into "ideal worker" notions that the longer I labored, the more dedicated and committed I would be and the better work I would produce. Once I became a mother, all of that was magnified, determined as I was to prove I could be *both/and* a great mother and a great worker rather than the more common options presented of *either/or,* or a muddling mediocrity at both.

Workaholics are seized by a compulsion to work, and may get an adrenaline charge from it, but they don't really enjoy it.[6] Was that me? Throughout my life, I've been plagued with doubt about whether I'm on the right path, doing the right thing with my life, doing enough, or missing the point. I can become paralyzed with anxiety. But I've always enjoyed learning, reporting, reading, writing, and sharing what I've found with others. Every day, it is my job to be surprised, outraged, or awed. As a reporter, people sharing their stories with me feels like they've given me their most precious gift. I love how those stories connect us to each other, shortening the distance between us and helping us better understand our lives in all their complexity, beauty, and imperfection. As the director of the Better Life Lab, I'm grateful that it's my *job* to strive to make work, care, and home better and fairer for everyone. I have a sense of responsibility to the people who work with me. And though I've had to learn hard and sometimes painful ways of how to better manage a team, there is such joy giving others opportunities and watching them thrive. So yes, I do enjoy my paid work. At home, I don't particularly love housework. But my unpaid care work is what makes me happy to be alive.

Still, it did seem that if I wasn't working, I was at least *thinking* about it all the time. My evenings, weekends, and even vacations have sometimes been polluted with actual work, or feeling guilty that I should be doing some, so I can finally "catch up." As if I am forever behind some elusive line of acceptable doneness. Why did I work and think about work so much? Was there always just too much to do? Were my expectations too high? Or was it fear driving it all?

Christine and I made a pact. I would spend fifteen minutes a day reading Workaholics Anonymous literature and she'd spend fifteen minutes each day cleaning and organizing one part of her house—a cluttered mess she'd been avoiding for years. Neither of us kept our end of the bargain for long. But I did begin calling in to occasional WA meetings. When Christine suggested I attend the annual conference, I went in person to Chicago before the pandemic and dialed in online after. Ultimately, while I could see the benefit of it, the quasi-religious nature of the program didn't work for me. But some of what I learned stayed with me.

Just as Christine could never sit still, workaholics can be addicted not just to work but to constant activity, even to puzzles and games.

Workaholics can also use work to avoid other things—filling the emptiness, as Christine had put it, trying to control fear and uncertainty—a revelation that hit me at my core. Avoiding pain, feelings of inadequacy or powerlessness. The existential questions of why we're here on Earth and how to make the most of our brief time.

Workaholics even use work to avoid work. One trait of workaholics is to turn to busywork and focus on safe, low-value tasks to avoid taking on the kinds of big projects, new ideas, or creative assignments that they might do well, and which would stretch them, but are also unfamiliar and could result in failure and humiliation.

This phenomenon of "work avoidance" brought to mind the day I cleaned out my desk when I left the *Washington Post*. I pulled out file after thick file stuffed with notebooks, studies, papers, ideas, and notes. Here were all the stories I began working on that I never finished, too busy being a good girl and agreeing to write a low-value weekend feature because the editors needed to fill space or to cover some breaking news story. I thought of all the late nights and long hours, the time my colleague had to run out to buy ice cream for my son's birthday party because I was stuck on deadline with some daily story I can no longer remember. I began to plonk each heavy manila file into the recycling pile, my heart sinking deeper into despair with every toss. "This would have made a great story." *Thunk*. "This would have made a great story." *Thunk*.

Though the origins of the word "workaholic" are debatable, some say psychologist Warren Oates was the first to popularize its use in 1968 to describe people, including apparently himself, with an "uncontrollable need to work incessantly."[7] He likened the condition to a substance abuse disorder, though one that was socially acceptable. The word has since become ubiquitous, though often used in jest, like in the TV sitcom of the same name that ran from 2011 to 2017, or on the July 5 U.S. National Workaholics Day, which pokes fun at those so chained to their desks that they rush back to work after July 4.[8] There are no solid measures for how many workaholics there are in the world. Some researchers estimated that in 1986, the number reached 23 percent among certain professions, such as doctors and lawyers.[9] About 30 percent of Canadians identify as workaholics, according to their rigorous 2009 General Social Survey.[10] In 2011, research considered that about 10 percent of U.S. adults may qualify.[11] Somewhat less scientifically, one 2019 investigation claimed that about half of all U.S. adults are workaholics.[12]

Malissa Clark, a professor of industrial and organizational psychology at the University of Georgia and author of *Never Not Working*, is one of the few researchers in the United States to study workaholism. Over the years of our ongoing conversation, she has pointed me to some of the best research on the topic, which is being done in Italy, of all places, something that always puzzled me. Isn't Italy one of the "beautiful countries" where people enjoy long vacations and afternoons sipping cappuccino? "It's funny to me, too," she said. "The culture does not seem to align with the hustle culture we have in America, and in countries like Japan and South Korea." Maybe "they see workaholism as so much more of a problem that it needs to be studied, whereas in the United States it seems acceptable, just part of a type A personality or the Protestant work ethic."

Clark, an overachiever from childhood, has struggled with where to draw the line between her devotion to work and workaholism, even as she authors research on how detrimental it is to one's health and to the quality of one's work. One of her major studies confirmed that workaholism is, not surprisingly, related to burnout, job stress, work-life conflict, and poor physical and mental health.[13] Women, she found, were just as likely to be workaholics as men, but they suffered more. She surmises that this is because they are more likely to be torn by the drive to prove themselves in the ideal worker world of paid work while also meeting the cultural expectation of devoting themselves to their "first duty" of the unpaid work of care and home. "Women are harder on themselves internally and other people are harder on them externally," Clark said. "So they're getting it from both ends."

Clark also found that, contrary to popular belief, workaholics are *not* more productive and workaholism does *not* produce better work. "You would think if someone's spending all this time at work, that they would be a better performer. But we actually didn't find that in our study," Clark told me. "We even found higher rates of *counterproductive* work, which is certainly not good for the organization"—the low-value tasks and busywork so common in overwork cultures. "That, frankly, is a lot of what drives my passion for this line of research. Not only to highlight workaholism as an important phenomenon but the paradox that if we keep finding such negative outcomes for individuals and no benefit to organizations, then *why* do we keep promoting this approach?"

It's not just putting in long hours that make for a workaholic, Clark and other researchers have seen. Some people can put in long hours and enjoy their work without obsessing about it or suffering negative consequences. That's called "work engagement."[14] But Clark cautions that there's often a fine line between being engaged and being a workaholic. "Anything taken to the extreme is going to be unhealthy," she said. Clark's research has led her to identify four leading drivers of workaholism:[15]

Motivational: Workaholics are driven by an internal motivation or compulsion to work. They don't enjoy it. They work because they feel they should be working.

Cognitive: Workaholics can't stop thinking about work and have difficulty disengaging from it.

Emotional: Workaholics feel anxious and guilty when they aren't working.

Behavioral: Workaholics work far more than could reasonably be expected of them at an organization.

But *where* that internal compulsion comes from is less well understood. Clark explained it could be personality, particularly what she calls a "maladaptive perfectionist"—setting expectations for oneself so impossibly high that they can never be achieved. Or one could be influenced by a role model or an early childhood experience. The tendency to workaholism could come from feelings of low self-worth. Or from the external environment and living in a culture where one's identity is defined by work and overwork is the norm. Or it could be driven by fear, particularly financial.

That financial fear has become acute. Millions of people in the United States struggle with financial precarity. Nearly 60 percent are unable to scrape together $1,000 to cover an emergency.[16] Nearly half of Black students owe more than they borrowed four years after graduating.[17] Close to half of those aged fifty-five to sixty-six have no retirement savings.[18]

Lonnie Golden is a labor economist at Pennsylvania State University who has spent his career researching work. I turned to Golden when I was writing about why Americans, so wedded to work, don't take vacation and instead revel in what the frustrated travel industry laments as "work martyrdom." Travel executives find that eschewing vacation is especially prevalent in millennials,[19] who have been raised on the myth that work should be a passion, which the writer Anne Helen Petersen captured so brilliantly in her book, *Can't Even: How Millennials Became the Burnout Generation.*

First, many workers don't have a choice whether to take time off or not. The United States is the only advanced economy with no paid vacation policy, and about one-third of the workforce doesn't get *any* paid vacation, most of whom work in low-wage jobs. Of those lucky enough to get paid vacation time through their employers, about half work while they're away, and many don't use all the days allotted, leaving an estimated 765 million days of unused vacation in 2018 alone.[20] Money fears, Golden said, may also be a big part of the reason, and not because vacations are expensive.

In 1910, President William Howard Taft said that vacations should no longer be for the wealthy only and that every American should have the right to *three months* away from paid work every year.[21] The idea went nowhere. Businesses fought against the national policy guaranteeing paid annual leave called for in the 1919 Treaty of Versailles, preferring, in the long tradition of corporate interests opposing government mandates and regulations, to give individual companies the right to decide whether to offer vacation time to workers. At the same time, union leaders like Samuel Gompers argued that benefits such as paid holidays, retirement savings, health care, and unemployment insurance served only to "weaken independence of the spirit," and that individuals should be responsible for their own economic security.[22] Thus was born the idea that what other countries consider workers' rights are, in the United States, seen as extraneous "fringe benefits," privileges, and perks.

The Great Depression, when millions of out-of-work and starving Americans could not be held responsible for their individual economic security, showed the deep flaws in that line of thinking. Some policymakers sought to include a national paid vacation policy in the Fair Labor Standards Act of 1938, which banned child labor and established the minimum wage and the forty-hour workweek. Many European countries had already adopted such policies. But union leaders wanted the right to negotiate for paid time off in union contracts and succeeded in securing about ten days a year of covered vacation time with employers. But as union membership and influence has waned, vacation policy has been stuck there ever since. (Some employers began offering health care during World War II as a way to make jobs more attractive at a time when government-mandated wage and price controls kept salaries low. What was thought to be a temporary emergency measure during wartime then got set in stone. U.S. employers have since been expected to provide health insurance for their workers and families and dependents.[23]) When it comes to paid time off, the International Labor Organization called for a minimum of three weeks of paid vacation every year in the 1970s.[24] Many European countries expanded their annual leave policies. The 1993 European Working Time Directive established a minimum of twenty days, or four weeks, of paid vacation, in addition to national holidays. Some countries have gone even farther: France requires thirty days; the UK, twenty-eight; Spain, Denmark, Norway, Austria, and others, twenty-five.[25] But in the United States, with no national standard, survey after survey shows American workers choosing money over time.[26] "There's good reason for it," Golden said. "We don't have the public sector paying for health care, transportation, education, and housing like many European countries do." Nor child care, nor higher education. Most Americans pay for their own health and wellbeing out of their own pockets. "So there's true *economic need* for money to come first, and time second."

Americans are, in fact, about *half* as likely to take paid vacation in any given week as they were forty years ago, the *Washington Post* reported after analyzing Bureau of Labor Statistics data. The longer one- or two-week vacations more common in the past have been replaced by smaller chunks of time off, a few days here and there. Elise Gould, an economist for the Economic Policy Institute, surmised that one reason for this falloff is that the United States also has no paid family leave or paid sick leave policies. So people may be saving up their vacation time to cover unanticipated health or other care emergencies.[27]

To my mind, the lack of health and wellbeing policies drives the overwork and workaholic culture so pervasive in the United States, with all of the people working harder and harder to keep from falling behind, or spiraling into an unforgiving pit of financial hardship. It is no wonder that the fear of running out of money and financial strain shows up as the number one source of stress.

Thus the United States has created the ideal, anxiety-provoking external conditions to push someone with internal workaholic tendencies right over the edge. Just as time scarcity drives panicked busyness, money scarcity drives panicked overwork.

When it comes to taking time off paid work for our unpaid work of care and our leisure, "we're in a perfect storm," Golden told me. "We shy away from having a national paid vacation standard, while there are more and more low-wage jobs that aren't covered by private employer policies. And, because of our bias toward work, the salaried people who do have paid vacation don't feel at liberty to use it and wind up leaving it on the table." Golden and others have been part of a decades-long push for a national paid vacation policy. "A national standard," he said, "might save us from ourselves."

It may not be coincidental that exhausted workaholics began seeking each other out to form Workaholics Anonymous in the 1980s, the era when long work hours became financially rewarding and a valued sign of the dedicated worker, according to scholars Claudia Goldin and Youngjoo Cha. In the decades before, a salaried worker putting in more than forty hours a week was simply gifting their time to their employer. There was no explicit financial reward. (Lower-wage hourly workers covered by the Fair Labor Standards Act, which excluded domestic and agricultural jobs until the 1970s, were guaranteed time and a half pay after forty hours to compensate them for their overwork.) That began to change in the 1980s as knowledge work got "greedy."[28] Professional and knowledge workers willing to be available 24/7 saw a wage premium and a faster track to promotions. "The relationship between the increase in compensation and the increase in hours is not linear," Cha told me. "It's exponential."

At the other end of the workforce spectrum, a "fissuring" occurred, with companies using more contract, temporary, and gig low-wage workers rather than employees, while offering those on staff part-time or erratic schedules and low pay. This meant that most low-wage workers have had to overwork, cobbling together several jobs or gigs to survive.

Who benefits from overwork culture? Cha and others have found that those who have been most able to take advantage of greedy overwork culture, with its high stakes and often lavish pay and prestige, are largely men. Workers with care responsibilities, who are still primarily women, are at a distinct disadvantage. Cha's research shows that increased compensation for overwork exacerbated the gender wage gap by 10 percent between 1979 and 2007.[29] Mothers are automatically seen as less competent at paid work than women without care responsibilities, research shows. They have less power, prestige, and authority and are often discriminated against in hiring and promotions. Mothers are unable to put in the hours expected in greedy paid work. One 2023 study found that they are much less likely to *be* in occupations perceived as time intensive, compared to women without children, and far less likely to be in positions of authority.[30] That keeps everyone stuck and serves to perpetuate male-dominated corporate monoculture.

Before the pandemic, American workers worked among the longest hours of any peer competitive productive nations, save for countries like South Korea and Japan, where brutal overwork is so common there are words to describe it as a cause of death: *karoshi* in Japan and *gwarosa* in South Korea.[31] A recent International Labor Organization report found that American workers clock four hundred more hours of work a year than their peers in Germany—that's *ten more weeks a year* of work.[32] A majority once told Gallup that they put in far more than forty hours of work each week, with nearly 40 percent attesting to extreme work. The pandemic did at least challenge some of the premises of overwork culture.[33] There were unprecedented quit rates, stories in the media of people confronting mortality and reevaluating their lives. There was the "quiet quitting" trend of doing the minimum of work, the protest movement in China—dubbed "lying flat"—against relentless work,[34] and the explosion of followers on a subreddit called "antiwork."[35] Amid persistent labor shortages, many people retired early, changed sectors, relocated,[36] or chose to work part-time.[37] Long Covid sidelined millions.[38] And national surveys show that workers, who are more stressed, disengaged, and burned out than ever,[39] want positions that will give them flexibility and time to live better lives, and they're willing to quit or refuse job offers that don't provide what they want.[40] The number of "desired hours" reported has dropped sharply,[41] even among the prime workaholic demographic: high-earning men.[42] Cha's research throughout the pandemic suggests that more people began putting less stock in long hours and workaholism as a badge of honor. "Which suggests the ideal worker norm has weakened," she said. "A lot of employees at least want something different from the way things were before."

With so much in flux, and the uphill effort required to change ideal worker standards, how does one overcome an inner compulsion to workaholism when the external environment encourages it? What can an individual do in the absence of legislation, regulation, litigation, business leadership, or worker risings that would truly transform work?

Tellingly, many work-life balance experts themselves struggle. Many I spoke with hadn't taken a vacation in years, even though they could cite chapter and verse the research showing that time off improves productivity, outlook, and health, and the absence of it is likely to cause coronary artery disease[43] and depression.[44] Michele Vancour, a professor of public health, is an expert on the stress and guilt of work-life conflict leading to sickness. The morning I spoke with her, she was in the throes of an intense headache and an attack of stress and guilt, having dropped her son off at school without the drums he needed for band class. "Every time I have to go give a talk, I always say, 'Do as I say, not as I do.'"[45] Phyllis Stewart Pires was working long hours on a mission to improve work-life balance for a major global tech company when she found herself in the hospital with a potentially fatal blood clot. "Why is it still so difficult," she asked, "when we know better?"[46]

I began to think of the problem as the Expert's Dilemma. Just like doctors who smoke and ethicists who steal library books,[47] work-life balance experts have a hard time balancing work and life. Why?

Many of the experts tended to blame themselves, saying they had bad overwork habits and just needed the willpower to change. Individual therapy can be helpful for workaholics, along with mindfulness practices and self-help strategies like those listed by work addict author and psychotherapist Bryan E. Robinson in his book *#Chill: Turn Off Your Job and Turn On Your Life*. But the behavioral scientists I sought out put the onus of changing workaholism fully on the environment. One of our foibles as humans is to get caught up in the moment, evidenced in present bias. So once we're in an environment of overwork, it can be hard to choose to stop. We may not think we have a choice. "If you spent some time in Europe, you'd think there are different ways to arrange civilization and work and family life. You'd get to see other choices are possible," social psychologist David Dunning told me. "I think a lot of Americans are stuck in the workplace overworking because that's where everyone else is. That's all you see. And unfortunately, in life, we're channeled into who we are by what we don't know is possible."

More individual willpower to cure workaholism is not what we need, Dunning and other behavioral scientists say. Instead, we need to change the environment to make it easier to choose not to overwork. "This sounds like such an American problem. I can assure you, my European colleagues have no such problem, or at least less of a problem," he said, referring to the guardrails of national policies to limit work hours, promote schedule control, make room for workers with care responsibilities and support them, and to cultures that embrace wellbeing and time rather than money. "So the question I have is: Is the real intervention here being Europe?"[48]

But for now, without those guardrails that can set the tone for the broader culture, Dunning and other behavioral scientists urge people to set up their own guardrails to change their own environments. Like the ideas42 work redesign intervention to plan and schedule summer breaks in January or February. Be transparent: if you send a late-night email, especially if you're a manager, make clear to colleagues that you were out walking the dog, had a doctor's appointment, or that you spent time with family during the day. Or just schedule it to go out the next day at a reasonable hour. Don't create an expectation of 24/7 work. Dunning himself, who lives by the dictates of his calendar, sets it up to make sure he won't overwork. He organizes his days to start early so he can knock off earlier in the evening and he plans his weekends with care, scheduling only limited time for errands or work on Saturday mornings, and ensuring the rest of the time is "sacred." If he struggles with procrastination, he makes what he calls "pre-commitment" agreements to keep him on track. Once, when he and a colleague were having trouble making time to write a paper, they agreed that if they didn't stick to their weekly writing schedule, they'd each have to donate money to causes they disliked. That was enough inducement to get the project done and without much fuss.

Iris Bohnet, a behavioral economist at Harvard's Kennedy School, knows she can get caught up at work. So to make sure she actually comes home for dinner with her family every night, she and her husband created their own precommitment device: they chose a child-care center with a set closing time rather than hiring a more flexible nanny. "That way, you actually have to go home," she said.

"Even though everyone loves their kids, it's just harder in the moment not to answer those ten emails, to make this one phone call. Then once we're home, we think, my God, it's so wonderful to be home, how could we have wanted to stay at the office?"[49]

One of the most powerful ways to change one's environment, social psychologists say, is to change one's choice architecture and stick with it—through informal peer networks.[50] Creating or putting ourselves in a community of like-minded people who want to make the same changes we do will help us set new norms and expectations and provide support at every step of the way to realize them. This sounds a lot like Workaholics Anonymous. Even in moments of despair, or in the midst of an emotional storm of shame, I was struck by how the WA workaholics I met were filled with grace and acceptance for each other. At the end of every meeting, they ask for and offer one another a powerful lifeline: "strength and hope."

Christine and I have kept in touch over the years. She sends me articles or guided meditations and has connected me to people to talk to. She was a willing ear as I struggled with the weight of feeling that I'm always working or thinking about work and yearned for some peace of mind. She became, if not an official sponsor, an understanding friend, part of my own peer network helping me to set new norms and expectations and to try to live up to them. I don't know if I qualify as a workaholic. Some days it feels like I do. Other days, well, I'm working on it. At a minimum, I have, as Malissa Clark herself admits, "workaholic tendencies."

One summer day, Christine came to my house for a visit. I was in the throes of work deadlines and she had since retired. She'd just turned seventy-one. "I have more time. I'll come to you," she offered. We sat at my kitchen table eating strawberries and reflecting on our struggles with work and how to overcome them. I wondered what life was like for a retired workaholic. She'd intended to work until she turned seventy, she explained, but two months before she turned sixty-eight, she was so completely burned out, she knew she couldn't make it.

At first, she struggled with unstructured time in retirement, feeling pressure to always be "productive," to make the "right" choices and do the things that people in retirement are "supposed" to do, like learn to paint with watercolors, play the piano, or tutor children.

She joined a WA group for retired workaholics who were also struggling with how to use their time. They filled it with activities, volunteering, taking on project after project, learning new languages, signing up for classes, taking care of family, overpromising—still unable to say no, hooked on achieving and people pleasing and being stressed out by doing. But Christine wanted to learn how to just be.

She went on long meditation retreats. With nothing to do but sit with the uncomfortable emptiness, Christine slowly came to see that all the seeking she'd done outside herself, using overwork as a way to find meaning or self-worth, never brought her what she was after: happiness. "I realized there is nothing in the external circumstances of my life that needs to change for me to be happy," she said. "I have enough. I am enough."

On her fiftieth college reunion website, she wrote: "Lots of cultural pressure to be active in retirement. But for me, the best retirement activity is recovering from years of workaholism by moving through my day slowly and doing as little as possible."

We both admitted we didn't have it all figured out. Still, she said, finishing the last of the sweet, plump strawberries on a gloriously sunny afternoon, "I've been happy for the first time in my life."

CHAPTER 7

FROM GRIEF TO RAGE TO ACTION: FIGHTING FOR A DECENT LIFE IN JAPAN'S KAROSHI CULTURE

Working conditions shall be those which should meet the needs of workers who live lives worthy of human beings.

—*Article 1, Japan's Labor Standards Law, 1947*[1]

24-Jikan 365-nichi shinu made hatarake.
24 hours a day, 365 days. Work till you die.

—*Watami Corporation's onetime motto*[2]

Hope is like a path in the countryside. First, there is nothing—but as people walk this way again and again, a path appears.

—*Lu Xun*[3]

Like many women of her generation, Yuko Mori had always thought of herself as a housewife. Creating and keeping a beautiful home, cooking labor-intensive traditional meals from scratch, and raising two daughters was her unpaid job, just as her husband's job was to venture out into the world of work as a teacher for pay. Small and unassuming, with wisps of gray streaking her deep black hair when I met her in June 2018, sixty-four-year-old, bespectacled

Mori seemed an unlikely warrior. Yet in her quiet, tenacious way, Mori took on one of the largest companies in Japan, one of the most charismatic corporate leaders, and the entire Japanese government to demand a change in Japan's relentless overwork culture. Losing a daughter to karoshi can do that.

Mori sips green tea as a light breeze ripples over the koi pond of Shirotori Garden in downtown Nagoya, a large industrial city that Western tourists usually speed by on the bullet train from the bustle of Tokyo to the temples of Kyoto. Sitting with me and journalist, translator, and labor activist Chie Matsumoto in the garden's teahouse, Mori speaks barely above a whisper as she tells the story of her daughter Mina, who at twenty-six, was overworked to the point of delirium and took her own life, becoming one of the most shocking cases of karoshi, or "death from overwork." After Mori and her husband, Tsuyoshi, joined a small but persistent group of labor lawyers, unions, and other families who'd lost loved ones to karoshi, Mina's death also became one of the most public and consequential catalysts for change.

In the United States, we tend to hear about the occasional sensational and horrific karoshi deaths like Mina's fleetingly, when they leap from the headlines, only to disappear a few days later. It's easy to write off such tragic events as a product of circumstances or a culture unique to Japan, or, with rising rates of *gwarosa* in South Korea[4] and *guolaosi* in China[5]—also death from overwork—to Asia. But were they?

I'd come to Japan to understand what it is like to live, work, and care in a culture where dying from overwork is so common that it has a name and has had one for decades.[6] Far from the isolated, troubling episodes the West hears about, karoshi had become normalized. But Mina's death catalyzed a movement of unions, labor lawyers, and families like the Moris to begin lobbying the government in 2008 for a law to prevent karoshi. That law finally passed in 2014. It acknowledges that karoshi is a social problem for which the government is responsible. The government is now required to thoroughly investigate and certify karoshi-related deaths and injuries and force companies to pay workers' compensation to bereaved families. It is also required to track overwork and publish annual reports. Its first white paper was published in 2016. The law is bolstered by a 2000 Supreme Court decision proclaiming that companies have a duty to care for employees. They must seek to prevent overwork or be forced to pay redress to families when they don't. There is also a proliferation of clinics, funded by the state universal health-care system, to retrain depressed and once-suicidal workers to gradually return to their jobs. At Project Rework, a popular clinic in Tokyo, people attend intensive retraining classes for six months to a year or more.[7] "We role-play and try to teach people how to say 'No,' in order to work safely," the director told me. The clinic aims to help individuals, much like the classic—and inadequate—American business response to stress and burnout. It can help, but doesn't solve the root cause of the problem. Even the director acknowledged that his methods can only do so much, and that overwork culture is a "structural" issue.

Not surprisingly, the clinics have not made much of a dent in karoshi, nor have the other interventions. There are legal and illegal workarounds to government regulations. Many are not enforced, are nonbinding, and demand no or laughably low penalties for offending companies. The overwork culture remains strong. The government reported in 2022 that about eight hundred people applied for compensation from the government for karoshi-related illness or death.[8] But labor lawyers I spoke with estimate that the real karoshi death and suicide toll is more like ten thousand a year,[9] even during and after the Covid-19 pandemic.[10] Of Japan's famously high suicide rate,[11] nearly three thousand were karoshi-related in 2022, higher than in previous years. The government also reported high rates of overwork, sleeplessness, and depression.[12]

Most people I spoke to had an inhuman overwork or karoshi story, even my Airbnb hosts and old friends from my years living in the country as an English teacher. Some people I interviewed related stories of never seeing their fathers growing up. One said hers left notes for the family to read at the breakfast table. Others didn't find it at all strange that they themselves were still in the office most nights at 11:00 p.m. A friend recounted how his uncle collapsed at his front door and died from a heart attack, coming home from another punishingly long workday. Nearly everyone knew someone who had overworked to the point of suffering a heart attack or a stroke. Or they knew people who had become too sick or depressed to work, or had even, as in Mina's case, become so despondent about the overwork culture that they committed *karojisatsu*, or karoshi suicide.[13]

In the Western press, karoshi deaths are often seen as the by-product of an exotic Eastern culture: there are frequent references to Japan's ancient warrior samurai ethos,[14] its feudal code of Bushido,[15] and the ritual of honor suicide, or seppuku.[16] But in Japan, I saw what I'd seen in the United States and elsewhere: the way we've organized paid work and, by extension, care and life, has stacked the deck against workers and people with care responsibilities. The story we tell ourselves, here and there, is about individual responsibility, personal failure, and blame. If people are becoming sick or dying from working too much, then it must be because they've chosen to do so, or they're not efficient, or they are too flawed to manage balancing work and care. I found the same blind faith in perpetual growth, the pursuit of short-term profit, and the belief that enriching those at the top will somehow make life better for everyone, which has only led to increasing inequality and misery. I saw the same disconnect between rising productivity and falling or stagnant wages, particularly for low-wage workers.[17] And I saw the same stubborn belief among the mostly male leaders who rose to power and prominence in an overwork system that this is the best and only way to organize work, despite overwhelming evidence that they're wrong. Just as in the United States, all of this makes change hard.

I attended a Workaholics Anonymous meeting in Tokyo where exactly one person showed up. Yuki, who asked that I not use her last name, had spent two and a half years in a hospital after nearly working herself to death. Since she started the WA chapter in 2013, the largest turnout she'd ever had was five people. "In Japan, working hard is considered a virtue," she said. "So people don't think of overwork as a negative."

In the United States, leaders stubbornly believe that overwork is the price of excellence.[18] In Japan, they believe that overwork is the only way for the country to remain competitive in the global economy.[19] Yet I saw inefficiency to the point of ridiculousness. As in the United States, the appearance of hard work mattered more than what was actually being done. Or as one researcher, Maki Umeda, put it to me, "In Japanese work culture, process is what matters. Not outcome." In the United States, the process is gummed up by a culture of meetings and a focus on long hours and the show of work rather than performance and deliverables—what I'd come to think of as stupid work. In Japan, the process is even more painstaking, ritualized, tedious, ambiguous, and also inefficient. Most jobs and tasks aren't well defined, so workers are never sure what to do or for how long—staying at work until an equally overworked boss says it's time to leave or go out drinking. One researcher called such work processes "waste."

Japanese workers put in some of the longest hours of paid work, yet they register among the lowest productivity rates of all advanced economies. So wedded is the corporate class to the virtue of long hours that dozing on the job is an admirable sign that someone's been grinding away.[20]

Notably, Japan's productivity is lower than Iceland's—a country with a commitment to short work hours and human well-being.[21] Microsoft Japan made headlines when it experimented with a four-day workweek in 2019. By shortening meetings to thirty minutes and implementing other process changes, it saw a 40 percent boost to productivity over the previous month,[22] dispelling the false equation of long work hours with high productivity. The experiment lasted only one month before it was back to business as usual.

On the whole, the Covid-19 pandemic did not significantly change Japan's culture of overwork or herald a shift to working digitally. What Japan is good at is manufacturing high-tech products like cars, bullet trains, robots, TVs, gadgets, and gaming systems. What it's not so good at is using software and digital work processes and trusting the cloud. Organizations instead rely on time-consuming analog paper and in-person systems.[23] Hiroshi Ono, a professor at Hitotsubashi University Business School, found that during the pandemic Japan ranked last of eight large economies, including the United States, the United Kingdom, Sweden, Germany, Italy, China, and South Korea, in the share of people who actually worked digitally in relation to the number of jobs that could allow for telework. Ono also found that, even as the world of work was forced to change around the world, Japanese corporations offered the fewest work-from-home policies.[24]

"We're stuck in this vicious cycle," Ono said. "Long work hours. Low happiness. Low productivity. There's something about Japan's work culture that just is averse to using flexible policies." To which Scott North, a sociology professor emeritus at Osaka University, responded: "Bosses. Old men. And younger people who can't stand up on their own behalf." North has spent his career researching karoshi and, like Ono, is someone I've turned to numerous times to better understand it. He was blunt in his assessment. "Karoshi doesn't 'happen.' It is caused by people who promote purposefully weak regulations, which are weakly enforced—the budget for inspections is small, the number of inspectors inadequate to the task," he told me. "The employers really have the upper hand."

The labor laws don't help. Although Japan, like the United States, ostensibly limits paid work hours to forty per week, a loophole in the country's Labor Standards Act, known as Article 36, allows labor and management to "agree" to longer hours. They're supposed to cap it, at least on paper. But in reality, the cap has meant little. Employers have the power to demand longer hours of paid work and of unpaid *sabisu zangyo,* or service overtime.[25] Most employee unions have little power to resist.[26] "Karoshi is the product of particular leaders and their taken-for-granted understanding of social order," Scott North concluded. "It's not a democratic vision."

Some Japanese companies *are* seeking to change.[27] Hosei University economist Koji Sakamoto, who has spent his career studying the best way to manage companies for high performance, has distilled one key element: putting a premium on human well-being. He calls it *goho yoshi*—managing companies for the benefit of five sides: employees and their families; suppliers and subcontractors; present and future customers; socially vulnerable people; and, last, shareholders.[28] He's found eight thousand companies making efforts—out of about nearly six million.[29] Of those eight thousand, there are about eight hundred that, he said, "truly cherish and respect people."

Sakamoto said the focus on short-term profits for shareholders and the view that treating workers well is a costly "indulgence"—both taught in business schools and embraced by corporations—have promoted this dangerous work culture. But as he acknowledged, he faces an uphill battle to transform it. Companies with a karoshi culture are the "absolute majority in Japan," he said. "I'm only one person and I have limited time. But people only have one short life and want to be happy."

In Japan, there is endless handwringing about the country's record low birth rate,[30] its restrictive immigration policies,[31] its long life expectancy and aging population—at nearly 30 percent, Japan has one of the highest ratios of people over sixty-five of any country in the world[32]—and how it could all lead to a downward "death spiral" in which the state will cease being able to function.[33] Yet the overwork culture bears some responsibility for the low birth rate, coupled with stubbornly held patriarchal beliefs that women should be primary unpaid caregivers at home and that men should do paid work—mothers of young children in Japan put in *seven times* the unpaid labor of care and home that fathers do, by far the widest gap of all advanced nations.[34] This makes it impossible for women to combine full-time paid work with unpaid care responsibilities. Who can put in sixty or more hours a week and then raise a family or care for loved ones on their own? The overwork culture leaves women few choices: work full-time, put in long hours and have no children, or rely on family or paid caregivers to care for them and rarely see them; choose low-paying precarious part-time or contract work that may offer some flexibility to manage care duties; or have no children at all.[35] The overwork culture keeps women dependent on men—the tax system also favors mothers who work part-time.[36] It keeps single mothers stuck in poverty.[37] It prevents Japanese men from sharing the unpaid work of care and home, even when surveys show that more of them want to.[38] It is also the main reason why Japan routinely scores near the bottom of international gender equality rankings: 125th of 146 countries in 2023.[39]

Yet despite the existential threat, the dangerously long hours and low productivity, the karoshi phenomenon is often met with a resigned *sho ga nai*. It can't be helped.[40]

Yuko Mori and a handful of karoshi fighters like her believe, against all odds, that a culture that values overwork to the point of death *can* be helped, and they are working to change it.

On the table before her, the delicate wagashi, the traditional sugar-dusted rice flour and bean paste sweet, is untouched. Yuko Mori explains as Chie Matsumoto translates that Mina was the elder of her two daughters. Because Yuko Mori was busy caring for her own mother and her husband worked long hours, Mina looked after and protected her younger sister from a young age. Mina got her sister up in the mornings and braided her hair before taking her to school, never having time to braid her own hair. Mina reminded her mother of the scrappy, brave elder daughter in Hayao Miyazaki's beloved animated film *My Neighbor Totoro*. After graduating from high school, Mina started studying at university but quit to work. She got what turned out to be a dead-end job in hospital administration. Disillusioned, she returned to school and studied painting through a correspondence course at an arts college in Kyoto. Then one day, seemingly out of the blue, Mina announced that she wanted to work for Watami, a big conglomerate that, in addition to agriculture, home delivery, waste management, renewable energy, and other businesses,[41] runs one of the largest pub chains, or *izakaya,* in Japan.[42] Yuko Mori was stunned. "I protested. I was opposed to her taking this job," she says quietly. She didn't like that the job required an eight-hour evening shift. "But Mina was determined."

Watami was founded and run by a charismatic CEO, Miki Watanabe, Mori explains, and Mina said she was drawn to his talk of "corporate social responsibility." This was a company where Mina thought she could work for the rest of her life, starting in the *izakaya,* then transferring to the agricultural sector. Later, after Mina's death, Yuko Mori read some of her daughter's journals. She wrote that "she'd been living in a two-dimensional world through painting," Mori says. "She wanted a fuller life, helping other people."

The position on offer was a highly coveted permanent job. These well-paying stable slots have become increasingly rare in Japan. Sought-after permanent jobs have always been rare for women.[43]

Permanent jobs, or the "lifetime employment" system, took off in Japan after the World War II era and helped turn the country into a global economic powerhouse that arose from the devastation of the war. From the 1940s to the 1980s, these jobs offered good benefits, often including housing and increasing promotions, wages, bonuses, and generous pensions based not on performance but on seniority—workers were ranked from the day they were hired to the day they retired. In exchange, the employees, who were known as *seishain* or "regular" workers, were expected to give firms their undying loyalty and, if requested, endless hours of work.

The philosophy of *messhi hoko,* or self-sacrifice for the sake of the group, became a way of life for both government and corporate employees.[44] Regular workers were to think of their organizations as family, and, as in any family, trust that their firms would take care of them, even in bad times.[45] For decades, these jobs were open only to men, white-collar "salarymen."[46] They were usually hired right out of college, so that companies could mold them in their image.[47] They worked long hours at least six days a week, even after the government legislated a two-day weekend in the late 1980s.[48] Long days were followed by long nights of mandatory heavy drinking—the *nomikai* culture.[49] In theory, and often in practice, no one quit. No one switched jobs mid-career. No one was laid off, even if there wasn't much to do.[50]

At the same time, women were expected to meet the Confucian ideal of "good wife/wise mother" and be home in their domain tending to the unpaid work of family and care. Women, if they worked in the market at all, were relegated to poorly paid "nonregular" positions and clerical "office lady" jobs, and, until a 1966 court ruling, were typically forced to "retire" after marrying.[51] It wasn't until the passage of an Equal Employment Opportunity Act in 1985—the result of intense international pressure[52]—and subsequent amendments that firms were encouraged to "endeavor" to end discrimination against women. The law lifted the ban on night work for women and put an end to most restrictions that limited their overtime hours.[53] Only then did permanent "lifetime employment" jobs open up to them. Even then, firms were slow to hire women or shunted them onto lower-paid dead-end tracks of clerical or support jobs with no room for advancement.[54] Instead of securing permanent positions, most women continue to be funneled into unstable contract or temp work that pays far less and offers no benefits, career growth, or stability—like Mina's first hospital administration job. These nonregular contracts last one, three, or five years and, while they may be renewable, are precarious.[55]

The traditional lifetime employment system began to fray with the oil shocks of the 1970s, when skyrocketing prices ended the rapid economic growth of the oil-dependent island nation.[56] The system imploded in the 1990s with the country's economic collapse.[57] What had always been an overwork culture that required workers to sacrifice time for their lives and families now became a karoshi culture, in which an astonishing number of people sacrificed not just their time but also their health and their wellbeing.

Firms seeking to survive in the downturn shed their lifetime workers, replacing them with cheaper temp and contract personnel.[58]

The remaining regular staff who weren't laid off, or moved to a subsidiary with a lower salary and fewer benefits, were expected to do the same amount of work with a smaller workforce. Fearing they could be the next ones fired, the regular workers began putting in even longer hours to demonstrate their self-sacrifice and dedication.[59] Nonregular employees also worked longer hours to show they were worthy of more stable positions—a promise rarely fulfilled but often dangled by firms as an incentive for overwork, labor activists told me. And much of this overwork is unpaid. Workers are expected to "gift" their time to their employers in *sabisu zangyo*.[60]

By 2022, poorly paid nonregular workers made up nearly 40 percent of the Japanese workforce[61]—about 70 percent of them women.[62] Of all the women in the workforce, more than half are nonregular workers[63] and most of them are part-time.[64]

So for young Mina Mori, yearning to be more engaged in the world and make her mark, the Watami job offer was irresistible: one of the few high-status permanent positions available with the promise of good pay, housing, benefits, and lifetime employment—for a woman? Mina was excited about the future such a job would give her. So in April 2008, Mina started working for Watami. The first thing the company did was transfer her to an *izakaya* in Yokosuka, two hundred miles away from home, and move her into a company dormitory about a thirty-minute train ride from the pub. That's another feature of permanent work in Japan: doing without question anything the firm asks of you, including moving wherever they want you to go, whenever they say, and as many times as they decide. As Mina was soon to find out, permanent work also meant putting in long hours of paid labor followed by long hours of unpaid *sabisu zangyo* overtime, even on evenings, weekends, and days that were supposed to be off. While the practice is described euphemistically as "service" in Japan, workers in other countries would call it wage theft.

As companies and even the courts have determined that *sabisu zangyo* doesn't count as part of official work hours, it can be difficult to prove that the employer mandated it.[65] But workers in

Japan, both Japanese and international, have told me that they are bullied and harassed if they don't do service overtime, even if it isn't explicitly requested—if everyone else is doing it, then they know they should, too. In famously subtle Japan, *kūki wo yomu*, or "reading the air," is a prized skill.[66]

For a time, Yuko Mori thought everything was going reasonably well for her daughter. When Mina called home, she'd sometimes complain about a manager or talk about a two-day company orientation she had to attend during her weekend off. Her mother dismissed these objections as hiccups, typical for anyone starting a new job, and Mina insisted she was well suited to the position, and she never mentioned how many hours she was working.

Before Mina took the job, she and her mother had watched a program on the alarming karoshi phenomenon, so Mina was aware of the danger. On one of her calls home, Mina confessed that she was feeling tired. Worried, Yuko Mori brought up the program they'd watched. She shakes her head at the memory. "Mina said, 'Don't worry. If it gets like that, I'll come home.' I believed her." Mina was like that, Mori says. "If she didn't like something, she'd leave." A few weeks later, when Mina's complaints about exhaustion became more frequent, a concerned Yuko Mori made arrangements to visit her. Mina had just sent her mother a spare key to her dormitory room.

"She said everything was fine," Yuko Mori says.

"When did you learn that everything was not fine?" I ask.

"After her death."

On June 12, just over two months after Mina had started working for Watami, and before Yuko Mori could leave to visit her, the Moris got a call from the police in the middle of the night. Mina had climbed up the outdoor staircase of a tall building near her dormitory and flung herself from it. She was dead. The Moris felt numb disbelief. They learned that, after another long workday, Mina had taken a walk to the ocean in the rain, bought snacks at a convenience store at around midnight, and by 2:00 a.m., she had jumped from the staircase. In Mina's purse, the police found receipts showing that, in the hours before she committed suicide, she'd bought shampoo, conditioner, cosmetics, and a new alarm clock. To Yuko Mori, that didn't seem like the behavior of someone about to end their life. "It looked like she was trying to cheer herself up," she says.

Mina had been in the habit of keeping notes and recording thoughts about her day. Later, police found a note she'd written not long before her death. "My body hurts. I feel exhausted. I feel emotionally numb. I can't move as fast as I want to. Please help me. Somebody help me."[67]

After her funeral, Watami executives came to visit the Moris. "My husband said, 'You were supposed to take care of her. You have a responsibility to explain what happened to her,'" Yuko Mori recalls. "They said they didn't know why Mina was so tired." Then they left. "I was afraid it was just going to end like that."

Yuko Mori began calling Watami every day. She called the food service department and the sales office. She called any number she could find, demanding an accounting of every minute of her daughter's time since joining the firm. "I was calling so much, they may have been afraid that I'd show up and ruin an opening ceremony somewhere." After several weeks, bowing to Yuko Mori's quiet yet fierce persistence, the company relented and Watami management agreed to talk to the family. Mori said they initially told her Mina had worked 80 hours overtime in each of the two months she was employed, meaning a 60-hour workweek. In 2001, the government had set 60-hour weeks—*80 hours of overtime a month*—as the "karoshi line,"[68] the point where people become too stressed and fatigued to function and stay healthy.[69] But the karoshi line wasn't enforced. In fact, at the Watami *izakaya* pub where Mina worked, the overtime cap was set at *120 hours* a month—a legal 70-hour workweek that employers could extend even further with demands for service overtime.[70]

Yuko Mori didn't believe their version of Mina's schedule. She began piecing together the story of her daughter's overwork on her own. That's when the Moris discovered that there are the *official* work hours that companies report to the government and show up in international data sets, which, though under the karoshi line and established union agreements, are still brutally long. Then there are the *real* work hours, which are simply unlivable. Workers, activists, and academics told me that it is common practice for companies to keep two sets of books, one for the "official" reported hours of work and the other for the real unreported, punishing long hours of paid overtime and unpaid service overtime.[71] "Companies report the number of hours they've planned to work, not the actual hours," academic Scott North explained. "A lot of people don't get paid for real overtime that they work because it wasn't planned." But Sam Timinsky, another academic who studies karoshi culture, takes a more cynical view. "There are massive incentives for people to lie, and they lie very aggressively," he has said in lectures. Work hours aren't getting any better. "What's getting better is the lying about it."[72]

Slowly, with the help of former Watami coworkers who had themselves become ill from overwork and quit, Yuko Mori discovered that in training, Mina was taught to prepare two items on the menu, but once on the job, she was expected to prepare and cook all the food. So Mina was coming in early to teach herself how to slice sashimi and make complicated dishes. Though the company showed records that she had regular breaks, former coworkers laughed when they saw the documentation. No one got breaks, they reported. Yuko Mori found out that Mina was also expected to stay to clean up, working often until 2:00 a.m. or later—sometimes so late that she missed the last train to her dorm. Then she slept at the pub, resting her head on a table, waiting for the first train at 5:00 a.m. to return to her dorm to sleep for a few hours before her next shift.

Mori learned that on her ostensible days off Mina was expected to go to Watami headquarters in Tokyo, a two-hour train ride, and participate in "study sessions." Workers read, memorized, and were quizzed on slogans from a book written by the CEO, Miki Watanabe, including his infamous motto: *"24 hours a day, 365 days. Work till you die."* Mina's former workers explained that she had also been expected to volunteer at one of the eldercare homes Watami owned, then write a report about the experience[73]—all service overtime and all for free. The more she heard, the more Yuko Mori thought of Watami as a cult that her daughter couldn't escape.

Yuko Mori ultimately discovered her daughter was on duty routinely from 2:00 p.m. to 5:00 a.m., including hours waiting for the first morning train, far exceeding the eighty overtime hours of the government's karoshi line.[74] It was an inhuman eighty-three-hour week that left little time for sleep or much of anything else. The day Mina died, she had spent a long day commuting to Tokyo and sitting through the mandatory unpaid Watami study session. Late that night, back in Yokosuka, she took her walk in the rain because she was so exhausted she probably couldn't sleep, her mother muses. By the time she climbed the staircase where she made her jump, Yuko Mori believes "she was so tired she couldn't think straight."

As the truth of Mina's punishing work schedule became clearer, the Moris' grief fused with rage. "I was so furious with Watami," Yuko Mori says. "At first, I thought this tragedy just happened to my daughter because her dorm was so far away, and she would miss the last train. But *everyone* was worked like that. It's impossible to live a decent life putting in that many hours."

The Moris decided to use their grief and fury to fight to change the system that normalizes karoshi and, in Tsuyoshi Mori's words, "murdered" their daughter.[75] The first step, they decided, was to use the system itself: to petition the Labor Standards Office to classify Mina's death as a karoshi suicide and file for workers' compensation. In Japan, the government recognized the first official karoshi death in 1988, and the number of certified karoshi deaths has only grown since then.[76] With the help of a labor lawyer, the Moris fought the Japanese government for four years. Finally, in February 2012, the Labor Standards Office officially classified Mina's death as due to karoshi.[77]

With that classification, the Moris were ready to take the struggle public. They wanted the world to know that Japan's overwork culture had killed their daughter, and they wanted to eradicate that culture entirely. One way to do that, they thought, was by suing the company itself, demanding a lot of money in compensation and tarnishing Watami's stellar reputation by making a very big stink.

CEO Watanabe, who had been building his visibility as a TV personality and burnishing his reputation to run for political office, took to social media to deny the company had anything to do with Mina's death. Instead, in what lawyers and researchers have found is a common tactic, he blamed Mina herself for working too much.[78]

Undeterred, the Moris began sharing Mina's story with the media, their somber faces set like stone behind an oversize photo of their daughter, dressed in white, with a sunny smile.[79] When Watanabe announced his political campaign, they protested at events and at Liberal Democratic Party headquarters demanding they drop Watanabe as a candidate.[80] The Moris were determined to show that Watanabe was a charlatan, as far as they were concerned, and that Watami was anything but the inspiring, progressive company it claimed to be—it was really one of the infamous *burakku kigyō*, or "black companies." These are companies that advocates like the Moris determine have no qualms working people to death. The advocates help publicize lists every year to shame these companies into changing. (After the Black Lives Matter protests of 2020, some advocates began calling the black companies "evil companies" or "karoshi companies" instead.)

"Watanabe was making glorious statements but treating people horribly," Yuko Mori explains.

The Moris hoped their suit would spur government action. But more than anything, they wanted the Japanese people to wake up: workers were being exploited to death by poor management practices and the loss of life was wholly unnecessary. They wanted workers to feel outraged, as they did, and to protest rather than continuing to accept karoshi culture with a fatalistic shrug. They wanted no more deaths, no more exhausted, half-lived lives of nothing but work. Winning in the court of public opinion, their protest succeeded in getting Watami labeled a "black company" and, in 2012 and 2013, it was voted the worst place to work in Japan.[81] But winning a legal battle was far from assured.

The family had a shot at successfully suing Watami only because another karoshi suicide paved the way. In 2000, the Japanese Supreme Court had ruled for the first time that companies have a duty to care for workers' health and are responsible for organizing work in such a way that employees don't experience excessive fatigue or stress.[82] The ruling came after a twenty-four-year-old man hanged himself in 1991. He had worked such long hours for Dentsu Inc., a large advertising company, that he sometimes arrived home at 6:00 a.m. with only enough time to shower and change before returning to the job—a not uncommon scenario I heard from a number of white-collar workers I spoke with. The young man's father blamed the company and its overwork culture for his son's death. The court agreed.[83]

Still, the Moris' lawyer at the time advised them to settle with Watami. In Japan taking legal action is taboo, condemned as subversive and rebellious as well as a betrayal of *wa*, the spirit of group harmony that is held as the highest ideal.[84] Instead of taking the lawyer's advice, and quietly conforming to the culture, the Moris fired him. They began working with lawyers at the National Defense Counsel for Victims of Karoshi, a small but dedicated group of attorneys who'd come together in 1988 to fight karoshi cases, and joined with the Tokyo east chapter of the National Union of General Workers to file a suit against Watami in December 2013. The Moris demanded 153 million yen (about $1 million in 2023) for failing to provide safe working conditions for their daughter.

Watanabe was elected to the national legislature, the Diet, that same year.

As the Moris battled in court, they met a nationwide network of other families who'd lost loved ones to karoshi and found that their experience was hardly unique. Those families had also been stonewalled or lied to by companies about work hours. They also had had to do their own sleuthing and re-create real overtime schedules and fight for years to get the karoshi deaths certified. They too had pushed to receive workers' compensation or see companies punished, although the fines amounted to a token few thousand dollars,[85] hardly enough to act as a disincentive to entrenched over-work culture.

This band of karoshi-fighting labor lawyers and the families of victims formed a group, *Zenkoku Karōshi wo Kangaeru Kazoku no Kai*, the Association of Families Affected by Karoshi. Not long after Mina Mori died in 2008, they began to push for a national law, the Basic Law to Prevent Karoshi. With Mina's case and others like it appearing more often in the press, with many of the stories drawn from calls to a public "Karoshi Hotline" event the lawyers hold every year, pressure mounted on the government to do something. It increased after a prominent 2012 newspaper survey of Japan's hundred largest firms showed that seventy had negotiated Article 36 overtime agreements far above the eighty overtime hours of the karoshi line. Some even demanded a perfectly legal two hundred hours of overtime a month—a ninety-hour workweek.[86]

As the Moris were fighting Watami in court, the victims' family group continued filing karoshi cases with the Labor Ministry and lobbying the national legislature. They gathered half a million signatures on a petition and pushed for local anti-karoshi laws. They even sent a delegation to Geneva to win international support. Finally, in 2014, the Basic Law to Prevent Karoshi passed. In addition to requiring the government to track karoshi cases and deaths and publish annual reports, the law mandates that the government raise awareness about karoshi and produce prevention plans. It did not, however, impose penalties on firms that fail to comply[87] nor put an end to the Article 36 loophole. The first white paper the government produced reported that one in five workers in Japan was at risk of karoshi.[88] "What families wanted was an enforceable law. What they got was 'moralsuasion,' education and research into the phenomenon," academic Scott North told me. "This was primarily a symbolic piece of legislation."

The following year, in 2015, nearly seven years after Mina Mori's death, the Watami Group admitted Mina's suicide was the result of their working conditions. The company—and Watanabe himself—apologized to the family and agreed to pay 133 million yen—an unprecedented punitive amount—to cover Mina's unpaid service overtime and as consolation to the Moris. Watanabe finally said he was "repentant" and would spend the rest of his life making up for Mina's death.[89] At Yuko Mori's insistence, the company also admitted that they failed to pay overtime to hundreds of other full-time employees and shelled out an additional 45 million yen ($316,000 in 2023) to reimburse them. By order of the court, Watami published the details of the settlement and an apology on its website. The company promised to cut down on overwork and to begin including seminars and study sessions as paid work, not service overtime. But as union leaders told me years later, without a strong union, they doubted the promises have had much impact.

Still, the Moris were not done. Unlike in other karoshi settlements, the Moris, the labor lawyers, and the union had refused to sign a nondisclosure clause. So they have continued to speak out about Mina and her case in their ongoing battle against the country's overwork culture.[90] "I wanted to put myself out front, to fight against Watami," Yuko Mori explains, a controversial stance against the cultural imperative of conforming to group harmony, especially for a housewife expected to steer the domestic ship at home. "But in the house, my younger daughter did not agree. She stopped talking to us for a long time." Yuko Mori pauses to take a breath.

The afternoon sun in the Shirotori Garden turns toward evening. Yuko Mori's teacup is empty and her wagashi sweet remains untouched. I ask if she feels vindicated by the 2014 law to prevent karoshi deaths they helped pass and the unprecedented court settlement they fought for. She smiles bitterly. "I think we were able to recover my daughter's honor," she says. "But that's it."

The Watami Group has since dropped its slogan "24 hours a day, 365 days. Work till you die" and replaced it with "Work Is Life Itself." Miki Watanabe, out of the legislature and serving as Watami Group's chairman and president, made headlines after the

Covid-19 pandemic for his push to go high-tech at the pub chain and replace frail humans and their need for sleep with automated food-serving conveyor belts and robots.[91]

The family is still struggling to heal. Every month, they chant prayers for Mina's soul at their local temple. It took ten years after her death before they were able to talk about Mina's life and reminisce about happier times. I ask Yuko Mori what she wants people to take from her daughter's death and their continued fight.

"Before you lose your life, raise your voice. Don't put up with this," she says. Workers must understand how important their lives are, regardless of their paid work and the hours they put into it, and exercise their rights to protect themselves.

"Do you see that happening?"

"It's difficult. But you can't ever give up," she says. "That would be the end."

The Moris used the Watami settlement they received to set up a fund to help other overworked workers and their families sue companies and continue their fight against the karoshi culture. They named the fund *Nozomi*. Hope.

The hot sun begins to set over a standing-room-only crowd gathered in Hibiya Park's open-air amphitheater in Tokyo one summer evening in 2018. The three-thousand-some people, many holding colorful union banners or handmade signs—along with thousands of others on an oversize screen who had joined virtually from around the country—have come together to protest then prime minister Shinzo Abe's proposed law, which he claimed would "reform" the deadly overwork culture. The Japanese government insists the new law will cut work hours and promote healthy work-life balance and gender equity.[92] The protesters argue that the "work style reform," as it's called, will only make overwork worse and karoshi cases harder to prove, given that the law would only reduce the overtime cap to sixty hours a month for most workers. Abe's plan would also exempt whole categories of workers from any overtime regulation, including doctors, for five years so businesses could "prepare." Truck drivers, for instance, have the highest rates of karoshi illness and death claims of any profession, government statistics show.[93] They work 20 percent longer hours and earn 10 percent less than the average Japanese worker. The 2018 "reform" proposal would exclude them from restrictions on overtime until 2024, and then cap overtime at eighty hours a month, right at the deadly karoshi line.[94]

Protesters call it the Karoshi Promotion Bill.[95] I sit next to two Buddhist monks dressed in bright yellow robes and ask them why they've come. "Suffering," they answer. "When we see people suffering, we feel the need to break out of the shell of the temple and take action."

The crowd hushes as a group of karoshi victim families files onto the stage. That morning, the group had testified against the reform proposal at the Diet and had just come from an afternoon sit-in protest outside Abe's office across the street from the park. Standing shoulder to shoulder facing the restive crowd, the families solemnly hold oversize photographs of loved ones who died from working too much. They take their seats, the photographs still displayed before them. Throughout the evening politicians, labor lawyers, and others take to the microphone to denounce Abe's proposal. The families sit stoic, like watchful avenging angels, resolute in their mission for justice.[96]

The photographs on display confirm that overwork culture is ubiquitous in just about every profession, every industry, and potentially every job. The karoshi images at this protest and at others are of truck drivers, doctors, chefs, teachers, building maintenance supervisors. They are of people who overworked in broadcasting, in advertising, in manufacturing, in agriculture, and in the service industry, in pubs like Mina Mori's. The list goes on and on.[97] The government's annual karoshi white papers typically show that the industries with the most reported long hours and the most compensated karoshi cases are transportation and postal services.[98] Teachers are not far behind. By law, there are virtually no limits on the mostly unpaid overtime work demanded of teachers, who are expected to teach, clean, distribute lunch, and do other tasks, as well as run weekend and after-school sports and clubs.[99] One 2018 survey by the Organisation for Economic Co-operation and Development of forty-eight advanced countries found that junior high school teachers in Japan averaged the longest hours—their fifty-six-hour workweeks were nearly twenty hours longer than the average for all survey participants.[100]

In its white papers, the Japanese government reports that it compensates several hundred people every year who've filed karoshi claims. But, advocates say, that barely scratches the surface. Those are just the cases that families reported and managed to get through a hostile bureaucracy and court system. The law enables companies to apologize and pay families privately for a karoshi death to avoid giving workers' compensation, labor inspectors told me, "so the numbers are no doubt much bigger."

Also missing from the government statistics is the fact that, unlike the Moris, many families decide not to report a karoshi death, labor lawyers say, or they get beaten down by a system that makes it so difficult to prove that a death or suicide was caused by overwork that they give up. Some families are too ashamed to file a workers' compensation claim to classify a death or breakdown as karoshi, fearing that they and their loved ones would be stigmatized as troublemakers. Many people who shared their karoshi stories with me asked that I not use their names. The father of one young teacher said his daughter, like so many others in that overworked profession, routinely worked from early morning until 2:00 or 3:00 a.m. One night, he found her collapsed on the floor. She'd had a debilitating stroke. The family never filed a karoshi claim, though years later she still had difficulty walking, thinking, and speaking. Worried that his daughter would be seen as weak, as someone who couldn't hack the unforgiving work culture, he didn't want to damage her reputation and hurt her chances of getting another job. "I want to avoid making trouble for my daughter's future," he told me when he requested anonymity.

In recent years, in compliance with the 2014 law, the Japanese government has approved claims for as many as six hundred cases a year of what it classifies as "mental health disorders" caused by overwork. Fewer than one hundred of these cases result in death.[101] But for many, the burnout, depression, or collapse is so intense that they're forced to drop out of work, possibly for years. This is what happened to Fumiyoshi Shimizu, a young man I met a few days before the Hibiya Park protest. For years after he graduated from high school, Shimizu worked on temporary contracts at various jobs until the twenty-four-hour convenience store where he had a position offered him a promotion to a coveted permanent spot as a manager. Shimizu was elated. "I thought this would be a great start to my new career," he told me. He was twenty-five at the time. As a contract worker, he'd been paid for overtime—typically about one hundred hours a month, he said. As a manager, however, overtime was expected. Even with a boost to his base salary, he began working more unpaid overtime, sometimes as much as 180 hours a month. He was putting in more hours and earning less.

With a turnover rate as high as 95 percent in the retail industry and frequent staff shortages, Shimizu said he often had to fill in on the cash register, stock shelves, receive deliveries, and perform other tasks on top of his management duties. He found he was on call twenty-four hours a day, with about one day off a month. Some nights, he never went home. "It was endless." (He showed me the official time card the company filed with the government, which listed eight or nine hours a day, and his "real time card," showing far more.) He was unable to sleep and felt nauseated all the time. He knew something was wrong, but he had no time to go to the doctor. He asked his bosses—both of whom he said had recently been hospitalized for overwork-related stress injuries—to demote him. They said he'd be expected to do the same amount of work for less pay.

After about a year on this schedule, Shimizu was working the cash register around 9:00 p.m. one night. He found he could no longer speak. "I tried to say thank you. But my mouth wouldn't move. I thought, 'This is it.' That's when I went to the hospital," he said. He was diagnosed with depression and advised to take unpaid sick leave. Doctors said if he continued with his schedule, he'd be a karoshi victim. For the next five years, Shimizu was unable to work. He lived with his parents, slept as much as fifteen hours a day, and took four different medications to ease his depression, curb his suicidal thoughts, boost his appetite, and help him stay asleep.

During the course of his sick leave, Shimizu joined a union and sued the company for making him a "manager in name only"[102]—a common tactic that enables companies to squeeze more labor at a lower cost[103]—and won, receiving 1.4 million yen (about $9,800 in 2023) to compensate him for his unpaid overtime and the injuries it caused. He returned to his former employer on a reduced schedule recommended by his doctors: six hours a day, four days a week. When I met Shimizu, more than ten years had passed since his collapse. He still had trouble sleeping, despite still taking pills, but he was determined to change the Japanese work system—somehow—and was struggling to find a way to be happy. For its part, the company continually gave him negative performance reviews. "They say my contribution . . . is very low," Shimizu told me. "I only feel angry."

To combat the entrenched karoshi culture, karoshi fighters like Shimizu and the victims' families have only a few tools available. One is working with labor lawyers to file karoshi claims with the government and sue companies. Another and often more powerful tool is sharing their stories of pointless work dedication and senseless death, over and over, until their message begins to sink in and, they hope, people begin to demand change.

The karoshi victim families have now been sharing their stories for three decades—with the public, with the press, and while lobbying the government for shorter hours and better regulations. When they're not speaking out, they're often sitting together in the gallery of the Diet, stonily holding the oversize photographs of their loved ones and serving as a very visible reminder to the politicians below of the cost of their policies. The families have shown up en masse at hearings, at meetings, in courtrooms, and at public events, even virtually during the pandemic, to express solidarity with a karoshi victim's family's compensation claim or lawsuit against a company. The families share their experiences with researchers at karoshi conferences, talk to schools, and give speeches to anyone who will listen.

Hearing their stories helped draw Makoto Iwahashi to the movement. When he started college in 2010, he joined POSSE, a labor rights organization battling against the karoshi culture. I met him in Tokyo at an extremely polite protest against karoshi companies—protesters bowed to passersby and asked if they would kindly take one of their pamphlets. He isn't surprised by Japan's high rates of depression and suicide, particularly among young people,[104] because so many his age feel hopeless. The idea of working a reasonable day, finding love, starting a family, or owning a home feels so out of reach. Yet seeing others like himself stand up and demonstrate, however politely, allows him to think that maybe they *could* begin to imagine a better way of living. "That's all we hope for," he told me. "We just want a decent life."

As the Hibiya Park protest goes on into the night, a labor lawyer takes to the stage to denounce Shinzo Abe's reform proposal as "full of poison." In its slick marketing campaign, the Abe government insists that the work style reform would reduce work hours and the possibility of karoshi. While cloaked as a benefit to workers, in reality it's a business-friendly proposal that would set the overtime limit to an average of eighty hours a month—which the government already deemed as the untenable karoshi line—or one hundred hours if employers decide that's necessary. The penalties for breaking the law are, critics say, "tiny." The most overworked professions, such as transportation and the health sector, would be exempt from overtime regulations for several years. The legislation would also create a new category of "elite career track" white-collar workers for those making more than 10 million yen a year (about $71,000 in 2023), which would, according to the government, reward performance, not hours, and bring much-needed "flexibility" to the

Japanese way of work. Crucially, the proposal would exempt these workers from any overtime regulations, making it easier for companies to blame workers if they put in long hours.

Tellingly, the twenty-four-member council that devised these reforms included just *one* labor representative. "Basically, it was twenty-three to one in favor of employers," sociologist Scott North told me.[105] Nowhere does the reform call for a wholesale rethinking of tasks and work processes to focus on value, performance, and outcomes, which the most successful work redesigns and four-day workweek movements do.

It is this very system, of blaming people for overwork when there are no regulations prohibiting it and the culture of work demands it, that Noriko Nakahara maintains killed her husband. A pediatrician, he put in endless hours. Nakahara saw him begin to break down and begged him to stop, but he insisted it was his duty. Until, at age forty-four, he put on a new white doctor coat and jumped off the roof of his hospital building. Nakahara fought for eight years to have his death classified as karoshi, and had been telling his story for nearly twenty years by the time I meet her at the Hibiya Park protest. The proposed work style reform law would exempt highly paid elite workers, like her husband, from overtime regulations. "No matter where I go, I want to say the same thing: 'Why, if you get paid a certain amount of money, is it okay to die?'" she says. "There's nothing that will bring him back," she adds, weeping. "The only thing I can do is tell . . . everyone we can't keep working like this." Nakahara's daughter is a pediatrician also, so her fight is not just to avenge her husband but to save her daughter from the same system that's pushing her beyond human limits. "It's too late when someone dies."

As part of its promise to reform the Japanese work style, the government also pledged equal pay provisions to close the country's infamously large gender wage gap. But they left it up to employers to decide what constitutes equal pay and allowed for wage gaps as long as companies can give "rational reasons" for them.[106] This is hardly the robust fix needed to close the largest gender wage gap of the G7 countries and almost double the OECD average.[107]

At the time, Abe was selling the work style reform as part of his "Womenomics" drive to revitalize the country's stagnant economy and falling birth rate. To do that, he promised to help "women shine" by bringing more women into the workforce, setting ambitious targets to promote them into leadership, investing in family-supportive policies like child care, and fostering a recognition that both men and women have care responsibilities—the only way for women to "shine" in the workforce is to enforce reasonable work hours that enable men to share the unpaid work of home and care. In 2020 Abe resigned because of ill health[108] and in 2022 he was assassinated. By 2023, little had changed for women.[109] While their participation in the workforce rose for a time during Abe's tenure, it fell dramatically during the pandemic, particularly for those with care responsibilities.[110]

Although Japan boasts one of the most generous paid parental leave policies in the world, particularly for men, less than 15 percent of eligible fathers used it in 2021—a far cry from the 50 percent target the government set for 2025.[111] This means that women are still shouldering the bulk of the unpaid work of care and home. And because they are disproportionately employed as nonregular and temporary workers, fewer women than men had access to the potentially life-changing ability to telework during the pandemic, labor economist Machiko Osawa reported. Also, as nonregular workers, many women don't qualify for the family-supportive benefits the government touts.[112] Both Osawa and social demographer Setsuya Fukuda blame the absence of progress squarely on Japan's culture of long work hours. "That hasn't changed much," Fukuda told me. "At the same time, the government is asking women to work more."

When Japan adopted its Equal Employment Opportunity Law in 1985,[113] leaders said that if women wanted to work for pay outside the home, they would have to work just like men.[114] For all the lip service to gender equality, the refusal to meaningfully regulate, legislate, and change the overwork culture, far from ensuring Japan's economic success or addressing its low birth rate, or enabling women to "shine," simply makes it possible for women, too, to work to the point of death.

As the Hibiya Park protest draws to a close, I turn to find translator Chie Matsumoto weeping, overcome by the weight of the human misery presented onstage. She introduces me to a longtime union organizer. I ask him what keeps him going in what feels like such a losing fight. He gives me a sharp look. "I imagine it's how you feel in the United States with your gun laws after another mass shooting," he says.

In June 2018, not long after the Hibiya Park protest, the Japanese government passed the new work style reform into law.[115]

In the years since the legislation passed, labor lawyers like Yoshimasa Obayashi say no real dent has been made in overwork culture. Although the law required more mandatory days off, it's unclear whether people are using them, he said, or if the data is being cooked. Though work hours do appear to be dropping, Obayashi and activists like Makoto Iwahashi are unsure whether the reporting can be trusted, or if it reflects the fact that more people are being hired on part-time contracts. As expected, Obayashi says that the law has made it harder to prove that someone was obliged to work long hours and thus get a karoshi workers' compensation case certified by the government. A 2022 Tokyo High Court ruling gives employers the right not to cooperate with families seeking to prove karoshi claims, he said, and to dispute any karoshi certification. "I'd have to say the law is causing more karoshi," he said. "The number of applications for workers' compensation continues to rise."

It's nearing 8:00 p.m. and the Toranomon Hills Café is beginning to fill with exhausted Japanese workers eager to explore a different way of toiling for their daily bread. They've come to the weekly Thursday gathering organized by the Tokyo branch of the Venture Café, a global nonprofit network that seeks to boost entrepreneurship, innovative start-ups, and more viable small business ownership through education and networking sessions.

Neoliberals like Margaret Thatcher and Ronald Reagan, who were intent on dismantling the way governments had historically promoted equity through policies, legislation, litigation, and regulation for the benefit of all, hailed entrepreneurship as the ultimate expression of freedom and the most lucrative way for societies to organize themselves.[116] Despite besotted policymakers' and the business community's obsession with it, entrepreneurship has a dark side: most start-ups and small businesses fail. Entrepreneurs take on intense personal risk, especially in countries without a functioning safety net, and crushing debt.[117] A majority suffer mental health consequences from the stress.[118] Success relies on the power and prestige of the networks you belong to, which favor those who also succeed in corporate monoculture: men. In the United States, white men.[119] Yet entrepreneurship appeals to some as a way out of intractable overwork culture, or even a lifeline. That's at least the argument I hear again and again at the Thursday gathering of hopeful workers at the Venture Café.

A woman who gives her name as Kana says she's tired of taking the first train to work and the last train home, never seeing her husband, working weekends, and getting four to five hours of sleep a night. "I fell asleep in the bathtub and woke up because it was cold," she confides. "I could've died. Been my own karoshi story." She'd come that evening with her friend, Rino, who also asked that I use only her first name. Rino had been out of a job for three months because she'd been so overworked and depressed that she was sick and her menstrual cycle never stopped. "I was constantly bleeding," she says. They wanted to see if there could be a different way to work and live in Japan.

Ryusuke Komura, the young project director for the Venture Café who greets them at the door, is living proof that there is.

From an early age, Komura was groomed for the Japanese "one path":[120] study for long hours, especially in junior high and at intensive after-school cram programs; get into the right high school; pass the university entrance exam; and get into an elite university. Then, in the spring before graduation, secure the right offer of a permanent lifetime job from a top-tier company during *shūkatsu*, the high-pressure job-hunting season,[121] and prepare for a lifetime of overwork.

Komura, who grew up in Osaka and studied in Kyoto and England during his college years, had his heart set on a lifetime position with a top Japanese advertising agency, knowing that it would mean working long hours. When the offer failed to materialize, he was devastated. He took a job at a large multinational IT company that he considered second tier. "I felt like a failure," he admitted. Once he started working, that feeling only intensified. "In Japan, we never get to learn how to set a goal for ourselves. We're never asked, 'What do *you* want to do?' or 'What's your dream?' The goal is already set, and all you have to do is just get there."

The terms of his employment, as with most corporate jobs in Japan, weren't well defined.[122] So Komura, like many corporate employees, didn't really know how much work was enough or when he should be done for the day. With so much ambiguity, there was no way to tell. And because the Japanese corporate monoculture also values strict hierarchy, no one is supposed to leave before the boss does or take time off unless the boss does.[123] Sometimes Komura stayed for twenty-four or forty-eight consecutive hours at his desk. One young worker I spoke to complained of routinely standing at the copy machine at 11:00 p.m. making blank copies because he had nothing to do, but he couldn't go home until his manager did and he needed to look productive. Komura recalled days of, essentially, busywork—going back and forth with his boss, quibbling over the placement of punctuation to make sure that a PowerPoint presentation was perfect. And then when the boss did finally decide to call it a day, everyone was expected to go out for a night of *nomikai*, excessive drinking. No one questioned the process, but Komura was burned out and miserable.

Hitotsubashi University Business School professor Hiroshi Ono said that Komura's first corporate job experience is common. The long work hours and low productivity are due to what he calls "waste": processes or expectations that eat up a lot of time but yield nothing of value—like the after-hours *nomikai* drinking culture, or long commutes for in-person work and the expectation, despite advances in technology, that work must be transacted in person, on paper, and carefully approved with bureaucratic layer after layer of fussy official *hanko* stamps.[124] "The first step toward higher productivity is to eliminate waste," Ono told me.

Haruno Yoshida, the first female president of BT Japan Corporation and the first woman to serve as vice chair of the Keidanren, Japan's powerful business lobby, had been trying to make this point, unsuccessfully, for years. I met Yoshida, a divorced single mother who had been pushing for telework and flexible work options as alternatives to the overwork culture, in 2018. With her designer pantsuit, long nails, and stiletto heels, Yoshida was as elegant as she was clear-eyed about the problems with Japan's overwork culture and its exacerbation of gender inequality. In straight-talking American-accented speech, laced freely with expert and pointed cursing, Yoshida complained about the endemic waste and stupid work.

"It's like we're using carrier pigeons instead of email. I mean, we're still using fax machines!"[125] she railed. "We refuse to use voicemail. Why? I don't know, maybe because people think it's rude not to answer the phone. But unless we get technology right," she went on, "unless we adopt telework, work from home, flexible, agile work, we can't have gender equality and work-life balance." For instance, it took until early 2024 for the Japanese government to finally agree to waive the requirement that documents be submitted on floppy disks—which haven't been manufactured since 2011—and even that change did not come without fierce resistance.[126]

Yoshida had harsh words for the performance of work, and what Ono and sociologists call "impression management"—the rewards that primarily male workers receive from just being physically present for long hours.[127] "Your contribution shouldn't be measured in sweat. It shouldn't be measured in tears," Yoshida went on. "It should be measured in numbers. In your performance." Yet like most humans wired to conform to our external environments, Yoshida acknowledged that she too was caught up in the overwork culture she sought to change. In 2019, at the age of fifty-five, she died of a heart attack.[128]

Even the Ministry of Labor inspectors I met, who are supposed to enforce shorter hours, are themselves caught up in overwork. Sometimes they stayed at their desks through the night, mainly answering the flurry of questions lawmakers send for ministers to answer at heavily scripted hearings. "We heard there were cots at the Agriculture Ministry. But we just sleep at our desks," one inspector told me. "My life's not so . . ." he paused, ". . . high quality." During the 2018 debate over the work style reforms, the inspectors logged up to three hundred hours of overtime every month, the inspectors said. When translator Chie Matsumoto and I left our interview at 6:00 p.m. one evening, everyone stood up to bow and then sat back down to work. As we passed rows and rows of paper time cards, Matsumoto lifted up one after another: each had a little red *hanko* stamp that signified working through the night.

It's not just office work that is inefficient and wasteful. Waste explains why Japanese truck drivers are so overworked and at such high risk of karoshi: Package sizes aren't standardized, so truckers themselves often have to load and unload cargo by hand, unable to use forklifts at loading docks. That causes huge backups, with long lines of truckers waiting hours to do the same. Hours for which they receive no pay.[129]

This is the fate that Ryusuke Komura wanted to escape. He quit his corporate job, got his MBA in the United States, and began working on his own terms as a consultant to an education start-up, teaching entrepreneurship at a university and working for the nonprofit Venture Café to promote entrepreneurial culture in Japan. Komura teleworks from his home office most days and helps his wife, a nurse working part-time, take care of their young son, often taking virtual meetings with the child on his lap. Unless it's a Thursday Venture Café gathering, he and his family have dinner together every night. "I'm in a situation where I can control my schedule," he said. "I'm pretty happy."

Komura's is an encouraging story of one. Tetsuya Ando is trying to change the story for millions. Ando is the founder of Fathering Japan, a nonprofit that has been working since 2006 to change Japan's karoshi culture and entrenched gender norms by encouraging men to take paid parental leave and become engaged caregivers. Since the early 1990s, Japan has had one of the most robust paid paternity leave policies in the world—up to a full year of paid leave at a generous level of salary replacement.[130] But men have rarely taken advantage of it. Even Ando, when he became a new father in 1997, was discouraged from using it. "My manager told me that if I was absent from work, I'd be shirking my responsibility and the work would suffer," he told me.

Ando didn't accept this. His role model was not his Japanese bosses or his own absent father but John Lennon, he said, who stepped back from his wildly successful music career to care for his newborn son Sean. Ando's paid leave with his daughter was life-changing. "My identity as a father clicked in. I did household chores. I read to her all the time. My love for her grew so much that I wanted to see her every minute of every day." Once he and his wife went back to work, he was often the only father at child-care pickup. He started to come home from work earlier and earlier just to be with her and took time off work when she got sick. "My boss kept saying, 'Why doesn't your wife do it?'" he recounted. "I got so frustrated. In Japan, men are supposed to live for work. But I wanted an identity as a man who cherishes work and also enjoys time with his family."

That's what led him to found Fathering Japan. What began as a small effort to bring like-minded men together to support one another has since grown into a cultural phenomenon. The group offers training and networking opportunities to support men willing to buck Japan's ideal worker culture to become caregivers. Ando and other Fathering Japan members speak to hundreds of organizations each year to raise awareness that cultural norms can and are changing. The organization has also expanded into the corporate sphere, with an *iku-boss* alliance (an iku-boss is a manager with an understanding of care responsibilities) and trainings and workshops to help companies promote work-life balance, reasonable work hours, and women's success at work. It also encourages men to take paid caregiving leave. Ando awards certificates and publicizes companies' efforts to raise awareness and spur more businesses to follow suit. In 2024, more than 270 organizations had joined Ando's alliance and took part in regular meetings to share successes and best practices.

Ando was particularly heartened by alliance members such as Sekisui House Ltd., one of the country's largest homebuilders. During a business trip to Sweden, the company's president was shocked to see so many caregiving fathers and decided to foster the same culture in his own company. Sekisui House joined Ando's alliance, brought him in for annual panels and workshops, began encouraging men to take leave, and included men's and women's ability to take paid leave in managers' performance evaluations. By 2023, 100 percent of the company's new fathers took at least one month of paid parental leave, a tenfold increase in five years, with no reduction in productivity. "That's the beginning of gender equality," Ando said.

Japan has a long way to go, Ando acknowledged. The Japanese government strengthened paternity leave laws in 2020 to make it easier for men to take it and to force large companies to publicize take-up rates. That helped boost rates from a meager 5 percent in 2018 to 17 percent in 2022.[131] The government, worried about declining fertility rates and spurred by research showing that overwhelmed women are more likely to want additional children when partners take parental leave, is aiming for a target of 85 percent by 2030.[132]

Ando said that the government and Japanese companies are finally waking up to the fact that both parents need to work and that more want to share paid work and unpaid care fairly. Change of that magnitude will take time. While transforming legislation is paramount, so too, he maintained, are everyday actions.

"When fathers change, families change. Then communities change, then companies change, then society changes," Ando said. "It may seem small, but I tell men that when they do the diapers or drop their children off at school, when they show others, every day, that there is joy in fathering, these are the things that transform society."

CHAPTER 8

SHORT WORK HOURS FOR ALL IN ICELAND

> The objective of this Act is to prevent discrimination on the basis of gender and to maintain gender equality and equal opportunities for the genders in all spheres of society. All people shall have equal opportunities to benefit from their own enterprise and to develop their skills irrespective of gender.
>
> —*Iceland's 2020 Act on Equal Status and Equal Rights Irrespective of Gender*[1]

It's nearly dusk by 2:00 p.m. on a Friday in mid-December when I meet Trausti Jónsson in front of the sleek concrete-and-glass Reykjavík City Hall building. The wan Icelandic winter light reflecting off the nearby Tjörnin Pond is already fading in the far northern latitude that offers, at most, five hours of daylight at this time of year. Although the heavy blanket of winter darkness and cold has been associated with Iceland's high rates of depression and antidepressant use,[2] Jónsson is in high spirits. Today is his short workday, when the fifty-five-year-old single father is on the job from 8:00 a.m. to noon. By midday, he's met his contractual obligation to work the thirty-six-hour week his union negotiated with the city a few years before, down from forty hours with no reduction in pay. Jónsson looks forward to Fridays all week. He calls it his "sacred" day. The four fewer hours of work mean four more hours with his three children: his sons Bjartur, eight, and Breki, three, and his twenty-six-year-old daughter, Bryndís.

On this particular Friday, Jónsson has already spent two hours after work running errands, shopping for groceries, and finishing preparations for the weekend. These are things he used to do in the evenings with his young children in tow, racing to pick them up from child-care and after-care programs before they closed. It's not that it wasn't possible, he explains, but it was stressful. He was exhausted after a long and often physically and emotionally draining forty-hour-plus workweek as a project manager for city youth prevention programs. So were his children, tired and cranky after their own long days. He felt the schlepping wasn't fair to them, and it didn't bring out the best in any of the family. They all just wanted to be home.

Now, shopping bags filled to the brim in the trunk of his car and his to-do list clear, Jónsson can do just that—be with his children at home. He has all the fixings to make pizza with them tonight, and he's stocked up on the ingredients to bake his grandmother's traditional holiday brown cake, or Brúnterta, this weekend. Wearing jeans and a thick wool sweater under a heavy black ski jacket, Jónsson reflects on this moment with satisfaction: his paid work is done for the week, the unpaid housework is under control. He's eager to begin the weekend solely focused on relaxing and having fun going to the woods with his family to find the perfect Christmas tree. "This time is a gift," he says of his shorter workweek. "People say it's all about the quality of time you spend with your children that counts, not the quantity. But it's both. Being together, it bonds us."

We hop in his car and, headlights on in the darkening afternoon, and make our way through traffic first to Breki's preschool. "He can stay until four fifteen or four thirty, but I don't want him there that long," Jónsson says. Even on regular workdays, Jónsson tries to get Breki by 3:30 at the latest. Sometimes, he'll pick him up earlier, just after naptime at 2:30, then take him back to work with him. "He really loves that." Bjartur, true to the burgeoning independence of an eight-year-old, often asks to stay longer at his after-school program to play with friends. Jónsson shares custody of the boys with two of his exes (his three children have three different mothers). The boys live with him every other week. So, on the weeks when they're with their mothers, Jónsson puts in longer hours at work. That way, he can be sure to work less during the weeks when the boys are with him.

"I make clear to everyone that, number one, I'm a dad. Number two come my friends. Then number three or four, I work for Reykjavík city," he says. "People know that my sacred time is with my kids." So much so that he finds himself quietly pining at times for the height of the pandemic lockdowns, when he and his boys, his daughter, and various family members were quarantining together in his small apartment. "I don't say it out loud, but I really loved those times," he says wistfully.

At the preschool, where Jónsson serves on the board now that he has the time, the windows are steaming from the heat of little bodies toddling in after playing outside in the cold. Breki rushes toward Jónsson and burrows into him, wrapping his tiny arms around his father's legs. As Jónsson bundles the child into a snowsuit, wrestling mittens onto his hands, tugging a woolen hat to sit snugly just above the child's eyes, and fitting his feet into tiny camo-patterned snow boots, Jónsson counts three other fathers and one mother at pickup, all here earlier than in previous years because a majority of workers in Iceland now have a shorter workweek.

A quick stop to pick up a reluctant Bjartur and the family is home. Bjartur helps carry the bags of groceries into Jónsson's apartment, picking his way past the row of shoes, boots, and bikes, electric and otherwise, stacked in the small hall near the front door, and stepping over the puzzles, paint easel, red ukulele, and various toys and trucks stacked on shelves and strewn about the floor. As Breki pounds on an electric piano, Jónsson pulls out the marinara sauce he'd made the night before and he and Bjartur begin working on the pizza dough. Daughter Bryndís, who lives fifteen minutes away by bike, shows up, as she often does. "I'm twenty-six and I'm still coming to dinner with my dad as much as I can," she says laughing.

Bryndís explains that she's always been close to her father—he's the one who cooked every night when she was a child, came to all her handball tournaments, and bought her her first pair of high heels as a teen. But there's something special happening, she says, now that he's working fewer hours. She sees how he's able to give more attention to each of his children. He takes the boys to football practice, theater, and painting lessons without feeling rushed, and he also has time—and energy—to help her study for her university classes, talk about her future, or just hang out. As the pizza cooks, Bjartur begins setting the small table in the kitchen nook, the walls decorated with brightly colored children's drawings. The eight-year-old remembers how everyone used to be so tired and stressed by Friday evening that they could barely do more than order takeout and plop in front of the TV. "I like it when he picks me up earlier," he says shyly of the sacred short workdays. "He's less tired. More fun to be around."

Jónsson pours everyone a glass of Malt og Appelsín, an Icelandic soda pop that combines malt and orangeade, a winter holiday treat, and the family sits down to share the pizza they've made together. "I love cheeeeeeese!" Breki says loudly in English, demanding another slice. When the laughter dies down, Jónsson sighs, a smile still on his lips. Outside, a light rain begins to fall and the festive white twinkle lights that festoon the windows and doors of the houses in his neighborhood shimmer in the wet darkness. It is a small moment. A simple, ordinary evening with his family on a Friday in winter. The kind, Jónsson thinks, that add up to a life well lived. "I love this time."

■

Jónsson's short workweek is available through union contracts that cover most workers in Iceland and is embraced by employees and many employers alike. His idyllic Friday evening with family is exactly what the architects of Iceland's short workweek were hoping for. The reduced hours are intended to reduce stress and burnout, improve health and wellbeing, and encourage the use of technology to do smarter, more productive work in less time. But the change is also aimed at gender equality and ensuring that *everyone* benefits from a better quality of life. The shorter week was designed as a nudge to men like Jónsson to spend fewer hours at paid work and more time at home doing unpaid housework and caring for children and family.

"This was always from the beginning a gender equality issue," Elín Oddný Sigurðardóttir told me one morning over coffee near her City Hall office. Sigurðardóttir, a social scientist and Left-Green Movement socialist, was an elected member of the Reykjavík City Council and part of the task force overseeing and analyzing the data from the city's pilot programs experimenting with shorter working hours that ran from 2015 to 2019. The national government began its own short work hours pilot in 2017. The overwhelmingly positive results from the pilots—improved productivity, less stress and burnout, more gender equity, better health and quality of life[3]—led to the widespread adoption of short work hours in labor agreements in 2019 and 2020 with trade unions that represent about 86 percent of the country's about two hundred thousand workforce, including blue- and white-collar workers.

The policies are designed to give organizations, leaders, managers, teams, and employees the autonomy to figure out how to shorten and streamline work processes for themselves. There are no grand fiats issued from on high or any one-size-fits-all mandates. Managers and workers are expected to do the hard task of figuring out the actual work they need to do and to experiment with different ways to make sure it's done and done well in thirty-five or thirty-six hours a week. Some people work shorter days, shaving off about forty-eight minutes to an hour every day. Some choose a short four-hour schedule on Fridays. Others prefer different days of the week for their short four-hour day or choose to take a full eight-hour day off every other week.

Iceland already had a reputation as a leader in gender equality, with long paid parental leaves and high women's labor force participation, Sigurðardóttir said. But under the surface, women are still doing more housework and caregiving. "It was apparent that it was mostly women cutting down their work hours in order to manage it," she said. She acknowledged that "there were concerns that a shorter workweek would just increase the time guys have to do something else, like go to the gym, and women would continue doing all the care. But one of the changes seems to be that men are taking up a bigger role in family life."

Coming home from paid work to the unpaid "second shift" of housework and caregiving is an idea that groundbreaking sociologist Arlie Hochschild introduced in her 1989 book of the same name. And although men have since increased the time they spend doing housework and child care, the second shift is still largely borne by women. Around the world, women spend two to ten times more hours than men doing the unpaid work of taking care of the home and children.[4]

And women still shoulder most of the unpaid and invisible mental labor of organizing and keeping track of family logistics—planning birthday parties, organizing children's activities and family trips, creating the holiday magic—and doing the emotional work that keeps families, friendships, and communities happy, functioning, and connected. It's exhausting, unsustainable, and unfair, and it happens everywhere. In Iceland, they call this mental labor the "third shift."

I wanted to come to Iceland to see whether a shorter workweek does improve productivity and wellbeing and ultimately pay for itself—arguments that advocates in the short work hours movement make. But I also wanted to see whether radically changing the way work is done and reducing the hours people are expected to do it—without cutting pay—makes a difference to gender equality, care, and quality of life. If men and women began to more equally spend time on paid and unpaid work, could the country close stubborn gender wage, power, promotion, and wealth gaps? And if shorter work hours combined with decent pay were made available to all kinds of workers—those on shifts, providing care, in factories, on front desks, in hospitals and schools—could the country create equitable conditions for everyone to live a good life? Could this lead to the fairer, more humane future I'd been searching for? If so, what would that look like and how would it *feel*?

Iceland isn't perfect, as critics gleefully point out.[5] And the United States is not and will never be Iceland. *I know that.* In sheer geographic and population size, much less diversity of people, divided politics, and complicated history, there is no comparison. But that's not the point of the investigation. I wondered if there were lessons to be drawn from the process of change, as well as the outcome.

To be fair, the global short work hours movement is an exciting and long-overdue development, with a growing body of research that shows reduced hours are often better for both workers' lives and for business productivity and profitability.[6] Experiments are already underway or planned in companies or public positions in a number of countries, including the United States, Canada, the UK, Scotland, Wales, Belgium, Spain, Sweden, and New Zealand.[7] Workers no longer toil on a factory assembly line, where the forty-hour week was piloted as an experiment in the 1920s.[8] So it is indeed long past time to declare that Monday through Friday, nine to five, is a relic of the past, and find something that works for twenty-first-century labor, care, and life.

All movements have to start somewhere. But I'd been getting increasingly annoyed by the short work hour movement's focus on companies that employ highly educated, white-collar workers, and in sectors where the majority of them are men. Clearly, these workers are often overworked and burned out. But they also have resources, education, choices, and a measure of agency to change jobs or professions. Largely absent from the conversation, just as they were from Covid-19-era return-to-office handwringing, are non–college educated, blue-collar manufacturing or construction workers, or people in low-wage retail, service, health, and care jobs, who make up such a large part of the workforce in the United States and elsewhere.[9]

Those who tend to have less education and fewer options are also more likely to be women and women of color.[10] Many of them in fact struggle to get *enough* hours or *enough* pay to make a decent living,[11] or they have no choice but to scrape by on poorly paid part-time or precarious gig work because of their care duties.[12]

I was worried that, rather than closing gaps and making life better for everyone, a short work hours movement focused on the most privileged could widen them. The world of work is already deeply segregated.[13] By gender, by race, by education. Just about in any way that we slice the data, men, white men in particular, always make more money.[14] In nearly every instance, men make more than women in the same profession, with the same background, years of experience, and education.[15] Men make more than women at every level of education.[16]

So imagine: Highly paid white-collar professionals, the majority of whom are men, begin to enjoy shorter work hours with no reduction in their handsome pay. They have sufficient income to enjoy stable lives and more leisure time and a higher quality of life. Maybe, like Jónsson, they become more active in their families' lives and more fairly share care and household work, which may help gender equality in the homes of the privileged. But if service workers are left out of the movement for shorter work hours for the same pay, then women in poorly paid hourly service or care jobs would be left to continue struggling with the chaos of paid work and heavy unpaid caregiving duties. Where would their time for leisure and ease be?

It was a concern Sigurðardóttir and the other short work hours architects sought to address from the outset. "We wanted short work hours not just in office settings," Sigurðardóttir said, "but also for shift workers, cleaners, people working with the elderly." In perhaps one of the most consequential outcomes, more women, who had been classified as working part-time at thirty-six hours, are now considered full-time employees. Many women working part-time chose to increase their hours each week to bring them up to thirty-six hours and full-time status.

That means they will make more money, receive better benefits, and, in the long run, have higher retirement pensions and greater financial independence. "Some women work slightly more now, but the satisfaction for everyone is quite high," explained Sigurðardóttir, who left office in 2022 and works for the city. "I don't think anyone would want to go back."

▬

The short work hours experiment got its start in 1998 when a new mother was shocked by her increased productivity working shorter hours after her maternity leave. Drífa Snædal, a self-described idealist, had been working as a technical assistant and had just had her first child. When she returned to the job after her paid maternity leave, she changed fields and negotiated an 80 percent workload for the same salary as her previous full-time position. "I had never been more productive," she said. That planted the idea that people could be more effective working fewer hours without a reduction in pay, and this could be wholly positive for businesses and workers. In 2010, Snædal moved with her daughter to Sweden for a few years to study for her master's degree in industrial relations.

A few years later, Sweden began experimenting with short work hours pilots in cities like Gothenburg, paying workers a full-time eight-hour-day wage for six hours. A Swedish Toyota service center had already adopted a six-hour day in 2002[17] with positive results, as had other Swedish municipalities, including the northern mining town of Kiruna.[18] Snædal said she "stumbled" on research and stories about how workers were happier, healthier, and more productive. She began to wonder if this would work in Iceland, which, though a Nordic country, is very different from the other Nordics. It relies on fishing, tourism, and aluminum to survive. She did what any Icelander who knows just about every other Icelander in the small country would do—she called a friend to share the data. Only this friend, Sóley Tómasdóttir, was a member of the Reykjavík City Council. The two of them then wrote up a short workweek pilot project proposal for the city, and its leaders decided to give it a try.

At the time, workers in Iceland logged far more hours on the job than in other Nordic countries, and, more like workers in the United States, they bought into a culture of overwork rather than time for care and life. "We are an old fishing society. We have a strong culture, a very strong moral, of hard work. We identify with the work we do," Snædal explained. "In the olden days, when there was enough fish, then everybody was mandated to work, even the children. I knew that if we were going to be successful, this would require a big cultural and generational shift."

On her return to Iceland, Snædal, always politically active, began to work for trade unions and launched an often lonely, yearslong effort to agitate to include demands for shorter work hours in their negotiated agreements. At first, her arguments fell on deaf ears. Union leaders were far more focused on raising wages than on shortening work hours. Skeptics and outright opponents seized on the fact that the Swedish city of Gothenburg, one of her inspirations, had wound up discontinuing its short work hours pilots. The Gothenburg pilot had been tried in a public care home. Studies found that the nurses working shorter hours were happier, healthier, more engaged, and more productive, and the quality of care improved, with nurses planning more and varied activities. But the city saw that shaving a few hours off already understaffed nurses' schedules meant that it had to hire more nurses. So the pilot appeared to cost more money. Conservatives on Gothenburg's city council attacked the pilots as a costly waste of taxpayer money.

But the city failed to look at the situation with a wider lens, taking into consideration the past and projecting farther into the future. The public care homes in Sweden, like nursing homes, hospitals, and other health and care facilities around the world, were already severely understaffed after years of cutting labor budgets in the name of "efficiency" in the public sector, and, in the private sector, in order to eke out more short-term profits. So the city had saved money by paying fewer people—namely women—and expecting them to overwork for years. This shortsighted approach, which is standard in a number of countries, including the United

States, has led to an epidemic of nurse, care, and health professional overwork and burnout around the globe.[19] What the Gothenburg conservatives missed was the fact that healthier, more productive care workers, earning good wages and staying in their jobs, would mean fewer burned-out people quitting, who might also need to rely on public benefits to survive.

Additionally, a healthier, happier care workforce means healthier, better-cared-for patients who may need less expensive support as a result. And more workers earning enough to buy the goods and services that others produce is what makes an economy healthy and growing. A stable middle class, not a handful of the 1 percent, are the real job creators in any economy.[20] The Toyota plant in Sweden was also forced to hire additional workers when it moved to its six-hour workday. But leaders found that that cost of additional labor was more than offset by the increased productivity, sales, and the company's greater profits.[21] Toyota and others participating in short work hours pilots also reported lower worker turnover, with a happier and more satisfied workforce, and so saved on rehiring and retraining, a benefit that's often invisible on typical business profit and loss balance sheets.

Snædal persisted—another key element in any change movement. By this time, she had been joined by another persistent fighter for short work hours, Sonja Thorbergsdóttir, a lawyer, single mother, and president of BSRB, the Icelandic Federation of State and Municipal Employees. It's the country's largest public-sector union, with more than twenty-four thousand members in 2023, the majority of whom are women. One-third of the women in the workforce worked part-time because of their heavier care responsibilities, Thorbergsdóttir explained. "If we wanted to reach full gender equality, we knew we had to do something about part-time jobs."

In 2014, the Pirate Party, which had formed in the wake of the 2008 economic collapse, entered into the short work hours fray and introduced a bill to cut the workweek to thirty-five hours. Critics shut down debate saying the bill would lead to hyperinflation.

Thorbergsdóttir's union and others spent hours researching this and other "scaremongering" campaigns, as she called them, and published reports methodically poking holes in the critiques. Unlike the United States, which legalized the forty-hour workweek standard in the 1938 Fair Labor Standards Act, Iceland didn't adopt it until 1971, though it would take until 2002 for actual workweeks to drop to forty hours.[22] There was indeed a period of high inflation, not just in Iceland but around the globe in the 1970s, but Thorbergsdóttir's research showed that the inflationary pressures that kicked in in the late 1960s and early 1970s had everything to do with the collapse of the herring fishery, not shorter work hours.

Their counterattack proved effective. When the city of Reykjavík began to roll out a handful of short work hours pilots for city employees in 2015, both Snædal and Thorbergsdóttir were on the steering committees overseeing them. Snædal ultimately took over leadership of the largest network of trade unions, the Icelandic Confederation of Labor, in 2018, and used her position to ensure that short work hours became part of regular union negotiations. After a ten-year fight, short work hours became standard in the labor contracts that cover the majority of the country's workforce. The long-awaited culture shift both women foresaw was underway.

Some industries, like hospitals and public health, did have to hire more workers to cover the extra shifts, and some workers complained that the shorter hours siphoned off time for lunch and breaks during the day. But the overall results gave Snædal and Thorbergsdóttir hope. The data confirmed that workers' wellbeing and stress levels improved, compared to a control group working a typical forty-hour week. Those in the pilots reported having more energy for exercise and time for friends, family, and hobbies, and that their higher energy had a positive impact on attitudes and productivity at work. They also felt more supported by their colleagues, that their managers were more encouraging and fair, that there was less confusion about people's roles, and that they had more control over the pace of their work. "It is like a gift from the heavens," one participant reported.[23]

Workers in the pilots noted less conflict between work and home than those in the control group, and more quality time and less stress with family, especially among shift workers and single parents. They spent less time in traffic and were able to volunteer and participate in civic life. "We were quite surprised to see that the older generation was just as happy as the younger one," Thorbergsdóttir told me. "Older workers used the free time to pick up their grandkids from preschool, drive them to sports, and take up long-forgotten hobbies." And as she had foreseen, paid work hours began to even out between men and women, the first step to closing gender wage gaps. True to the original intent, more men, like Jónsson, were taking on bigger roles or feeling less stress about doing the unpaid work of cooking, cleaning, running errands, and providing care to children or other family members.[24]

Gradually, a new narrative of good, hard work began to emerge, one that emphasizes how changing work processes to work effectively creates more time and space for life, replacing the old story of punishing overwork as the way to prove one's worth and identity.

Snædal and Thorbergsdóttir were not the only dogged idealists with a vision to change the country's work culture. As they organized within the union movement to help workers demand shorter hours without losing pay, and to help them believe they could do their work in less time, Gudmundur Haraldsson, a software developer, was getting restless about his own overwork patterns. "I just felt stuck at work, not able to have any serious hobbies or side projects. I felt frustrated. I was seeing people really stressed and also stuck. This is the twenty-first century, when we have so much technology to help us do our work, yet we still have all these long hours."

I meet Haraldsson one evening at Hressingarskálinn, a traditional Icelandic coffeehouse near the center of town. Haraldsson's own exhaustion and frustration with the culture of long work hours coincided with the global financial meltdown in 2008 and the banking collapse that bankrupted the country. The catastrophe broke people's trust in the old system, which cleared the way for them to create something new. "I started seeing all these companies going bankrupt, and yet we didn't see any change in living standards to speak of. I began to think, is all of this work really necessary?" Haraldsson explains. He began to imagine what the country would look like if people worked shorter hours but could still maintain a good standard of living. "I realized that we seem to be inventing a lot of work to just maintain a model that was essentially not providing quality of life."

He joined the Icelandic think tank Alda, the Association for Sustainable Democracy, and began, in his spare time, researching shorter paid work hours. Like Snædal's experience, his first research brief, compiled in 2012 and sent to media outlets, political parties, and employers with the power to make change, fell on deaf ears. "The response was nil," he tells me. But as Haraldsson persisted, trying to drum up attention, attitudes to shorter work hours were changing.

Haraldsson carefully compiled the data from the short work hours pilots and pulled it all into one report. He wanted to make sure the results were translated into English and shared widely, so he and Alda partnered with Autonomy, a UK-based progressive research organization focused on shorter work hours and the future of work. They published a report in the summer of 2021 that reverberated in the media around the world. A host of international writers gushed that Iceland had somehow managed to cut hours without reducing pay and remained just as productive while improving gender equality, health, happiness, and wellbeing.[25] It seemed too good to be true. "The pilots really had a huge impact on people's lives," Haraldsson says as he drains the last of his tea. "It was amazing what having just sixteen more hours a month can mean to people."

What I wanted to know was *how*. How exactly did they accomplish this change? With my own workaholic tendencies, and shaped by the American overwork environment, I was skeptical. Can you really cut your paid work hours and still get your work done, and done well? If it's possible, as someone who struggles to keep paid work from spilling into every hour, stray thought, and corner of life, I wanted to understand the strategies that turn a good idea into an everyday reality.

Over a lunch of global tacos at a funky restaurant called Punk, I meet with the two people probably most responsible for making short work hours succeed in Iceland: Aldís Magnúsdóttir, who serves as head of the personnel policy department at the government's Ministry of Finance and Economic Affairs, and union leader Sonja Thorbergsdóttir. Once the shorter work hours with no reduction in pay standard was enshrined in trade union agreements, the two women began the hard task of figuring out how to make it happen. It felt impossible at first. Different unions wanted different things. Various governmental departments had conflicting ideas.

So Thorbergsdóttir and Magnúsdóttir put together a small working group of experts, mediators, and project managers to draw on the research, "get all the cats in line," as they described it, and then find consensus. This was particularly important when it came to shift workers, who tend to live shorter, sicker, more sleep-deprived lives than others.[26] Many old-timers didn't believe shift workers could operate differently or were simply resistant to the idea that anything about paid work could or should change. The first thought the working group had was to reframe the movement: It wasn't short working hours that they were pushing for. It was, they said, about improving effectiveness. They dubbed their project the Better Work Week. "We were saying, we need to think differently about how to design work and organize the workday," Magnúsdóttir said. "This is about better work, not less work, in fewer hours.'"

The group quickly hit upon a crucial realization—the same realization that the Work Family and Health Network had grasped when researching work redesigns: while leaders are important, *middle managers are the key.* They make or break turning any big idea into a daily practice. The group began collaborating intensively with these managers, sharing research and ideas, holding workshops, and asking and answering questions. They invited managers to analyze work, workflows, and individual jobs.

"We asked, 'Can you ease any tasks? Can you organize shifts differently?'" Magnúsdóttir said.

"We asked people to think about what they were doing and why they were doing it that way," Thorbergsdóttir added. "The answer we often got was, 'It's always been done like this.'"

"The biggest shock was that some organizations hadn't changed anything in thirty years," Magnúsdóttir said, "though work had changed a lot in the meantime."

Once the group had hammered out how shorter paid hours could work in a variety of settings, including for the shifts where so many women are employed, they planned a bus tour around the country to spread the word and help organizations implement the change. But then the pandemic shut everything down. So instead, the group organized virtual meetings with more than five hundred business leaders and managers every Wednesday. They also began the long, hard slog of making change happen: saying the same thing over and over again until it began to sink in, until people trusted that change was possible and they were willing to try something new. "Sometimes it feels like we're on repeat. If I've said it once, I've said it fifty thousand times," Thorbergsdóttir said. "It's a big culture change. Some managers are all in. Others don't see the point. So we have to keep working on that."

To help me better understand the mechanics of change, Thorbergsdóttir connected me to a host of workers all over the country. I spent days traveling around Iceland asking the same question: *How* do shorter hours work? I interviewed people in child care, police officers, social workers, office staff, frontline counter workers, union leaders, pool attendants, politicians and policymakers, managers and business leaders. Though every workplace is different and the demands of each job vary, key patterns emerged: The most successful transformations included everyone and their ideas in reimagining work. They forced people to figure out their purpose and prioritize that. They questioned assumptions about the way work gets done, experimented with new processes, used data, and made continuous improvements. More, they had leaders willing to try something new who believed change was possible and acted as role models.

Arna Ýr Sævarsdóttir's experience is a case in point. Sævarsdóttir, the service and digital transformation manager for the city of Reykjavík, manages frontline service workers for the city. The first thing her team did was undertake an intensive process of mapping out their entire workflow. In every instance, they asked whether what they were doing was absolutely necessary. In response, they dropped tasks they realized weren't, that no one had ever questioned before. Like many workplaces, they had digitized many processes over the years, but instead of dropping the old analog way of doing things, they'd just added another layer of complexity. Communications over Slack, email, and instant platforms adding to rather than replacing meetings and phone calls. Paper filing systems and organizers in addition to digital tools, for example. Now, she said, "we're not printing and scanning hundreds of documents." When you really look, "you can find waste—of time, of resources. And when you don't fill up your time with crap, you have an opportunity to shorten work hours, upskill, and focus on education and being more human." In this way, managers like Sævarsdóttir in Iceland cut out stupid work, the "waste," as Hiroshi Ono would say, that managers elsewhere cling to.

For the frontline workers she manages, Sævarsdóttir said they first tried giving everyone a day off every other week on rotating days. But if someone else happened to get sick, they found they didn't have enough people to help clients at the counter or on the phone. So they turned to data. They began tracking when clients were coming in for services or calling for help. The office had always been open from 8:20 a.m. to 4:15 p.m., but the data showed that no one came in or called between 8:20 and 8:30 a.m. It was similarly quiet between 4:00 and 4:15 p.m. So they shortened the entire staff's hours by twenty-five minutes every day. The team decided that Friday would be their short work hour day. Part of the team takes every other Friday off. Another group, herself included, work a short Friday every week. To accommodate clients, half the frontline team starts at 8:30 a.m. and finishes at 2:00 p.m. and the other half starts at 10:00 a.m. and finishes at 4:00 p.m. The team decided to make Friday a meeting-free day. "They were skeptical at first, but we gave it a try," Sævarsdóttir said. She's come to look forward to the Fridays when most people are out of the office and her mornings are quiet. "It has become a day of reflection and focus on intense work for me."

To shift the culture, instead of praising people who overworked, she and other managers began talking about the importance of work-life balance and commending people who got their jobs done efficiently. Sævarsdóttir also realized she needed to lead by example, so she made sure she worked short hours, too. Sævarsdóttir used data to track how well they were doing their jobs. In all cases, she said, productivity either stayed the same or improved. "This is about courage," she said. "Leaders have to be courageous enough to make this decision."

When I told her that many in the United States assume that the work will suffer, or that people wouldn't be able to get their work done in a shorter period of time, Sævarsdóttir shook her head. "It's a question of mindset. It's not that you work faster. It's all about prioritization. A well-rested person is in balance and more efficient than a stressed-out person, tired, and on the point of burnout. I think the goal should be to achieve a culture in the workplace that gives you space and time to be a person."

As in Sævarsdóttir's department, nurses are managing shorter work hours by creatively rearranging shifts at the Landspitali National University Hospital, not far from the soaring Hallgrímskirkja church, the national landmark that sits atop Skólavörðuholt hill at Reykjavík's highest point.

Coleen Lastimosa, a nurse with the cardiology unit—the only one in Iceland—used to work what was considered part-time to have time to care for her family. But when her union negotiated a short work hours contract, her part-time hours were considered full-time. She's earning the same pay, she's putting in the same number of hours but, as a full-time worker, she'll build up a healthier pension. She can choose her own schedule and the union contract no longer allows back-to-back morning and evening shifts, so she's finally sleeping better. "I'm more alert and quicker and make better decisions," she told me. "I have more energy to engage my patients." However, some wards are struggling to cover all patients with a staff on short hours, said Valdis Gardarsdóttir, director of the outpatient cardiac clinic. She started the transition there by asking all the staff at the clinic for their ideal short schedule. Then she sat down with the clinic's scheduler and carefully mapped out a plan. In the end, "everyone got their wish," she said. She herself typically works a short day on Wednesdays. Even though some shifts can get busier and the workload heavier when fewer staff are on duty, people are willing to pitch in because they feel that they're all part of making work better for everyone. "People are really happy."

For project manager Arna Hrönn Aradóttir, who works for the city with Trausti Jónsson, the key wasn't so much rearranging shifts as taming a bloated meeting culture. She and her team turned to a consultant to reorganize their operations. The consultant zeroed in on the team's meeting-heavy culture and forced them to rethink the goal of each meeting. They prioritized in-person meetings with students and parents. Other internal or organizational meetings were switched to virtual, long before it became the norm during the pandemic, which freed up often lengthy commutes with time that could then be put to better use. The consultant helped them define what constituted a good meeting, focusing on setting an agenda, coming prepared, getting the most out of each one, and allocating time afterward to process and act on the outcome. "That has worked very well," she said, surprised by how these seemingly small tweaks brought about a wholesale change in the way the team works, how they feel about what they do, and how well they do it.

"Before, people were always sick. But six months after we started shortening the workweek, people had more energy. They were happier because they had more time with their families and fewer sick days," she explained. The shorter hours gave the soft-spoken Aradóttir time to go running—with spikes on her running shoes in winter to manage the ice—and take her children to one of several thermal outdoor swimming pools and "hot pots" in the evenings after dinner. And she's using her extra time on Fridays to get a master's degree in public health. "It feels like it's no longer just work work work, everyone stressed all the time."

The transition to short paid work hours has meant letting go of old ways of thinking about work as well as the old ways of doing it. Halldóra Gunnarsdóttir, the equality officer for the city of Reykjavík, and her husband, Hreinn Hreinsson, who works in IT, participated in the city's pilots. Over a delicious home-cooked meal of lamb shank with traditional Icelandic laufabrauð, they explain they were used to an overwork culture when they joined the city staff in the 1990s. "It was competitive—like if you put in long hours you were the hero. People would ask, 'When did you get home last night? Ah eleven p.m.?' Or say, 'You were sending emails at twelve o'clock at night. Great!'" Hreinsson said. "It was really exhausting. Looking back, it's like black and white compared to what's going on today."

For Gunnarsdóttir, the change to shorter work hours required her team to think differently about the role of a civil servant: the job is providing services to citizens rather than "shuffling paper," she said. And they had to confront the performance signaling of overwork while not actually producing good results. When she first began at city hall, it was a male-dominated worksite, she said, and going in on Saturdays was a common expectation. But when she started working on Saturdays, she was dismayed to see that many of the men hardly did any work. "Maybe they wrote a letter. They didn't have any duties at home because they were all just relaxing at work and getting paid for it. I used to think, what about the families?" she said. "A lot of the work ethic was just being at the workplace, but not working, and that's so stupid." Now they both have more time for their daughters and grandchildren at their little house in the countryside.

At the national police headquarters, detective Albert Sigurðsson similarly spent years overworking. "The people who did that were the golden boys," he said. Sigurðsson noted that this was terrible for gender equality—women who were expected to care for children couldn't possibly work like that. He began to chafe at the culture when he became a father to two sons and, later, when his wife was diagnosed with breast cancer. Now both he and his wife finish at noon on Fridays and spend that time together as a family. Sigurðsson cooks and for the first time is involved in the unpaid second and third shifts, planning and organizing home life, buying the children's clothes, and signing them up for classes and sports teams, as well as driving them to and from practice.

But how did the police manage to cut down hours, when crime continues around the clock? Sigurðsson explained that officers can choose three different short hours schedules, just as the city's workers do, either shaving off time every day, working a half day every week, or taking a day off every other week. This way, each department is always covered. They are also trying to make use of technology and automation to smooth workflows, encouraging people to book appointments online for nonemergency complaints rather than dropping in unexpectedly at any time. As a detective focusing on intelligence gathering, Sigurðsson has the ability to schedule meetings and interviews at any time other than Friday afternoons.

All the police know that an emergency is different. "Sometimes we're in the middle of a big case. And then we just work," Sigurðsson said. But that isn't all the time. The extra breathing room has given him time to reflect on the kind of police work he really wants to do as well as what's most important to him in life. He's now studying psychology, having come to recognize that people who commit crime have a life story, identities beyond their crimes, and experiences that have shaped them along the way. He wants to do more to help people. "I have the same goal—to do good, to get justice for what's wrong," he said. "I've changed a bit in the priorities of what I think police should do."

In the private sector, some business leaders have been less than enthusiastic about shortening work hours, and others are outright hostile. But there are those who welcomed the opportunity to reimagine paid work and harness technology to make their employees' lives better and improve their cultures as well as their bottom lines. Marel is a global company, headquartered in Iceland, that invents and manufactures cutting-edge equipment, software, and systems for the food-processing industry. It's also one of the country's largest employers. In recent years, Marel, which has fairly equal numbers of men and women on both its executive team and its board of directors, began to expand and wanted to recruit the best people. In 2019, they decided to organize around the principles of sustainability, equality, and equilibrium, prioritizing work-life balance and people's wellbeing.

"We thought, how can we leverage that? Why does that have to be a threat? Why can't that be our strength?" Ketill Magnússon, Marel's human resources director, told me. In a dramatic move, they decided to stop the clock and no longer focus on the input, the hours someone worked, but instead on their output. Magnússon remembers the worried response of managers and staff at the time. People had been clocking in their whole lives; it's all they knew. Managers worried they'd lose control. But the company asked teams to, in essence, deconstruct the work and focus on what was most important, setting tangible tasks and goals. "The reason we made this shift is for business," Magnússon said. "Having a more tangible idea of what comes out of my day is more important than how many minutes I spend in front of my computer. This is a very, very huge shift. It allows you to think as an individual: 'How can I organize my day so my output is optimal?'"

At around the same time, after the release of the successful results of the city and state pilot programs, Iceland's national government began to negotiate short work hours with public-sector trade unions. Private-sector unions under Drifa Snædal began to demand short work hours in their contracts, too. For Marel, that meant negotiating with the twenty-five different unions that represent their nine hundred workers. The company was enthusiastic about short hours from the start, Magnússon said, using it as an opportunity to continue to focus on effective work and wellbeing. At a town hall meeting, the company asked six employees to help draft a plan that would cover all twenty-five unions.

The company also consulted with the most progressive union, thinking that if it could come up with conditions to satisfy them, the other unions would agree. They wound up agreeing to a thirty-five-hour week, with teams working a short day every third Friday. Workers shared ideas for how to make their time more effective, reducing waste and effort from the manufacturing floor to the corner office. "We want to be a role model for Icelandic companies on this," Magnússon said.

I meet Ásberg Jónsson, the youthful, energetic CEO and owner of the travel agency Nordic Visitor, one afternoon in his Scandi-style wood-paneled company headquarters. Staffers are just finishing one of the regular company-wide lunches in the cafeteria. Jónsson is an enthusiastic private-sector evangelist for shorter work hours. He began questioning assumptions around work and his own proclivity to put in long hours when he became a father. If he was struggling, he wondered about the people working for him. Then the company started to struggle. "The profit was not acceptable at all," he explains. "We were doing way too much manual work and the output was not acceptable."

He brought the staff together and challenged them to think about how to use technology to make things more efficient. "My thinking was, people would get this carrot—if we improved output, we can reduce work hours," he says. As they analyzed their processes, they realized that most of their time was taken up by receiving information and requests via email, and then inputting data, and then calling hotels and elsewhere to make reservations and bookings. So they created systems with forms that automatically sync to hotel inventories and make bookings. They found better software solutions to automate invoicing and billing. As the company became more efficient, Jónsson shortened workdays from eight to seven hours, with flexible start and stop times, without a reduction in pay. "Becoming more efficient, you could expect that this would mean we would fire people or lay them off," he says. "Not in our case. We just had more time to market ourselves . . . which led to growth, which created more jobs, but different types of jobs. We began working more with our heads rather than our hands."

After a dip during the height of the Covid-19 pandemic and travel lockdown, company profits more than doubled from pre-pandemic levels by 2023; Jónsson acquired three new companies; productivity and performance increased; and employee satisfaction went way up. "This strategy of giving employees the benefit of automation—making them part of it—and helping them see they get something back from it—helped us create a better culture," he told me. "It can be done."

▬

Prime Minister Katrín Jakobsdóttir is one of the country's biggest believers that short work hours can indeed be done and that the change is not only possible but required for a better future. My meeting with the young and much-loved prime minister is set for 9 o'clock one morning at the prime minister's official office, Stjórnarráðshusið. In the pitch-black winter morning and pouring rain, the little white house is so unassuming, so easily mistaken for, say, a municipal history museum, that it's easy to miss. Which is exactly what I do, with no help at all from my soaked iPhone's wonky GPS. When I show up late, disheveled and rain-sodden, a composed Jakobsdóttir meets me herself at the barely guarded door and ushers me into a warm, cozy reception room with overstuffed chairs and welcoming soft lights. At the time we meet, the diminutive prime minister and head of the Left-Green Movement party has just been elected to a second term and voted one of the most trusted politicians in the country.[27] She's dressed in a simple jumper dress and white shirt, her long brown hair pulled back into a messy bun. She pours us cups of steaming black coffee from a French press and immediately launches into an explanation of how gender equality and short work hours are central to her left-right-center coalition government and to the wellbeing of the island nation. Though she herself doesn't work a shorter week, she says, her staff have chosen to work half days on Fridays, alternating hours so that she always has staff available. "We're obsessed with gender equality in Iceland," Jakobsdóttir says matter-of-factly.

On her watch, progress on the issue and on work-life balance for everyone have become key metrics that the government tracks as two of the country's thirty-nine "Wellbeing Economy" indicators designed to capture the nation's health, wealth, and quality of life. The government surveyed residents to ask what they most valued and most wanted their representatives to deliver. Topping the list were good health and more time with family.[28]

A common theme among change agents striving to improve paid work is the quest to establish metrics that measure and judge the wealth and success of nations that go beyond the market-driven gospel of Gross Domestic Product growth. Ironically, it was Iceland's adherence to GDP and material gain that many say led to the catastrophic collapse of its entire banking sector in 2008.[29] That and, some argued,[30] a testosterone-heavy, reckless masculine culture.

Yet Jakobsdóttir maintains that the painful economic and political crisis, with mass street protests and calls for accountability and transparency, is what sparked the shift from GDP to a Wellbeing Economy and the focus on shorter paid work hours. The heads of three banks, all men, went to jail and two were replaced by women. Government leaders, also men, resigned, and Jóhanna Sigurðardóttir became the world's first openly gay female prime minister.[31] "It was a watershed moment" that challenged old assumptions, Jakobsdóttir says, opening up a broader spectrum of ideas and a rethinking of what matters as a society. Gender equality and wellbeing, rather than peripheral extras, began to be seen as central drivers of economic prosperity. Thinking long-term about people's happiness started to gain ground. "It's considered to be a little soft approach to politics," she tells me, "but maybe this is the most important thing."

That's certainly been true in Jakobsdóttir's own case. A mother of three boys, she was pregnant with her second child when she was first elected to parliament in 2007. She was minister for education, culture, and research in 2009 when she gave birth to her third child. With both births, she took four or five months of paid leave, becoming the first government minister to do so (her husband took longer paid parental leaves)."There were a lot of people who predicted that I would leave politics." She laughs. "But I'm still here." She views herself as an important role model, enabling other government ministers, including men, to take paid leave from paid work when they need to care for loved ones. Jakobsdóttir is the first to admit that she wouldn't be where she is without shared paid parental leave, universal child care, or the groundbreaking work of so many women who came before her who laid the foundation for better gender equality.

In 1850, Iceland was the first country in the world to grant unconditional equal inheritance rights to both men and women.[32] (In the United States, it would take until 1900 for every state to grant married women the right to receive an inheritance, keep their own wages, and own property in their own name.)[33]

In 1975, Iceland's women went out on their famous *kvennafrí*, or "day off" strike.[34] At the time, women earned about 60 percent of men's salaries and still shouldered the bulk of care at home. So on October 24, nearly 90 percent of women stopped working in protest, in their jobs and at home. Many schools had to close because most of the teachers were women, as did shops and factories. With flight attendants on strike, flights were canceled. Bank executives became tellers to keep banks open. Grocery stores reported a run on hot dogs, a favorite ready-meal that men could cook easily. Men, for the first time experiencing the daily reality for most women who juggle paid work and unpaid care, took to calling the strike "The Long Friday."[35]

The strike led to a series of unprecedented and ongoing efforts to change public policies, workplace practices, and cultural attitudes. Jakobsdóttir, born in 1976, recalls a childhood in which women's and men's roles and rights in society were common dinner table topics. She also remembers an all-women's party in the 1980s that was initially ridiculed but whose platform has since become established policy. The result of their work, the Equal Status Act, is designed to "promote gender equality in all spheres of society." The act, passed in 2000 and later amended, requires employers to provide flexible arrangements so people can combine paid work and family life, pay men and women equal wages, and ensure that they are equally represented in management and influential roles. No public company board, government council, or committee may have less than 40 percent gender equality.[36] Tough anti-discrimination laws that prohibit workplace gender, racial, and ethnic harassment went into effect in 2018.

Iceland invests about 1 percent of its GDP in early care and education, compared to about 0.4 percent in the United States, one of the lowest of all advanced competitive economies.[37] Iceland's generous support has led to low children-to-staff ratios; high enrollment levels and low costs to parents (5 percent of median household income,[38] compared to an average of 10 percent of married couple families' income in the United States and 35 percent of single-parent incomes).[39] The result is high-quality care with long-lasting benefits to economic development, women's employment and gender equality, and children's healthy growth and development.[40]

Iceland also has one of the most generous and gender-equal paid family leave policies. Jakobsdóttir's government increased from four to six months the allotment of paid leave for each parent after the birth or adoption of a child. Mothers and birthing parents are obligated to take at least two weeks of leave after giving birth. Beyond that, parents have up to two years to take advantage of their six-month leave allocations each, which they can use all at once or intermittently. Parents receive 80 percent of their pay from the previous year, up to about 143,963 ISK, or about $4,561 per month, with a minimum of about $1,094 per month for part-time workers. Single parents are entitled to twelve months of paid leave. Parents who've suffered miscarriages or stillbirths also receive two to three months of paid leave. In addition, each parent can take four months of unpaid "child-care leave" to handle emergencies or sickness until a child is eight.[41]

In a brilliantly designed move to change entrenched gender roles and nudge more men to become active caregivers, most of the paid leave is "nontransferable." If one parent doesn't use the bulk of their allotted six months, then the family loses that time. The "use it or lose it" policy, which was put forward by a right-of-center government, is modeled on what started as a "Fatherhood Quota" experiment in Norway and Sweden and has since been adopted by several Nordic and other countries. Almost overnight, norms began changing. No longer were you considered a good father by working longer and harder and providing more money as the breadwinner for your family, as in the United States. You were considered a good father if you spent time with your new child and family and used your paid leave allotment. Going back to work early was no longer seen as a positive sign of commitment to work but rather a negative mark of depriving your new child and growing family.[42]

In contrast, in the United States, research has documented how the masculine "distant breadwinner" norm is still in force. As we've seen, men tend to earn a "fatherhood bonus" when they have a child,[43] as employers assume they'll be more committed to provide for their families. Mothers run into the maternal wall and suffer a motherhood penalty,[44] a financial cut that gets deeper with each child[45] and hits mothers of color especially hard,[46] as employers assume their first duties are, or should be, caring for their families at home. (One hedge fund billionaire famously said of a working mother's work ethic, "As soon as that baby's lips touched that girl's bosom, forget it."[47])

In the research we did at the Better Life Lab on men and care, one of the most striking findings is that the *experience* of giving hands-on care can transform men's beliefs and behaviors and make them not only comfortable but willing to buck social norms to do more of it.[48] Yet, in a frustrating Catch-22, most men say that even if they value and want to be active caregivers, they can't. So they never have the immersive caring experience that could change behaviors and break traditional gender norms.

That's why the "use or lose it" policies have been so transformative.

In late 2021, when I met with Jakobsdóttir, she was the country's second female prime minister. The gender pay gap was among the smallest in the world. Women made up nearly 47 percent of parliament. Companies were newly legally required to prove that men and women receive equal pay for equal work and be certified or face fines.[49] And the share of men taking time away from paid work to care for their families had skyrocketed, from the single digits in 2000 to close to 90 percent.[50] "A lot of people predicted fathers wouldn't want to use it, but this has not proven to be the case," Jakobsdóttir says.

It's a transformation that Trausti Jónsson has seen and experienced firsthand. Men of his father's generation typically left the caring of children to the women. His father, a banker, took one week off when Jónsson's oldest sister was born. The social "response was, 'What the hell? What's wrong with you?'" he told me. "Like it was an indulgence."

Even two decades ago, when Jónsson and his first wife had their daughter, Bryndís, Iceland, like many other countries at the time, provided paid maternity leave only to women after a child's birth.[51] Fathers tended to take, at most, a few days off before heading back to work.[52] (The United States is still virtually alone in the world in failing to guarantee paid maternity leave, much less paid parental or family leave, despite the widespread need[53] and overwhelming support for it.[54])

But Jónsson and his family were living in Sweden at the time.

With that country's new fatherhood quota leave policy in force,[55] Jónsson wound up taking several months and learned to care for his daughter. "The time we had with her as a newborn was *amazing*. I felt like it was such a privilege," he said. "In Sweden, they made it so easy." This started him on the path to being a hands-on caregiver and ultimately a single father managing the first, second, and third shifts on his own. "Any man can father a child," he told me. "I use the term 'dad' for the kind of father I am. There's a big difference in my mind." After Bjartur was born in 2013, Jónsson took a three-month intermittent paid parental leave every other week. By that time, Icelandic law guaranteed mothers and fathers three months each of paid leave, and three months that the family could ostensibly share, although mothers wound up taking the bulk of it.[56]

Though the laws had changed, the culture was slow to catch on. It still wasn't easy for men. Jónsson was working at a senior center back then and many of his clients viewed caregiving as a woman's job. "They thought I was just being lazy" by taking leave, he said. "I'd tell them, yes, he's got a mother, but he's got a dad, too. He's my responsibility, too. That's why I'm at home with him.'" By the time Breki arrived in 2018, Iceland's work culture and attitudes toward gender equality had shifted. The child was due to be born in June but was delivered prematurely in February. Jónsson made sure to be in the neonatal intensive care unit, holding the child on his bare chest, for at least three hours a day, as doctors requested, to bond and keep him warm. Knowing he had to save his paid leave for the months before Breki could go to child care, Jónsson used his vacation and unpaid time to be at the hospital, making the choice of time over money that many mothers are forced to do in the United States. Still, that experience forged a deep connection between the two that, Jónsson hopes, will last a lifetime. He eventually took his full three months of paid parental leave when the child was nine months old, "almost as much as Breki's mother," he said proudly.

In 2021, under Jakobsdóttir, Iceland's parliament expanded the law once again, guaranteeing each parent at least six full months of paid leave that they either must use or the family will lose, with only six weeks that they can split.[57]

Jónsson isn't the only father who's changed in tandem with work culture and public policy. I met with Ingólfur Gíslason, an associate professor of sociology at the University of Iceland. In a handful of grainy black-and-white PowerPoint slides, he showed how a carefully crafted gender-neutral policy, done right, can transform society. Research has long found that when fathers are involved in caregiving early on, they're more likely to remain engaged throughout a child's life, he said. Before the "use it or lose it" policy, women provided the majority of care, not only just after birth but three years later, as the child grew. A few years after the policy passed, women were still doing most of the care just after birth. But once a child turned three, 70 percent of married and cohabitating partners were equally sharing care responsibilities.[58] As he came to the end of his slides, Gíslason shook his head ruefully. "People say that caring fatherhood is now part of their image of masculinity," he said. "I envy them. I wish this had been available when I was a young father."[59]

▬

It's just after lunch and nap time, and the Sólborg preschool is alive with riotous play and joyful noise. Outside the cheerful aquamarine school building, toddlers bundled up against the cold scamper around the large open playground, digging in the sand, riding bright orange tricycles, bouncing on teeter-totters, and swinging on hammocks, sending the pom-pom tassels flying. Inside, children, aged eighteen months to five years, paint and draw, jump on tiny trampolines, take turns on an indoor slide, or curl up with books on cozy oversize pillows tucked into the corners of the rooms. Some teachers sit on the floor or at tiny desks with the children, helping with puzzles, playing with blocks, asking and answering questions. Others work quietly in empty classrooms planning lessons. Because the school welcomes and specializes in teaching children with hearing impairment, sign language is ubiquitous. What isn't immediately apparent in all the bustle is that the short work hours experiment has left its mark on virtually everyone here: teachers either do fewer hours each day or one shorter day every week. Directors have longer breaks in the summers or on holidays. The children are dropped off later or picked up earlier by parents who are also working fewer hours than before. And everyone says they have more energy.

When the city first proposed short hours experiments, preschools like Sólborg were some of the earliest places change agents wanted to target in order to make better schedules available to the majority of women who work in the care sector. Yet few believed it was possible. Many preschool directors said outright that shorter hours would never work in care settings and refused to try, said Guðrún Jóna Thorarensen, Sólborg's director. She was not one of them. She'd been reading about artificial intelligence, how technology is rapidly changing work, and had been reflecting on how care and the human connection it requires will never be replaced by automation. She'd thought for years that care jobs needed to become good jobs to draw a more stable, high-quality workforce. The Icelandic government has worked to standardize the training required for anyone to teach at any level, from preschool through primary and secondary school, and to ensure that teaching jobs at all levels have similarly good pay, good benefits, and good working conditions.[60] (In the United States, turnover is high in early education, largely because preschool teachers and child-care workers earn a fraction of what primary school teachers make and are as much as seven times more likely to live in poverty.[61]) Shorter work hours, Thorarensen thought, could be another step in the right direction toward making care jobs good jobs.

She herself had been skeptical at first. In her preschool, some teachers are married with young children and tend to work part-time hours. Others are single, or are single parents who've always worked full-time. It was the latter group, many of them well over fifty, who were eager to try the pilot. "They said, 'I would very much like to have some years that I didn't have to work 100 percent in my life. And this is my chance,'" Thorarensen told me. "That changed my mind."

The preschool began an intensive process to reimagine its work and workload. Thorarensen had the teachers come together as a team and comb through each day in fifteen-minute increments, asking what they could change, do differently or better, how they could achieve the same quality of teaching in thirty-six hours, not forty. They analyzed their operating schedule and realized virtually no child arrived at the 7:30 a.m. start time, and all of them were long gone before the traditional 5:00 p.m. closing time. So they moved the opening time to 7:45 a.m. and closing time to 4:30 p.m. They rearranged shifts and streamlined planning and other tasks. The transition wasn't easy. "But now, when people come in, they're focused. They already know what they're going to do for the next hour, and the hour after that, and don't have to start their day thinking about it," she said. The school embraced flexibility, giving teachers the option of doing their planning from home or a remote setting rather than expecting them to be at the school, which has reduced stress and improved quality. "The first thing I found as a manager was that the staff were more relaxed," Thorarensen said. "They were more into their work because their minds were not constantly somewhere else."

Teachers, including her, had more dedicated time to attend to their lives. Thorarensen works a half day on Wednesday and arranges all her medical and other appointments and errands for Wednesday afternoons. Before the change, teachers were sick nearly 10 percent of the time, she said. After shortening the workweek, it's hovered at 2 to 4 percent. Likewise, turnover had been high, at about 20 to 30 percent a year before the pilot. Now, it's down to about 10 percent.

"Look, being a preschool teacher is hard work. It's noisy. It's difficult to be in a big group for eight or nine hours a day. Teachers get tired. For small children, it can be difficult," she said. "It's not that it's not great to be here, it's just too much." The shorter weeks have given families more quality time together when parents and children aren't tired. Thorarensen has become a believer. "I think you get so much out of the hours you take off working time," she said. "Better work, better staff, happy people."

EPILOGUE

Beyond Work

All constitutions of government, however, are valued only in proportion as they tend to promote the happiness of those who live under them. This is their sole use and end.

—*Adam Smith,* The Theory of Moral Sentiments[1]

Our paradigm for value is production. But most work is actually about maintaining things, it's about care. So we need to start over. We should take the ideas of production and consumption, throw them away, and substitute for them care and freedom.

—*David Graeber*[2]

Catherine is easy to spot as I walk into Ronzio Coffee House in Glasgow's West End. I'd been forewarned that her favorite color is pink. So when I see a young woman in a pink shirt, with pink nails, a pink scrunchy holding her dark blond hair in a ponytail, and a pink jeans jacket festooned with pink buttons with slogans like "Oh yeah!" I make my way to her table.

She sits with two other women. "Hiya," one says and gestures for me to take a seat. "We're regulars here."

"I like to come sometimes for tea," a cheery Catherine begins to tell me. "Sometimes for cake. Sometimes after church. The girls are nice here." The coffee shop isn't far from the cozy flat she shares with two roommates. She begins to show me her Minnie Mouse earrings, a gift from her sister, when she breaks off to enthusiastically greet one of her neighbors by name who's just walked in. He tells her he's been away on holiday. "I thought you were avoiding me!" she teases with a wicked smile. She turns to gush over his dogs, who are clearly taken with her, too. "Nan and Lacey are happy today," she says, laughing.

"She never forgets a name," one of the women with her, Lesley Williamson, says of Catherine. "Her memory's amazing."

Catherine, twenty-seven when I met her in the summer of 2022, has been diagnosed with autism, severe learning disabilities, developmental delays, and a type of bipolar mental health disorder. The two women with her at the coffeehouse, Williamson and Karen Buist, are caregivers, part of her personal care team. They are also the reason she's here at this coffee shop on this fine summer morning, a bubbly effervescence in pink, rather than psychotic, heavily medicated, and confined to a psychiatric hospital, as she has been at three different times for prolonged periods up until 2020. Catherine is, in fact, celebrating her second anniversary of living in her own flat when I meet her. "I'm happy there," Catherine says. "I was on a locked ward before that. With all men. I didn't like it." She begins to get visibly agitated. "It wasn't for me."

"That's all in the past," Buist says calmly.

"You're getting more independent now," Williamson chimes in.

"That's right," Catherine says. She brightens. "I made my own lunch the other day. Chicken on bread with a drop of mayo. I even make tea," she asserts, for her flatmates.

"Not very often," Buist teases.

Catherine giggles.

I'd come to Scotland not because it's home to Adam Smith, forefather of capitalism and the free market, but because it's an early leader in a nascent global Wellbeing Economy movement that's trying to right the wrongs unleashed by Smith's more shortsighted and rapacious followers. A wellbeing economy bases its policy and investment decisions and measures success and a nation's wealth in terms of the health, wellbeing, and happiness of its people and the planet,[3] not by GDP, consumption, corporate profits, growth, and production. I wanted to see what paid work and the unpaid work of care and home might look like in a society organized with such different priorities.

"GDP measures the output of all of our work, but it says nothing about the nature of that work, about whether that work is worthwhile or fulfilling," Scotland's then first minister Nicola Sturgeon said in a 2019 TED Talk that has since been viewed more than 2.5 million times.[4] "It puts a value, for example, on illegal drug consumption but not on unpaid care. It values activity in the short term that boosts the economy, even if that activity is hugely damaging to the sustainability of our planet in the longer term."[5] She could have pointed to the fossil fuel sector or the gasoline-powered car manufacturers. These industries are enormously profitable in the short term but over time contribute to climate change, spur natural disasters such as floods, droughts, severe storms, and fires (which cost the United States an estimated $165 billion in 2022 alone),[6] and pose an existential threat to survival on the planet.[7] GDP counts the paid caregiving of child-care teachers and home health aides, as we've seen, but not the unpaid child and family care that is mostly done by women.

GDP's narrow focus on income fails to capture grotesque inequality in human wellbeing, so that a country like the United States can be considered one of the wealthiest on Earth while having among the highest rates of child poverty[8] and maternal,[9] infant,[10] and child[11] mortality, particularly in the Black community, of any advanced economy. By failing to measure human and planetary health and wellbeing, Sturgeon argues, governments, businesses, and societies are less inclined to act to make them better.

Under Sturgeon, Scotland became the secretariat for a new Wellbeing Economy Governments group in 2018, sharing ideas and strategies to birth a new approach to the economy with a network of like-minded countries—New Zealand, Iceland, Finland, Wales, and others. "When we focus on wellbeing, we start a conversation that provokes profound and fundamental questions," Sturgeon said in her TED Talk. "What really matters to us in our lives? What do we value in the communities we live in? What kind of country, what kind of society, do we really want to be?"

As a result, Scotland's National Performance Framework and Wellbeing economy monitor[12] now tracks not just GDP, unemployment, and other traditional economic indicators but income inequality, the happiness of children, the country's carbon footprint, renewable energy production, green spaces, access to housing, the child poverty rate, in-work poverty, the gender pay gap, the level of cultural engagement, life expectancy, and a host of other markers of a happy, healthy society[13]—the very qualities that make life worth living.[14]

Given Scotland's relationship to the United Kingdom, there's only so much that the country can do to make this transformation. Scotland was granted some devolved powers from the UK in 1999 when it reestablished its own parliament.[15] When the center-left pro-independence Scottish National Party came into power in 2007, its leaders made the wellbeing economy a key part of its agenda.[16] But with only partial powers, the Scottish government has control over the economy and education but not labor and employment. So many of the Scottish government's wellbeing economy efforts to make all jobs good jobs, including creating a cabinet-level secretary for the wellbeing economy, fair work, and energy in 2023,[17] rely more on its powers of persuasion, using pressure campaigns, seed investments, and voluntary compliance.

These efforts have drawn heat from both the left and the right. Conservatives favoring traditional economic growth models, regardless of the burgeoning inequality and long-term cost to the planet, have denigrated the idea as "almost totally meaningless."[18] On the left, labor leaders wanting bolder action say the initiative is little more than an exercise in rhetoric. But transformation has to start somewhere, and a good place is helping people see why the current system isn't working, painting a vision for a different future, and shaping a different story of what a healthy economy and society could and should look like. Peter Kelly, director of the Poverty Alliance, along with more than two hundred Scottish leaders who are part of the global Wellbeing Economy Alliance, or WEAll, has called for the Scottish government to make a robust plan to turn the rhetoric into action.[19] "There's a lot of cynicism out there. But I take the long view," he told me. "These efforts are important symbolically. And they're having more impact than people realize. The rhetoric is creating momentum for change."

Just ask the people who work at Jerba Campervans in the quaint coastal town of North Berwick on Scotland's Firth of Forth. In 2018, the government set out to increase the number of employee-owned businesses, a wellbeing economy initiative that leaders believe will boost productivity and profitability and ensure that the profits are distributed fairly while improving the lives of workers and their communities.[20] That year, Jerba Campervans co-owner Simon Poole and his partner, Cath Brookes, decided to transition their firm to employee-owned. Poole, who cofounded the company in 2006, had been thinking about a succession plan and, when he considered selling the company, found he couldn't sleep at night. "I live in a small community. How could I hold my head up in Tesco? I'd have a few more pounds for my pocket but all my workers would be out of jobs," he said when I visited the shop one day. The worker-owners were busy converting vans into compact custom holiday campers, tricked out with beds, flushing toilets, and showers.

"These workers committed to me," he went on, "so I wanted to be committed to them. I live a very average life and I'm quite happy with what I've got. There's a limit to what one person can consume, you know? So why not share it with the people who've helped you get there?" Instead of Poole and Brookes keeping the profits, the firm now pays out an annual bonus to its employees. Poole even paid the bonus out of his own pocket during the pandemic when the shop had to close for a time. Once it opened back up, the business became more productive and profitable than ever, with better-quality work and fewer returns, Poole said proudly. He now travels widely helping other companies set up or convert to employee-owned businesses and co-ops. "With employee ownership, everyone's a winner," he said. "The only slight loser is the owner who might not make as much. But money doesn't make you happy."

Jill Forrest, who staffs the front office, spent twenty-three years working in a job for less pay than her male colleagues, although she is her family's sole breadwinner. Her experience as an employee-owner, where all pay and financials are transparent and fair, has been life-changing. "It makes you work harder," she said. "There's so much trust. Everyone works as a team because we're all going to benefit." Prior to coming to Jerba Campervans, Ian Adkins had a lifetime of experience as a furniture maker only to be put out of work by IKEA, followed by "work-till-you-drop" low-wage jobs installing hardwood floors to support his family. Now he not only feels more fulfilled, he has more control over his time outside work as well as something he thought he'd never attain: a sense of ease. "I'm probably the happiest I've been in my whole life," he said.

As I traveled in Scotland, I interviewed scores of people on the wellbeing economy efforts getting off the ground—community wealth-building initiatives[21] to create local economies of shared prosperity, gender-based budgeting to promote policies that further equality,[22] a Fair Work Convention,[23] and a Just Transition Commission[24] committed to ensuring that good jobs with living wages are tied to net zero carbon emissions, "purpose-driven business" discussions,[25] government investment to encourage employee ownership,[26] and flexible work policies.[27] But I kept coming back to the story of Catherine and her caregivers.

Their experience shows that it's entirely possible to reimagine how we define work to encompass both paid and unpaid work and make them better.

Catherine didn't have much of a childhood. Born to parents struggling with addiction and in no way ready to care for a child with psychiatric and mental challenges, Catherine was placed in different foster cares starting when she was eight years old. At nineteen, her mental health deteriorated to the point where she was committed to a psychiatric hospital, a pattern that would repeat off and on for nearly a decade. Catherine's legal welfare guardian, Joyce, who asked me not to use last names to protect Catherine's privacy and safety, said, "A huge chunk of really young years that she should have been out living and enjoying she kind of lost."

Joyce and her husband, Allan, are Catherine's younger sister's foster parents. From the two girls' earliest days in care, Joyce and Allan sought to keep close ties between them. Though Catherine was placed with other foster families, Joyce and Allan included Catherine in holiday gatherings and on vacations and visited her regularly whenever she was institutionalized. A previous attempt at independent living in 2017 lasted just three months and ended disastrously. Catherine had another mental health breakdown and returned to a psychiatric hospital. She became psychotic, Joyce remembered. Catherine thought there were bodies lurking under the floorboards and that people were coming to murder her. She could be defiant, sometimes refusing to take her medication. She could be unpredictable, running away, flying off the handle, or suddenly lashing out violently, cursing, even at her beloved younger sister, convinced that no one cared about her. Sometimes her medications would leave her sedated, quiet, and foggy. "It was horrible to see her like that," Joyce said. "We thought we were losing the Catherine we knew."

Then three things changed that gave Catherine her life back. First, the Scottish government began reweaving its social safety net, a precursor to its drive toward a wellbeing economy and the role care plays in it. In 2002 it passed the first in a series of laws that guarantee free "social care" services for the elderly and disabled.[28] In the UK, as in the United States, social care, or home care, is means tested and available only to those with the lowest incomes or the greatest need.[29] The system leaves millions of middle-income families—too poor to afford the staggering cost of care on their own and too rich to qualify for public services like Medicaid—"drowning,"[30] as one U.S. family caregiver said. Many family caregivers—the majority of whom are women—are forced to reduce work hours, cut back on career ambitions, or leave the workforce entirely, costing them over their lifetimes between $122,000 and $420,000 in 2021 dollars, the U.S. Department of Labor found.[31] Some families are forced to "spend down" their assets in order to qualify for Medicaid and the long-term care.[32] No wonder so many people are terrified of aging in the United States.

In Scotland, the government committed to[33] radically change the way it delivered public benefits, including social care services, promising to design them with people and communities, rather than by bureaucrats for top-down administrative ease. A scathing independent commission report found that 40 percent of the country's safety net budget was spent on interventions that could have been avoided with a preventative approach. Investing in high-quality child care, for example, leads to better education, health, job prospects, and economic security in the long term and can reduce spending on entrenched poverty or crime. Investing in high-quality social care that enables people like Catherine to stay stable, living in their homes and communities, keeps them out of higher-cost institutions or requiring more costly and intensive care after a breakdown.[34]

The commission found that focusing on the wellbeing of people and communities made sense not only for those receiving care but for the taxpayers who fund the system and the economy as a whole. "As taxpayers, this is probably the best pound-for-pound investment we could make. Unless we spend money at the outset, we end up paying ten times as much. The cost of failure is massive," said former social care commission member Stuart Currie, whose own mother worked in social care for forty years. "Obviously, there's a financial cost. But the human cost is even greater."

With this focus on prevention, the Scottish government vowed to embrace independent living for disabled people and affirmed their right to freedom, choice, dignity, and control over their lives, as well as the right to the practical assistance and support to be part of society and have an ordinary life.[35] This included giving people control over their own care budgets rather than have them dictated by a series of local authorities. Now the local authorities perform a care assessment and set individual budgets for services based on need. But it's up to the recipients to decide how to spend these care packages. They can take the funds as a direct payment and hire their own caregivers or do with the money what they choose. They can pay an organization from the charitable or "third sector" to make and provide those arrangements. Or they can ask their local authorities to provide the care for them, as before. Those receiving public support wind up spending up to 80 percent of it in their local shops and businesses and on local services, Currie explained. "The longer people can live in their own homes, the better it is not just for themselves and their families but for the local economy." That's community wealth building.

Delivering on the promise of reforming the system also meant making care jobs—as we've seen, one of the fastest-growing professions in many countries[36]—good jobs. The government raised wages, made schedules fair and predictable, and set out to value, professionalize, and stabilize a largely female workforce[37] that, like in the United States and elsewhere, typically earns poverty wages, receives few if any benefits, and is expected to put up with bad job conditions out of the goodness of their hearts. "The Scottish government has been clear that they see social care as really important to the economy," John Mooney, head of UNISON, the largest union of social care workers, told me. There's even an effort underway in the Scottish parliament to form a universal National Care Service, much like the UK's National Health Service.[38] "The good news is there's been a real focus in driving frontline wages up within social care. Now it's still nowhere near enough, don't get me wrong. It's going in the right direction, toward a real living wage. But the workers in the social care sector are still struggling, and turnover is still high," he said. "So it needs to move much faster."

For people like Catherine, who thrive on predictable routines and trusted relationships, a disruptive parade of poorly paid and poorly trained caregivers who don't know her and what she needs can spell the difference between a healthy, happy life in the community or a psychotic break. The caregivers involved in her first failed attempt at independence didn't understand her, Joyce explained. They didn't have much of a relationship with her and put her in a flat by herself. "It was too much for Catherine. Too intense," Joyce said. "I can't overstate enough how important continuity is for Catherine. And unless you're paying people a reasonable salary, you won't keep the good ones. For Catherine, even with a change of staff, you have to be careful. She gets very, very anxious, and that impacts her mental health and can escalate. Unfortunately, Catherine pays the price when we get it wrong."

The second event that changed Catherine's life came when Joyce and Allan won a long court battle to become Catherine's legal welfare guardians, which ensured that they would have a say in Catherine's care arrangements.

The final significant change for Catherine was the decision to work with Enable, one of the largest social care providers in the charitable "third sector" in Scotland and a pioneer in transforming care jobs into good jobs. Long before the Scottish government began to raise wages, Enable had been on a mission to improve conditions for the twenty-five hundred people it employs. While the organization campaigned for the government to pay living wages, it also reorganized its own internal operation to direct more funds to frontline worker salaries. It was the first large social care charity accredited by Living Wage Scotland[39] and became the highest-paying one in the nation.

"It's hugely insulting not to pay care workers well," Enable CEO Theresa Shearer told me at her office in Glasgow. "People say they come into care work because they value doing the work. But that doesn't mean they shouldn't be able to pay their bills. They shouldn't have to live a life of poverty. Our golden thread, if you will, is good work leads to a good life: supporting the wellbeing of caregivers leads to brilliant outcomes for the people who need care." Enable pays for training and for referring a friend as a new caregiver, gives four weeks' notice for shifts, and was also one of the first to pay living hourly wages, rather than an insultingly low flat fee, for overnight shifts. In 2017, Scotland also began to pay hourly wages for overnight shifts. Until then, the practice throughout the United Kingdom was to pay about 30 pounds (approximately 38 U.S. dollars in 2023) for an entire twelve-hour sleepover shift.[40] In 2021, the UK Supreme Court ruled that a low flat rate was permissible, reasoning that care workers slept overnight so didn't deserve to be paid by the hour, even though they were on the job and usually woke several times to tend to clients, and weren't at home with their families or in control of their time. "We said, if you leave your house, that's work," Shearer said. "And you should be paid a living wage for every hour of it."

Enable is also committed to ensuring that those in need of care have a right to live independently in their communities and decide how to arrange their care. Enable was an early adopter of a "personal assistant" model, which gives people like Catherine and their families choice and control, Shearer explained, in setting goals to enable those in need of care to live full and rich lives, and in choosing and hiring their own caregivers.[41] "Enable does its best to match personalities, but the person has to *want* you to care for them," Enable caregiver Andrew Robertson told me.

Robertson had worked unpredictable and precarious hours in the service industry for years before the pandemic forced him to reassess what he wanted out of life. The competitive pay and stable hours drew him to Enable, he said, while the sense of vocation kept him there. "As a personal assistant, you're there to give as much independence as possible to the person you're helping. You're there to facilitate their aspirations. I really like that. It's extremely rewarding." With a more stable workforce because of the improved job quality, and the personal assistant approach, an independent inspectorate rated 88 percent of Enable's social care services "very good" or "excellent" in 2022, compared to a sector average of 62 percent.[42]

In 2020, when it was time for Catherine to leave the psychiatric hospital and try independent living again, Joyce and Catherine's sister worked with a small team of Enable's well-trained and long experienced personal assistants, who began to visit Catherine in the hospital. Among them were Karen Buist, who managed Catherine's team and has worked in social care for sixteen years, and Lesley Williamson, one of her personal care assistants, who's been in the field for ten. For both of them, the stability, higher pay, and better working conditions at Enable have allowed them to stay in jobs they love. "I love to see people coming from hospital, moving on and changing their lives," Williamson said. "I like making a difference," Buist added.

The care team spent time at the hospital getting to know Catherine, what she likes, what she needs, what kind of life she wants, developing a relationship with her before they began talking about moving. "It wasn't them and us. We were all working together," Joyce said. "It took a couple of months. We were all focused on Catherine having a quality of life she truly deserved. Having a life and a home, really."

At Ronzio Coffee Shop, Buist and Williamson explain that the initial hospital visits made clear that Catherine thrives on being around other people. So they made sure to find a flat with two roommates who are also supported by Enable personal assistants. They taught Catherine coping skills for her anxiety, like going into her room and listening to music when she gets upset. They also worked on a predictable routine, which Catherine helped put together.

"I like to go walk in the park," Catherine says. "It's not far from my flat. Or go to the cinema."

"What about Mondays and Thursdays?" Buist prompts.

"Oh yes, we go to the social club. I sing karaoke and dance." Catherine smiles. "I love to sing Beyoncé's 'Put a Ring on It.' And Lady Gaga. And I like going to visit family on a Wednesday."

"Busy, busy," Williamson teases. "You're the social butterfly in the group."

"I love getting my nails done," Catherine goes on with her list, as excited as if she were opening her birthday presents.

"Yes, you and your sister like your wee girlie days, don't you?" Williamson says.

"I like my bed. My room's nice and tidy. I have my own bathroom."

"You love your lotions and potions," Williamson encourages.

An animated Catherine describes her dance and yoga classes and moves on to her favorite TV shows, her FaceTime chats with her sister, Joyce, and Allan, and their trips to the theater and elsewhere. She lists the neighbors she knows, the names of their dogs and their children, her roommates, and the little gifts she likes to give them. She recounts how her days start at 7:00 a.m., how she knows her "wee schedule" and what to expect every day and who she'll be spending it with.

Midstream, Catherine wonders if it's time for lunch.

"Can we have tuna pasta?" she asks.

"Of course," Williamson says. "Anything for you."

Catherine smiles brightly.

Because Catherine doesn't work for pay or contribute to the market economy, she and people like her are sometimes characterized as "burdens" on our work-focused societies.[43] But what happens if more and more of us fall into that category? As technology, automation, and AI rapidly remake the nature of paid work, what happens when there may not be enough of it to go around?

As with any massive, disruptive shift, we can't know for certain what's to come. Change has a way of delivering the unexpected. Yet we know of a few different futures that may await us as we adapt to that change. Which one will unfold and how will depend in large part on the choices we begin to make now.

In one scenario, we continue on our current trajectory. We follow the neoliberal or conservative course and denigrate and limit the role the public sector plays in our lives. We let the market run free, creating ever more inequality and insecurity. We stick with economic systems that funnel most of the wealth to the few at the top. We watch passively as technology and market forces hollow out the middle and create either very good or very bad jobs, both of which demand overwork to survive, draining time for family, relationships, care, joy, and leisure. We continue to blame individuals for burnout and stress and tell them to meditate or manage their time better rather than overhaul dysfunctional work systems and cultures. We go on expecting unpaid or poorly paid caregivers—mostly women—to impoverish themselves to provide care for our youngest children, our disabled and ill, and our growing aging population. We view poverty as a sign of moral failing, bad choices, or laziness and skimp on the social safety net. In the process, we create what MIT economist David Autor has described as unequal societies of "the servers and the served."[44] This is what I call the dystopian Blade Runner scenario.

In another future, as Autor and other economists argue, technology will certainly destroy some jobs but create others we can't yet imagine.[45] Perhaps, like Warren Valdmanis's investment strategy, the state of Washington's home care system, or the efforts underway in Scotland, we will choose to make these new jobs good jobs—stable, with living wages and hours, family-sustaining benefits, and time for care and life—so we can all share in the prosperity of technology-driven increased productivity.

And in this more hopeful future, if there aren't enough of these good jobs to go around, perhaps we'll come together to invest our common resources intentionally to sustain human life and support the common good. We've done it before. At the turn of the twentieth century, when 40 percent of the U.S. workforce labored in the agricultural sector, Midwest farm states were forced to do just that. With the advent of mechanized technologies, people in farm states realized that in the coming years there would be few if any jobs for their children and grandchildren. (In 2021, farmworkers made up less than 2 percent of the workforce.[46]) In what economists Claudia Goldin and Lawrence Katz argue was perhaps one of the most consequential public investments of the past hundred years, the farm states put their public dollars into their educational systems and required students to stay in school rather than work on family farms. That led to the creation of one of the most educated workforces in the world, ready to take on the challenges of the Second World War and advanced industrialization.[47] "Our success in adapting to technological change in the past has come from deliberate decisions to invest in our human capital," Autor said.[48] So perhaps we'll invest in our human capital by strengthening the safety net to make sure that those without paid work or with still-lousy jobs can at least survive and find a different way to thrive.

That's the idea behind some public initiatives, such as Guaranteed Basic Income or Job Guarantee programs. In the work-focused United States, where lawmakers have added paid work requirements to public benefits for those living in poverty, regardless of whether that person is able to get a job or whether that job pays enough to survive,[49] a job guarantee may be more palatable. After all, the United States has done something like it before with the Depression-era Work Projects Administration. But most people don't realize that we have a similar history with a Guaranteed Basic Income. In 1969, Dutch historian and author Rutger Bregman writes, then president Richard M. Nixon was about to enact a program to grant a family of four living in poverty $1,600 a year (more than $10,000 in 2023)[50]—not enough to live on, certainly, but enough to take the edge off. The Nixon administration had piloted Guaranteed Basic Income controlled trials with more than eighty-five hundred people in seven states. The results were impressive: work hours remained largely the same for those receiving the pay, Bregman writes, while those who cut back on their hours used the time to care for family or to acquire education that yielded better jobs. In his 1971 State of the Union address, Nixon, while falling back on the familiar Republican trope of work requirements, also called on lawmakers to "place a floor under the income of every family with children in America."[51]

Though Nixon's plan fell through, the idea has taken on new life in recent years, with successful pilots in Stockton, California,[52] and through a Mayors for a Guaranteed Income initiative, which has piloted programs in towns in Alabama, Georgia, Wisconsin, Virginia, and New Jersey, among other states.[53] In 2020, John Summers qualified for the eighteen-month basic income pilot in Cambridge, Massachusetts, and began receiving $500 a month. The monthly direct deposit payment was extended for another eighteen months when the city allocated $22 million and expanded the program in June 2023 to all families with children under twenty-one who earn at or below 250 percent of the federal poverty line, with the hopes of making payments permanent.[54]

Summers doesn't fit the misinformed stereotype that many Americans hold regarding who uses public safety net programs.[55] Far from being lazy or making poor choices, Summers has a PhD in history, once lectured at Harvard, and, when he can, runs a small research institute out of his house. Summers quit his higher-paying full-time job in 2016 when a sudden divorce left him with sole custody of his two children, one of whom, his son, Misha, has seven different diagnoses, including nonspeaking autism. Summers couldn't find anyone to help him care for his son, so he took on the task. Summers loves the choice he made to be a full-time caregiver for his son and daughter, though not the impoverishment that has come with it. In his first year as a caregiver, he estimates that his income dropped by $100,000. He often wonders why the unpaid work he does raising his children isn't as valued as the paid work he tries to cram into the early morning hours and late evening when they're asleep. (A question mothers have asked for . . . centuries.)

I meet Summers with his ten-year-old son and thirteen-year-old daughter on a stormy summer afternoon in their tidy, book-lined second-floor apartment. The basic income payment has helped him pay their mortgage, Summers explains. It has served as a hedge against what he calls "economic whiplash" without destroying their souls. "It's solidarity. It says there are other people who care about us and who want us to be able to live without taking a hit to our self-worth or our value. Because that's the way income works in this country: 'You get what you deserve.' That's the message,"

Summers says. "So the relationship between income and personal worth or dignity is broken with a guaranteed basic income." It also offers the assurance of feeling that there's something solid under one's feet, instead of what can feel like shifting sand, if not quicksand. "It enables you to conceive of a future," he adds, including a future for Misha.

In addition to autism, Misha has been diagnosed with intellectual disability and a sensory processing disorder. Doctors have found two genetic mutations that had never been reported until they tested him, and no one quite knows how they affect him, putting him on what Summers calls "the far edge of science." Although Misha is not blind, he's been diagnosed with cerebral vision impairment, and it's unclear, exactly, what he sees. He sits by the window gazing out at the streetlamps for hours. "S!" Misha interrupts. "S!" Summers has figured out that "s" stands for the sprinklers in a nearby park where he likes to play. "T" means Target, another place he loves to go. "S!" Misha insists again. Each time, Summers responds patiently. "We're not going to go to the sprinklers right now. It's raining. Can you say *rain*? It's raining?" Like Catherine in Glasglow, Misha will never be able to work in the market for pay and make his way in life through labor. A basic income—much like Scotland's individual social care budgets—would give Misha a lifeline, Summers says, and provide him with "economic citizenship." It would signify that he belongs in society, that he matters.

Which leads to one more possible future scenario, one that involves a wellbeing economy. Technological progress is expected to create more productivity and wealth, even as it will likely mean fewer jobs and less paid work. What if we shared that wealth? What if the very meaning of work shifted and we came to value not just productivity in the market but how we care for each other?

In the United States, as across the globe, there's a firm belief that paid work is what gives our lives shape, meaning, and purpose.[56] Without it, as legendary theoretical physicist Stephen Hawking once argued, our lives would be empty.[57] Management literature is littered with assertions that the more meaning workers find in their jobs, the more engaged and productive they are at work and the more satisfied outside of work.[58] Fear of what the masses would do with too little work and too much leisure has long been a worry to those in power.[59] And as we have seen, unemployment, at least in the workism-worshipping United States, as writer Derek Thompson calls it, can destroy one's health and wellbeing and damage one's soul.[60] "I think many of us know what gainful employment looks like," the economist Daniel Susskind has said. "I don't think lots of us know what gainful unemployment looks like."[61]

I have argued for overhauling the way we think about work to give value to what people do in the market for pay and the unpaid labor of care and home. But what if we opened the aperture and enlarged the scope even further? What if we defined work as the *contributions* we make to our families, communities, and society? What if we calculated work as the care we give, the joy and delight we bring to our communities, and the art and creative expression we share to help us understand one another and connect with the awe and wonder of life? Doing that would radically expand the notion of work and meaning. "I think about ways to organize ourselves so that the full range of contributions can be counted as hard work," Rinku Sen told me. Sen is a writer, social justice organizer, and executive director of the Narrative Initiative, which aims to change the stories we tell ourselves to foster a shared vision for the common good. "Volunteering at the food bank. That's hard work. Taking care of your elderly parent. Hard work. I think many Americans recognize a lot of different kinds of work as being work because they live it. When more of us are willing to do that, then we can have a different conversation about compensation beyond what employers are willing to pay."

It will be a hard sell. More than people in any other country, Americans are steadfast in the belief that hard work pays off.[62] We've been told work for pay is the surest path to achieving the American dream of economic independence, self-determination, and fulfilling one's aspirations for a good life. One 2019 survey by the libertarian Cato Institute found that 80 percent of Americans, regardless of political affiliation or demographic, believed that "hard work is its own reward," and it is central to the American ethos.[63] This helps explain why the more fervently Americans believe in the American ideal of unbridled opportunity, the more negatively they view people who live in poverty, who must just not be working hard enough.[64] It's also why Republican lawmakers in states like Arizona, South Dakota, Iowa, Texas, and others are pushing legislation to ban guaranteed basic income programs, calling them "socialism on steroids" that will only guarantee government dependence.[65]

Social psychologist Azim Shariff and his colleagues call this thinking "the moralization of effort."[66] How, they wondered, "have so many humans reached the point where they accept that even miserable, unnecessary work is actually morally superior to no work at all?"[67] To test the hypothesis, Shariff and his colleagues designed a few experiments. They found that people who make more of an effort, who struggle, are deemed morally admirable and rewarded monetarily, even when that effort is inefficient, unnecessary, or doesn't create any value. In one experiment, participants were asked to rate two people, one who did a task easily and another who had greater difficulty and took longer to do it. The participants judged the worker who struggled as more moral. Tellingly, they weren't only from the workaholic United States but also from work-'til-you drop South Korea *and* the more joie de vivre France. In another scenario, participants were asked to rate a medical scribe who was automated out of a job and took his full salary for a year while doing nothing and a medical scribe also automated out of his job who kept coming into the office even though he had nothing to do. Participants rated the person who came in to work as significantly warmer and more moral.

Shariff argues that the moralization of effort made sense in our human evolution. Humans always have had to rely on one another and cooperate in order to survive. So it's only logical that we would want to surround ourselves with team players—people who'll join us on the hunt, watch our children while we gather food, help us bring in the harvest before the snows, and lend a hand to raise the barn. We evolved because we found people to count on for help when we needed it. But in the modern world, our belief that hard work is its own reward has led us off the rails. "Our intuition that effort is good for its own sake, regardless of what it produces, has created a work environment with perverse incentives. So when we start attaching worth to *activity* rather than to *productivity*, we start caring more about whether somebody is a hard worker than whatever it is that that work was supposed to achieve," Shariff said in a 2023 TED Talk. Ah—the showy performance of work! The obsession with inputs of hours worked rather than outputs! Virtuous busyness! The ideal worker! "This can come at a very steep human cost," Shariff says. Our obsession with showing our effort to prove that we're hard workers and build our moral reputations, and our admiration of the same in others, is, he says, nothing short of "effort porn."[68]

In a future with potentially less work, Shariff and his colleagues argue, like Sen, that we will need to expand our notions of hard work and effort to include the many different kinds of voluntary and unpaid contributions we make to the world. This, too, can give us a sense of fulfillment and belonging to something greater than ourselves.

Isolation and the threat of death during the global pandemic pushed many to begin reassessing the meaning of paid work and care in their lives. The realization dawned that the injunction to follow one's passion at paid work, to treat it like a holy calling, was often little more than an invitation to be exploited—overworked, underpaid, and expected to be grateful for it. "People are beginning to see there are other aspects of life as important or more important than work," Jae Yun Kim, a business ethics professor, told the *New York Times*.[69] Could that enlarged sense of meaning extend to the contributions we make beyond paid work?

I admit that, with my workaholic tendencies, I wrestle with this idea of finding meaning, purpose, and identity beyond paid work. I, too, wonder how we could organize this larger vision, much less afford it. As I sat with my discomfort, writer and essayist Maria Popova's *Marginalian* newsletter popped into my inbox. Popova's work is dedicated to chronicling how writers and artists have struggled through the ages to find meaning in our brief lives here on Earth. This particular newsletter addressed Aesop's fable about the hard-working ant and the lazy grasshopper. In Aesop's stern telling, an ant spends all summer diligently collecting and storing food for the coming winter while the grasshopper sings and plays. When winter comes, the grasshopper lies dying of hunger while the ant has plenty to eat. The moral? "Then the grasshopper knew," one imagines too late, that "it is best to prepare for the days of necessity."[70]

Popova writes about poet and etymologist John Ciardi's reimagining of the tale. In it, the ant, John J. Plenty, is driven not just by hard work but by the gnawing sense that he'll never have enough, that he'll always need more. The grasshopper, Fiddler Dan, Popova writes, is one of those "unpurchasable, unstorable emblems of aliveness that abound the moment we look up from our ledger of lack."[71] As in the original fable, the grasshopper spends his summer days carefree, filling the world with beautiful music. So much so that the ant's sister falls in love with him and they elope. Winter comes and the ant gloats when the music stops—that will teach them, he thinks. Then, seized with fear that he might not have worked hard enough or stored enough, the ant barely touches his food. When spring arrives, the ant, hungry despite his full larder, vows to work even harder and store even more. He opens his door to begin his drudging toil, barely noticing the spring in his determination to prepare for a far-off future. He finds that the grasshopper is once again making the world sing and dance with his joyful music. Ciardi ends his poem:

> Say what you like as you trudge along,
> The world won't turn without a song.[72]

Like Ciardi, we can recast the meaning of work, and one place to start is with the questions posed by Nicola Sturgeon: What really matters in our lives? What do we value in our communities? What kind of society or world do we want to create? How do we reconceive the core human principles of meaning, fairness, and cooperation beyond paid work?

The vision of a new and better way of living is just beyond the horizon and still out of focus, but we can imagine it. Imagine if more CEOs thought the way Jerba Campervan's Simon Poole does, that they have enough to live a good life and are willing to share their great slice of the pie more fairly. Imagine workers being as happy and trusted as Jill Forrest and Ian Adkins, with a voice, power, mutual respect, and peace of mind. Imagine being free of the gnawing insecurity produced by our GDP-focused, profits-for-the-powerful system.[73] Imagine having time to live wholeheartedly, to love, to care for families and each other, to be deeply involved in communities and civic life. Imagine enjoying leisure to refresh the soul, as the Greek philosophers said.

The shape of the economy is the result of political choices we have made about what we value. We in fact already have the resources to make it fairer and healthier. In his stirring book *Poverty, by America,* author Matthew Desmond argues that a $177 billion investment would ensure that every person in America has a safer and more affordable place to live and enough to eat, and it would give every child a fairer shot at security and success. The money to pay for that, Desmond suggests, could come from the $1 trillion a year in unpaid taxes owed by multinational corporations and wealthy families.[74] "We can always find money to go to war," Scottish social care commissioner Stuart Currie told me. "It's unbelievable when you think about it, but you can find billions overnight to kill people. We're not quite as good at finding money to help people live."

What if we became good at it? What if we put people and their wellbeing at the center of our economy and recognized that all good things flow from there? What if we decided to live up to the original promise of that most idealistic American document, the Declaration of Independence, and dedicated ourselves to Higher Progress and unleashing our collective abundance?[75]

In this hopeful vision, our society is less transactional and places greater value on human morality than on money. It celebrates the individual and our multitude of differences yet recognizes that we're all in this together. In this better world, the grasses might not dance to the grasshopper's music. But transformation is possible. We can begin by following the path these change agents have started to clear. If enough of us do that, like hope, the way will appear. The choice has always been ours.

APPENDIX I

HOW TO CHANGE: TOOLS AND STRATEGIES TO MAKE WORK BETTER

Research, evidence, and common sense for cooperation, fairness, and meaning for individuals, organizational leaders, and policymakers

Throughout human history, we have organized work in an infinite number of ways. There is no one right way to do it. Work is arranged and the fruits of our labor distributed based on what we believe and the stories we tell ourselves. For several decades now we have subscribed to the version that those at the top deserve a lot more than everyone else, and that they will use their plenty wisely for the benefit of all. That hasn't happened. It's led instead to grotesque inequality, misery, resentment, strife, and suffering.

The future is a choice. We have the power to change and transform the way we work and live to make it better for everyone. Dutch historian Jan Lucassen writes that three principles have always defined good work, both the paid work of the market and the unpaid labor of home and care: cooperation, fairness, and meaning. We all have a role to play implementing those core principles. Here are ten strategies that can begin to transform the way we work and live—ten each for individuals; business leaders, managers, and organizations; and policymakers:

Individuals: Change What You Can Control

BECOME AWARE OF THE STORY YOU'RE IN

- Awareness is often the first step toward transformation. The biggest journey you can take may be in your own mind. Go beyond the headlines, the sound bites, the political spin, the hot takes, and the old stories we tell ourselves. Find trusted sources to help you understand how the economy works and the policy and business decisions that have led to gross inequality.

DON'T BLAME YOURSELF

- Understand that burnout and work stress are driven by *organizational* problems, not individual failings. Yes, deep breathing, long baths, and mindfulness can help you manage the stress, but burnout is driven by leaders and cultures. So drop the guilt and begin setting and communicating your priorities and boundaries, which can also help spark change from the middle out.

SEE AND FREE YOURSELF FROM THE BUSY TRAP

- Many cultures prize busyness and overwork, assuming that longer work hours show greater dedication and more commitment. While that may be true for some, research shows that longer hours are typically associated with *less* productivity, fewer innovative ideas, and higher levels of stress-related illness and even death. Take time to pause. Get clear on what's most valuable in your work and focus on that. Do one thing. Multitasking is really just task switching and consumes far too much bandwidth.

TIME AND ATTENTION ARE YOUR MOST PRECIOUS FINITE RESOURCES

- Recognize that you can't manage time. But you can manage your expectations for what you do with it. Watch for overpromising and overdoing. Try to do one big, meaningful thing a day, not one hundred.
- Use intentional scheduling. That big work project? When are you actually going to get to it? That field trip you want to chaperone? The physical therapist you need to see? The vacation you hope to take? Place the priorities of your full life on your calendar. That way, you avoid getting trapped in busy culture triage, which can lead to focusing on low-value tasks.[1]
- Instead of cramming more into an already crowded schedule, the way we may shove stuff into an overly full closet, behavioral scientist Sendhil Mullainathan suggests you think of your calendar as an art gallery.[2] Intentionally choose where to place your time, energy, and attention, and give yourself blank space to recover, respond, and plan for what comes next.
- Schedule slack into your calendar. Remember the planning fallacy—fallible human beings have a difficult time estimating how long things actually take. So allocate time to handle the work that didn't get done when an emergency flared or that was more complicated or demanding than you initially thought.

- Use rituals and boundary management, especially in hybrid settings, to mitigate what can feel like endless "shapeless work" and help you know when it's time to end your paid workday. Use timers. Reward progress.

SHARE FAIRLY THE UNPAID WORK OF CARE AND HOME

- Understand that deeply held and often unconscious gender norms continue to shape policies and culture, policing us into male breadwinner and female caregiver roles. But change can start at home. For different-sex couples, take a page from same-sex couples who have much less conflict over sharing unpaid care and housework. Because there are no traditional gender roles to fall back on, research shows they are forced to express their preferences and to negotiate a fair division of labor.[3] Do that. Involve children in chores. For single parents, build a network of support.

GET HELP FROM FRIENDS

- Change is hard to do on your own. So, just like Workaholics Anonymous and other support groups, find supportive friends and peers and help each other with the journey against the inertia of the status quo toward the rich and full life you envision for yourselves.

EMBRACE THE FACT THAT CARE IS AN ESSENTIAL PART OF LIFE

- Whether paid or unpaid, the care you give, receive, and provide is essential to living a full and rich life. The time we spend connecting with other people, with loved ones, getting to know our neighbors, participating in the civic life of our communities, is part of that care and not only does it make us resilient in the face of emergencies, it helps us live longer, healthier lives and is the source of human happiness.[4] Make time for it. Honor and value it and the people who do it for a living.

REST AND PLAY

- Take time for joy, leisure, and fun. Drop into the present moment and be fully present and alive. Don't put it off until you get all your paid and unpaid work done. Give yourself the gift of permission to have fun right now.

USE YOUR POWER

- You have power as a consumer to do research and use your money to support the companies that value the wellbeing of humans and the planet. Encourage others to do the same. Join a union or worker organization, or support those that do. Use the law to protect your rights. Call local, state, and national policymakers and let them know you support policies and investments that support families and better lives. Keep calling. Demand that work-life enrichment be recognized, not as a perk but as a fundamental human right.

BE PART OF BIGGER CHANGE

- Look for bright spots and *believe* change is possible. Join activist groups, advocacy movements, or political campaigns. Reach out to others to share stories of struggle and strategies for changing both paid work and the unpaid work of home and care. Work within organizations for change. Speak out for public action for more equitable universal laws, regulations, and policies. Run for office.

Organizational Change: An Agenda for Business Leaders and Managers

GET THE BASICS RIGHT

- Commit to creating good jobs with living wages and hours, stable schedules, and the supports—let's stop calling them fringe benefits—that people need to survive and thrive. As MIT's Zeynep Ton says and the Good Jobs Institute's research shows, it's better for business when jobs are good.[5] Recognize that businesses can do a lot on their own, but they can't do it all. Publicly support universal, portable family-supportive public policies such as paid leave, health care, and public investments in care infrastructure, and back the policymakers working toward that. Let's stop trapping people in jobs just so they can get life-sustaining employer-provided benefits.

COMMIT TO DESIGNING BIAS-FREE, INCLUSIVE SYSTEMS

- Create bias-free procedures for recruiting, hiring, retaining, and promoting at all levels, including the C-suite and boards. This can include structured interviews to mitigate confirmation bias, with questions centered on skills and specific tasks the job requires. Set standards that recognize and reward performance and structure teams, projects, and decision-making based on the broader perspectives and deeper emotional and collective intelligence that comes with diverse teams.[6] This will go a long way to muting the effects of the good old boy network and self-perpetuating white male corporate monoculture.

FOSTER CULTURES OF TRUST AND TRANSPARENCY

- Research shows that this leads to innovation and productivity.[7] Remember, too, that research also shows that when people have choice, challenge, a sense of purpose, and connection to a larger mission, when they are well supported, trusted, and feel respected, then workers are happy, businesses are profitable, and society flourishes.[8] Take a page from Warren Valdmanis and Two Sigma Impact and create equitable high-performing *and* wellbeing cultures that are predicated on:
    * Fair treatment
    * A promising future
    * Psychological safety
    * A sense of mission and purpose

COUNT LABOR AS VALUABLE HUMAN CAPITAL

- Invest in labor for the long run. Stop implementing layoffs to make the books look good for Wall Street in the short run. Wharton Business School professor Peter Cappelli argues that companies look more valuable to investors when they adopt a financial accounting system that sees humans as assets, not liabilities, and share data on their investments to help workers do their jobs better, from providing decent pay and benefits to training and professional development.[9]

RECOGNIZE THAT CARE IS ESSENTIAL

- Track employee care responsibilities and provide supports. Caregiving has been considered a private responsibility borne primarily by women. Most businesses don't collect data on the caregiving status of their employees, one Harvard Business School survey found, even though 73 percent of workers have some kind of caregiving responsibility and feel it adversely affects them and their careers at work. Business leaders who, the authors write, are "oblivious" to the care crises their workers face need to evolve beyond masculine "ideal worker" norms that reward an all-work all-the-time ethic. By systematically collecting employee caregiver data, companies can create policies and cultures that support workers and their caregiving while meeting business objectives of productivity and profit.[10]

DITCH IDEAL WORKER BUSYNESS CULTURES

- Eliminate cultures that reward long hours and the performance of work and instead focus on value. Measure actual output. Don't surveil, spy on, and reward input. "It makes me extremely distrustful of the company and also just feeling like a child getting monitored all the time," Madi Swenson, a copywriting specialist and strategist, told me. She became so anxious and stressed from the constant "bossware"—software that takes screenshots of the computer every ten minutes—that she quit her job. "What are we trying to measure here? Is it that the work is getting done or is it that we're sitting at our desks all day?"

BELIEVE WORK REDESIGN IS POSSIBLE

- Drop stupid work and waste. Learn from successful work redesign pilots, pandemic-induced transformations, and short work hours movements, such as those in Iceland. As Joe O'Connor, founder of the Work Time Reduction Center of Excellence, said of successful short hours transformations, "It's an operational excellence mission in disguise. It's as much an opportunity to change the way you work as well as the hours you work."
- Start by defining the purpose of the organization and the real output required to create value.
- Map out your workflow. What's working? What time-wasters could be dispensed with? (Usually lots of meetings.)
- Design new systems *with* workers. Give teams the authority to design solutions based on work output.
- Challenge assumptions that long hours make for better work and question status quo ways of working.
- Prioritize giving workers more autonomy and control over the time, manner, and place of work and workloads.
- Center work-life enrichment and equity as goals.
- Model effective work practices and work-life balance.
- Experiment. Learn. Gather Data. Adapt. Repeat.

LEAVE THE MONOCULTURE ECHO CHAMBER

- Recognize that the workforce doesn't look like you or have your experiences. Embrace the notion that giving workers more say and control in where, when, and how they work is better for them, particularly those with care responsibilities or disabilities, or workers of color, and it's better for businesses.[11] Most desk workers prefer shorter paid hours and some combination of flexible hybrid in-person work to collaborate with others and digital work for uninterrupted concentrated time to think and focus on bigger projects.[12] Giving essential workers more control over their schedules is part of creating good jobs as well as good for the bottom line.[13] Digital work is not "morally wrong" (Elon Musk), an "aberration" (David Solomon), or "inefficient" (Jamie Dimon).[14] It's not the way *you* worked. But it's the way future work will be done.

INVEST IN GOOD MANAGER TRAINING

- Provide training that gives concrete tools and strategies for how to use data to measure performance and output to drive decisions. It's too easy to default to the status quo of rewarding long hours and presence in the workplace and manage by walking around. Working and managing in a flexible way and navigating often-unconscious biases are skills that can be developed and practiced.

RECOGNIZE THE BROAD PURPOSE OF A CORPORATION

- It is so much bigger than generating profits for shareholders and enriching CEOs. Invest in human capital. Share the wealth with workers, stakeholders, and the communities in which you operate. Stop promoting grotesque inequality and commit to strengthen the middle class, stabilize democracy, and create a better, more equitable, and sustainable future.

Societal Change: Recommendations for Policymakers

- Design equitable family-sustaining policies *with* the people who need them, with the goals of human health, wellbeing, and thriving, and of elevating the value of care. Implement them well. That means:

    * Guaranteeing equitable, universal paid annual leave, paid sick days, and paid family and medical leave. Additional measures, such as job protection, adequate wages, and equal "use it or lose it" provisions help encourage and normalize men breaking breadwinner norms and taking time to give care.
    * Reweaving a robust safety net, including a functioning unemployment system that does not punish or stigmatize those out of work but provides adequate time, wages, and training to help people find their way forward and move to stability. And starting from the premise that humans are *not* inherently lazy but all yearn for dignity, meaning, and belonging.
    * Taking the long view to creatively design efficient, equitable systems to serve humans, drawing lessons from

Washington State, the private sector, and labor unions to create care and safety net systems that work for everyone. Washington State recognized that making home care jobs good jobs improves the stability of the workforce and the quality of care. This in turn makes life better for those in need and enables more people to remain at home rather than be transferred to expensive nursing homes, which saves money and benefits taxpayers.

  * Reviving a social contract with the public and private sectors and labor that does not leave workers shouldering the risks and vicissitudes of the market on their own, while fostering social mobility and a stable middle class.

- Pass legislation barring discrimination against workers with care responsibilities.
- Ratify the Equal Rights Amendment to fully embrace the personhood of women and laws that protect women's bodily autonomy over their own reproductive futures.
- Invest in high-quality care infrastructure, from prenatal care through child care to disability and elder to end-of-life care. Use public dollars to pay care workers well, make care accessible, high quality, and affordable, and ease the financial burden on families and unpaid family caregivers. Use the data to show that these supports pay for themselves many times over in a healthier, more equitable society.
- Commit to making all jobs good jobs, with stable schedules, living wages and hours, and portable, universal benefits not tied to employers, including paid leave, health care, and retirement.
- Measure the success of the nation based on human wellbeing and the good of the planet, not the shortsighted and often destructive production and consumption measured by GDP.
- End tax cuts for the wealthy and trickle-down economic policies that funnel wealth to the top, foster inequality, and starve public infrastructure and civil society, thereby undermining democracy. Invest in people and communities. Collect taxes on the wealthy and multinational corporations and use those dollars to equitably improve health, wellbeing, and happiness.
- Reform the tax code to end rewarding investment in machines and technology over human beings and their labor. The current code taxes investment in people at between 25 and 33 percent, while the rate for investment in capital equipment, software, and technology hovers between 0 and 5 percent.[15] This accelerates investment in automation and contributes to the view that human labor is a liability and cost to cut. "That's a clear distortion

in the market," Rep. Jim Himes, D-Connecticut and former chair of the House Select Committee on Economic Disparity and Fairness in Growth, told me.[16]

- Enforce a new psychosocial work stress health and safety standard. Measure and track its consequences. Use legislation, regulation, and litigation to punish those who foster work stress, as well as tax incentives and rewards to encourage equitable and healthy work systems, practices, and cultures.
- Overhaul punitive labor laws to give workers voice and power.
- As technology and automation remake work, prioritize humans and use creative approaches, such as universal basic income or guaranteed jobs programs, to provide people with dignity, economic citizenship, and belonging.

APPENDIX II

THE PROBLEM WITH WORK STRESS AND HOW TO SOLVE IT

It's not you. It's the systems and cultures that need to change.

In modern hustle culture, work stress is often seen as an individual failure of someone who just can't hack the pressure, which means it's the individual's responsibility to fix. Executives who have long proclaimed that overwhelmed, stressed-out employees are one of their top concerns[1] have tended to turn to stress management and "wellness" programs such as lunchtime yoga or meditation apps for the burned-out "talent" they seek to retain. Workers in low-wage or precarious work are often just supposed to be grateful they have a job.

But decades of occupational health and safety research confirm that stress on the job is the result of the way work is organized. Solving the problem of work stress requires work itself to change.

What is work stress? Research shows that what drives much of it is an effort–reward imbalance, a mismatch between the effort workers put into the job and the rewards they receive in return for their labors. The less say or control a worker has—what's known as decision latitude—the higher the stress. It's therefore rooted in inequality and power.

Here are the ten most studied psychosocial work stressors taking a toll on human health and life[2] and that need to change:

1. **Long Work Hours:** People working long hours are two and a half times more likely to experience depression than those who work an eight-hour day[3] and have a 60 percent increased risk of coronary heart disease.[4] A 2021 study by the World Health Organization and the International Labor Organization reported that working fifty-five hours or more per week is associated with a 35

percent higher risk of stroke and a 17 percent higher risk of dying from coronary heart disease, compared to those working a thirty-five-to-forty-hour week.[5]

Solutions: Paid annual leaves and cultures that encourage workers to take breaks and rest. Stable, predictable schedules with flexibility in time, manner, and place of work as the default. Shorter work hours with decent pay.

2. **Work-Family Conflict:** The struggle to combine work and care increases the odds of reporting poor physical health by 90 percent.[6] The American Institute of Stress reports that the stress of juggling work and family responsibilities is one of the top three work stressors.[7] Workers with care responsibilities often experience family-to-work conflict and feel stress when family duties pull them away from the job, particularly in unforgiving employment environments. When work spills over into family life, stealing time from home, availability for loved ones, or personal enjoyment, research shows that it can lead to burnout and increase anxiety and depressive symptoms.[8]

Solutions: When workers with care responsibilities do feel supported at work, research reveals that they sleep better, spend more quality time with family, and are more loyal and productive at work, among other benefits.[9] Supervisors trained in managing workers with care responsibilities help, as do family-supportive paid leave, stable, predictable schedules, and flexible policies as the default.

3. **Low Job Control:** Low job control increases mortality by almost 45 percent.[10] Greater worker control involves having autonomy and agency to do the job and the ability to organize to demand better work environments. Worker power has eroded in recent decades. Unlike in many other competitive advanced economies, where membership in trade unions is high and workers often have a seat at the bargaining table, in the United States, just about 6 percent of the private-sector workforce belongs to a union, and union membership has been on the decline. Research shows that unionized workers enjoy better work schedules than nonunionized workers[11] and are happier, with greater job satisfaction and wellbeing.[12]

Solutions: Increase job control and worker autonomy. Make tasks clearer, set expectations, listen to workers, and give them the ability to meet reasonable expectations and deadlines. "Job control is seen as a health protective mechanism. The more job control, the more you have 'decision latitude'—choice in what projects and tasks you want to take on," Marnie Dobson, codirector of the Healthy Work Campaign, explained in an interview. "Low job control is more common in low-wage work. But as physicians, for instance, have more and more of their decision latitude whittled away by insurance companies, physician burnout has gone through the roof."[13]

4. **Shift Work:** Rotating shifts, night shifts, unpredictable shifts, and on-call or just-in-time shifts have been associated with sleep disruptions, which robs the body of recovery time.[14] That can lead to an increase in cortisol, the stress hormone that can create inflammation and lead to chronic illness, such as cardiovascular issues. Nurses, for instance, are at high risk for sleep interruptions. Dobson and Peter Schnall, her codirector at the Healthy Work Campaign, have studied work stress and firefighters, who work in shifts.[15] "Most people think firefighters die from fighting fires or exposure to fumes," Dobson said. "But we found they were at much higher risk for hypertension, obesity, and having a heart attack on the job. Part of it is they have twenty-four-hour shifts and get constantly interrupted, and part is that they have to be constantly 'on.'"

   For workers with unpredictable schedules, Dobson said, the uncertainty and low wages create intense stress. "It's hard to manage or plan for child care, or, if you're in school, plan for classes," she said. "And because these are also low-wage jobs—which in itself is a stressor—you may be more willing to take on-call shifts to get extra hours so you can pay the rent. Uncertainty is a major stressor for human beings in general, and can cause burnout and mental health problems."

Solutions: Research has found that stable schedules improve subjective wellbeing, sleep quality, and economic security.[16] Other solutions include getting the basics right on good jobs, and providing living wages and life-sustaining benefits.

5. **High Job Demands:** If you have a demanding job but have some control over your work pace and load, the research is mixed on whether the demands are bad for your health. What *is* bad, however, is a mix of high job demands and low job control. "When your job demands are high, to the point where it exceeds your ability to cope, that's when job strain kicks in," Dobson said. "And it is related to burnout,[17] higher blood pressure,[18] heart disease,[19] and depressive symptoms."[20]

It's not just knowledge workers, doctors, medical professionals, engineers, journalists, and other white-collar employees who are likely to have high job demands—anyone taking on more tasks or duties, often as a result of "lean staffing,"[21] labor cuts, or tight labor budgets, is at risk, as is any worker in a job with high physical demands, such as farmworkers and construction workers.

An emotionally demanding job may not necessarily be a negative influence, Dobson said, and some studies have found that emotionally demanding work can be beneficial to your health "because there's some value people get out of it, a sense of contribution and meaning," she noted. Where emotional labor begins to harm health, she added, is when workers are expected to display positive emotions on an ongoing basis, especially in the face of hostile customers or clients, such as flight attendants, care workers, or restaurant staff, who must suppress their feelings and put on a good face, particularly if they are working for tips to make a living wage. Workers expected to "surface act"[22] in that way experience emotional dissonance, which is linked to burnout and other mental health issues.

Working under tight or unrealistic deadlines in which the employee has no say can also lead to chronic stress, Dobson and Schnall said, as does the "always on" culture of late-night emails or physical or virtual presence.

Solutions: Manage for performance and output, don't spy on or calculate input. Focus on job tasks and goals, then right-size staff and workloads to meet them. Support workers' emotional wellbeing and give them recovery time. The Healthy Work Campaign offers an anonymous survey[23] for workers to measure their own work demands compared to a nationally representative sample.

6. **Job Insecurity:** Precarious work has been on the rise, with more contract, freelance, and gig jobs, temp jobs, involuntary part-time jobs—poorly paid temporary adjunct professors, for instance—as employers focus on cutting labor costs to boost profits or survive. High levels of job insecurity have been associated with higher incidence of mental health symptoms, such as depression, cardiovascular disease, and mortality.[24]

   Research done in organizations in the midst of restructuring has found that workers experienced high stress anticipating a job loss or awaiting firm decisions.[25] "Anticipation of job loss is a major form of insecurity," Dobson said. "But the people who survive layoffs often experience high levels of job insecurity and mental health issues as well.[26] They're left with the feeling that this might happen again." Next time, it might be them.[27]

Solutions: It's time to rethink the social contract, with businesses committing to provide good jobs and seeing workers as assets to invest in rather than liabilities to cut. In the public sector, this means reinvigorating safety net programs such as unemployment insurance, with adequate time and funding as well as education and training to help workers thrive, rather than spiral into financial instability and mental health crises.

7. **Low organizational justice:** Human dignity and the concept of moral injury lies behind this psychosocial stressor. In such circumstances, a worker can't do the best job possible because of the way the organization or industry functions—nurses assigned too many patients, for instance, or warehouse workers who are expected to meet ever-higher quotas, without explanation, because of an algorithm that they can't challenge, all while cameras surveil their every move.[28]

   "The experience of unfairness and disrespect is a major stressor," Dobson said. Toxic cultures and bosses who allow bullying, microaggressions, gender and racial harassment, and discrimination can lead to work stress and chronic ill health, as do cultures that don't handle hiring, allocating plum assignments, or promotions in a fair way. Low organizational justice is linked to burnout and poor mental health, as well as cardiovascular disease, according to Dobson.[29]

Solutions: Create civil and respectful work cultures of psychological safety and trust where harassment isn't tolerated and all workers can thrive. Set clear goals, expectations, and deadlines and give workers autonomy to meet them. Focus on job tasks and manage for performance and output, not input, such as hours spent in the office. Embrace flexibility, giving workers more agency over time, manner, and place of work, as the default. Adopt equitable best practices for hiring, promotions, and handing out assignments. Rightsize workloads to staff levels.

8. **Low social support at work:** Research shows that low social support at work, combined with job strain, is the strongest risk factor for mental distress at work.[30]

Solutions: This is all about relationships at work. "Social support is one of the primary ways in which we cope with stress—emotional support from family and friends, but also the information and resources we have access to," Dobson explained. "So having a supportive supervisor, someone who cares about your welfare, who you are as a person, and provides you with the information and resources you need to get your job done . . . is critical," as is feeling accepted by coworkers. "The presence of social support can buffer stressful job situations and job strain." Without the buffer of social support, job strain is more likely to be associated with cardiovascular disease, Dobson added.

Research on the pioneering approach of "family-supportive supervisor training" shows that worker health, wellbeing, job satisfaction, and engagement improve when workers feel supported at work.[31]

9. **No health insurance:** It should come as no surprise that like low wages, the lack of health insurance can be a major stressor[32] and is linked to poorer health.[33] Without health insurance, people put off early treatment for illness, which means they "will potentially get seriously sick," Dobson said. "If you have health insurance and can take care of your health conditions, you're likely to live much longer. It also speaks to uncertainty and whether workers feel they're treated with respect and dignity. It all fits together."

Solutions: Unlike in other countries, where health care is seen as a universal right, and where many have universal health care systems, in the United States, individual employers can choose to provide health insurance often at vastly different levels and set conditions that can make it difficult to qualify. Many employers keep worker hours below thirty hours per week to avoid offering insurance under the Affordable Care Act. Expecting employers to provide health insurance—a relatively recent artifact of wage freezes during World War II[34]—also locks workers in jobs they may hate just to keep their insurance.[35] It also makes U.S. jobs more expensive[36] and increases the lure of moving jobs overseas where labor is cheaper.

In the United States, explore universal Medicare for All proposals and expand access to the Affordable Care Act and Medicaid. When everyone has access to quality health care, everyone benefits.

10. **Unemployment:** Layoffs have become more common in recent decades as organizations adopt a business strategy to keep costs low and profits high by squeezing labor. A raft of research has found that being laid off more than doubles the risk of heart attack and stroke among older workers,[37] can increase the chance

of developing stress-related diabetes, arthritis, or mental health issues by 83 percent,[38] and even shortens life expectancy.[39] Losing a job also often means losing access to health care. Unemployment is also linked to a higher risk of suicide.[40]

Even anticipating being unemployed can be a major stressor, said Sarah Damaske, a sociologist at Penn State whose most recent book, *The Tolls of Uncertainty*, explores the unemployment experience. "Just the thought . . . stresses people out," Damaske said. "And once you are unemployed, it really isn't good for your health." First, there's the financial shock. Each state has developed its own unemployment insurance system. Some reimburse as much as 50 percent of one's previous salary, while in others it's as little as 25 percent. Then come the physical and mental health costs, feeling a loss of identity and the sense that what you do matters.[41] "Being unemployed can have a negative effect on your health for years and years, and sometimes decades to come."

Solutions: On the business side, recognize that layoffs are a bad way to do business, the result of short-term thinking. Squeezing labor costs might make balance sheets and earnings reports look better in the immediate term, but most firms lose workers with valuable skills and knowledge, run up high turnover and training costs, contend with lower morale and productivity among remaining workers, and often wind up rehiring some of the same people in more precarious contract positions[42]—all of which is bad for business in the long run. So take a long view. Build loyalty and resilience by creatively meeting downturns with job sharing or shortened work hours rather than resorting to layoffs.[43]

On the policy side, reinvigorate, update, and invest in an unemployment insurance program that truly works, with enough time, access to education and training, and a high enough reimbursement rate to help workers find not just a new job but potentially a better one.[44] With coming automation, and the potential for widespread unemployment, consider the benefits of Guaranteed Basic Income[45]—an idea even Republican president Richard M. Nixon supported back in 1969.[46]

NOTES

Prologue

1. International Labor Organization. “Declaration of Philadelphia,” May 10, 1944. Accessed April 9, 2023. https://www.ilo.org/global/about-the-ilo/newsroom/news/WCMS_698995/lang-en/index.htm.
2. Wong, Felicia, and Michael Tomasky. ”How Feminist Economics Brought Us the Care Agenda (with Nancy Folbre).” *How to Save a Country* (podcast), May 25, 2023. https://rooseveltinstitute.org/2023/05/25/how-feminist-economics-brought-us-the-care-agenda-with-nancy-folbre/.
3. Terkel, Studs. *Working: People Talk About What They Do All Day and How They Feel About What They Do*. New York: Pantheon Books, 1974.
4. Henderson, Kaitlyn. “Where Hard Work Doesn’t Pay Off: An Index of US Labor Policies Compared to Peer Nations.” Oxfam Research, 2023. Accessed February 4, 2024. https://webassets.oxfamamerica.org/media/documents/Where_Hard_Work_Doesnt_Pay_Off.pdf?_gl=1*1t3dm42*_ga*MTQ4NTQyOTAyNS4xNjkzMzQ4ODQ1*_ga_R58YETD6XK*MTY5MzM0ODg0NC4xLjAuMTY5MzM0ODg0NC42MC4wLjA.
5. U.S. Department of Labor. “Minimum Wages for Tipped Employees,” January 1, 2023. Accessed April 9, 2023. https://www.dol.gov/agencies/whd/state/minimum-wage/tipped.
6. Hofverberg, Elin. “Kvennafridagurinn—The Day Icelandic Women Went on Strike | In Custodia Legis.” Library of Congress, March 8, 2022. Accessed August 30, 2023. https://blogs.loc.gov/law/2022/03/kvennafridagurinn-the-day-icelandic-women-went-on-strike/.
7. Global Women’s Strike. “A Brief History: From Wages for Housework to Global Women’s Strike.” Accessed August 30, 2023. https://globalwomenstrike.net/history/.
8. Ruppanner, Leah, Maria Brandén, and Jani Turunen. “Does Unequal

Housework Lead to Divorce? Evidence from Sweden." *Sociology* 52, no. 1 (February 1, 2018): 75–94. https://doi.org/10.1177/0038038516674664.

9. Frisco, Michelle L., and Kristi Williams. "Perceived Housework Equity, Marital Happiness and Divorce in Dual-Earner Households." *Journal of Family Issues* 24, no. 1 (January 2003): 51–73. https://journals.sagepub.com/doi/abs/10.1177/0192513x02238520.
10. Ruppanner et al. "Does Unequal Housework Lead to Divorce? Evidence from Sweden."
11. MBO Partners. "COVID-19 and the Rise of the Digital Nomad." Accessed April 9, 2023. https://s29814.pcdn.co/wp-content/uploads/2021/05/MBO-Partners-Digital-Nomad-Report-2020.pdf.
12. Smith, Molly. "Disabled Americans Reap Remote-Work Reward in Record Employment." Bloomberg, October 3, 2022. Accessed April 9, 2023. https://www.bloomberg.com/news/articles/2022-10-03/disabled-us-workers-see-highest-ever-employment-figures-from-remote-work?leadSource=uverify%20wall.
13. Tulshyan, Ruchika. "Return to Office? Some Women of Color Aren't Ready." *New York Times*, July 23, 2021. Accessed April 9, 2023. https://www.nytimes.com/2021/06/23/us/return-to-office-anxiety.html.
14. Galanti, Teresa, Gloria Guidetti, Elisabetta Mazzei, Salvatore Zappala, and Ferdinando Toscano. "Work from Home During the COVID-19 Outbreak." *Journal of Occupational and Environmental Medicine* 63, no. 7 (July 1, 2021): e426–32. https://doi.org/10.1097/jom.0000000000002236.
15. Barrero, Jose Maria, Nick Bloom, William D. Eberle, and William H. Abbott. "60 Million Fewer Commuting Hours Per Day: How Americans Use Time Saved by Working from Home." Becker Friedman Institute for Economics at the University of Chicago Working Paper (September 18, 2020). Accessed February 4, 2024. https://bfi.uchicago.edu/wp-content/uploads/2020/11/60-Million-Fewer-Commuting-Hoursv2.pdf.
16. Molla, Rani. "Americans Who Work from Home Are Getting More Productive." *Vox*, May 30, 2022. Accessed April 9, 2023. https://www.vox.com/recode/23129752/work-from-home-productivity.
17. Aksoy, Cevat Giray, Jose Maria Barrero, Nicholas Bloom, Steven J. Davis, Mathias Dolls, and Pablo C. Zarate. "Time Savings When Working from Home." National Bureau of Economic Research Working Paper Series, no. 30866 (January 2023). https://doi.org/10.3386/w30866.
18. Dam, David, Davide Melcangi, Laura Pilossoph, and Aidan Toner-Rogers. "What Have Workers Done with the Time Freed Up by Commuting Less?" Liberty Street Economics, October 18, 2022. Accessed April 9, 2023. https://libertystreeteconomics.newyorkfed.org/2022/10/what-have-workers-done-with-the-time-freed-up-by-commuting-less/.
19. Federal Reserve Bank of St. Louis. "Timely Topics Podcast: Retirements Increased During the COVID-19 Pandemic. Who Retired and Why?"

March 30, 2022. Accessed April 9, 2023. https://www.stlouisfed.org/timely-topics/retirements-increased-during-pandemic.

20. Utz, Annabel, Julie Yixia Cai, and Dean Baker. "The Pandemic Rise in Self-Employment: Who Is Working for Themselves Now?" Center for Economic and Policy Research, August 29, 2022. Accessed April 9, 2023. https://cepr.net/the-pandemic-rise-in-self-employment-who-is-working-for-themselves-now/.
21. Richter, Felix. "The 'Great Resignation' Isn't Over Yet." Statista, January 5, 2023. Accessed April 9, 2023. https://www.statista.com/chart/26186/number-of-people-quitting-their-jobs-in-the-united-states/.
22. Landivar, Liana Christin, and Mark deWolf. "Mothers' Employment Two Years Later: An Assessment of Employment Loss and Recovery During the COVID-19 Pandemic." Women's Bureau, U.S. Department of Labor, 2022. Accessed April 9, 2023. https://www.dol.gov/sites/dolgov/files/WB/media/Mothers-employment-2%20-years-later-may2022.pdf.
23. Bhattarai, Abha. "Caring for Aging Parents, Sick Spouses Is Keeping Millions out of Work." *Washington Post*, April 4, 2022. Accessed April 9, 2023. https://www.washingtonpost.com/business/2022/04/04/caregiving-economy-adults-work/.
24. Glynn, Sarah Jane. "Coronavirus Paid Leave Exemptions Exclude Millions of Workers from Coverage." Center for American Progress, April 17, 2020. Accessed April 9, 2023. https://www.americanprogress.org/article/coronavirus-paid-leave-exemptions-exclude-millions-workers-coverage/.
25. Corbyn, Zoë. "'Bossware Is Coming for Almost Every Worker': The Software You Might Not Realize Is Watching You." *Guardian*, April 27, 2022. Accessed April 9, 2023. https://www.theguardian.com/technology/2022/apr/27/remote-work-software-home-surveillance-computer-monitoring-pandemic.
26. Work, Stress and Health. "Schedule," 2021. Accessed August 28, 2023. https://workstressandhealth.com/schedule/.
27. *Washington Post*. "Transcript: Race in America: The Costs of Racism with Heather McGhee, Author, 'The Sum of Us,'" July 21, 2022. Accessed April 16, 2023. https://www.washingtonpost.com/washington-post-live/2022/07/21/transcript-race-america-costs-racism-with-heather-mcghee-author-sum-us/.
28. Fuller, Joseph, and Manjari Raman. "The High Cost of Neglecting Low-Wage Workers." *Harvard Business Review*, May–June 2023. Accessed February 4, 2024. https://hbr.org/2023/05/the-high-cost-of-neglecting-low-wage-workers#:~:text=No%20matter%20how%20hard%20or,remained%20stuck%20in%20such%20positions.
29. Economic Policy Institute. "The Productivity–Pay Gap," October 2022. Accessed April 9, 2023. https://www.epi.org/productivity-pay-gap/.
30. Economic Policy Institute. "CEO Pay Has Skyrocketed 1,460% Since

1978: CEOs Were Paid 399 Times as Much as a Typical Worker in 2021," October 4, 2022. Accessed April 9, 2023. https://www.epi.org/publication/ceo-pay-in-2021/#:~:text=CEO%20pay%20has%20skyrocketed%201%2C460,in%202021%20%7C%20Economic%20Policy%20Institute.

31. Constant, Paul. "The Wealthiest 1% Has Taken $50 Trillion from Working Americans and Redistributed It, a New Study Finds. Here's What That Means." *Business Insider*, September 18, 2020. Accessed April 9, 2023. https://www.businessinsider.com/wealthiest-1-percent-stole-50-trillion-working-americans-what-means-2020-9.
32. Fischer, Amanda. "The Rising Financialization of the U.S. Economy Harms Workers and Their Families, Threatening a Strong Recovery." Washington Center for Equitable Growth, May 2021. Accessed September 3, 2023. https://equitablegrowth.org/wp-content/uploads/2021/05/051121-dignity-work-ib.pdf; Benmelech, Efraim, Nittai Bergman, and Hyunseob Kim. "Strong Employers and Weak Employees: How Does Employer Concentration Affect Wages?" NBER Working Paper Series, no. 24307, February 1, 2018. https://doi.org/10.3386/w24307; Schmitt, John, Elise Gould, and Josh Bivens. "America's Slow-Motion Wage Crisis: Four Decades of Slow and Unequal Growth." Economic Policy Institute, September 13, 2018. Accessed September 3, 2023. https://www.epi.org/publication/americas-slow-motion-wage-crisis-four-decades-of-slow-and-unequal-growth-2/.
33. Schaeffer, Katherine. "6 Facts About Economic Inequality in the U.S." Pew Research Center, February 7, 2020. Accessed April 9, 2023. https://www.pewresearch.org/fact-tank/2020/02/07/6-facts-about-economic-inequality-in-the-u-s/.
34. Edwards, Kathryn A. "A $2.5 Trillion Question: What If Incomes Grew Like GDP Did?" The RAND Blog, October 2020. Accessed April 6, 2023. https://www.rand.org/blog/2020/10/a-25-trillion-question-what-if-incomes-grew-like-gdp.html.
35. Stuart, Bryan A. "Intergenerational Economic Mobility: America Is Known as the Land of Opportunity, but Our Children Are Not Destined to Do Better Than Us." Inequality Research Review: Intergenerational Economic Mobility, 2023 Q3. Accessed February 4, 2024. https://www.philadelphiafed.org/-/media/frbp/assets/economy/articles/economic-insights/2023/q3/eiq323-inequality-research-review-intergenerational-economic-mobility.pdf.
36. Organisation for Economic Co-operation and Development. "Wage Levels (Indicator)," 2023. Accessed April 9, 2023. https://data.oecd.org/earnwage/wage-levels.htm.
37. ROC United. "Restaurant Opportunities Centers United." Accessed April 20, 2023. https://rocunited.org/.
38. "The Impact of Covid-19 on Restaurant Workers Across America." ROC United, January 2022. Accessed April 20, 2023. https://rocunited.org/wp-content/uploads/sites/7/2022/06/ROC_COVID_Impact_2.pdf.

39. Henderson, Kaitlyn. "Where Hard Work Doesn't Pay Off: An Index of US Labor Policies Compared to Peer Nations." Oxfam Research, 2023. Accessed August 30, 2023. https://webassets.oxfamamerica.org/media/documents/Where_Hard_Work_Doesnt_Pay_Off.pdf?_gl=1*1t3dm42*_ga*MTQ4NTQyOTAyNS4xNjkzMzQ4ODQ1*_ga_R58YETD6XK*MTY5MzM0ODg0NC4xLjAuMTY5MzM0ODg0NC42MC4wLjA.
40. International Labor Organization. "Working Time and Work-Life Balance Around the World," January 6, 2023. Accessed April 10, 2023. https://www.ilo.org/global/publications/books/WCMS_864222/lang—en/index.htm.
41. Hamermesh, Daniel S., and Elena Stancanelli. "Long Workweeks and Strange Hours." National Bureau of Economic Research Working Paper Series, no. 20449 (September 2014). Accessed February 5, 2024. https://www.nber.org/system/files/working_papers/w20449/w20449.pdf.
42. Cropley, Mark, Fred R. H. Zijlstra, Dawn Querstret, and Sarah R. Beck. "Is Work-Related Rumination Associated with Deficits in Executive Functioning?" *Frontiers in Psychology* 7 (September 30, 2016). https://doi.org/10.3389/fpsyg.2016.01524.
43. VTx Virginia Tech. "Employer Expectations on Off-Hours Email: New Study Shows Adverse Health Effects on Workers and Families," August 10, 2018. Accessed April 9, 2023. https://vtx.vt.edu/articles/2018/08/pamplin-employer-emailexpectations.html.
44. Cascio, Wayne. "Employment Downsizing and Its Alternatives." SHRM Foundation, 2009. Accessed April 9, 2023. https://www.shrm.org/hr-today/trends-and-forecasting/special-reports-and-expert-views/documents/employment-downsizing.pdf.
45. Miller, Claire Cain. "Women Did Everything Right. Then Work Got 'Greedy.'" *New York Times*, April 26, 2019. Accessed April 9, 2023. https://www.nytimes.com/2019/04/26/upshot/women-long-hours-greedy-professions.html.
46. Thompson, Derek. "The Religion of Workism Is Making Americans Miserable." *Atlantic*, February 24, 2019. Accessed April 9, 2023. https://www.theatlantic.com/ideas/archive/2019/02/religion-workism-making-americans-miserable/583441/.
47. Varanasi, Lakshmi, Sarah Jackson, Jordan Hart, Jyoti Mann, Beatrice Nolan, Hannah Getahun, Geoff Weiss, and Aaron Mok. "The Full List of Major US Companies Slashing Staff This Year, from UPS to Google and Microsoft." *Business Insider*, February 5, 2024. Accessed February 5, 2024. https://www.businessinsider.com/layoffs-sweeping-us-these-are-companies-making-cuts-2024#google-laid-off-hundreds-more-workers-in-2024-1.
48. Ross, Martha, and Nicole Bateman. "Meet the Low-Wage Workforce." Brookings, November 7, 2019. Accessed April 9, 2023. https://www.brookings.edu/research/meet-the-low-wage-workforce/.

49. Aurand, Andrew, Dan Emmanuel, Ikra Rafi, Dan Threet, and Diane Yentel. "Out of Reach: The High Cost of Housing 2021." National Low Income Housing Coalition, 2021. Accessed April 9, 2023. https://nlihc.org/sites/default/files/oor/2021/Out-of-Reach_2021.pdf.
50. U.S. Government Accountability Office. "Federal Social Safety Net Programs: Millions of Full-Time Workers Rely on Federal Health Care and Food Assistance Programs," October 19, 2020. Accessed April 9, 2023. https://www.gao.gov/products/gao-21-45.
51. Bhattarai, Abha, and Maggie Penman. "Restaurants Can't Find Workers Because They've Found Better Jobs." *Washington Post,* February 3, 2023. Accessed April 9, 2023. https://www.washingtonpost.com/business/2023/02/03/worker-shortage-restaurants-hotels-economy/.
52. Bogage, Jacob, and María Luisa Paúl. "The Conservative Campaign to Rewrite Child Labor Laws." *Washington Post,* May 1, 2023. Accessed August 8, 2023. https://www.washingtonpost.com/business/2023/04/23/child-labor-lobbying-fga/.
53. Heigl, Lillie, Elana Silva, and Kimberly Knackstedt. "Pennies on the Dollar: The Use of Subminimum Wage for Disabled Workers Across the United States." Education Policy Program, New America Foundation, February 14, 2024. Accessed February 14, 2024. https://www.newamerica.org/education-policy/reports/the-use-of-subminimum-wage-for-disabled-workers-across-the-us/.
54. Bogage, Jacob. "In a Tight Labor Market, Some States Look to Another Type of Worker: Children." *Washington Post,* February 11, 2023. Accessed April 9, 2023. https://www.washingtonpost.com/business/2023/02/11/child-labor-iowa/.
55. Bureau of Labor Statistics, U.S. Department of Labor. "History of Child Labor in the United States—Part 2: The Reform Movement," January 2017. Accessed April 9, 2023. https://www.bls.gov/opub/mlr/2017/article/history-of-child-labor-in-the-united-states-part-2-the-reform-movement.htm#:~:text=It%20was%20not%20until%201938,be%20upheld%20by%20the%20Court.
56. Dua, André, Kweilin Ellingrud, Bryan Hancock, Ryan Luby, Anu Madgavkar, and Sarah Pemberton. "Freelance, Side Hustles, and Gigs: Many More Americans Have Become Independent Workers." McKinsey & Company, August 23, 2022. Accessed April 9, 2023. https://www.mckinsey.com/featured-insights/sustainable-inclusive-growth/future-of-america/freelance-side-hustles-and-gigs-many-more-americans-have-become-independent-workers; Atske, Sara. "The State of Gig Work in 2021." Pew Research Center, December 8, 2021. Accessed September 21, 2023. https://www.pewresearch.org/internet/2021/12/08/the-state-of-gig-work-in-2021/.
57. Oddo, Vanessa M., Castiel Chen Zhuang, Sarah B. Andrea, Jerzy Eisenberg-

Guyot, Trevor Peckham, Daniel Jacoby, and Anjum Hajat. "Changes in Precarious Employment in the United States: A Longitudinal Analysis." *Scandinavian Journal of Work, Environment & Health* 47, no. 3 (April 1, 2021): 171–80. https://doi.org/10.5271/sjweh.3939.

58. Cha, Youngjoo, and Kim A. Weeden. "Overwork and the Slow Convergence in the Gender Gap in Wages." *American Sociological Review* 79, no. 3 (April 8, 2014): 457–84. https://doi.org/10.1177/0003122414528936.
59. Sullivan, Daniel C., and Till Von Wachter. "Mortality, Mass-Layoffs, and Career Outcomes: An Analysis Using Administrative Data." National Bureau of Economic Research Working Paper Series, no. 13626 (November 28, 2007). https://doi.org/10.3386/w13626.
60. Sucher, Sandra J., and Marilyn Morgan Westner. "What Companies Still Get Wrong About Layoffs." *Harvard Business Review*, December 8, 2022. Accessed April 9, 2023. https://hbr.org/2022/12/what-companies-still-get-wrong-about-layoffs.
61. Acemoglu, Daron, Alex Jingwei He, and Daniel Le Maire. "Eclipse of Rent-Sharing: The Effects of Managers' Business Education on Wages and the Labor Share in the US and Denmark." National Bureau of Economic Research Working Paper Series, no. 29874 (March 1, 2022). https://doi.org/10.3386/w29874.
62. Sull, Donald, Charles Sull, William Cipolli, and Caio Brighenti. "Why Every Leader Needs to Worry About Toxic Culture." *MIT Sloan Management Review*, March 16, 2022. Accessed April 9, 2023. https://sloanreview.mit.edu/article/why-every-leader-needs-to-worry-about-toxic-culture/.
63. Sull, Donald, Charles Sull, and Ben Zweig. "Toxic Culture Is Driving the Great Resignation." *MIT Sloan Management Review*, January 11, 2022. Accessed April 9, 2023. https://sloanreview.mit.edu/article/toxic-culture-is-driving-the-great-resignation/.
64. McFeely, Shane, and Ben Wigert. "This Fixable Problem Costs U.S. Businesses $1 Trillion." Gallup, March 13, 2019. Accessed April 9, 2023. https://www.gallup.com/workplace/247391/fixable-problem-costs-businesses-trillion.aspx.
65. Williams, Joan B. "The Pandemic Has Exposed the Fallacy of the 'Ideal Worker.'" *Harvard Business Review*, May 11, 2020. Accessed February 6, 2024. https://hbr.org/2020/05/the-pandemic-has-exposed-the-fallacy-of-the-ideal-worker.
66. New America. "Sexual Harassment: A Severe and Pervasive Problem." Accessed April 9, 2023. https://www.newamerica.org/better-life-lab/reports/sexual-harassment-severe-and-pervasive-problem/summary-of-findings/.
67. Bureau of Labor Statistics, U.S. Department of Labor. "Employment Characteristics of Families—2021," April 20, 2022. Accessed April 9, 2023. https://www.bls.gov/news.release/pdf/famee.pdf.

68. Glass, Jennifer, Kelly Raley, and Joanna Pepin. "Mothers Are the Primary Earners in Growing Numbers of Families with Children." Council on Contemporary Families, November 2, 2021. Accessed April 9, 2023. https://sites.utexas.edu/contemporaryfamilies/2021/11/02/breadwinning-mothers-brief-report/.
69. Bureau of Labor Statistics. "Table 4. Families with Own Children: Employment Status of Parents by Age of Youngest Child and Family Type, 2021–2022 Annual Averages." Accessed February 4, 2024. https://www.bls.gov/news.release/famee.t04.htm.
70. Hunt, Sabastian. "The Case Against GDP, Made by Its Own Creator." Gross National Happiness USA, March 5, 2021. Accessed April 24, 2023. https://gnhusa.org/gpi/the-case-against-gdp-made-by-its-own-creator/.
71. Brenan, Megan. "Women Still Handle Main Household Tasks in U.S." Gallup, November 29, 2020. Accessed April 9, 2023. https://news.gallup.com/poll/283979/women-handle-main-household-tasks.aspx.
72. Miller, Andrea, and Eugene Borgida. "The Separate Spheres Model of Gendered Inequality." *PLOS One* 11, no. 1 (January 22, 2016): e0147315. https://doi.org/10.1371/journal.pone.0147315.
73. Bureau of Labor Statistics, U.S. Department of Labor. "May 2021 National Occupational and Wage Estimates United States: 39-9011 Childcare Workers," *Occupational Employment and Wage Statistics*, March 31, 2022. Accessed April 9, 2023. https://www.bls.gov/oes/current/oes399011.htm.
74. Whitebook, Marcy, Deborah Philipps, and Carollee Howes. "Worthy Work, STILL Unlivable Wages: The Early Childhood Workforce 25 Years After the Child Care Staffing Study." Center for the Study of Child Care Employment, University of California, Berkeley, 2014. Accessed September 21, 2023. https://cscce.berkeley.edu/wp-content/uploads/publications/Executive-Summary-Final.pdf.
75. Bureau of Labor Statistics, U.S. Department of Labor. "Employment Projections—2021–2031," September 8, 2022. Accessed April 9, 2023. https://www.bls.gov/news.release/pdf/ecopro.pdf.
76. Fuller, Joseph, and Manjari Raman. "The Caring Company: How Employers Can Cut Costs and Boost Productivity by Helping Employees Manage Caregiving Needs." Harvard Business School, January 17, 2019. Accessed April 9, 2023. https://www.hbs.edu/managing-the-future-of-work/research/Pages/the-caring-company.aspx.
77. Reid, Erin. "Why Some Men Pretend to Work 80-Hour Weeks." *Harvard Business Review*, April 28, 2015. Accessed April 9, 2023. https://hbr.org/2015/04/why-some-men-pretend-to-work-80-hour-weeks.
78. Heppner, Rebekah. "The Ideal Worker." In *The Lost Leaders: How Corporate America Loses Women Leaders*, pp. 75–91. New York: Palgrave Macmillan, 2013. https://doi.org/10.1057/9781137350701_9.
79. Rashid, Rebecca, and Arthur C. Brooks. "A New Formula for Happi-

ness." *Atlantic*, November 14, 2022. Accessed April 9, 2023. https://www.theatlantic.com/podcasts/archive/2022/11/happiness-formula-howto-age/672109/?utm_source=substack&utm_medium=email.

80. Collins, Caitlyn, Leah Ruppanner, and William J. Scarborough. "Why Haven't U.S. Mothers Returned to Work? The Child-Care Infrastructure They Need Is Still Missing." *Washington Post*, November 8, 2021. Accessed April 19, 2023. https://www.washingtonpost.com/politics/2021/11/08/why-havent-us-mothers-returned-work-child-care-infrastructure-they-need-is-still-missing/.
81. D'Souza, Karen. "Is the Child Care Crisis Escalating?" EdSource, May 3, 2023. Accessed September 3, 2023. https://edsource.org/2023/is-the-child-care-crisis-escalating/689487.
82. Coffey, Maureen, and Rose Khattar. "The Child Care Sector Will Continue to Struggle Hiring Staff Unless It Creates Good Jobs." Center for American Progress, September 2, 2022. Accessed September 3, 2023. https://www.americanprogress.org/article/the-child-care-sector-will-continue-to-struggle-hiring-staff-unless-it-creates-good-jobs/.
83. Glynn, "Coronavirus Paid Leave Exemptions Exclude Millions of Workers from Coverage."
84. Company communication provided to author by Kari McCracken.
85. World Policy Center. "Is Paid Annual Leave Available to Workers?" Accessed April 9, 2023. https://www.worldpolicycenter.org/policies/is-paid-annual-leave-available-to-workers.
86. LaRocco, Lori Ann. "Deadline to Avoid a National Rail Strike Which Could Cost Economy $2 Billion a Day Is Near." CNBC, September 8, 2022. Accessed April 9, 2023. https://www.cnbc.com/2022/09/08/deadline-for-rail-strike-which-could-cost-2-billion-a-day-nears.html.
87. Levitz, Eric. "Why America's Railroads Refuse to Give Their Workers Paid Leave." *Intelligencer*, November 30, 2022. Accessed April 9, 2023. https://nymag.com/intelligencer/2022/11/rail-strike-why-the-railroads-wont-give-in-on-paid-leave-psr-precision-scheduled-railroading.html.
88. Cohen, Josh. "Why Can't WA Rail Workers Use State Sick Leave?" *Crosscut*, December 9, 2022. Accessed April 9, 2023. https://crosscut.com/news/2022/12/why-cant-wa-rail-workers-use-state-sick-leave.
89. Kanno-Youngs, Zolan, and Emily Cochrane. "Biden Signs Legislation to Avert Nationwide Rail Strike." *New York Times*, December 2, 2022. Accessed September 3, 2023. https://www.nytimes.com/2022/12/02/us/politics/rail-strike-biden.html.
90. Mark, Julian. "Why Paid Sick Leave Became a Big Issue in Rail Labor Talks." *Washington Post*, December 3, 2022. Accessed April 9, 2023. https://www.washingtonpost.com/business/2022/12/03/rail-workers-paid-sick-leave/.
91. Shepardson, David. "Most Unionized US Rail Workers Now Have New

Sick Leave." Reuters, June 6, 2023. Accessed September 21, 2023. https://www.reuters.com/world/us/most-unionized-us-rail-workers-now-have-new-sick-leave-2023-06-05/.

92. U.S. Bureau of Labor Statistics. "What Data Does the BLS Publish on Family Leave?" September 21, 2023. Accessed October 14, 2023. https://www.bls.gov/ebs/factsheets/family-leave-benefits-fact-sheet.htm.
93. Kliff, Sarah. "1 in 4 American Moms Return to Work Within 2 Weeks of Giving Birth—Here's What It's Like." *Vox*, August 22, 2015. Accessed April 9, 2023. https://www.vox.com/2015/8/21/9188343/maternity-leave-united-states.
94. Schulte, Brigid. "Caring for Dying Loved Ones Is a Luxury Few Can Afford. I Was Lucky." *Washington Post*, April 9, 2021. Accessed April 9, 2023. https://www.washingtonpost.com/outlook/dying-family-time-off-work/2021/04/08/045da710-97b7-11eb-a6d0-13d207aadb78_story.html.
95. Organisation for Economic Co-operation and Development. "PF3.1: Public Spending on Child Care and Early Education," February 2023. Accessed April 9, 2023. https://www.oecd.org/els/soc/PF3_1_Public_spending_on_child care_and_early_education.pdf.
96. Women's Bureau, U.S. Department of Labor. "Fact Sheet: Childcare Prices in Local Areas," January 2023. Accessed February 21, 2024. https://www.dol.gov/sites/dolgov/files/WB/NDCP/Fact-sheet-English-508-compliant.pdf.
97. U.S. Government Accountability Office. "Child Care: Subsidy Eligibility and Use in Fiscal Year 2019 and State Program Changes During the Pandemic," March 29, 2023. Accessed February 4, 2024. https://www.gao.gov/products/gao-23-106073.
98. Hanson, Melanie. "U.S. Public Education Spending Statistics." Education Data Initiative, September 8, 2023. Accessed February 16, 2024. https://educationdata.org/public-education-spending-statistics.
99. "Remarks by Secretary of the Treasury Janet L. Yellen on Shortages in the Child Care System." U.S. Department of the Treasury press release, September 15, 2021. Accessed March 8, 2024. https://home.treasury.gov/news/press-releases/jy0355.
100. Collins, Caitlyn. "In Germany, Parents Can Sue the Government for Failing to Provide Child Care." *Atlantic*, January 10, 2017. Accessed February 21, 2024. https://www.theatlantic.com/business/archive/2017/01/german-childcare/512612/.
101. Cohen, Rachel M. "Canada Is Promoting Child Care for $10 a Day." *Vox*, December 18, 2023. Accessed February 21, 2024. https://www.vox.com/24002791/child-care-daycare-canada-parenting-children-policy.
102. Carrazana, Chabeli. "1 in 4 Parents Report Being Fired for Work Interruptions Due to Child Care Breakdowns." 19th, February 2, 2023. Accessed Sep-

tember 3, 2023. https://19thnews.org/2023/02/child-care-crisis-economy-parents-jobs/.

103. *HomeCare* magazine. "Study: Families Shoulder Burden of Care for Seniors," November 29, 2022. Accessed April 9, 2023. https://www.homecaremag.com/news/study-families-shoulder-burden-care-seniors.
104. American Association of Retired Persons. "AARP Research Shows Family Caregivers Face Significant Financial Strain, Spend on Average $7,242 Each Year," June 29, 2021. Accessed April 9, 2023. https://press.aarp.org/2021-6-29-AARP-Research-Shows-Family-Caregivers-Face-Significant-Financial-Strain,-Spend-on-Average-7,242-Each-Year.
105. Harknett, Kristen, and Daniel Schneider. "Precarious Work Schedules and Population Health." *Health Affairs*, February 12, 2020. Accessed April 9, 2023. https://www.healthaffairs.org/do/10.1377/hpb20200206.806111/#:~:text=Exposure%20to%20unstable%20and%20unpredictable,increased%20psychological%20distress%20in%20adults.
106. Lynch, Shana. "Why Your Workplace Might Be Killing You." Stanford Graduate School of Business, February 23, 2015. Accessed April 9, 2023. https://www.gsb.stanford.edu/insights/why-your-workplace-might-be-killing-you.
107. U.S. Department of Health and Human Services. "The U.S. Surgeon General's Framework for Workplace Mental Health & Well-Being," 2022. Accessed August 28, 2023. https://www.hhs.gov/sites/default/files/workplace-mental-health-well-being.pdf.
108. Deloitte. "Work and Wellbeing Still Aren't Working Well Together," August 2, 2023. Accessed August 28, 2023. https://action.deloitte.com/insight/3455/work-and-wellbeing-still-arent-working-well-together.
109. Gallup. "State of the Global Workplace Report," August 24, 2023. Accessed August 28, 2023. https://www.gallup.com/workplace/349484/state-of-the-global-workplace.aspx.
110. Perry, Mark, J. "Quotation of the Day on the 'Magic of the Marketplace.'" American Enterprise Institute, September 26, 2013. Accessed February 5, 2024. https://www.aei.org/carpe-diem/quotation-of-the-day-on-the-magic-of-the-marketplace/.
111. Haynie, Devon. "Report: American Quality of Life Declines over Past Decade." *US News & World Report*, September 11, 2020. Accessed April 9, 2023. https://www.usnews.com/news/best-countries/articles/2020-09-11/a-global-anomaly-the-us-declines-in-annual-quality-of-life-report.
112. Pew Research Center. "Public Trust in Government: 1958–2023," September 19, 2023. Accessed February 6, 2024. https://www.pewresearch.org/politics/2023/09/19/public-trust-in-government-1958-2023/.
113. Simmons-Duffin, Selena. "'Live Free and Die?' The Sad State of U.S. Life Expectancy." NPR, March 25, 2023. Accessed April 9, 2023. https://www

.npr.org/sections/health-shots/2023/03/25/1164819944/live-free-and-die-the-sad-state-of-u-s-life-expectancy.

114. Schulte, Brigid. "Trump's New Rule to Punish Immigrants Just Shows How Bad American Jobs Are." *Washington Post*, September 5, 2019. Accessed April 9, 2023. https://www.washingtonpost.com/outlook/the-cruel-irony-of-the-newpublic-charge-rule/2019/09/05/37f51896-cf5a-11e9-9031-519885a08a86_story.html.
115. McLean, Caitlin, Lea Austin, Marcy Whitebook, and Krista Olson. "Early Childhood Workforce Index 2020." Center for the Study of Child Care Employment, University of California, Berkeley, 2021. Accessed April 9, 2023. https://cscce.berkeley.edu/workforce-index-2020/the-early-educator-workforce/early-educator-pay-economic-insecurity-across-the-states/.
116. Schulte, Brigid. "Crisis Conversations: Is Our Childcare System Nearing Its Breaking Point?" New America, May 1, 2020. Accessed April 9, 2023. https://www.newamerica.org/better-life-lab/podcasts/crisis-conversations-our-childcare-system-nearing-its-breaking-point/.
117. Autor, David, David Mindell, and Elisabeth Reynolds. "The Work of the Future: Building Better Jobs in an Age of Intelligent Machines." MIT Task Force on the Work of the Future, November 17, 2020. Accessed April 9, 2023. https://workofthefuture.mit.edu/research-post/the-work-of-the-future-building-better-jobs-in-an-age-of-intelligent-machines/.
118. Gray, Mary. "Ghost Work: How to Stop Silicon Valley from Building a New Global Underclass." Data & Society, May 8, 2019. https://datasociety.net/library/databite-no-119-mary-l-gray/.
119. Reich, Robert. "3 Economic Myths," video, March 10, 2015. Accessed April 9, 2023. https://robertreich.org/post/113280648985.
120. Lu, Chunlong. "Middle Class and Democracy: Structural Linkage." *International Review of Modern Sociology* 31, no. 2 (2005): 157–78.
121. Schulte, Brigid. "Rage Against the Machine: The Future of Work Is Already Here, and It Isn't Robots We Should Be Stressed Out About." New America, March 22, 2022. Accessed April 16, 2023. https://www.newamerica.org/better-life-lab/podcasts/rage-against-the-machine-the-future-of-work-is-already-here/.
122. Lucassen, Jan. *The Story of Work: A New History of Humankind*. New Haven, CT: Yale University Press, 2021, pp. 5, 74, 437.
123. Rashid and Brooks, "A New Formula for Happiness."
124. Lucassen, *The Story of Work*, p. 72.
125. Schwartz, Barry. *Why We Work*. TED Books. New York: Simon & Schuster, 2015, p. 70.
126. Horowitz, Juliana Menasce, and Kim Parker. "How Americans View Their Jobs." Pew Research Center, March 30, 2023. Accessed February 24, 2024. https://www.pewresearch.org/social-trends/2023/03/30/how-americans-view-their-jobs/.

127. General Social Survey, National Opinion Research Center, NORC, at the University of Chicago. Accessed February 24, 2024. https://gssdataexplorer.norc.org/variables/4493/vshow.
128. Schwartz, *Why We Work*, pp. 24–30.
129. Schwartz, *Why We Work*, p. 10.
130. Schulte, Brigid. *Overwhelmed: Work, Love, and Play When No One Has the Time*. New York: Sarah Crichton Books, Farrar, Straus and Giroux, 2014.

Chapter 1: American Karoshi

1. Yale Law School Career Development Office. "The Truth About the Billable Hour." Accessed September 3, 2023. https://law.yale.edu/sites/default/files/area/department/cdo/document/billable_hour.pdf.
2. Heart and Stroke Foundation of Canada. "Spontaneous Coronary Artery Dissection (SCAD)." Accessed April 23, 2023. https://www.heartandstroke.ca/heart-disease/conditions/spontaneous-coronary-artery-dissection#:~:text=Ninety%20percent%20of%20SCAD%20cases,women%20under%2060%20years%20old.
3. Saw, Jacqueline, Eve Aymong, Tara Sedlak, Christopher E. Buller, Andrew Starovoytov, Donald R. Ricci, Simon P. Robinson, et al. "Spontaneous Coronary Artery Dissection." *Circulation: Cardiovascular Interventions* 7, no. 5 (October 7, 2014): 645–55. https://doi.org/10.1161/circinterventions.114.001760; Tanabe, Junya, Yuzo Kagawa, Akihiro Endo, and Kazuaki Tanabe. "Spontaneous Coronary Artery Dissection Associated with Psychological Stress." *BMJ Case Reports* 14, no. 8 (August 25, 2021): e245414. https://doi.org/10.1136/bcr-2021-245414.
4. Miller, Claire Cain. "Women Did Everything Right. Then Work Got 'Greedy.'" *New York Times*, April 26, 2019. Accessed April 10, 2023. https://www.nytimes.com/2019/04/26/upshot/women-long-hours-greedy-professions.html.
5. Schwartz, Jeff, Tom Hodson, and Ian Winstrom Otten. "The Overwhelmed Employee." *Deloitte Insights*, March 8, 2014. Accessed April 10, 2023. https://www2.deloitte.com/us/en/insights/focus/human-capital-trends/2014/hc-trends-2014-overwhelmed-employee.html; Unhealthy Work. "Unhealthy Work: Causes, Consequences, Cures Archives," January 26, 2012. Accessed September 3, 2023. https://unhealthywork.org/category/unhealthywork/; *Corporate Wellness Magazine*. "The Top 20 Corporate Wellness Apps You Need to Know About." Accessed September 3, 2023. https://www.corporatewellnessmagazine.com/article/the-top-20-corporate-wellness-apps-you-need-to-know-about; Place Lab. "Wellness 2.0: Beyond Lunchtime Yoga." EQ Office, February 20, 2020. Accessed September 3, 2023. https://www.eqoffice.com/placelab/wellness-2-0-beyond-lunchtime-yoga.
6. Fleming, William J. "Employee Well-Being Outcomes from Individual-Level

Mental Health Interventions." *Industrial Relations Journal*, January 2024. Accessed February 7, 2024. https://wellbeing.hmc.ox.ac.uk/publications/employee-well-being-outcomes-from-individual-level-mental-health-interventions-cross-sectional-evidence-from-the-united-kingdom/.

7. Tsutsumi, Akizumi. "Prevention and Management of Work-Related Cardiovascular Disorders." *International Journal of Occupational Medicine and Environmental Health* 28, no. 1 (2015): 4–7. https://doi.org/10.2478/s13382-014-0319-z.
8. Dunleavy, Brian P. "People with Mental Health Disorders 76% More Likely to Be Out Sick Due to Stress." UPI, April 1, 2020. Accessed April 10, 2023. https://www.upi.com/Health_News/2020/04/01/People-with-mental-health-disorders-76-more-likely-to-be-out-sick-due-to-stress/3961585750522/; Garefelt, Johanna, Loretta G. Platts, Martin Hyde, Linda L. Magnusson Hanson, Hugo Westerlund, and Torbjörn Åkerstedt. "Reciprocal Relations Between Work Stress and Insomnia Symptoms: A Prospective Study." *Journal of Sleep Research* 29, no. 2 (December 2, 2019): e12949. https://doi.org/10.1111/jsr.12949.
9. McGregor, Jena. "This Professor Says the Workplace Is the Fifth Leading Cause of Death in the U.S." *Washington Post*, March 22, 2018. Accessed April 10, 2023. https://www.washingtonpost.com/news/on-leadership/wp/2018/03/22/this-professor-says-the-workplace-is-the-fifth-leading-cause-of-death-in-the-u-s/.
10. Schnall, Peter L., Joseph E. Schwartz, Paul Landsbergis, Katherine E. Warren, and Thomas G. Pickering. "A Longitudinal Study of Job Strain and Ambulatory Blood Pressure." *Psychosomatic Medicine* 60, no. 6 (November 1, 1998): 697–706. https://doi.org/10.1097/00006842-199811000-00007; Healthy Work Campaign. "Introducing 'Working on Empty.'" Medium, February 8, 2017. Accessed September 3, 2023. https://healthyworknow.medium.com/introducing-working-on-empty-aa884df0d25b; Unhealthy Work. "Unhealthy Work: Causes, Consequences, Cures Archives—Unhealthy Work," January 26, 2012. Accessed September 3, 2023. https://unhealthywork.org/category/unhealthywork/; Schnall, Peter L., Paul Landsbergis, and Dean Baker. "Job Strain and Cardiovascular Disease." *Annual Review of Public Health* 15, no. 1 (January 1, 1994): 381–411. https://doi.org/10.1146/annurev.pu.15.050194.002121.
11. World Health Organization. "Psycho-Social Risks and Mental Health." Accessed September 3, 2023. https://www.who.int/tools/occupational-hazards-in-health-sector/psycho-social-risks-mental-health; American Psychological Association. "Coping with Stress at Work," October 14, 2018. Accessed September 3, 2023. https://www.apa.org/topics/healthy-workplaces/work-stress; European Agency for Safety and Health at Work. "Psychosocial Risks and Stress at Work." Accessed September 3, 2023. https://osha.europa.eu/en/themes/psychosocial-risks-and-stress.

12. Garton, Eric. "Employee Burnout Is a Problem with the Company, Not the Person." *Harvard Business Review,* April 6, 2017. Accessed September 3, 2023. https://hbr.org/2017/04/employee-burnout-is-a-problem-with-the-company-not-the-person; Edú-Valsania, Sergio, Ana Laguía, and Juan Antonio Moriano León. "Burnout: A Review of Theory and Measurement." *International Journal of Environmental Research and Public Health* 19, no. 3 (February 4, 2022): 1780. https://doi.org/10.3390/ijerph19031780.
13. Moss, Jennifer. "Burnout Is About Your Workplace, Not Your People." *Harvard Business Review,* December 11, 2019. Accessed April 10, 2023. https://hbr.org/2019/12/burnout-is-about-your-workplace-not-your-people.
14. Stewart, Emily. "The American Unemployment System Is Broken by Design." *Vox,* May 13, 2020. Accessed February 7, 2024. https://www.vox.com/policy-and-politics/2020/5/13/21255894/unemployment-insurance-system-problems-florida-claims-pua-new-york.
15. Autor, David, David Mindell, and Elisabeth Reynolds. "The Work of the Future: Building Better Jobs in an Age of Intelligent Machines." MIT Task Force on the Work of the Future, November 17, 2020. Accessed April 9, 2023. https://workofthefuture.mit.edu/wp-content/uploads/2021/01/2020-Final-Report4.pdf, p. 65.
16. Gallo, William T., Hsun-Mei Teng, Tracy Falba, Stanislav V. Kasl, Harlan M. Krumholz, and Elizabeth H. Bradley. "The Impact of Late Career Job Loss on Myocardial Infarction and Stroke: A 10 Year Follow Up Using the Health and Retirement Survey." *Occupational and Environmental Medicine* 63, no. 10 (October 1, 2006): 683–87. https://doi.org/10.1136/oem.2006.026823.
17. Preidt, Robert. "After Job Loss, People Report More Health Issues." ABC News, May 8, 2009. Accessed April 10, 2023. https://abcnews.go.com/Health/Healthday/story?id=7540442&page=1.
18. Roelfs, David J., Eran Shor, Karina W. Davidson, and Joseph E. Schwartz. "Losing Life and Livelihood: A Systematic Review and Meta-Analysis of Unemployment and All-Cause Mortality." *Social Science & Medicine* 72, no. 6 (March 1, 2011): 840–54. https://doi.org/10.1016/j.socscimed.2011.01.005; Singh, Gopal K., and Mohammad Siahpush. "Inequalities in US Life Expectancy by Area Unemployment Level, 1990–2010." *Scientifica* 2016 (January 1, 2016): 1–12. https://doi.org/10.1155/2016/8290435.
19. Ramchand, Rajeev, Lynsay Ayer, and Stephen O'Connor. "Unemployment, Behavioral Health, and Suicide." *Health Affairs,* April 7, 2022. https://doi.org/10.1377/hpb20220302.274862.
20. Wood, Alexander M., Mark Graham, Vili Lehdonvirta, and Isis Hjorth. "Good Gig, Bad Gig: Autonomy and Algorithmic Control in the Global Gig Economy." *Work, Employment & Society* 33, no. 1 (February 1, 2019): 56–75. https://doi.org/10.1177/0950017018785616.
21. Marmot, Michael, Stephen Stansfeld, Chetan K. Patel, Fiona M. North, James W. Head, Ian H. White, Eric J. Brunner, A. Feeney, and Geoffrey

Smith. "Health Inequalities Among British Civil Servants: The Whitehall II Study." *Lancet* 337, no. 8754 (June 8, 1991): 1387–93. https://doi.org/10.1016/0140-6736(91)93068-k.

22. Schieman, Scott, Yuko Whitestone, and Karen T. Van Gundy. "The Nature of Work and the Stress of Higher Status." *Journal of Health and Social Behavior* 47, no. 3 (September 1, 2006): 242–57. https://doi.org/10.1177/002214650604700304.
23. Pudrovska, Tetyana, Deborah Carr, Michael J. McFarland, and Caitlyn Collins. "Higher-Status Occupations and Breast Cancer: A Life-Course Stress Approach." *Social Science & Medicine* 89 (July 1, 2013): 53–61. https://doi.org/10.1016/j.socscimed.2013.04.013.
24. Virtanen, Marianna, Stephen Stansfeld, Rebecca Fuhrer, Jane E. Ferrie, and Mika Kivimäki. "Overtime Work as a Predictor of Major Depressive Episode: A 5-Year Follow-Up of the Whitehall II Study." *PLOS One* 7, no. 1 (January 25, 2012): e30719. https://doi.org/10.1371/journal.pone.0030719; Virtanen, Marianna, Jane E. Ferrie, Archana Singh-Manoux, Martin J. Shipley, Jussi Vahtera, Michael Marmot, and Mika Kivimäki. "Overtime Work and Incident Coronary Heart Disease: The Whitehall II Prospective Cohort Study." *European Heart Journal* 31, no. 14 (July 1, 2010): 1737–44. https://doi.org/10.1093/eurheartj/ehq124; Wong, Kapo, Alan H. S. Chan, and Shing-Chung Ngan. "The Effect of Long Working Hours and Overtime on Occupational Health: A Meta-Analysis of Evidence from 1998 to 2018." *International Journal of Environmental Research and Public Health* 16, no. 12 (June 13, 2019): 2102. https://doi.org/10.3390/ijerph16122102.
25. Anderson, Pauline. "Physicians Experience Highest Suicide Rate of Any Profession." Medscape, May 7, 2020. Accessed April 10, 2023. https://www.medscape.com/viewarticle/896257; Weston, Caitlin. "Burning Out: International Approaches to Clinician Wellbeing." Churchill Trust, 2018. Accessed September 3, 2023. https://doctorshealthsa.com.au/uploads/C_Weston-Report_Churchill-Trust-Roadshow_Burning-Out_doctors-health-report.pdf.
26. Carmichael, Sarah Green. "The Research Is Clear: Long Hours Backfire for People and for Companies." *Harvard Business Review*, August 28, 2015. Accessed April 19, 2023. https://hbr.org/2015/08/the-research-is-clear-long-hours-backfire-for-people-and-for-companies.
27. Healthy Work Campaign. "Healthy Work Stats and Infographs," December 22, 2022. Accessed April 10, 2023. https://www.healthywork.org/resources/statistics-infographs/.
28. Gallup. "State of the Global Workplace 2021 Report," 2021. Accessed September 3, 2023. https://bendchamber.org/wp-content/uploads/2021/12/state-of-the-global-workplace-2021-download.pdf, p. 40.
29. Aronsson, Gunnar, Töres Theorell, Tom Grape, Anne Hammarström,

Christer Hogstedt, Ina Marteinsdottir, Ingmar Skoog, Lil Träskman-Bendz, and Charlotte Hall. "A Systematic Review Including Meta-Analysis of Work Environment and Burnout Symptoms." *BMC Public Health* 17, no. 1 (March 16, 2017). https://doi.org/10.1186/s12889-017-4153-7.

30. Landsbergis, Paul, Marnie Dobson, George W. Koutsouras, and Peter L. Schnall. "Job Strain and Ambulatory Blood Pressure: A Meta-Analysis and Systematic Review." *American Journal of Public Health* 103, no. 3 (February 6, 2013): e61–71. https://doi.org/10.2105/ajph.2012.301153.
31. Theorell, Töres, Katarina Jood, Lisbeth Slunga Järvholm, Eva Vingård, Joep Perk, Per-Olof Östergren, and Charlotte L. Hall. "A Systematic Review of Studies in the Contributions of the Work Environment to Ischaemic Heart Disease Development." *European Journal of Public Health* 26, no. 3 (June 1, 2016): 470–77. https://doi.org/10.1093/eurpub/ckw025.
32. Theorell, Töres, Anne Hammarström, Gunnar Aronsson, Lil Träskman-Bendz, Tom Grape, Christer Hogstedt, Ina Marteinsdottir, Ingmar Skoog, and Charlotte Hall. "A Systematic Review Including Meta-Analysis of Work Environment and Depressive Symptoms." *BMC Public Health* 15, no. 1 (August 1, 2015). https://doi.org/10.1186/s12889-015-1954-4.
33. Bureau of Labor Statistics, U.S. Department of Labor. "Employed Persons by Detailed Occupation, Sex, Race, and Hispanic or Latino Ethnicity." Labor Force Statistics from the Current Population Survey, January 25, 2023. Accessed April 10, 2023. https://www.bls.gov/cps/cpsaat11.htm.
34. New America. "Working While Black," April 26, 2023. Accessed August 28, 2023. https://www.newamerica.org/better-life-lab/podcasts/working-while-black/.
35. World Health Organization: WHO. "Burn-out an 'Occupational Phenomenon': International Classification of Diseases," May 28, 2019. Accessed April 10, 2023. https://www.who.int/news/item/28-05-2019-burn-out-an-occupational-phenomenon-international-classification-of-diseases.
36. Mayo Clinic. "Breaking Down Burnout in the Workplace," April 6, 2023. https://mcpress.mayoclinic.org/mental-health/breaking-down-burnout-in-the-workplace/.
37. Mayo Clinic. "Coping with Stress: Workplace Tips," June 16, 2021. Accessed April 16, 2023. https://www.mayoclinic.org/healthy-lifestyle/stress-management/in-depth/coping-with-stress/art-20048369.
38. Boyd, Danielle. "Workplace Stress." American Institute of Stress, February 15, 2023. Accessed April 10, 2023. https://www.stress.org/workplace-stress.
39. McKinsey & Company. "Employee Burnout Is Ubiquitous, Alarming—and Still Underreported," April 16, 2021. Accessed April 10, 2023. https://www.mckinsey.com/featured-insights/sustainable-inclusive-growth

/chart-of-the-day/employee-burnout-is-ubiquitous-alarming-and-still-underreported.

40. Abramson, Ashley. "Burnout and Stress Are Everywhere." American Psychological Association, January 1, 2022. Accessed April 10, 2023. https://www.apa.org/monitor/2022/01/special-burnout-stress.
41. Eley Law Firm. "Can Coloradans Seek Workers' Compensation for Job-Related Heart Attacks?" Accessed April 10, 2023. https://www.eleylawfirm.com/articles/can-coloradans-seek-workers-compensation-for-job-related-heart-attacks/.
42. MacLaury, Judson. "The Job Safety Law of 1970: Its Passage Was Perilous." U.S. Department of Labor. Accessed September 3, 2023. https://www.dol.gov/general/aboutdol/history/osha.
43. MacLaury, "The Job Safety Law of 1970: Its Passage Was Perilous."
44. Chirico, Francesco, Tarja Heponiemi, Milena Pavlova, Salvatore Zaffina, and Nicola Magnavita. "Psychosocial Risk Prevention in a Global Occupational Health Perspective. A Descriptive Analysis." *International Journal of Environmental Research and Public Health* 16, no. 14 (July 11, 2019): 2470. https://doi.org/10.3390/ijerph16142470.
45. Occupational Safety and Health Administration, U.S. Department of Labor. "Workplace Stress—Understanding the Problem." Accessed April 10, 2023. https://www.osha.gov/workplace-stress/understanding-the-problem.
46. European Agency for Safety and Health at Work, "Psychosocial Risks and Stress at Work."
47. European Agency for Safety and Health at Work. "Managing Stress and Psychological Risks E-Guide." Accessed September 3, 2023. https://osha.europa.eu/sites/default/files/Eguide_stress_ENGLISH.pdf.
48. Occupational Safety and Health Administration, U.S. Department of Labor. "Workplace Stress—Guidance and Tips for Employers." Accessed April 10, 2023. https://www.osha.gov/workplace-stress/employer-guidance.
49. Goh, Joel, Jeffrey Pfeffer, and Stefanos A. Zenios. "The Relationship Between Workplace Stressors and Mortality and Health Costs in the United States." *Management Science* 62, no. 2 (February 1, 2016): 608–28. https://doi.org/10.1287/mnsc.2014.2115.
50. Goh, Joel, Jeffrey Pfeffer, and Stefanos A. Zenios. "Exposure to Harmful Workplace Practices Could Account for Inequality in Life Spans Across Different Demographic Groups." *Health Affairs* 34, no. 10 (October 1, 2015): 1761–68. https://doi.org/10.1377/hlthaff.2015.0022.
51. Kern, Merilee. "What Is the True Cost of Work-Related Stress?" American Institute of Stress, April 20, 2022. Accessed April 10, 2023. https://www.stress.org/what-is-the-true-cost-of-work-related-stress.
52. Harvard Business School Working Knowledge. "Workplace Stress Responsible for Up to $190B in Annual U.S. Healthcare Costs." *Forbes*, January 26, 2015. Accessed April 10, 2023. https://www.forbes.com/sites

/hbsworkingknowledge/2015/01/26/workplace-stress-responsible-for-up-to-190-billion-in-annual-u-s-heathcare-costs/?sh=11aa7cbc235a.

53. Goh, Pfeffer, and Zenios, "Exposure to Harmful Workplace Practices Could Account for Inequality in Life Spans Across Different Demographic Groups."
54. Blanding, Michael. "How a Company Made Employees So Miserable, They Killed Themselves." Harvard Business School, November 16, 2021. Accessed April 10, 2023. https://hbswk.hbs.edu/item/how-a-company-made-employees-so-miserable-they-killed-themselves.
55. Carucci, Ron, and Ludmila Praslova. "Employees Are Sick of Being Asked to Make Moral Compromises." *Harvard Business Review*, February 21, 2022. Accessed April 10, 2023. https://hbr.org/2022/02/employees-are-sick-of-being-asked-to-make-moral-compromises.
56. National Institute for Occupational Safety and Health. "The Changing Organization of Work and the Safety and Health of Working People: Knowledge Gaps and Research Directions." U.S. Department of Health and Human Services, April 2002. Accessed April 23, 2023. https://doi.org/10.26616/nioshpub2002116.
57. National Institute for Occupational Safety and Health. "NIOSH Total Worker Health Program." Centers for Disease Control and Prevention. Accessed April 30, 2023. https://www.cdc.gov/niosh/twh/.
58. Office of the U.S. Surgeon General. "Addressing Health Worker Burnout." U.S. Department of Health and Human Services, 2022. Accessed April 10, 2023. https://www.hhs.gov/surgeongeneral/priorities/health-worker-burnout/index.html.
59. International Organization for Standardization. "ISO 45003:2021 Occupational Health and Safety Management—Psychological Health and Safety at Work—Guidelines for Managing Psychosocial Risks," June 2021. Accessed April 23, 2023. https://www.iso.org/standard/64283.html.
60. Howell, Lydia P., Laurel A. Beckett, and Amparo C Villablanca. "Ideal Worker and Academic Professional Identity: Perspectives from a Career Flexibility Educational Intervention." *American Journal of Medicine* 130, no. 9 (September 1, 2017): 1117–25. https://doi.org/10.1016/j.amjmed.2017.06.002.
61. Patel, Rikinkumar S., Ramya Bachu, Archana Adikey, Meryem Malik, and Mansi Shah. "Factors Related to Physician Burnout and Its Consequences: A Review." *Behavioral Sciences* 8, no. 11 (October 25, 2018): 98. https://doi.org/10.3390/bs8110098.
62. Berg, Sara. "Pandemic Pushes U.S. Doctor Burnout to All-Time High of 63%." American Medical Association, September 15, 2022. Accessed April 10, 2023. https://www.ama-assn.org/practice-management/physician-health/pandemic-pushes-us-doctor-burnout-all-time-high-63.
63. Harvey, Samuel B., Ronald M. Epstein, Nick Glozier, Katherine Petrie, Jessica Strudwick, Aimée Gayed, Kimberlie Dean, and M. Todd Henderson. "Mental

Illness and Suicide Among Physicians." *Lancet* 398, no. 10303 (September 1, 2021): 920–30. https://doi.org/10.1016/s0140-6736(21)01596-8.

64. Lee, Kathryn A., and Christopher R. Friese. "Deaths by Suicide Among Nurses: A Rapid Response Call." *Journal of Psychosocial Nursing and Mental Health Services* 59, no. 8 (August 1, 2021): 3–4. https://doi.org/10.3928/02793695-20210625-01.
65. Andrew, Louise B. "Physician Suicide." Medscape, July 13, 2022. Accessed April 10, 2023. https://emedicine.medscape.com/article/806779-overview.
66. Sansone, Randy A., and Lori A. Sansone. "Physician Suicide: A Fleeting Moment of Despair." *Psychiatry (Edgmont)* 6, no. 1 (January 2009): 18–22. Accessed February 8, 2024. https://www.ncbi.nlm.nih.gov/pmc/articles/PMC2719447/.
67. Knoll, Corina, Ali Watkins, and Michael Rothfeld. "'I Couldn't Do Anything': The Virus and an E.R. Doctor's Suicide." *New York Times*, July 11, 2020. Accessed April 10, 2023. https://www.nytimes.com/2020/07/11/nyregion/lorna-breen-suicide-coronavirus.html.
68. Ventriglio, Antonio, Cameron Watson, and Dinesh Bhugra. "Suicide Among Doctors: A Narrative Review." *Indian Journal of Psychiatry* 62, no. 2 (March 1, 2020): 114. https://doi.org/10.4103/psychiatry.indianjpsychiatry_767_19.
69. Watkins, Ali, Michael Rothfeld, William K. Rashbaum, and Brian M. Rosenthal. "Top E.R. Doctor Who Treated Coronavirus Patients Dies by Suicide." *New York Times*, April 29, 2020. Accessed April 10, 2023. https://www.nytimes.com/2020/04/27/nyregion/new-york-city-doctor-suicide-coronavirus.html.
70. "Dr. Lorna Breen Heroes' Foundation." Accessed April 10, 2023. https://drlornabreen.org/.
71. American Hospital Association. "Suicide Prevention in the Health Care Work Force." Accessed February 8, 2024. https://www.aha.org/suicideprevention/health-care-workforce.
72. Dr. Lorna Breen Heroes' Foundation. "Remove Intrusive Mental Health Questions from Licensure and Credentialing Applications: A Toolkit to Audit, Change, and Communicate," May 23, 2023. Accessed February 8, 2024. https://drlornabreen.org/wp-content/uploads/2023/05/ALLIN_Audit-Change-Communicate-Toolkit_5.3.23.pdf.
73. Flynn, Meagan. "Bill Named in Memory of Lorna Breen, Doctor Who Died by Suicide on Frontline of Pandemic, Passes Congress." *Washington Post*, February 18, 2022. Accessed April 10, 2023. https://www.washingtonpost.com/dc-md-va/2022/02/18/lorna-breen-kaine-bill/.
74. The White House. "Fact Sheet: Biden-Harris Administration Highlights Strategy to Address the National Mental Health Crisis," May 31, 2022. https://www.whitehouse.gov/briefing-room/statements-releases/2022/05

/31/fact-sheet-biden-harris-administration-highlights-strategy-to-address-the-national-mental-health-crisis/.

75. Jasani, Greg. "The Breen Bill to Protect Health Providers Is Well-Intentioned. But It Won't Stop Burnout." STAT, March 21, 2022. Accessed April 10, 2023. https://www.statnews.com/2022/03/21/lorna-breen-act-health-providers-burnout/.
76. Sindhu, Kunal K., and Eli Y. Adashi. "The Dr Lorna Breen Health Care Provider Protection Act." *JAMA Health Forum* 3, no. 9 (September 30, 2022): e223349. https://doi.org/10.1001/jamahealthforum.2022.3349.
77. Dr. Lorna Breen Heroes Foundation. "Top 5 Actions to Support Care Team Well-Being," January 20, 2022. Accessed April 10, 2023. https://drlornabreen.org/support-care-team-well-being-release/.
78. Kane, Leslie. "Medscape Physician Compensation Report 2023: Your Income vs Your Peers.'" Medscape, April 14, 2023. Accessed August 8, 2023. https://www.medscape.com/slideshow/2023-compensation-overview-6016341?reg=1#25.
79. Kane, Leslie. "'I Cry but No One Cares': Physician Burnout & Depression Report 2023." Medscape, January 27, 2023. Accessed August 8, 2023. https://www.medscape.com/slideshow/2023-lifestyle-burnout-6016058?faf=1#6.
80. Workplace Change Collaborative. "Strategies for Health Organizations: Improving Workload and Workflows." Accessed February 8, 2024. https://www.wpchange.org/strategies/sub-strategies/workload-workflows.
81. Kane, "'I Cry but No One Cares.'"

Chapter 2: Yearning for a Great Reimagination

1. Eastman, Crystal. "Now We Can Begin." Archives of Women's Political Communication, December 1, 1930. Accessed April 23, 2023. https://awpc.cattcenter.iastate.edu/2017/03/09/now-we-can-begin-1920/.
2. Casetext Search + Citator. "Sprague v. Ed's Precision Mfg., LLC, 548 F. Supp. 3d 627," July 9, 2021. Accessed April 18, 2023. https://casetext.com/case/sprague-v-eds-precision-mfg-llc.
3. Casetext Search + Citator. "Yiyu Lin v. CGIT Sys., Civil Action 20–11051-MBB," September 21, 2021. Accessed April 18, 2023. https://casetext.com/case/yiyu-lin-v-cgit-sys/.
4. Harwood, Alaina. "Caregiver Discrimination in the Wake of the COVID-19 Pandemic." UC Hastings Scholarship Repository, 2022. Accessed April 18, 2023. https://repository.uchastings.edu/hwlj/vol33/iss1/6/.
5. Casetext Search + Citator. "Collazo v. Ferrovial Construccion PR, LLC, CIVIL 20–1612 (DRD)," September 30, 2021. Accessed April 18, 2023. https://casetext.com/case/collazo-v-ferrovial-construccion-pr-llc-1.
6. Casetext Search + Citator. "Jarry v. ECC Corp., 581 F. Supp. 3d 376,"

January 24, 2022. Accessed April 18, 2023. https://casetext.com/case/jarry-v-ecc-corp.

7. Calvert, Cynthia Thomas. "Caregivers in the Workplace." WorkLife Law, 2016. Accessed April 18, 2023. https://worklifelaw.org/publications/Caregivers-in-the-Workplace-FRD-update-2016.pdf.
8. Calvert, "Caregivers in the Workplace"; Harwood, "Caregiver Discrimination in the Wake of the COVID-19 Pandemic."
9. Calarco, Jessica. "The US Social Safety Net Has Been Ripped to Shreds—and Women Are Paying the Price." CNN, November 18, 2020. Accessed April 18, 2023. https://www.cnn.com/2020/11/18/opinions/social-safety-net-women-paying-price-opinion-calarco/index.html.
10. Glynn, Sarah Jane. "Coronavirus Paid Leave Exemptions Exclude Millions of Workers from Coverage." Center for American Progress, April 17, 2020. Accessed April 9, 2023. https://www.americanprogress.org/article/coronavirus-paid-leave-exemptions-exclude-millions-workers-coverage/.
11. Administration for Children and Families Office of Child Care. "American Rescue Plan Child Care Stabilization Program," September 20, 2023. Accessed February 8, 2024. https://www.acf.hhs.gov/sites/default/files/documents/occ/National_ARP_Child_Care_Stabilization_Program_Fact_Sheet_Sept_2023.pdf.
12. Arundel, Kara. "Child Care Experts Offer Optimism amid Growing Challenges." K-12 Dive, January 10, 2024. Accessed February 8, 2024. https://www.k12dive.com/news/child-care-fiscal-cliff/704154/.
13. The White House. "Build Back Better Framework," October 28, 2021. https://www.whitehouse.gov/briefing-room/statements-releases/2021/10/28/build-back-better-framework/.
14. World Policy Center. "Is Paid Annual Leave Available for Both Parents of Infants?" Accessed April 9, 2023. https://www.worldpolicycenter.org/policies/is-paid-leave-available-for-both-parents-of-infants.
15. Hickey, Christopher. "Not the Year for Women and Parents: Child Care Provisions Were Cut from the Inflation Reduction Act. It's Not the First Time." CNN, August 12, 2022. Accessed April 18, 2023. https://www.cnn.com/2022/08/12/politics/inflation-reduction-children-families/index.html.
16. Keith, Tamara. "Paid Parental Leave: How Republicans Learned to Love a Democratic Priority." NPR, December 13, 2019. Accessed September 5, 2023. https://www.npr.org/2019/12/13/787631029/paid-parental-leave-how-republicans-learned-to-love-a-democratic-priority.
17. Holpuch, Amanda. "Pentagon Expands Military Parental Leave to 12 Weeks." *New York Times*, January 5, 2023. Accessed September 5, 2023. https://www.nytimes.com/2023/01/05/us/us-military-parental-leave.html.
18. U.S. Army. "Military Parental Leave Program (MPLP)." My Army Benefits. Accessed September 5, 2023. https://myarmybenefits.us.army.mil

/Benefit-Library/Federal-Benefits/Military-Parental-Leave-Program-(MPLP)?serv=122.

19. U.S. Department of Defense. "Service Members Get Extended Parental Leave," March 29, 2023. Accessed September 5, 2023. https://www.defense.gov/News/News-Stories/Article/Article/3345492/service-members-get-extended-parental-leave/.
20. U.S. Government Accountability Office. "Military Child Care: DOD Efforts to Provide Affordable, Quality Care for Families," February 2, 2023. Accessed September 5, 2023. https://www.gao.gov/products/gao-23-105518.
21. World Policy Center. "For How Long Are Workers Guaranteed Paid Sick Leave?" Accessed April 9, 2023. https://www.worldpolicycenter.org/policies/for-how-long-are-workers-guaranteed-paid-sick-leave.
22. Maclean, Catherine, Stefan Pichler, and Nicolas R. Ziebarth. "Paid Sick Leave Improves Public Health Outcomes and Supports U.S. Workers at a Relatively Low Cost to Employers." Equitable Growth, January 12, 2022. https://equitablegrowth.org/paid-sick-leave-improves-public-health-outcomes-and-supports-u-s-workers-at-a-relatively-low-cost-to-employers/.
23. Pichler, Stefan, and Nicolas R. Ziebarth. "The Pros and Cons of Sick Pay Schemes: Testing for Contagious Presenteeism and Noncontagious Absenteeism Behavior." *Journal of Public Economics* 156 (December 1, 2017): 14–33. https://doi.org/10.1016/j.jpubeco.2017.07.003.
24. Equitable Growth. "Factsheet: New Study Shows That Emergency Paid Sick Leave Reduced COVID-19 Infections in the United States," October 26, 2020. https://equitablegrowth.org/factsheet-new-study-shows-that-emergency-paid-sick-leave-reduced-covid-19-infections-in-the-united-states/.
25. Bureau of Labor Statistics, U.S. Department of Labor. "A Look at Paid Family Leave by Wage Category in 2021." TED: The Economics Daily, January 10, 2022. Accessed April 18, 2023. https://www.bls.gov/opub/ted/2022/a-look-at-paid-family-leave-by-wage-category-in-2021.htm#:~:text=Lower%20wage%20workers%20were%20less,in%20the%20highest%2010%20percent.
26. Fuller, Joseph, and Manjari Raman. "The Caring Company: How Employers Can Cut Costs and Boost Productivity by Helping Employees Manage Caregiving Needs." Harvard Business School, January 17, 2019. Accessed April 19, 2020. https://www.hbs.edu/managing-the-future-of-work/research/Pages/the-caring-company.aspx.
27. Buchholz, Katharina. "Female Labour-Force Participation in the US Has Stalled. Is Anywhere Doing Better?" World Economic Forum, May 18, 2022. Accessed April 19, 2023. https://www.weforum.org/agenda/2022/03/female-labor-force-participation-gender-gap-pandemic/#:~:text=The%20

labor%20force%20participation%20rate,back%20down%20to%20 1993%20levels.

28. Gonzales, Matt. "Nearly 2 Million Fewer Women in Labor Force." SHRM, February 17, 2022. Accessed April 18, 2023. https://www.shrm.org/resources andtools/hr-topics/behavioral-competencies/global-and-cultural -effectiveness/pages/over-1-million-fewer-women-in-labor-force.aspx #:~:text=Federal%20data%20shows%20that%20men,the%20ongoing%20 COVID%2D19%20pandemic.
29. Tüzemen, Didem, and Thao Tran. "Women Take a Bigger Hit in the First Wave of Job Losses Due to COVID-19." Federal Reserve Bank of Kansas City, April 16, 2020. Accessed April 18, 2023. https://www.kansascityfed.org /Economic%20Bulletin/documents/5434/2020-eb20tuzementran0416.pdf.
30. Landivar, Liana Christin, and Mark deWolf. "Mothers' Employment Two Years Later: An Assessment of Employment Loss and Recovery During the COVID-19 Pandemic." Women's Bureau, U.S. Department of Labor, 2022. Accessed April 9, 2023. https://www.dol.gov/sites/dolgov/files/WB/media /Mothers-employment-2%20-years-later-may2022.pdf.
31. World Bank Open Data. "Labor Force, Female (% of Total Labor Force)." Accessed October 14, 2023. https://data.worldbank.org/indicator/SL.TLF .TOTL.FE.ZS?locations=OE&most_recent_value_desc=true.
32. Statistics Canada, Government of Canada. "Employment Growth in Canada and the United States During the Recovery from COVID-19," December 22, 2022. Accessed April 19, 2023. https://www150.statcan.gc.ca/n1 /pub/36-28-0001/2022012/article/00001-eng.htm.
33. Swenson, Haley. "Equality Within Our Lifetimes? Top Four Policy Takeaways for Making Global Gender Equality a Reality." New America, March 6, 2023. Accessed April 18, 2023. https://www.newamerica.org/better-life -lab/blog/equality-within-our-lifetimes-top-four-policy-takeaways-for -making-global-gender-equality-a-reality/.
34. Armstrong, Martin. "It Will Take Another 136 Years to Close the Global Gender Gap." World Economic Forum, April 12, 2021. Accessed April 18, 2023. https://www.weforum.org/agenda/2021/04/136-years-is-the-estimated -journey-time-to-gender-equality/.
35. Swenson, "Equality Within Our Lifetimes? Top Four Policy Takeaways for Making Global Gender Equality a Reality," 7:12.
36. Yu, Wei-Hsin, and Yuko Hara. "Motherhood Penalties and Fatherhood Premiums: Effects of Parenthood on Earnings Growth Within and Across Firms." *Demography* 58, no. 1 (February 1, 2021): 247–72. https://doi.org /10.1215/00703370-8917608.
37. Shaw, Elyse, and C. Nicole Mason. "Holding Up Half the Sky: Mothers as Workers, Primary Caregivers, & Breadwinners During COVID-19." Institute for Women's Policy Research, May 2020. Accessed April 18, 2023.

https://iwpr.org/wp-content/uploads/2020/07/Holding-Up-Half-the-Sky-Mothers-as-Breadwinners.pdf.

38. Leamaster, Reid J., and Andres Bautista. "Understanding Compliance in Patriarchal Religions: Mormon Women and the Latter Day Saints Church as a Case Study." *Religions* 9, no. 5 (April 27, 2018): 143. https://doi.org/10.3390/rel9050143.
39. Glass, Jennifer, R. Kelly Raley, and Joanna Pepin. "Mothers Are the Primary Earners in Growing Numbers of Families with Children," November 2, 2021. Accessed April 19, 2023. https://sites.utexas.edu/contemporaryfamilies/2021/11/02/breadwinning-mothers-brief-report/.
40. Boushey, Heather, and Kavya Vaghul. "Women Have Made the Difference for Family Economic Security." Equitable Growth, April 4, 2016. https://equitablegrowth.org/women-have-made-the-difference-for-family-economic-security/.
41. Miller, Claire Cain. "Why Mothers' Choices About Work and Family Often Feel Like No Choice at All." *New York Times*, January 17, 2020. Accessed February 10, 2024. https://www.nytimes.com/2020/01/17/upshot/mothers-choices-work-family.html.
42. Weisser, Cybele. "Richer, Together." *Money*, June 2014.
43. Center for WorkLife Law, UC Hastings Law and State Innovation Exchange. "At a Glance: Family Caregiver Discrimination," September 21, 2021. Accessed April 19, 2023. https://stateinnovation.org/at-a-glance-family-caregiver-discrimination/.
44. Center for WorkLife Law, UC Hastings Law. "Laws Protecting Family Caregivers at Work," 2021. Accessed April 19, 2023. https://worklifelaw.org/wp-content/uploads/2022/11/FRD-Law-Table.pdf.
45. Waxman, Olivia B. "In Previously Unseen Interview, Ruth Bader Ginsburg Shares How Legal Pioneer Pauli Murray Shaped Her Work on Sex Discrimination." *Time*, October 16, 2020. Accessed April 19, 2023. https://time.com/5896410/ruth-bader-ginsburg-pauli-murray/.
46. Author interview with Daphne Delvaux, July 21, 2022.
47. Minnesota Legislative Reference Library. "Minnesota Women's Legislative Timeline." Accessed April 19, 2023. https://www.lrl.mn.gov/womenstimeline/details?recid=61.
48. U.S. Department of Labor. "Section 7(r) of the Fair Labor Standards Act—Break Time for Nursing Mothers Provision." Accessed April 19, 2023. https://www.dol.gov/agencies/whd/nursing-mothers/law.
49. A Better Balance. "The PUMP for Nursing Mothers Act: What You Should Know," January 13, 2023. Accessed April 19, 2023. https://www.abetterbalance.org/resources/pump-for-nursing-mothers-act-explainer/.
50. Morgan, Kate. "Pay Secrecy: Why Some Workers Can't Discuss Salaries." BBC, July 11, 2021. Accessed April 19, 2023. https://www.bbc.com

/worklife/article/20210708-pay-secrecy-why-some-workers-cant-discuss-salaries.

51. Morris, Liz, Jessica Lee, and Joan C. Williams. "Exposed: Discrimination Against Breastfeeding Workers." Center for WorkLife Law, UC Hastings Law, 2019. Accessed April 19, 2023. https://worklifelaw.org/publication/exposed-discrimination-against-breastfeeding-workers/.
52. Spiggle, Tom. *You're Pregnant? You're Fired! Protecting Mothers, Fathers and Other Caregivers in the Workplace*. Raleigh, NC: Morgan and Dawson, 2014.
53. Meek, Joan Younger, and Lawrence Noble. "Policy Statement: Breastfeeding and the Use of Human Milk." *Pediatrics* 150, no. 1 (June 27, 2022). https://doi.org/10.1542/peds.2022-057988.
54. American Civil Liberties Union. "Freyer v. Frontier and Hodgkins v. Frontier," September 30, 2021. Accessed April 19, 2023. https://www.aclu.org/cases/freyer-v-frontier-and-hodgkins-v-frontier?redirect=cases/frontier-airlines-eeoc-complaint.
55. ACLU. "Pilots Reach Settlement with Frontier Airlines over Lactation and Pregnancy Policies." December 4, 2023. Accessed February 8, 2024. https://www.aclu.org/press-releases/pilots-reach-settlement-with-frontier-airlines-over-lactation-and-pregnancy-policies.
56. Utz, Annabel, Julie Yixia Cai, and Dean Baker. "The Pandemic Rise in Self-Employment: Who Is Working for Themselves Now?" Center for Economic and Policy Research, August 29, 2022. Accessed April 19, 2023. https://cepr.net/the-pandemic-rise-in-self-employment-who-is-working-for-themselves-now/.
57. Timmons, Heather. "The Support Ivanka Trump Wants for Women Entrepreneurs Already Exists—and Her Dad Is Destroying It." *Quartz*, April 27, 2017. Accessed April 19, 2023. https://qz.com/969161/while-ivanka-trump-touts-women-entrepreneurs-president-trump-is-destroying-programs-that-support-them.
58. Auguste, Daniel, Stephen Roll, and Mathieu R. Despard. "The Precarity of Self-Employment Among Low- and Moderate-Income Households." *Social Forces* 101, no. 3 (February 7, 2022): 1081–115. https://doi.org/10.1093/sf/soab171.
59. Petras, George, Jennifer Borresen, and Janet Loehrke. "Congress Is Steadily Getting Older, and Some Members Have Been in Office for Decades." *USA Today*, September 29, 2023. Accessed February 9, 2024. https://www.usatoday.com/story/graphics/2023/09/12/how-congress-is-getting-older/70797524007/.
60. Reeves, Martin, and Adam Job. "The Case for Intergenerational C-Suite: Why Companies Need More Age Diversity in Their Leadership Ranks." *Fortune*, December 18, 2023. Accessd February 9, 2024. https://fortune.com/2023/12/18/future-50-ceos-leadership-age-diversity-bcg/.

61. Pew Research Center. "Few Say Having Two Full-Time Working Parents Is the Ideal Situation for Children in Two-Parent Households," October 2, 2018. Accessed February 9, 2024. https://www.pewresearch.org/social-trends/2017/03/23/gender-and-caregiving/psdt-10-02-18_paid_leave_update-00/.
62. Walker, Kristi, Kristen Bialik, and Patrick van Kessel. "Strong Men, Caring Women." Pew Research Center, July 24, 2018. Accessed February 9, 2024. https://www.pewresearch.org/social-trends/interactives/strong-men-caring-women/.
63. Haspel, Elliot. "Opinion: Here Come the Tired Arguments Against Universal Child Care—Reject Them." *Early Learning Nation*, February 5, 2021. Accessed February 9, 2024. https://earlylearningnation.com/2021/02/opinion-here-come-the-tired-arguments-against-universal-child-care-reject-them/.
64. Cohen, Nancy L. "Why America Never Had Universal Child Care." *New Republic*, April 24, 2013. Accessed February 16, 2024. https://newrepublic.com/article/113009/child-care-america-was-very-close-universal-day-care.
65. Pfannestiel, Kyle. "Idaho Lawmakers Evaluate How to Financially Respond After Audit into State Health Department." *Idaho Capital Sun*, November 3, 2023. Accessed February 9, 2024. https://idahocapitalsun.com/2023/11/09/idaho-lawmakers-evaluate-how-to-financially-respond-after-audit-into-state-health-department/#:~:text=The%20Idaho%20Legislature%20appropriated%20%2436,aged%20children%2C%20including%20learning%20loss.
66. Holmes, Brian. "Idaho Republican Votes Against Using Federal Funds for Early Education, Says It Makes It 'Easier for Mothers to Come out of the Home.'" KTVB7, March 3, 2021. Accessed February 9, 2024. https://www.ktvb.com/article/news/local/208/idaho-republican-votes-against-education-funds-convenient-for-mothers-to-come-out-of-the-home/277-645ae7a7-601e-4557-9d7c-f8df5c22949c.
67. Covert, Bryce. "There's a Reason We Can't Have Nice Things." *New York Times*, July 21, 2022. Accessed February 10, 2024. https://www.nytimes.com/2022/07/21/opinion/racism-paid-leave-child-care.html.
68. Nadasen, Premilla. "From Widow to 'Welfare Queen': Welfare and the Politics of Race." *Black Women, Gender + Families* 1, no. 2 (Fall 2007): 52–77. Accessed February 15, 2024. https://www.jstor.org/stable/10.5406/blacwomegendfami.1.2.0052.
69. Parolin, Zach. "Welfare Money Is Paying for a Lot of Things Besides Welfare." *Atlantic*, June 13, 2019. Accessed February 15, 2024. https://www.theatlantic.com/ideas/archive/2019/06/through-welfare-states-are-widening-racial-divide/591559/.
70. Sawhill, Isabel V., Morgan Welch, and Chris Miller. "It's Getting More Expensive to Raise Children. And Government Isn't Doing Much to

Help." Brookings, August 30, 2022. Accessed April 19, 2023. https://www.brookings.edu/blog/up-front/2022/08/30/its-getting-more-expensive-to-raise-children-and-government-isnt-doing-much-to-help/.

71. Landivar, Liana Christin, Nikki L. Graf, and Giorleny Altamirano Rayo. "Child Care Prices in Local Areas: Initial Findings from the National Database of Child Care Prices." Women's Bureau, U.S. Department of Labor Issue Brief. January 2023. Accessed February 9, 2024. https://www.dol.gov/sites/dolgov/files/WB/NDCP/508_WB_IssueBrief-NDCP-20230213.pdf.
72. Peck, Emily. "Household Child Care Costs Have Spiked More Than 30% Since 2019." *Axios*, November 1, 2023. Accessed February 9, 2024. https://www.axios.com/2023/11/01/child-care-costs-average-chart-inflation.
73. Brown, Anna. "Growing Share of Childless Adults in U.S. Don't Expect to Ever Have Children." Pew Research Center, November 19, 2021. Accessed April 19, 2023. https://www.pewresearch.org/fact-tank/2021/11/19/growing-share-of-childless-adults-in-u-s-dont-expect-to-ever-have-children/; Miller, Claire Cain. "Americans Are Having Fewer Babies. They Told Us Why." *New York Times*, July 5, 2018. Accessed September 5, 2023. https://www.nytimes.com/2018/07/05/upshot/americans-are-having-fewer-babies-they-told-us-why.html.
74. American Association of Retired Persons. "Caregiving in the United States 2020," May 14, 2020. Accessed April 19, 2023. https://www.aarp.org/ppi/info-2020/caregiving-in-the-united-states.html.
75. Chari, Amalavoyal V., John Engberg, Kristin Ray, and Ateev Mehrotra. "The Opportunity Costs of Informal Elder-Care in the United States: New Estimates from the American Time Use Survey." RAND, January 1, 2014. Accessed April 19, 2023. https://www.rand.org/pubs/external_publications/EP66196.html.
76. Truskinovsky, Yulya, and Nicole Maestas. "Caregiving and Labor Force Participation: New Evidence from the American Time Use Survey." *Innovation in Aging* 2, suppl. 1 (November 1, 2018): 580. https://doi.org/10.1093/geroni/igy023.2149; Johnson, Richard, Karen Smith, and Barbara Butricia. "Lifetime Employment-Related Costs to Women of Providing Family Care," Urban Institute, February 2023. Accessed August 28, 2023. https://www.dol.gov/sites/dolgov/files/WB/Mothers-Families-Work/Lifetime-caregiving-costs_508.pdf.
77. Stanczyk, Alexandra B. "Does Paid Family Leave Improve Household Economic Security Following a Birth? Evidence from California." *Social Service Review* 93, no. 2 (June 26, 2019): 262–304. https://doi.org/10.1086/703138.
78. New America. "Eight Lessons from Quebec on Designing Universal Early Care and Learning in the U.S." Accessed September 5, 2023. https://s3.amazonaws.com/newamericadotorg/documents/One_Pager_-_Lessons_from_Quebec.pdf; Canadian Press. "Quebec Offers Striking Daycare Workers an Immediate Pay Hike." *Montreal Gazette*, October 14,

2021. Accessed September 5, 2023. https://montrealgazette.com/news/local-news/quebec-daycare-strike-extends-to-csn-union-members-on-thursday-friday.

79. Fortin, Pierre, Luc Godbout, and Suzie St-Cerny. "Impact of Quebec's Universal Low-Fee Childcare Program on Female Labour Force Participation, Domestic Income and Government Budgets." Université de Sherbrooke: Sherbrooke, Quebec. Working Paper 2012/02 (2012). https://cffp.recherche.usherbrooke.ca/wp-content/uploads/2018/12/cr_2012-02_impact_of_quebecs_universal_low_fee.pdf.
80. Solomon, Catherine. "13% ROI Research Toolkit." Heckman Equation, October 14, 2021. https://heckmanequation.org/resource/13-roi-toolbox/#:~:text=Professor%20Heckman%20and%20colleagues%20find,to%20work%20due%20to%20childcare.
81. Verniers, Catherine, and Jorge Vala. "Justifying Gender Discrimination in the Workplace: The Mediating Role of Motherhood Myths." *PLOS One* 13, no. 1 (January 9, 2018): e0190657. https://doi.org/10.1371/journal.pone.0190657.
82. Williams, Joan C. "The Maternal Wall." *Harvard Business Review,* October 2004. Accessed April 19, 2023. https://hbr.org/2004/10/the-maternal-wall.
83. Heilman, Madeline E., and Tyler G. Okimoto. "Motherhood: A Potential Source of Bias in Employment Decisions." *Journal of Applied Psychology* 93, no. 1 (January 1, 2008): 189–98. https://doi.org/10.1037/0021-9010.93.1.189.
84. Williams, Joan C. "Opinion | Employers Are Discriminating Against Mothers During the Coronavirus Pandemic." *New York Times,* August 8, 2020. https://www.nytimes.com/2020/08/06/opinion/mothers-discrimination-coronavirus.html.
85. Fairie, Paul. "A List of Things People Blamed on Working Women." Twitter, August 10, 2023. Accessed August 30, 2023. https://twitter.com/paulisci/status/1689758753472790528; LiveWire Calgary. "British People Are Lazy, Women Ruin Everything, and Kids Today Are Too Spoiled: A Century of Hot Takes from Newspapers Coming to Book Form," March 16, 2023. Accessed August 30, 2023. https://livewirecalgary.com/2023/03/16/british-people-are-lazy-women-ruin-everything-and-kids-today-are-too-spoiled-a-century-of-hot-takes-from-newspapers-coming-to-book-form/.
86. Williams, Joan C., Jennifer L. Berdahl, and Joseph A. Vandello. "Beyond Work-Life 'Integration.'" *Annual Review of Psychology* 67, no. 1 (January 4, 2016): 515–39. https://doi.org/10.1146/annurev-psych-122414-033710.
87. Waller, Allyson. "Woman Says She Was Fired Because Her Children Disrupted Her Work Calls." *New York Times,* July 8, 2020. Accessed April 19, 2023. https://www.nytimes.com/2020/07/08/us/drisana-rios-lawsuit-hub-international.html.
88. Author interview with Daphne Delvaux, July 21, 2022.
89. Yavorsky, Jill, Yue Qian, and Rebecca Glauber. "Workplace Productivity:

Gender, Parenthood, and Career Consequences." Presented at the American Sociological Association 2023 Annual Meeting, Philadelphia, PA, 2023.

90. Thébaud, Sarah. "Cultural Stereotypes About Gender, Parenting, and Work: Content, Dynamics, and Implications for Inequality in a Post-Pandemic Society." Paper presented at the Council on Contemporary Families Gender Equality Symposium, Washington, DC, March 9, 2023.
91. Liner, Emily. "A Dollar Short: What's Holding Women Back from Equal Pay?" Third Way, March 18, 2016. Accessed April 19, 2023. https://www.thirdway.org/report/a-dollar-short-whats-holding-women-back-from-equal-pay.
92. Miller, Claire Cain. "As Women Take Over a Male-Dominated Field, the Pay Drops." *New York Times*, March 27, 2016. Accessed October 14, 2023. https://www.nytimes.com/2016/03/20/upshot/as-women-take-over-a-male-dominated-field-the-pay-drops.html.
93. Durana, Alieza, Amanda Lenhart, Roselyn Miller, Brigid Schulte, and Elizabeth Weingarten. "Sexual Harassment: A Severe and Pervasive Problem." New America, September 26, 2018. Accessed April 19, 2023. https://www.newamerica.org/better-life-lab/reports/sexual-harassment-severe-and-pervasive-problem/introduction/.
94. National Women's Law Center. "Hard Work Is Not Enough: Women in Low-Paid Jobs," July 20, 2023. Accessed September 5, 2023. https://nwlc.org/resource/when-hard-work-is-not-enough-women-in-low-paid-jobs.
95. Hu, Jane C. "Even in Female-Dominated Fields, Men Make More Than Women." *Slate*, June 18, 2015. Accessed April 19, 2023. https://slate.com/human-interest/2015/06/men-in-female-dominated-fields-they-still-make-more-than-women.html.
96. Miller, "As Women Take Over a Male-Dominated Field, the Pay Drops."
97. Poo, Ai-Jen. "The Work That Makes All Other Work Possible," TED Talk, December 7, 2018. Accessed April 19, 2023. https://www.ted.com/talks/ai_jen_poo_the_work_that_makes_all_other_work_possible?language=en.
98. CNN. "'We Started Something New Here': Factory Gets Influx of Workers with Unique Offer," May 9, 2022. Accessed April 20, 2023. https://www.cnn.com/videos/business/2022/05/09/kawasaki-factory-attracts-new-workers-newday-mcmorris-santoro-pkg-vpx.cnn.
99. Kaplan, Juliana, and Madison Hoff. "1 in 7 US Businesses Raised Wages Last Year Because of the Pandemic." *Business Insider*, February 9, 2022. Accessed April 20, 2023. https://www.businessinsider.com/how-many-businesses-raised-wages-last-year-due-to-pandemic-2022-2.
100. Tucker, Jasmine, and Kayla Patrick. "Low-Wage Jobs Are Women's Jobs: The Overrepresentation of Women in Low-Wage Work." National Women's Law Center, August 2017. Accessed April 20, 2023. https://nwlc.org/wp-content/uploads/2017/08/Low-Wage-Jobs-are-Womens-Jobs.pdf.

101. MSNBC. "Americans Staying at Home Struggle to Balance Work and Family," May 12, 2020. Accessed August 28, 2023. https://www.msnbc.com/know-your-value/5-step-plan-reset-unfair-division-labor-home-during-covid-n1204491.
102. Schulte, Brigid. "An Unexpected Upside to Lockdown: Men Have Discovered Housework." *Guardian*, June 17, 2020. Accessed April 20, 2023. https://www.theguardian.com/us-news/2020/jun/17/gender-roles-parenting-housework-coronavirus-pandemic; New America. "The Future of Gender Equality Three Years into the Global Pandemic," March 10, 2023. Accessed April 20, 2023. https://www.youtube.com/watch?v=6wy4PisOyD0.
103. Miller, Claire Cain. "Fathers Gained Family Time in the Pandemic. Many Don't Want to Give It Back." *New York Times*, March 13, 2023. Accessed April 20, 2023. https://www.nytimes.com/2023/03/12/upshot/fathers-pandemic-remote-work.html.
104. Montes, Joshua, Christopher Smith, and Isabel Leigh. "Caregiving for Children and Parental Labor Force Participation During the Pandemic." Federal Reserve, November 5, 2021. Accessed April 20, 2023. https://www.federalreserve.gov/econres/notes/feds-notes/caregiving-for-children-and-parental-labor-force-participation-during-the-pandemic-20211105.html.
105. Organisation for Economic Co-Operation and Development. "Net Replacement Rate in Unemployment." Accessed April 20, 2023. https://stats.oecd.org/Index.aspx?DataSetCode=NRR.
106. Grunau, Philipp, and Julia Lang. "Retraining for the Unemployed and the Quality of the Job Match." *Applied Economics* 52, no. 47 (May 22, 2020): 5098–114. https://doi.org/10.1080/00036846.2020.1753879.
107. Economic Policy Institute. "Reforming Unemployment Insurance: Stabilizing a System in Crisis and Laying the Foundation for Equity." Accessed April 20, 2023. https://files.epi.org/uploads/Reforming-Unemployment-Insurance.pdf.
108. O'Leary, Christopher J. "How to Fix a Broken Unemployment Insurance System." Upjohn Institute. Accessed September 13, 2023. https://www.upjohn.org/research-highlights/how-fix-broken-unemployment-insurance-system.
109. Edwards, Kathryn A. "Unemployment's History with Black Workers," October 5, 2020. Accessed September 5, 2023. https://www.rand.org/blog/2020/10/holes-just-big-enough-unemployments-history-with-black.html.
110. Alcalá Kovalski, Manuel, and Louise Sheiner. "How Does Unemployment Insurance Work? And How Is It Changing During the Coronavirus Pandemic?" Brookings, July 20, 2022. Accessed September 5, 2023. https://www.brookings.edu/articles/how-does-unemployment-insurance-work-and-how-is-it-changing-during-the-coronavirus-pandemic/.

111. Economic Policy Institute, "Reforming Unemployment Insurance: Stabilizing a System in Crisis and Laying the Foundation for Equity."
112. Rowan, Lisa. "The States with the Best and Worst Unemployment Benefits—and Why They're So Different." *Forbes Advisor*, February 14, 2023. Accessed April 20, 2023. https://www.forbes.com/advisor/personal-finance/best-and-worst-states-for-unemployment/.
113. Renahy, Emilie, Christiane Mitchell, Agnes Molnar, Carles Muntaner, Edwin Ng, Farihah Ali, and Patricia O'Campo. "Connections Between Unemployment Insurance, Poverty and Health: A Systematic Review." *European Journal of Public Health* 28, no. 2 (January 18, 2018): 269–75. https://doi.org/10.1093/eurpub/ckx235.
114. Robert Wood Johnson Foundation. "How Does Employment—or Unemployment—Affect Health?" March 2013. Accessed April 20, 2023. https://www.hivlawandpolicy.org/sites/default/files/How%20Does%20Employment%20%C3%A2%E2%82%AC%E2%80%9C%20or%20Unemployment%20%C3%A2%E2%82%AC%E2%80%9C%20Affect%20Health%20%28RWJF%29.pdf.
115. Amiri, Sohrab. "Unemployment Associated with Major Depression Disorder and Depressive Symptoms: A Systematic Review and Meta-Analysis." *International Journal of Occupational Safety and Ergonomics* 28, no. 4 (August 5, 2021): 2080–92. https://doi.org/10.1080/10803548.2021.1954793.
116. Ramchand, Rajeev, Lynsay Ayer, and Stephen O'Connor. "Unemployment, Behavioral Health, and Suicide." *Health Affairs*, April 7, 2022. Accessed April 20, 2023. https://doi.org/10.1377/hpb20220302.274862.
117. Norlander, Peter. "Addressing Long-Term U.S. Unemployment Requires Confronting the Stigma Against the Unemployed amid the Coronavirus Recession." Washington Center for Equitable Growth, October 22, 2020. https://equitablegrowth.org/addressing-long-term-u-s-unemployment-requires-confronting-the-stigma-against-the-unemployed-amid-the-coronavirus-recession/.
118. Congressional Research Service. "Unemployment Rates During the COVID-19 Pandemic," August 20, 2021. Accessed April 20, 2023. https://sgp.fas.org/crs/misc/R46554.pdf.
119. Topping, Alexandra. "Firms Told to Tackle Flexible-Working 'Stigma' Faced by Men." *Guardian*, February 2, 2022. Accessed April 20, 2023. https://www.theguardian.com/global-development/2022/feb/02/firms-told-to-tackle-flexible-working-stigma-faced-by-men.
120. New America. "Men and Care in the United States," June 17, 2020. Accessed April 20, 2023. https://www.newamerica.org/better-life-lab/better-life-lab-collections/men-and-care-united-states/; Schulte, Brigid. "Providing Care Changes Men." New America, February 4, 2021, p. 2. Accessed April 18, 2023. https://www.newamerica.org/better-life-lab/reports/providing-care-changes-men/introduction/.

121. Gonalons-Pons, Pilar, and Markus Gangl. "Marriage and Masculinity: Male-Breadwinner Culture, Unemployment, and Separation Risk in 29 Countries." *American Sociological Review* 86, no. 3 (May 26, 2021): 465–502. https://doi.org/10.1177/00031224211012442.

Chapter 3: The Wicked Problem of Redesigning Work

1. Twain, Mark. *Mark Twain's Notebook*. New York: Harper & Brothers, 1935, p. 344.
2. Monnig, Jennifer. "Transforming Hiring and Work Habits at Intel." *Innovation Leader*, Spring 2018.
3. Merelli, Annalisa. "The Only Reason More Americans Haven't Quit Their Jobs Is Healthcare." *Quartz*, November 2, 2021. Accessed April 16, 2023. https://qz.com/2082849/one-in-three-americans-would-quit-if-it-wasnt-for-healthcare.
4. Todd, Sarah. "The Short but Destructive History of Mass Layoffs." *Quartz*, July 12, 2019. Accessed April 16, 2023. https://qz.com/work/1663731/mass-layoffs-a-history-of-cost-cuts-and-psychological-tolls.
5. Peck, Emily. "How Layoffs Can Have Negative Long-Term Consequences for Companies." *Axios*, March 3, 2023. Accessed April 16, 2023. https://www.axios.com/2023/03/03/how-layoffs-can-have-negative-long-term-consequences-for-companies; Knowledge at Wharton. "How Layoffs Hurt Companies," April 12, 2016. Accessed April 16, 2023. https://knowledge.wharton.upenn.edu/article/how-layoffs-cost-companies/.
6. Gavett, Gretchen. "The Problem with 'Greedy Work.'" *Harvard Business Review*, September 28, 2019. Accessed April 16, 2023. https://hbr.org/2021/09/the-problem-with-greedy-work#:~:text=Greedy%20work%20can%20be%20defined,vacation%20day%20for%20the%20project.
7. Tawadrous, Paul. "Freelance Nation Brings More Flexible Work Options to Intel." Intel.com, March 18, 2016. Accessed April 16, 2023. https://community.intel.com/t5/Blogs/Intel/We-Are-Intel/Freelance-Nation-Brings-More-Flexible-Work-Options-to-Intel/post/1334264.
8. Kandell, Jonathan. "Andrew S. Grove Dies at 79; Intel Chief Spurred Semiconductor Revolution." *New York Times*, March 21, 2016. Accessed April 16, 2023. https://www.nytimes.com/2016/03/22/technology/andrew-grove-intel-obituary.html?utm_source=pocket&utm_medium=email&utm_campaign=pockethits&_r=0.
9. Rogoway, Mike. "Intel Plans Sharp Focus to Fix Management Problems." OregonLive, January 31, 2017. Accessed April 16, 2023. https://www.oregonlive.com/silicon-forest/2017/01/intel_plans_sharp_focus_to_sol.html.
10. Travers, Mark. "What Percentage of Workers Can Realistically Work from Home? New Data from Norway Offer Clues." *Forbes*, April 24, 2020.

Accessed April 16, 2023. https://www.forbes.com/sites/traversmark/2020/04/24/what-percentage-of-workers-can-realistically-work-from-home-new-data-from-norway-offer-clues/?sh=4504b83678fe.

11. Goldberg, Emma. "After Two Years of Remote Work, Workers Question Office Life." *New York Times*, March 10, 2022. Accessed April 16, 2023. https://www.nytimes.com/2022/03/10/business/remote-work-office-life.html.
12. Slaughter, Anne-Marie. "Forget the Trump Administration. America Will Save America." *New York Times*, March 21, 2020. Accessed April 16, 2023. https://www.nytimes.com/2020/03/21/opinion/sunday/coronavirus-governors-cities.html.
13. Benson, Alan P. "Rethinking the Two-Body Problem: The Segregation of Women into Geographically Dispersed Occupations." *Demography* 51, no. 5 (September 5, 2014): 1619–39. https://doi.org/10.1007/s13524-014-0324-7.
14. Bernhagen, Lindsay. "Why Even the Most Rigorously Educated Women Put Their Spouses' Careers First." *Slate*, November 30, 2017. Accessed April 16, 2023. https://slate.com/human-interest/2017/11/trailing-spouses-what-female-ph-d-s-teach-us-about-lasting-workplace-gender-inequality.html.
15. Waller, Graham. "Think Hybrid Work Doesn't Work? The Data Disagrees." Gartner, November 21, 2022. Accessed April 16, 2023. https://www.gartner.com/en/articles/think-hybrid-work-doesnt-work-the-data-disagrees.
16. Blackbaud. "Blackbaud Transitions to a Remote-First Workforce Approach," November 1, 2021. Accessed April 16, 2023. https://www.blackbaud.com/newsroom/article/2021/11/01/blackbaud-transitions-to-a-remote-first-workforce-approach.
17. Blackbaud. "Blackbaud Recognized as One of the Best Companies for Remote Workers by Quartz," September 12, 2022. Accessed April 16, 2023. https://www.blackbaud.com/newsroom/article/2022/09/12/blackbaud-recognized-as-one-of-the-best-companies-for-remote-workers-by-quartz.
18. Hansen, Stephen, Peter John Lambert, Nicholas Bloom, Steven Davis, Raffaella Sadun, and Bledi Taska. "Remote Work Across Jobs, Companies, and Space." National Bureau of Economic Research Working Paper Series, no. 31007 (March 2023). https://doi.org/10.3386/w31007.
19. Mercer. "Navigating the New World at Work," January 2024. Accessed February 10, 2024. https://www.mercer.com/assets/us/en_us/shared-assets/local/attachments/pdf-2023-2024-inside-employees-minds-study-navigating-the-new-world-at-work.pdf.
20. Danziger, Anna, and Shelley Waters Boots. "The Business Case for Flexible Work Arrangements." Georgetown University Law Center, 2008. Accessed April 17, 2023. https://scholarship.law.georgetown.edu/legal/4.
21. Kossek, Ellen Ernst, Patricia Gettings, and Kaumudi Misra. "The Future of Flexibility at Work." *Harvard Business Review*, September 28, 2021. Accessed April 17, 2023. https://hbr.org/2021/09/the-future-of-flexibility-at-work.
22. "The Benefits of Flexible Working Arrangements." Future of Work Institute,

August 2012. https://www.bc.edu/content/dam/files/centers/cwf/individuals/pdf/benefitsCEOFlex.pdf.

23. Chung, Heejung. "Flexible Working Is Making Us Work Longer." *Quartz*, April 27, 2017. Accessed April 16, 2023. https://qz.com/765908/flexible-working-is-making-us-work-longer.
24. Bauer, Lauren, and Sarah Yu Wang. "Prime-Age Women Are Going Above and Beyond in the Labor Market Recovery." Hamilton Project, August 30, 2023. Accessed August 31, 2023. https://www.hamiltonproject.org/publication/post/prime-age-women-are-going-above-and-beyond-in-the-labor-market-recovery/.
25. Future Forum. "Leveling the Playing Field in the Hybrid Workplace," January 2022. Accessed April 16, 2023. https://futureforum.com/wp-content/uploads/2022/01/Future-Forum-Pulse-Report-January-2022.pdf.
26. Williams, Joan, and Cynthia Thomas Calvert. "Balanced Hours: Effective Part-Time Policies for Washington Law Firms: The Project for Attorney Retention, Final Report, Third Edition." William & Mary Law School Scholarship Repository, 2002. https://scholarship.law.wm.edu/wmjowl/vol8/iss3/2.
27. Emanuel, Natalia, Emma Harrington, and Amanda Pallais. "The Power of Proximity: Office Interactions Affect Online Feedback and Quits, Especially for Women and Young Workers." Working Paper (March 23, 2023). https://scholar.harvard.edu/pallais/publications/power-proximity-office-interactions-affect-online-feedback-and-quits-especially.
28. Cullen, Zoë B., and Ricardo Perez-Truglia. "The Old Boys' Club: Schmoozing and the Gender Gap." Social Science Research Network, December 1, 2019. https://doi.org/10.3386/w26530.
29. Schulte, Brigid. "Designing Equitable and Effective Workplaces for a 'Corona-Normal' Future of Work." New America, March 17, 2022. Accessed April 16, 2023. https://www.newamerica.org/better-life-lab/reports/designing-equitable-workplaces-for-a-post-pandemic-world-a-toolkit-for-digital-hybrid-essential-work/.
30. Schulte, "Designing Equitable and Effective Workplaces for a 'Corona-Normal' Future of Work."
31. McKeever, Vicky. "Goldman Sachs CEO Solomon Calls Working from Home an 'Aberration.'" CNBC, February 25, 2021. Accessed April 16, 2023. https://www.cnbc.com/2021/02/25/goldman-sachs-ceo-solomon-calls-working-from-home-an-aberration-.html.
32. Business Insider. "The Many Ways JPMorgan Keeps Tabs on Its Workers—from Their Zoom Calls to In-Office Attendance," August 8, 2022. Accessed April 16, 2023. https://www.businessinsider.com/how-jpmorgan-tracks-employees-zoom-calls-id-swipes-2022-8.
33. King, Hope. "JPMorgan Directs Senior Execs Back to Office 5 Days a Week." *Axios*, April 12, 2023. Accessed August 8, 2023. https://www.axios.com/2023/04/12/jpmorgan-back-to-office-hybrid.

34. Wells, Charlie. "Remote Workers Need a New Plan." Bloomberg, February 1, 2024. Accessed February 10, 2024. https://www.bloomberg.com/news/newsletters/2024-02-01/are-remote-workers-more-likely-to-be-laid-off?embedded-checkout=true.
35. Chen, Te-Ping. "Remote Workers Bear the Brunt When Layoffs Hit." *Wall Street Journal*, January 26, 2024. Accessed February 10, 2024. https://www.wsj.com/lifestyle/careers/layoffs-remote-work-data-980ed59d.
36. Slack. "The State of Work 2023," 2023. Accessed August 8, 2023. https://slack.com/resources/why-use-slack/state-of-work.
37. Hatfield, Steve, Tara Mahoutchian, Nate Paynter, Nic Scoble-Williams, John Forsythe, Shannon Poynton, Martin Kamen, Lauren Kirby, Michael Griffiths, and Yves Van Durme. "2023 Global Human Capital Trends." Deloitte Insights, January 9, 2023. Accessed April 16, 2023. https://www2.deloitte.com/us/en/insights/focus/human-capital-trends.html#activating-the-future.
38. Yost, Cali. "'How Do You DO It?' High Performance Flexibility 2023." Flex + Strategy Group, January 26, 2023. Accessed April 16, 2023. https://flexstrategygroup.com/blog/2023/01/how-do-you-do-it-high-performance-flexibility-2023.
39. Schwartz, Jeff, Tom Hodson, and Ian Winstrom Otten. "The Overwhelmed Employee." Deloitte Insights, March 7, 2014. Accessed April 16, 2023. https://www2.deloitte.com/us/en/insights/focus/human-capital-trends/2014/hc-trends-2014-overwhelmed-employee.html.
40. Bacic, William K. "Hyper-Connectivity Inhibits Work-Life Balance." Deloitte United States. Accessed September 13, 2023. https://www2.deloitte.com/us/en/pages/about-deloitte/articles/the-wonders-of-work-life-balance-and-well-being.html.
41. Berdahl, Jennifer L., Marianne Cooper, Peter Glick, Robert B. Livingston, and Joan C. Williams. "Work as a Masculinity Contest." *Journal of Social Issues* 74, no. 3 (September 1, 2018): 422–48. https://doi.org/10.1111/josi.12289.
42. Groysberg, Boris, and Robin Abrahams. "Manage Your Work, Manage Your Life." *Harvard Business Review*, March 2014. Accessed April 16, 2023. https://hbr.org/2014/03/manage-your-work-manage-your-life.
43. Pandurangi, Nidhi. "Elon Musk's Productivity Hack Is Taking 2 or 3 Days Off a Year, Working 7 Days a Week, and Getting 6 Hours of Sleep a Night." *Business Insider*, May 17, 2023. Accessed February 10, 2024. https://www.businessinsider.com/elon-musk-tesla-twitter-productivity-days-off-year-work-week-2023-5.
44. Siddiqui, Faiz, and Jeremy B. Merrill. "Musk Issues Ultimatum to Staff: Commit to 'Hardcore' Twitter or Take Severance." *Washington Post*, November 16, 2022. Accessed February 10, 2024. https://www.washingtonpost.com/technology/2022/11/16/musk-twitter-email-ultimatum-termination/.

45. McGregor, Jena. "Elon Musk's 'Morally Wrong' Remote Work Gripe Misses Its Many Upsides." *Forbes*, May 19, 2023. Accessed February 10, 2024. https://www.forbes.com/sites/jenamcgregor/2023/05/19/elon-musks-morally-wrong-remote-work-gripe-misses-its-many-upsides/?sh=4333f25a5965.
46. Hawkins, Andrew J. "Tesla's 'Ultra Hardcore' Work Culture—as Told by Its Employees." *The Verge* (podcast), August 16, 2023. Accessed February 10, 2024. https://www.theverge.com/2023/8/16/23833447/tesla-elon-musk-ultra-hardcore-employees-land-of-the-giants.
47. Spangler, Todd. "One Year After Elon Musk Bought Twitter, X Monthly Users Are Down 15% and Ad Revenue Has Slumped 54%." *Variety*, October 27, 2023. Accessed February 10, 2024. https://variety.com/2023/digital/news/musk-twitter-x-acquisition-one-year-user-revenue-decline-1235770297/; Duhigg, Charles, "Dr. Elon & Mr. Musk: Life Inside Tesla's Production Hell." *Wired*, December 13, 2018. Accessed February 10, 2024. https://www.wired.com/story/elon-musk-tesla-life-inside-gigafactory/.
48. Sherwin, Galen. "Discriminatory Return to In Office Work Mandates Could Push Women and People of Color out of the Workforce." American Civil Liberties Union, May 13, 2021. Accessed April 16, 2023. https://www.aclu.org/news/womens-rights/discriminatory-return-to-in-office-work-mandates-could-push-women-and-people-of-color-out-of-the-workforce; American Civil Liberties Union. "SC EO Return in Person Fact Sheet," May 13, 2021. Accessed October 14, 2023. https://www.aclu.org/documents/sc-eo-return-person-fact-sheet.
49. Telford, Taylor, and Danielle Abril. "Companies' Hard-line Stance on Returning to the Office Is Backfiring." *Washington Post*, February 2, 2024. Accessed February 10, 2024. https://www.washingtonpost.com/technology/2024/02/02/return-to-office-punishments-remote-hybrid-work/.
50. Jones, Anna. "The Problem with Losing 'Osmosis Learning.'" BBC, October 4, 2021. Accessed April 17, 2023. https://www.bbc.com/worklife/article/20211004-the-problem-with-losing-osmosis-learning.
51. Abril, Danielle. "Gen Z Workers Demand Flexibility, Don't Want to Be Stuffed in a Cubicle." *Washington Post*, August 11, 2022. Accessed April 17, 2023. https://www.washingtonpost.com/technology/2022/08/11/gen-z-workforce-hybrid/.
52. Mercer. "Navigating the New World at Work," January 2024. Accessed February 10, 2024. https://www.mercer.com/assets/us/en_us/shared-assets/local/attachments/pdf-2023-2024-inside-employees-minds-study-navigating-the-new-world-at-work.pdf.
53. Isos Karian and Box. "Hybrid Working: The Never-Ending Search for the Right Approach," July 10, 2022. Accessed September 13, 2023. https://ipsoskarianandbox.com/insight/43/hybrid-working-the-never-ending-search-for-the-right-approach.

54. *Harvard Business Review*. "Tsedal Neeley on Why We Need to Think of the Office as a Tool, with Very Specific Uses," January 14, 2022. Accessed April 17, 2023. https://hbr.org/2022/01/tsedal-neeley-on-why-we-need-to-think-of-the-office-as-a-tool-with-very-specific-uses.
55. Daisley, Bruce. "Clear Thinking for 2022," January 25, 2022. Accessed April 17, 2023. https://eatsleepworkrepeat.com/clear-thinking-for-2022/.
56. Bergen, Mark. "Google's Ex-HR Chief Says Hybrid Work Won't Last." Bloomberg, April 1, 2022. Accessed April 17, 2023. https://www.bloomberg.com/news/newsletters/2022-04-01/google-s-ex-hr-chief-says-hybrid-work-won-t-last.
57. Bloom, Nicholas. "To Raise Productivity, Let More Employees Work from Home." *Harvard Business Review*, January 2014. Accessed April 17, 2023. https://hbr.org/2014/01/to-raise-productivity-let-more-employees-work-from-home.
58. Delaney, Kevin J. "What We Know Now About the Business Impact of Hybrid Work." *Time*, September 6, 2022. Accessed April 17, 2023. https://time.com/charter/6211250/hybrid-work-nicholas-bloom/.
59. Harrington, Emma, and Matthew E. Kahn. "Has the Rise of Work-from-Home Reduced the Motherhood Penalty in the Labor Market?" October 31, 2023. Accessed February 20, 2024. ttps://drive.google.com/file/d/1Z1J2GHZjqkWzRV5ygA02yzSemwkAmzne/view.
60. Waller, "Think Hybrid Work Doesn't Work? The Data Disagrees."
61. Wigert, Ben, and Jessica White. "The Advantages and Challenges of Hybrid Work." Gallup, September 14, 2022. Accessed April 17, 2023. https://www.gallup.com/workplace/398135/advantages-challenges-hybrid-work.aspx.
62. Integrated Benefits Institute. "Remote and Hybrid Employees Report Improved Productivity, Satisfaction, and Engagement, According to IBI Analysis," October 20, 2022. Accessed April 17, 2023. https://www.prnewswire.com/news-releases/remote-and-hybrid-employees-report-improved-productivity-satisfaction-and-engagement-according-to-ibi-analysis-301655030.html.
63. Ding, Yuye, and Mark (Shuai) Ma. "Return-to-Office Mandates." Social Science Research Network, December 25, 2023. Accessed February 10, 2024. https://papers.ssrn.com/sol3/papers.cfm?abstract_id=4675401.
64. Furman, Jason, and Wilson Powell III. "Record US Productivity Slump in First Half of 2022 Risks Higher Inflation and Unemployment." PIIE, August 9, 2022. Accessed April 17, 2023. https://www.piie.com/blogs/realtime-economics/record-us-productivity-slump-first-half-2022-risks-higher-inflation-and?utm_source=npr_newsletter&utm_medium=email&utm_content=20220909&utm_term=7224424&utm_campaign=money&utm_id=5861281&orgid=88&utm_att1=.
65. Murphy, Aislinn. "BlackRock CEO Larry Fink Discusses Inflation, ESG Investing in the Energy Sector." Fox Business, September 6, 2022. Accessed

April 17, 2023. https://www.foxbusiness.com/markets/blackrock-ceo-larry-fink-discusses-inflation-esg-investing-energy-sector.

66. Social Security Administration. "The House Passes H.R. 139, 'SHOW UP Act of 2023.'" *Social Security Legislative Bulletin*, February 6, 2023. Accessed April 17, 2023. https://www.ssa.gov/legislation/legis_bulletin_020123.html#:~:text=On%20February%2001%2C%202023%2C%20the,call%20vote%20of%20221%2D206.
67. Tsipursky, Gleb. "The Return to the Office Could Be the Real Reason for the Slump in Productivity. Here's the Data to Prove It." *Fortune*, February 16, 2023. Accessed April 17, 2023. https://fortune.com/2023/02/16/return-office-real-reason-slump-productivity-data-careers-gleb-tsipursky/.
68. Future Forum. "Future Forum Pulse Winter Snapshot," February 2023. Accessed April 17, 2023. https://futureforum.com/research/future-forum-pulse-winter-2022-2023-snapshot/.
69. Tsipursky, Gleb. "Remote Work Can Be Better for Innovation Than In-Person Meetings." *Scientific American*, October 14, 2021. Accessed April 17, 2023. https://www.scientificamerican.com/article/remote-work-can-be-better-for-innovation-than-in-person-meetings/.
70. Smith, Morgan. "Employees Are Twice as Likely as Executives to Work from the Office Full-Time, Despite Return-to-Office Mandates." CNBC, April 19, 2022. Accessed April 17, 2023. https://www.cnbc.com/2022/04/19/employees-are-twice-as-likely-as-executives-to-work-in-office-full-time.html.
71. Future Forum. "Future Forum Pulse Winter Snapshot," February 2023. Accessed April 17, 2023. https://futureforum.com/research/future-forum-pulse-winter-2022-2023-snapshot/.
72. MacLellan, Lila. "70% of Top Male Earners in the US Have a Spouse Who Stays Home." *Quartz*, April 30, 2019. Accessed April 17, 2023. https://qz.com/work/1607995/most-men-in-the-top-1-of-us-earners-have-a-spouse-who-stays-home.
73. Fuller, Joseph, and Manjari Raman. "The Caring Company: How Employers Can Cut Costs and Boost Productivity by Helping Employees Manage Caregiving Needs." Harvard Business School, January 17, 2019.
74. Diversity Research Institute. "U.S. Fortune 500 Corporate Governance Report," 2023. Accessed August 28, 2023. https://nationaldiversityconference.com/2023/wp-content/uploads/2023/01/2023-diversity-first-top-50-companies-furtune-500-overview.pdf.
75. *Economist*. "Welcome to the Era of the Hyper-Surveilled Office," May 14, 2022. Accessed April 17, 2023. https://www.economist.com/business/welcome-to-the-era-of-the-hyper-surveilled-office/21809219.
76. Kohn, Melvin L., and Carmi Schooler. "Job Conditions and Personality: A Longitudinal Assessment of Their Reciprocal Effects." *American Journal of Sociology* 87, no. 6 (1982): 1257–86. Accessed February 24, 2024. https://psycnet.apa.org/record/1983-03470-001.

77. BehavioralEconomics.com. "Present Bias." Accessed April 17, 2023. https://www.behavioraleconomics.com/resources/mini-encyclopedia-of-be/present-bias/#:~:text=The%20present%20bias%20refers%20to,Donoghue%20%26%20Rabin%2C%201999.
78. Malito, Alessandra. "Nobel Prize Winner Richard Thaler May Have Added $29.6 Billion to Retirement Accounts." MarketWatch, January 6, 2018. Accessed April 17, 2023. https://www.marketwatch.com/story/nobel-prize-winner-richard-thaler-may-have-added-296-billion-to-retirement-accounts-2017-10-09.
79. Feeney, Mary K., and Barry Bozeman. "Staying Late." *American Review of Public Administration* 39, no. 5 (September 1, 2009): 459–77. https://doi.org/10.1177/0275074008327293.
80. Gallup. "Too Many Interruptions at Work?" March 24, 2022. Accessed April 17, 2023. https://news.gallup.com/businessjournal/23146/too-many-interruptions-work.aspx.
81. Boyle, Matthew. "Bosses Say Nearly Half of Meetings Should Disappear." Bloomberg, March 13, 2023. Accessed April 17, 2023. https://www.bloomberg.com/news/articles/2023-03-13/bosses-say-nearly-half-of-meetings-should-disappear?utm_source=website&utm_medium=share&utm_campaign=linkedin.
82. Mankins, Michael. "Is Technology Really Helping Us Get More Done?" Bain, February 24, 2016. Accessed April 17, 2023. https://www.bain.com/insights/is-technology-really-helping-us-get-more-done-hbr.
83. Schulte, Brigid. "Even Work-Life Balance Experts Are Awful at Balancing Work and Life." *The Cut,* March 28, 2017. Accessed September 13, 2023. https://www.thecut.com/2017/03/work-life-balance-experts-are-bad-at-balancing-work-and-life.html.
84. Gurchiek, Kathy. "Work Martyrdom: The Road to Burnout." SHRM, September 29, 2021. Accessed April 17, 2023. https://www.shrm.org/resourcesandtools/hr-topics/employee-relations/pages/work-martyrdom-the-road-to-burnout.aspx.
85. Mullainathan, Sendhil, and Eldar Shafir. "Freeing Up Intelligence." *Scientific American Mind,* January 2014.
86. Schulte, Brigid. "Preventing Busyness from Becoming Burnout." *Harvard Business Review,* August 27, 2021. Accessed April 17, 2023. https://hbr.org/2019/04/preventing-busyness-from-becoming-burnout.
87. Reid, Erin. "Why Some Men Pretend to Work 80-Hour Weeks." *Harvard Business Review,* April 28, 2015. Accessed April 9, 2023. https://hbr.org/2015/04/why-some-men-pretend-to-work-80-hour-weeks.
88. Connolly, Dan, Uyhun Ung, Matthew Darling, Ted Robertson, and Suman Gidwani. "Work and Life: A Behavioral Approach to Solving Work-Life Conflict." Ideas42, March 2017. Accessed August 30, 2023. https://

www.ideas42.org/wp-content/uploads/2017/03/I42-863_RWJ_Report_DesignSolution_final.pdf.

89. Buehler, Roger, Dale W. Griffin, and Johanna Peetz. "The Planning Fallacy." In Mark P. Zanna and James M. Olson, eds., *Advances in Experimental Social Psychology*, pp. 1–62. Amsterdam: Elsevier, 2010. https://doi.org/10.1016/s0065-2601(10)43001-4.
90. Mankins, Michael. "This Weekly Meeting Took Up 300,000 Hours a Year." *Harvard Business Review*, November 2, 2014. Accessed April 17, 2023. https://hbr.org/2014/04/how-a-weekly-meeting-took-up-300000-hours-a-year.
91. Hartig, Terry, Ralph Catalano, Michael K. Ong, and S. Leonard Syme. "Vacation, Collective Restoration, and Mental Health in a Population." *Society and Mental Health* 3, no. 3 (August 7, 2013): 221–36. https://doi.org/10.1177/2156869313497718.
92. Connolly et al., "Work and Life: A Behavioral Approach to Solving Work-Life Conflict."
93. Work, Family & Health Network. "STAR: Office." Accessed April 17, 2023. https://workfamilyhealthnetwork.org/star.
94. Grand View Research. "Corporate Wellness Market Size, Share & Trends Analysis Report." Accessed April 17, 2023. https://www.grandviewresearch.com/industry-analysis/corporate-wellness-market.
95. Hammer, Leslie, and Ellen Ernst Kossek. "Family Supportive Supervisor Behaviors (FSSB) Training Manual," 2013. Accessed April 17, 2023. https://projects.iq.harvard.edu/files/wfhn/files/fssb_training_manual10_13.pdf.
96. Work, Family & Health Network. "Publications." Accessed April 17, 2023. https://workfamilyhealthnetwork.org/publications?page=2.
97. Barnes, Andrew. *The 4 Day Week: How the Flexible Work Revolution Can Increase Productivity, Profitability and Well-Being, and Help Create a Sustainable Future*. London: Piatkus, 2020, p. 2.
98. Delaney, Helen. "Research: Perpetual Guardian's 4-Day Workweek Trial: Qualitative Research Analysis," 4 Day Week Global. Accessed April 17, 2023. https://www.4dayweek.com/research-perpetual-guardians-4day-workweek-trial-qualitative-research-analysis.
99. White Paper—The Four Day Week. "Guidelines for an Outcome-Based Trial—Raising Productivity and Engagement," 2019.
100. Olds, Danielle M., and Sean P. Clarke. "The Effect of Work Hours on Adverse Events and Errors in Health Care." *Journal of Safety Research* 41, no. 2 (April 1, 2010): 153–62. https://doi.org/10.1016/j.jsr.2010.02.002.
101. C.W. and A.J.K.D. "Get a Life." *Economist*, September 24, 2013. Accessed April 17, 2023. https://www.economist.com/free-exchange/2013/09/24/get-a-life.
102. Pencavel, John. "The Productivity of Working Hours." *Economic Journal* 125, no. 589 (December 1, 2015): 2052–76. https://doi.org/10.1111/ecoj.12166.

103. Whaples, Robert. "Hours of Work in U.S. History." EH.net, August 14, 2001. Accessed August 8, 2023. https://eh.net/encyclopedia/hours-of-work-in-u-s-history/.
104. Cubicle Therapy. "Who the Fuck Created the 8 Hour Workday?" Accessed September 13, 2023. https://cubicletherapy.com/8-hour-workday/; Ruggeri, Christine. "Most Workers Want to Work Less, So Why Does the 40-Hour Workweek Exist?" Leaders.com, June 28, 2023. Accessed September 13, 2023. https://leaders.com/articles/company-culture/40-hour-workweek/;
105. Crowther, Samuel. "Henry Ford: Why I Favor Five Days' Work with Six Days' Pay." In Wikisource, the Free Online Library, July 2, 2022. Accessed September 13, 2023. https://en.wikisource.org/wiki/Henry_Ford:_Why_I_Favor_Five_Days%27_Work_With_Six_Days%27_Pay.
106. Jacobson, Louis. "Does the 8-Hour Day and the 40-Hour Week Come from Henry Ford, or Labor Unions?" Politifact, September 9, 2015. Accessed August 8, 2023. https://www.politifact.com/factchecks/2015/sep/09/viral-image/does-8-hour-day-and-40-hour-come-henry-ford-or-lab/.
107. History.com. "Ford Factory Workers Get 40-Hour Week," April 29, 2020. Accessed April 17, 2023. https://www.history.com/this-day-in-history/ford-factory-workers-get-40-hour-week.
108. Wynn, Alison T., Magali Fassiotto, Caroline Simard, Jennifer K. Raymond, and Hannah A. Valantine. "Pulled in Too Many Directions: The Causes and Consequences of Work-Work Conflict." *Sociological Perspectives* 61, no. 5 (May 21, 2018): 830–49. https://doi.org/10.1177/0731121418774568.
109. Ericsson, K. Anders. "Training History, Deliberate Practice and Elite Sports Performance: An Analysis in Response to Tucker and Collins Review—What Makes Champions?" *British Journal of Sports Medicine* 47, no. 9 (June 1, 2013): 533–35. https://doi.org/10.1136/bjsports-2012-091767; Ericsson, K. Anders, Michael J. Prietula, and Edward T. Cokely. "The Making of an Expert." *Harvard Business Review*, July 2007. Accessed September 13, 2023. https://hbr.org/2007/07/the-making-of-an-expert.
110. McGregor, Jena. "In Overworked Japan, Microsoft Tested a Four-Day Workweek. Productivity Soared 40 Percent." *Washington Post*, November 4, 2019. Accessed April 17, 2023. https://www.washingtonpost.com/business/2019/11/04/overworked-japan-microsoft-tested-four-day-workweek-productivity-soared-percent/.
111. MacFarlane, Scott, and Analisa Novak. "End of the 5-Day Workweek? Some States Consider Legislation Making 4-Day Workweeks More Common." CBS News, February 27, 2023. Accessed April 17, 2023. https://www.cbsnews.com/news/4-day-workweek-states-considering-legislation/.
112. Thorpe, Devin. "Why Bill Gates Partners with Rotary to Eradicate Polio." *Forbes*, May 31, 2019. Accessed September 5, 2023. https://www.forbes.com/sites/devinthorpe/2019/05/31/why-bill-gates-partners-with-rotary-to-eradicate-polio/?sh=79cb53b95c02.

113. AmeriCorps. "Volunteering and Civic Life in America: Research Summary." Accessed September 5, 2023. https://americorps.gov/sites/default/files/document/volunteering-civic-life-america-research-summary.pdf.
114. Autonomy. "The Results Are In: The UK's Four-Day Week Pilot." 4 Day Week Global, 2023. Accessed April 17, 2023. https://autonomy.work/wp-content/uploads/2023/02/The-results-are-in-The-UKs-four-day-week-pilot.pdf.
115. Tanaka, Chris. "4-Day Work Week Trial Seen as Overwhelming Success." CBS News, February 21, 2023. Accessed April 17, 2023. https://www.cbsnews.com/boston/news/4-day-work-week-trial-results/.

Chapter 4: Workers Rising: More than Clapping for Essential Work

1. Lincoln, Abraham. "An Address by Abraham Lincoln Before the Wisconsin State Agricultural Fair," September 30, 1859. https://quod.lib.umich.edu/l/lincoln/lincoln3?id=3_471_1;note=ptr;rgn=div1;view=trgt.
2. Ross, Martha, and Nicole Bateman. "Meet the Low-Wage Workforce." Brookings, November 7, 2019. Accessed April 27, 2023. https://www.brookings.edu/research/meet-the-low-wage-workforce/.
3. McKinsey & Company. "Freelance, Side Hustles, and Gigs: Many More Americans Have Become Independent Workers," August 23, 2022. Accessed April 27, 2023. https://www.mckinsey.com/featured-insights/sustainable-inclusive-growth/future-of-america/freelance-side-hustles-and-gigs-many-more-americans-have-become-independent-workers; Anderson, Monica, Colleen McClain, Michelle Faverio, and Risa Gelles-Watnick. "The State of Gig Work in 2021." Pew Research Center, December 8, 2021. Accessed September 21, 2023. https://www.pewresearch.org/internet/2021/12/08/the-state-of-gig-work-in-2021/.
4. Glynn, Sarah Jane. "Coronavirus Paid Leave Exemptions Exclude Millions of Workers from Coverage." Center for American Progress, April 17, 2020. Accessed April 27, 2023. https://www.americanprogress.org/article/coronavirus-paid-leave-exemptions-exclude-millions-workers-coverage/.
5. Cohen, Patricia. "We All Have a Stake in the Stock Market, Right? Guess Again." *New York Times*, February 8, 2018. Accessed April 27, 2023. https://www.nytimes.com/2018/02/08/business/economy/stocks-economy.html.
6. Nieman Foundation for Journalism at Harvard. "Reviving the Labor Beat: 'Every One of Us Is a Worker.'" Nieman Foundation, March 4, 2022. Accessed April 27, 2023. https://nieman.harvard.edu/articles/reviving-labor-beat-twitter-space/.
7. Pierce, Michael. "How Bill Clinton Remade the Democratic Party by Abandoning Unions: An Arkansas Story." Labor and Working-Class History Association, November 23, 2016. Accessed April 27, 2023. https://

www.lawcha.org/2016/11/23/bill-clinton-remade-democratic-party-abandoning-unions-working-class-whites/.

8. Kaplan, Juliana, Madison Hoff, and Ayelet Sheffey. "The Labor Market Is Still Really Strong, but That Means a Recession Next Year Could Hurt Even More." *Business Insider*, December 3, 2022. Accessed September 21, 2023. https://www.businessinsider.com/recession-forecast-outlook-job-market-strong-downturn-next-year-hurt-2022-12.
9. Fins, Amanda. "Women in Leisure and Hospitality Are Among the Hardest Hit by Job Losses and Most at Risk of Covid-19 Infection." Women's National Law Center, November 2020. Accessed April 27, 2023. https://nwlc.org/wp-content/uploads/2020/11/LeisureFS.pdf.
10. Bureau of Labor Statistics, U.S. Department of Labor. "Industries at a Glance: Leisure and Hospitality," April 23, 2023. Accessed April 27, 2023. https://bls.gov/iag/tgs/iag70.htm.
11. Stevenson, Betsey, and Benny Docter. "November Jobs Report: Strong Job Growth Continues, but There Are Hints of Weakness," December 2, 2022. Accessed April 27, 2023. https://poverty.umich.edu/2022/12/02/november-jobs-report-strong-job-growth-continues-but-there-are-hints-of-weakness/; U.S. Bureau of Labor Statistics, "Industries at a Glance: Leisure and Hospitality."
12. Cooper, David, and Dan Essrow. "Low-Wage Workers Are Older Than You Think: 89 Percent of Workers Who Would Benefit from a $12 Minimum Wage Are at Least 20 Years Old." Economic Policy Institute, April 27, 2015. Accessed April 27, 2023. https://www.epi.org/publication/low-wage-workers-are-older-than-you-think.
13. Sherk, James. "Most Minimum-Wage Jobs Lead to Better-Paying Opportunities." Heritage Foundation, January 21, 2014. Accessed September 21, 2023. https://www.heritage.org/jobs-and-labor/report/most-minimum-wage-jobs-lead-better-paying-opportunities.
14. Fuller, Joseph, and Manjari Raman. "Building from the Bottom Up." *Harvard Business Review*, January 2022. Accessed April 27, 2023. https://www.hbs.edu/managing-the-future-of-work/Documents/research/Building%20From%20The%20Bottom%20Up.pdf.
15. Gabe, Todd, Jaison Abel, and Richard Florida. "Can Low-Wage Workers Find Better Jobs?" Federal Reserve Bank of New York, April 2018. Accessed April 27, 2023. https://www.newyorkfed.org/research/staff_reports/sr846.
16. Begley, Steven, Bryan Hancock, Thomas Kilroy, and Sajal Kohli. "Automation in Retail: An Executive Overview for Getting Ready." McKinsey & Company, May 23, 2019. Accessed April 27, 2023. https://www.mckinsey.com/industries/retail/our-insights/automation-in-retail-an-executive-overview-for-getting-ready.
17. Gould, Elise, and Jori Kandra. "State of Working America 2021: Measuring Wages in the Pandemic Labor Market." Economic Policy Institute,

April 27, 2022. Accessed April 27, 2023. https://www.epi.org/publication/swa-wages-2021/.

18. Zundl, Elaine, Daniel Schneider, Kristen Harknett, and Evelyn Bellew. "Still Unstable: The Persistence of Schedule Uncertainty During the Pandemic." Shift Project, January 2022. Accessed April 24, 2023. https://shift.hks.harvard.edu/still-unstable/.
19. Scott, Ellen, Mary King, and Raahi Reddy. "The Impact on Oregonians of the Rise of Irregular Scheduling." University of Oregon Labor Education and Research Center, February 2017. Accessed April 27, 2023. https://lerc.uoregon.edu/files/2017/03/SchedulingReport-Web-10qk39n.pdf.
20. Lambert, Susan J., Julia R. Henly, and Jaeseung Kim. "Precarious Work Schedules as a Source of Economic Insecurity and Institutional Distrust." *RSF: The Russell Sage Foundation Journal of the Social Sciences* 5, no. 4 (September 1, 2019): 218. https://doi.org/10.7758/rsf.2019.5.4.08.
21. Storer, Adam, Daniel Schneider, and Kristen Harknett. "What Explains Race/Ethnic Inequality in Job Quality in the Service Sector?" Equitable Growth, October 16, 2019. Accessed April 27, 2023. https://equitablegrowth.org/working-papers/what-explains-race-ethnic-inequality-in-job-quality-in-the-service-sector/.
22. Scheiber, Noam. "Despite Labor Shortages, Workers See Few Gains in Economic Security." *New York Times*, February 1, 2022. Accessed April 28, 2023. https://www.nytimes.com/2022/02/01/business/economy/part-time-work.html.
23. Retail Dive. "The Running List of Major Retail Bankruptcies," February 27, 2023. Accessed April 28, 2023. https://www.retaildive.com/news/running-list-major-retail-bankruptcies/624502/.
24. Retail Dive, "The Running List of Major Retail Bankruptcies."
25. Hartmans, Avery. "The Pandemic Didn't Kill Stores but They'll Never Be the Same Again." *Business Insider*, December 30, 2022. Accessed April 28, 2023. https://www.businessinsider.com/how-pandemic-changed-brick-and-mortar-retail-stores-fulfillment-returns-2022-12; Pisani, Joseph. "Amazon's Profit More Than Triples as Pandemic Boom Continues." AP News, April 29, 2021. Accessed September 21, 2023. https://apnews.com/article/lifestyle-health-coronavirus-technology-business-16a950ba630045281458500081d562e6; U.S. Census Bureau and Mayumi Brewster. "Annual Retail Trade Survey Shows Impact of Online Shopping on Retail Sales During COVID-19 Pandemic." Census.gov, April 27, 2023. Accessed September 21, 2023. https://www.census.gov/library/stories/2022/04/ecommerce-sales-surged-during-pandemic.html.
26. Affine. "In-Store Traffic Analytics: Retail Sensing with Intelligent Object Detection." *Medium*, April 27, 2021. Accessed April 28, 2023. https://affine.medium.com/in-store-traffic-analytics-retail-sensing-with-intelligent-object-detection-51f7aea13a1a; O'Neil, Cathy. *Weapons of Math Destruction:*

How Big Data Increases Inequality and Threatens Democracy. New York: Crown Publishers, 2016.

27. Boushey, Heather, and Bridget Ansel. "Working by the Hour: The Economic Consequences of Unpredictable Scheduling Practices." Equitable Growth, September 2016. Accessed September 21, 2023. https://equitablegrowth.org/working-by-the-hour-the-economic-consequences-of-unpredictable-scheduling-practices/.
28. Schulte, Brigid. "Why Today's Shopping Sucks." *Washington Monthly*, January 12, 2020. Accessed April 28, 2023. https://washingtonmonthly.com/2020/01/12/why-todays-shopping-sucks/.
29. Schulte, "Why Today's Shopping Sucks."
30. O'Neil, *Weapons of Math Destruction*, pp. 128–29.
31. Greenhouse, Steven. "A Part-Time Life, as Hours Shrink and Shift for American Workers." *New York Times*, October 27, 2012. Accessed April 28, 2023. https://www.nytimes.com/2012/10/28/business/a-part-time-life-as-hours-shrink-and-shift-for-american-workers.html.
32. Retail Action Project. "Retail Action Project." Accessed April 29, 2023. https://www.retailactionproject.org/.
33. National Women's Law Center. "Reporting Time Pay: A Key Solution to Curb Unpredictable and Unstable Scheduling Practices," January 2015. Accessed April 29, 2023. https://nwlc.org/wp-content/uploads/2015/08/reporting_time_pay_fact_sheet_jan_2015.pdf.
34. UCLA Labor Center. "Hour Crisis: Unstable Schedules in the Los Angeles Retail Sector," 2018. Accessed April 28, 2023. https://www.labor.ucla.edu/publication/hourcrisisreport.
35. Freedberg, Eli, Andy Klaben-Finegold, and Joy Rosenquist. "Los Angeles Adopts Fair Workweek Measures." SHRM, February 14, 2023. Accessed April 28, 2023. https://www.shrm.org/ResourcesAndTools/legal-and-compliance/state-and-local-updates/Pages/los-angeles-fair-workweek.aspx.
36. Deitch, Rachel. "On-Call Is Being Called Off: Attorneys General Inquiry Leads Several Retailers to End On-Call Scheduling." *Georgetown Journal on Poverty Law & Policy*, April 19, 2017. Accessed April 28, 2023. https://www.law.georgetown.edu/poverty-journal/blog/on-call-is-being-called-off-attorneys-general-inquiry-leads-several-retailers-to-end-on-call-scheduling/.
37. "Ward v. Tilly's, Inc.," 2019. Accessed April 28, 2023. https://law.justia.com/cases/california/court-of-appeal/2019/b280151.html.
38. Schulte, "Why Today's Shopping Sucks."
39. Ballotpedia. "Oregon Increase State Minimum Wage, Measure 25 (2002)." Accessed April 29, 2023. https://ballotpedia.org/Oregon_Increase_State_Minimum_Wage,_Measure_25_(2002).
40. Parker, Doug, and Don Stait. "Oregon Becomes Fourth State to Pass Paid Sick Leave Law." Littler Mendelson P.C., June 15, 2015. Accessed April 29, 2023. https://www.littler.com/publication-press/publication/oregon

-becomes-fourth-state-pass-paid-sick-leave-law#:~:text=On%20June%20 12%2C%202015%2C%20the,year%20of%20paid%20sick%20leave.

41. Ben-Ishai, Liz. "Oregon Becomes First State to Pass Comprehensive Fair Scheduling Law." Center for Law and Social Policy, June 29, 2017. Accessed April 28, 2023. https://www.clasp.org/blog/oregon-becomes-first-state-pass-comprehensive-fair-scheduling-law/.
42. Scott, Stephen, and Alexander Wheatley. "Oregon Passes Nation's Most Generous Paid Family Leave Law." SHRM, July 16, 2019. Accessed April 29, 2023. https://www.shrm.org/resourcesandtools/legal-and-compliance/state-and-local-updates/pages/oregon-passes-generous-paid-family-leave-law.aspx.
43. Ben-Ishai, "Oregon Becomes First State to Pass Comprehensive Fair Scheduling Law."
44. Oregon Bureau of Labor and Industries. "Predictive Scheduling." Accessed April 28, 2023. https://www.oregon.gov/boli/workers/pages/predictive-scheduling.aspx.
45. *Crain's Chicago Business*. "Walgreens Earnings Miss Estimates," June 27, 2023. Accessed September 3, 2023. https://www.chicagobusiness.com/health-care/walgreens-earnings-miss-estimates.
46. Schneider, Daniel, and Kristen Harknett. "It's About Time: How Work Schedule Instability Matters for Workers, Families, and Racial Inequality." Shift Project, October 16, 2019. Accessed April 28, 2023. https://shift.hks.harvard.edu/its-about-time-how-work-schedule-instability-matters-for-workers-families-and-racial-inequality/.
47. Schneider, Daniel, and Kristen Harknett. "Consequences of Routine Work-Schedule Instability for Worker Health and Well-Being." *American Sociological Review* 84, no. 1 (February 1, 2019): 82–114. https://doi.org/10.1177/0003122418823184.
48. Schneider and Harknett, "Consequences of Routine Work-Schedule Instability for Worker Health and Well-Being."
49. U.S. Government Accountability Office. "Federal Social Safety Net Programs: Millions of Full-Time Workers Rely on Federal Health Care and Food Assistance Programs," November 19, 2020. Accessed April 28, 2023. https://www.gao.gov/products/gao-21-45.
50. Jacobs, Ken. "Americans Are Spending $153 Billion a Year to Subsidize McDonald's and Wal-Mart's Low Wage Workers." *Washington Post*, April 15, 2015. Accessed April 28, 2023. https://www.washingtonpost.com/posteverything/wp/2015/04/15/we-are-spending-153-billion-a-year-to-subsidize-mcdonalds-and-walmarts-low-wage-workers/.
51. Zundl et al., "Still Unstable: The Persistence of Schedule Uncertainty During the Pandemic."
52. Harknett, Kristen, Daniel Schneider, and Sigrid Luhr. "Who Cares If Parents Have Unpredictable Work Schedules? Just-in-Time Work Schedules and Child Care Arrangements." *Social Problems* 69, no. 1 (2022): 164–83.

53. Harknett, Kristen, Daniel Schneider, and Sigrid Luhr. "Who Cares If Parents Have Unpredictable Work Schedules? The Association Between Just-in-Time Work Schedules and Child Care Arrangements." Washington Center for Equitable Growth, October 16, 2019. Accessed April 28, 2023. https://equitablegrowth.org/working-papers/who-cares-if-parents-have-unpredictable-work-schedules-the-association-between-just-in-time-work-schedules-and-child-care-arrangements/.
54. Shift Project. "Homepage." Accessed April 28, 2023. https://shift.hks.harvard.edu/.
55. Ananat, Elizabeth O., Anna Gassman-Pines, and John A. Fitz-Henley II. "The Effects of the Emeryville Fair Workweek Ordinance on the Daily Lives of Low-Wage Workers and Their Families." *RSF: The Russell Sage Foundation Journal of the Social Sciences* 8, no. 5 (2022): 45–66. muse.jhu.edu/article/862640.
56. Gould-Werth, Alix, Emilie Openchowski, and Raksha Kopparam. "New Study in the Proceedings of the National Academy of Sciences Shows Schedule Stability Supports U.S. Workers and the Broader Economy." Washington Center for Equitable Growth, October 12, 2021. Accessed April 28, 2023. https://equitablegrowth.org/new-study-in-the-proceedings-of-the-national-academy-of-sciences-shows-schedule-stability-supports-u-s-workers-and-the-broader-economy/; Harknett, Kristen, Daniel Schneider, and Véronique Irwin. "Improving Health and Economic Security by Reducing Work Schedule Uncertainty." *Proceedings of the National Academy of Sciences* 118, no. 42 (October 19, 2021). https://doi.org/10.1073/pnas.2107828118.
57. Williams, Joan C., Saravanan Kesavan, and Lisa McCorkell. "Research: When Retail Workers Have Stable Schedules, Sales and Productivity Go Up." *Harvard Business Review*, March 29, 2018. Accessed April 28, 2023. https://hbr.org/2018/03/research-when-retail-workers-have-stable-schedules-sales-and-productivity-go-up.
58. Schulte, "Why Today's Shopping Sucks."
59. Schulte, "Why Today's Shopping Sucks."
60. McKinsey & Company. "Personalizing the Customer Experience: Driving Differentiation in Retail," April 28, 2020. Accessed April 30, 2023. https://www.mckinsey.com/industries/retail/our-insights/personalizing-the-customer-experience-driving-differentiation-in-retail.
61. Howland, Daphne. "Retailers Are Understaffing Stores—and Losing Sales." Retail Dive, December 14, 2017. Accessed April 28, 2023. https://www.retaildive.com/news/retailers-are-understaffing-stores-and-losing-sales/513055/.
62. Fisher, Marshall, Santiago Gallino, and Serguei Netessine. "Retailers: Stop Thinking of Salespeople as Expendable." *Harvard Business Review*, January 2019. Accessed April 28, 2023. https://hbr.org/2019/01/retailers-are-squandering-their-most-potent-weapons.

63. Fisher, Marshall. "Retail Rage." *Harvard Business Review*, January 6, 2012. Accessed April 28, 2023. https://hbr.org/2012/01/retail-rage.
64. HR Dive. "A Running List of States and Localities with Predictive Scheduling Mandates," February 13, 2023. Accessed April 28, 2023. https://www.hrdive.com/news/a-running-list-of-states-and-localities-with-predictive-scheduling-mandates/540835/.
65. Greenhouse, Steven. "'The Success Is Inspirational': The Fight for $15 Movement 10 Years On." *Guardian*, November 23, 2022. Accessed April 28, 2023. https://www.theguardian.com/us-news/2022/nov/23/fight-for-15-movement-10-years-old.
66. Lerner, Stephen, and Jono Shaffer. "25 Years Later: Lessons from the Organizers of Justice for Janitors." *Nation*, June 16, 2015. Accessed April 28, 2023. https://www.thenation.com/article/archive/25-years-later-lessons-from-the-organizers-of-justice-for-janitors/.
67. Lempinen, Edward. "A $15 Minimum Wage Would Cost Jobs, Right? Probably Not, Economists Say." Berkeley News, March 18, 2021. Accessed April 28, 2023. https://news.berkeley.edu/2021/03/18/a-15-minimum-wage-would-cost-jobs-right-probably-not-economists-say/.
68. The White House. "The State of Our Unions," September 5, 2022. Accessed April 28, 2023. https://www.whitehouse.gov/cea/written-materials/2022/09/05/the-state-of-our-unions/.
69. Scheiber, Noam. "McDonald's Franchise Settles Suit Involving 'Dog Diaper' Masks." *New York Times*, August 12, 2021. Accessed April 28, 2023. https://www.nytimes.com/2021/08/12/business/mcdonalds-dog-diapers.html.
70. Chen, Yea-Hung, Alicia R. Riley, Kate A. Duchowny, Mujahid Iqbal, Ruijia Chen, Mathew V. Kiang, Alyssa C. Mooney, Andrew Stokes, M. Maria Glymour, and Kirsten Bibbins-Domingo. "COVID-19 Mortality and Excess Mortality Among Working-Age Residents in California, USA, by Occupational Sector: A Longitudinal Cohort Analysis of Mortality Surveillance Data." *Lancet Public Health* 7, no. 9 (September 1, 2022): e744–53. https://doi.org/10.1016/s2468-2667(22)00191-8.
71. Green, Ken. "How the Media Depicts Labor Issues and How Unions Can Set the Record Straight." UnionTrack, June 13, 2019. Accessed April 28, 2023. https://uniontrack.com/blog/media-depicts-labor-issues.
72. Green, "How the Media Depicts Labor Issues and How Unions Can Set the Record Straight"; Schmidt, Diane E. "Public Opinion and Media Coverage of Labor Unions." *Journal of Labor Research* 14 (June 1993): 151–64. https://doi.org/10.1007/bf02685662.
73. Paulas, Rick. "Unions Are Cool." *Vice*, October 27, 2017. Accessed April 28, 2023. https://www.vice.com/en/article/j5jp4d/unions-are-cool.
74. McCarthy, Justin. "U.S. Approval of Labor Unions at Highest Point Since 1965." Gallup, August 30, 2022. Accessed April 28, 2023. https://news

.gallup.com/poll/398303/approval-labor-unions-highest-point-1965.aspx.

75. Gramlich, John. "Majorities of Americans Say Unions Have a Positive Effect on U.S. and That Decline in Union Membership Is Bad." Pew Research Center, September 3, 2021. Accessed April 28, 2023. https://www.pewresearch.org/short-reads/2021/09/03/majorities-of-americans-say-unions-have-a-positive-effect-on-u-s-and-that-decline-in-union-membership-is-bad/.
76. Bogage, Jacob. "Teamsters Approve UPS Contract with Raises for Drivers, Package Sorters." *Washington Post*, August 22, 2023. Accessed September 21, 2023. https://www.washingtonpost.com/business/2023/08/22/ups-teamsters-contract-vote/.
77. Fisk, Catherine L. "What's at Stake in the Hollywood Writers' Strike." American Prospect, July 28, 2023. Accessed September 21, 2023. https://prospect.org/labor/2023-07-28-whats-at-stake-hollywood-writers-strike; *Los Angeles Times*. "What to Know About the SAG-AFTRA Actors' Strike," September 20, 2023. Accessed September 21, 2023. https://www.latimes.com/entertainment-arts/business/story/2023-06-29/what-to-know-sag-aftra-strike-actors-hollywood.
78. Kuttner, Robert. "Kuttner on TAP: Labor's Militant Creativity." American Prospect, September 18, 2023. Accessed September 21, 2023. https://americanprospect.bluelena.io/index.php?action=social&chash=635440afdfc39fe37995fed127d7df4f.234&s=71d26fabe63341819933683ad410722b.
79. Kaye, Danielle. "The UAW Launches a Historic Strike Against All Big 3 Automakers." NPR, September 15, 2023. Accessed September 21, 2023. https://www.npr.org/2023/09/15/1199673197/uaw-strike-big-3-automakers.
80. Brownstein, Ronald. "COVID-19 Has Highlighted Worker-Protection Issues." *Atlantic*, May 7, 2020. Accessed April 29, 2023. https://www.theatlantic.com/politics/archive/2020/05/coronavirus-minimum-wage-paid-leave-biden/611281/.
81. Bivens, Josh, and Jori Kandra. "CEO Pay Has Skyrocketed 1,460% Since 1978: CEOs Were Paid 399 Times as Much as a Typical Worker in 2021." Economic Policy Institute, October 4, 2022. Accessed April 29, 2023. https://www.epi.org/publication/ceo-pay-in-2021/.
82. Fuhrmann, Ryan. "How Large Corporations Avoid Paying Taxes." Investopedia, February 7, 2023. Accessed April 29, 2023. https://www.investopedia.com/financial-edge/0512/how-large-corporations-get-around-paying-less-in-taxes.aspx#.
83. Pickert, Reade. "US Corporate Profits Soar with Margins at Widest Since 1950." Bloomberg.com, August 25, 2022. Accessed April 29, 2023. https://www.bloomberg.com/news/articles/2022-08-25/us-corporate-profits-soar-taking-margins-to-widest-since-1950#xj4y7vzkg?leadSource

=uverify%20wall; Statista. "U.S. Corporate Profits 2012–2022, by Quarter," March 21, 2023. Accessed April 29, 2023. https://www.statista.com/statistics/222127/quarterly-corporate-profits-in-the-us/.

84. The White House, "The State of Our Unions."
85. Sainato, Michael. "Feel the Benefit: Union Workers Receive Far Better Pay and Rights, Congress Finds." *Guardian*, June 10, 2022. Accessed April 29, 2023. https://www.theguardian.com/us-news/2022/jun/10/us-union-workers-report-congress.
86. Walters, Matthew, and Lawrence Mishel. "How Unions Help All Workers." Economic Policy Institute, August 26, 2003. Accessed September 21, 2023. https://www.epi.org/publication/briefingpapers_bp143/.
87. Finnigan, Ryan, and Jo Mhairi Hale. "Working 9 to 5? Union Membership and Work Hours and Schedules." *Social Forces* 96, no. 4 (June 1, 2018): 1541–68. https://doi.org/10.1093/sf/sox101.
88. Rosalsky, Greg. "You May Have Heard of the 'Union Boom.' The Numbers Tell a Different Story." NPR, February 28, 2023. Accessed September 21, 2023. https://www.npr.org/sections/money/2023/02/28/1159663461/you-may-have-heard-of-the-union-boom-the-numbers-tell-a-different-story.
89. Gurley, Lauren Kaori. "Union Membership Rate Hit Record Low in 2023, Though Unions Picked Up Workers." *Washington Post*, January 23, 2024. Accessed February 11, 2024. https://www.washingtonpost.com/business/2024/01/23/union-membership-low-strikes-labor/.
90. Combs, Robert. "Analysis: Labor's Triumphant Organizing Year May Not Be Its Last." Bloomberg Law, February 7, 2023. Accessed August 30, 2023. https://news.bloomberglaw.com/bloomberg-law-analysis/analysis-labors-triumphant-organizing-year-may-not-be-its-last.
91. Bureau of Labor Statistics, U.S. Department of Labor. "The Employment Situation—August 2023," August 4, 2023. Accessed September 21, 2023. https://www.bls.gov/news.release/archives/empsit_01062023.pdf.
92. Gurley, "Union Membership Rate Hit Record Low in 2023, Though Unions Picked Up Workers."
93. U.S. Department of Labor. "Good Jobs Initiative." Accessed April 29, 2023. https://www.dol.gov/general/good-jobs.
94. Families & Workers Fund. "Good Jobs Champions Statement"; Families & Workers Fund. "The Families and Workers Fund Aims to Help Build a More Equitable Economy That Uplifts All," October 4, 2022. Accessed April 29, 2023. https://familiesandworkers.org/news/good-jobs-champions/.
95. Nilsen, Ella. "How Home Care Workers Were Left Out of FDR's New Deal." *Vox*, May 18, 2021. Accessed April 29, 2023. https://www.vox.com/22423690/american-jobs-plan-care-workers-new-deal.
96. Brooks, David. "One Road to Character: Frances Perkins and the

Triangle Shirtwaist Factory Fire." *Atlantic*, April 14, 2015. Accessed April 29, 2023. https://www.theatlantic.com/politics/archive/2015/04/frances-perkins/390003/; "Lecture by Frances Perkins," September 30, 1964. Accessed April 29, 2023. https://trianglefire.ilr.cornell.edu/primary/lectures/.

97. Potts, Monica. "Unions Have Been Under Attack for Decades, but Michigan Just Gave Them a Big Win." FiveThirtyEight, March 24, 2023. Accessed April 29, 2023. https://fivethirtyeight.com/features/unions-have-been-under-attack-for-decades-but-michigan-just-gave-them-a-big-win/.
98. Madland, David. "New Zealand's New Sectoral Bargaining Law Holds Lessons for the United States." OnLabor, December 22, 2022. Accessed April 29, 2023. https://onlabor.org/new-zealands-new-sectoral-bargaining-law-holds-lessons-for-the-united-states/.
99. OnLabor. "Historic New EU Law Part of Growing Push for Sectoral Bargaining," January 19, 2023. Accessed April 29, 2023. https://onlabor.org/historic-new-eu-law-part-of-growing-push-for-sectoral-bargaining/.
100. McNicholas, Celine, Margaret Poydock, and Lynn Rhinehart. "How the PRO Act Restores Workers' Right to Unionize: A Chart of the Ways the PRO Act Fixes Major Problems in Current Labor Law." Economic Policy Institute, February 4, 2021. Accessed April 29, 2023. https://www.epi.org/publication/pro-act-problem-solution-chart/.
101. Belsie, Laurent. "Worker Representation on Company Boards Raises Investment." National Bureau of Economic Research, February 2020. Accessed April 29, 2023. https://www.nber.org/digest/feb20/worker-representation-company-boards-raises-investment; Holmberg, Susan R. "Opinion | Workers on Corporate Boards? Germany's Had Them for Decades." *New York Times*, January 6, 2019. Accessed April 29, 2023. https://www.nytimes.com/2019/01/06/opinion/warren-workers-boards.html.
102. Colvin, Alexander J. S. "The Growing Use of Mandatory Arbitration: Access to the Courts Is Now Barred for More Than 60 Million American Workers." Economic Policy Institute, April 6, 2018. Accessed April 29, 2023. https://www.epi.org/publication/the-growing-use-of-mandatory-arbitration-access-to-the-courts-is-now-barred-for-more-than-60-million-american-workers/.
103. Scheiber, Noam. "You're Now a 'Manager.' Forget About Overtime Pay." *New York Times*, March 6, 2023. Accessed April 29, 2023. https://www.nytimes.com/2023/03/06/business/economy/managers-overtime-pay.html.
104. International Trade Union Congress. "Global Rights Index 2022," 2022. Accessed April 29, 2023. https://www.globalrightsindex.org/en/2022/countries/usa.
105. Schulte, Brigid. "Essential—and Invisible." New America, March 21, 2020. Accessed April 29, 2023. https://www.newamerica.org/weekly/essentialand-invisible/; Child Care Providers United. "Governor New-

som Signs Law That Allows Child Care Providers to Have Their Union Formally Recognized," September 30, 2019. Accessed April 29, 2023. https://childcareprovidersunited.org/news/press/california_child_care_providers_governor_newsom/.

106. Chien, Nina. "Factsheet: Estimates of Child Care Eligibility & Receipt for Fiscal Year 2019." Office of the Assistant Secretary for Planning & Evaluation, U.S. Department of Health & Human Services, September 2022. Accessed April 29, 2023. https://aspe.hhs.gov/sites/default/files/documents/1d276a590ac166214a5415bee430d5e9/cy2019-child-care-subsidy-eligibility.pdf.
107. Workman, Simon. "The True Cost of High-Quality Child Care Across the United States." Center for American Progress, June 28, 2021. Accessed April 29, 2023. https://www.americanprogress.org/article/true-cost-high-quality-child-care-across-united-states/.
108. "Subsidy Reimbursement Rates in Texas Remain Far Below the True Cost of Providing Child Care." Prenatal-to-3 Policy Impact Center, February 2023. Accessed April 29, 2023. https://pn3policy.org/wp-content/uploads/2023/02/PN3PIC_ChildCareinCrisis-TexasCaseStudy_4.pdf.
109. Women's Bureau, U.S. Department of Labor. "Child Care Remains out of Financial Reach for Many Families, US Department of Labor Data Shows," January 24, 2023. Accessed April 29, 2023. https://www.dol.gov/newsroom/releases/wb/wb20230124.
110. Stavely, Zaidee. "California Family Child Care Providers Vote to Join Union." EdSource, July 27, 2020. Accessed April 29, 2023. https://edsource.org/2020/california-family-child-care-providers-vote-to-join-union/637229.
111. Loewenberg, Aaron, and Abbie Lieberman. "Valuing Family Child Care Providers: Supporting Organizing, Empowerment, and Prosperity." New America, July 6, 2021. Accessed April 29, 2023. https://www.newamerica.org/education-policy/edcentral/valuing-family-child-care-providers-supporting-organizing-empowerment-and-prosperity/.
112. Thompson, Don. "California Inks Contract with New 40,000-Member Child Care Union." *Los Angeles Times*, July 23, 2021. Accessed April 29, 2023. https://www.latimes.com/california/story/2021-07-23/california-inks-contract-with-new-40-000-member-child-care-union; Loewenberg and Lieberman, "Valuing Family Child Care Providers: Supporting Organizing, Empowerment, and Prosperity."
113. Hussain, Suhauna. "A New Law Could Raise Fast-Food Wages to $22 an Hour—and Opponents Are Trying to Halt It." *Los Angeles Times*, September 12, 2022. Accessed April 29, 2023. https://www.latimes.com/business/story/2022-09-12/ab-257-explainer-how-does-it-work-referendum.
114. SEIU 1021. "Gov. Newsom Signs AB 257 into Law on Labor Day in Major Victory for Fast-Food Workers," September 2, 2022. Accessed April 29,

2023. https://www.seiu1021.org/article/gov-newsom-signs-ab-257-law-labor-day-major-victory-fast-food-workers.

115. Browning, Kellen. "California Court Mostly Upholds Prop. 22 in Win for Uber and Other Gig Companies." *New York Times*, March 13, 2023. Accessed April 29, 2023. https://www.nytimes.com/2023/03/13/business/prop-22-upheld-california.html.
116. Covert, Bryce. "Like Uber, but for Gig Worker Organizing." American Prospect, March 30, 2020. Accessed April 29, 2023. https://prospect.org/labor/like-uber-but-for-gig-worker-organizing/.
117. Romero-Alston, Laine, and Sarita Gupta. "Worker Centers: Past, Present, and Future." American Prospect, August 30, 2021. Accessed April 29, 2023. https://prospect.org/labor/the-alt-labor-chronicles-america-s-worker-centers/worker-centers-past-present-and-future/.
118. Jobs With Justice. "Our History," 2015. Accessed April 29, 2023. https://www.jwj.org/about-us/our-history.
119. Parrott, Max. "To Crush Unions, Starbucks Targets Employee Communications." *Lever*, March 28, 2023. Accessed April 29, 2023. https://www.levernews.com/to-crush-unions-starbucks-targets-employee-communications-2/.
120. Eidelson, Josh. "The Undercover Organizers Behind America's Union Wins." Bloomberg.com, April 3, 2023. Accessed April 29, 2023. https://www.bloomberg.com/news/features/2023-04-03/starbucks-amazon-labor-union-wins-helped-by-undercover-salts?leadSource=uverify%20wall#xj4y7vzkg.
121. Lamb, Natasha, and Michael Passoff. "Racial and Gender Pay Scorecard," March 2023. Accessed April 29, 2023. https://static1.squarespace.com/static/5bc65db67d0c9102cca54b74/t/640f22770d7c0634287c57c3/1678713464204/Racial+and+Gender+Pay+Scorecard+2023.pdf.
122. Neumann, Wolfgang, Shane M. Dixon, and Anna-Carin Nordvall. "Consumer Demand as a Driver of Improved Working Conditions: The 'Ergo-Brand' Proposition." *Ergonomics* 57, no. 8 (July 4, 2014): 1113–26. https://doi.org/10.1080/00140139.2014.917203; Hiscox, Michael J., Michael Broukhim, Claire Litwin, and Andrea Woloski. "Consumer Demand for Fair Labor Standards: Evidence from a Field Experiment on eBay." Social Science Research Network, April 12, 2011. https://doi.org/10.2139/ssrn.1811788.
123. U.S. Bureau of Labor Statistics. "Home Health and Personal Care Aides." Occupational Outlook Handbook, September 8, 2022. Accessed April 29, 2023. https://www.bls.gov/ooh/healthcare/home-health-aides-and-personal-care-aides.htm.
124. Bureau of Labor Statistics, U.S. Department of Labor. "Employment Projections—2021–2031," September 8, 2022. Accessed April 9, 2023. https://www.bls.gov/news.release/pdf/ecopro.pdf.
125. Snyder, Rani. "Unpaid Family Caregivers Lose $522B in Wages Every

Year." Route Fifty, December 21, 2021. Accessed April 29, 2023. https://www.route-fifty.com/health-human-services/2021/12/unpaid-family-caregivers-need-support/360022/.

126. *Better Aging.* "Will Robots Become Caretakers for Seniors?," January 23, 2021. Accessed April 29, 2023. https://www.betteraging.com/aging-technology/will-robots-become-caretakers-for-seniors/.
127. Bureau of Labor Statistics, U.S. Department of Labor. "Occupational Employment and Wages, May 2022: Home Health and Personal Care Aides," May 2023. Accessed September 13, 2023. https://www.bls.gov/oes/current/oes311120.htm.
128. SEIU 775. "The Union Difference: SEIU 775 Caregivers Experience." Accessed September 13, 2023. https://seiu775.org/union-difference/.
129. Donlan, Andrew. "After 3-Year Dip, Home Care Turnover Soars to 77%." Home Health Care News, May 24, 2023. Accessed September 13, 2023. https://homehealthcarenews.com/2023/05/after-dipping-for-three-years-home-care-turnover-rate-soared-to-77-in-2022/.
130. Schulte, Brigid. "Crisis Conversations: For Elder-Care Workers in the Pandemic, One State (Mostly) Gets It Right." New America, May 22, 2020. Accessed April 29, 2023. https://www.newamerica.org/better-life-lab/podcasts/crisis-conversations-elder-care-workers-pandemic-one-state-mostly-gets-it-right/.
131. Tolbert, Jennifer, and Meghana Ammula. "10 Things to Know About the Unwinding of the Medicaid Continuous Enrollment Provision." KFF, August 23, 2023. Accessed September 13, 2023. https://www.kff.org/medicaid/issue-brief/10-things-to-know-about-the-unwinding-of-the-medicaid-continuous-enrollment-provision/.
132. New America. "Caregiving in America—the Dignity Gap," April 5, 2022. Accessed April 29, 2023. https://www.newamerica.org/better-life-lab/podcasts/caregiving-in-america-the-dignity-gap/.

Chapter 5: Unlikely Allies and the Business Case for Responsible Capitalism

1. Benioff, Marc. "We Need a New Capitalism." *New York Times*, October 14, 2019. Accessed February 11, 2024. https://www.nytimes.com/2019/10/14/opinion/benioff-salesforce-capitalism.html.
2. Valdmanis, Warren. "What Makes a Job 'Good'—and the Case for Investing in People." TED Talk, September 2021. Accessed April 29, 2023. https://www.ted.com/talks/warren_valdmanis_what_makes_a_job_good_and_the_case_for_investing_in_people?language=en.
3. Cappelli, Peter. *Our Least Important Asset: Why the Relentless Focus on Finance and Accounting Is Bad for Business and Employees*. New York: Oxford University Press, 2023, p. 3.
4. O'Leary, Michael, and Warren Valdmanis. *Accountable: The End of*

Fiduciary Absolutism and the Rise of Citizen Capitalism. New York: Harper Business, 2020, pp. 3, 249; Edmond, Charlotte. "Employees Are a Company's Best Asset—and Healthiest Investment." World Economic Forum, October 21, 2020. Accessed April 29, 2023. https://www.weforum.org/agenda/2020/10/shareholder-capitalism-oleary-valdmanis-economy-worker/.

5. Sull, Donald, Charles Sull, and Ben Zweig. "Toxic Culture Is Driving the Great Resignation." *MIT Sloan Management Review*, January 11, 2022. Accessed April 29, 2023. https://sloanreview.mit.edu/article/toxic-culture-is-driving-the-great-resignation/.
6. Heller, Nathan. "The Bullshit-Job Boom." *New Yorker*, June 7, 2018. Accessed April 29, 2023. https://www.newyorker.com/books/under-review/the-bullshit-job-boom.
7. Bloomberg Live. "Work Shifting 2.0: Redefining Normal," March 9, 2022. Accessed April 29, 2023. https://www.youtube.com/watch?v=KoEBs23iu9c.
8. Stewart, Emily. "What Is Private Equity, and Why Is It Killing Everything You Love?" *Vox*, January 6, 2020. Accessed April 29, 2023. https://www.vox.com/the-goods/2020/1/6/21024740/private-equity-taylor-swift-toys-r-us-elizabeth-warren.
9. Bloomberg Live, "Work Shifting 2.0: Redefining Normal."
10. Bloomberg Live, "Work Shifting 2.0: Redefining Normal."
11. O'Leary and Valdmanis, *Accountable: The End of Fiduciary Absolutism and the Rise of Citizen Capitalism*, p. 250.
12. Melé, Domènec, and César González Cantón. "The *Homo Economicus* Model." In *Human Foundations of Management: Understanding the Homo Humanus*, pp. 9–29. London: Palgrave Macmillan, 2014. https://doi.org/10.1057/9781137462619_2.
13. Sorkin, Andrew Ross. "A Free Market Manifesto That Changed the World, Reconsidered." *New York Times*, September 11, 2020. Accessed April 29, 2023. https://www.nytimes.com/2020/09/11/business/dealbook/milton-friedman-doctrine-social-responsibility-of-business.html.
14. Cha, Youngjoo, and Kim A. Weeden. "Overwork and the Slow Convergence in the Gender Gap in Wages." *American Sociological Review* 79, no. 3 (April 8, 2014): 457–84. https://doi.org/10.1177/0003122414528936.
15. Ton, Zeynep. *The Case for Good Jobs: How Great Companies Bring Dignity, Pay, and Meaning to Everyone's Jobs*. Boston: Harvard Business Review Press, 2023, p. 225.
16. Sandel, Michael J. *What Money Can't Buy: The Moral Limits of Markets*. New York: Farrar, Straus and Giroux, 2012, p. 9.
17. O'Leary and Valdmanis, *Accountable: The End of Fiduciary Absolutism and the Rise of Citizen Capitalism*, p. 248.

18. O'Leary and Valdmanis, *Accountable: The End of Fiduciary Absolutism and the Rise of Citizen Capitalism*, p. 251.
19. New America. "The Future of Wellbeing in an Automated World," May 27, 2022. Accessed April 29, 2023. https://www.newamerica.org/better-life-lab/podcasts/the-future-of-wellbeing-in-an-automated-world/.
20. Two Sigma. "Two Sigma Impact Partners with Pediatric Therapy Leader Circle of Care," July 12, 2022. Accessed September 13, 2023. https://www.twosigma.com/articles/two-sigma-impact-partners-with-pediatric-therapy-leader-circle-of-care/.
21. Schultz, Abby. "Future Returns: Two Sigma Impact Aims to Create Quality Jobs and Better Businesses." *Barron's*, May 2, 2023. Accessed September 13, 2023. https://www.barrons.com/articles/future-returns-two-sigma-impact-aims-to-create-quality-jobs-and-better-businesses-ca7517b0.
22. Bloomberg Live, "Work Shifting 2.0: Redefining Normal," 59:00.
23. Bhagat, Sanjai. "An Inconvenient Truth About ESG Investing." *Harvard Business Review*, March 31, 2022. https://hbr.org/2022/03/an-inconvenient-truth-about-esg-investing.
24. Ungarino, Rebecca. "Republicans Went After BlackRock and Sustainable Investing in 2022. Meet 12 Officials Crusading Against 'Woke Capitalism.'" *Business Insider*, December 28, 2022. Accessed February 12, 2024. https://www.businessinsider.com/conservative-politicians-esg-sustainable-investing-2022-6?utm_medium=referral&utm_source=yahoo.com; De Mott, Filip. "Republicans in New Hampshire Want to Make ESG Investment of State Funds a Crime Punishable by Up to 20 Years in Jail." Yahoo Finance, January 18, 2024. Accessed February 12, 2024. https://finance.yahoo.com/news/republicans-hampshire-want-esg-investment-023407912.html.
25. Gelles, David. "How Environmentally Conscious Investing Became a Target of Conservatives." *New York Times*, February 28, 2023. Accessed April 29, 2023. https://www.nytimes.com/2023/02/28/climate/esg-climate-backlash.html.
26. Whittaker, Martin. "Walmart's Recent $14 Billion Investment Is a Reminder That We Need More Eyes on the Long-Term." *Forbes*, February 25, 2021. Accessed April 29, 2023. https://www.forbes.com/sites/martinwhittaker/2021/02/25/walmarts-recent-14-billion-investment-is-a-reminder-that-we-need-more-eyes-on-the-long-term/?sh=7441639d58a2.
27. Steady. "A Conversation with Author and Workforce Expert Rick Wartzman (Moderated by Harold Meyerson)," February 17, 2023. Accessed April 29, 2023. https://www.youtube.com/watch?v=4jImFwHjEIk.
28. Bloomberg Live. "Event Highlights: Work Shifting 2.0: Redefining Normal." Bloomberg Live, March 10, 2022. Accessed April 29, 2023. https://www.bloomberglive.com/blog/event-highlights-work-shifting-march9/.

29. PricewaterhouseCoopers. "ESG-Focused Institutional Investment Seen Soaring 84% to US$33.9 Trillion in 2026, Making Up 21.5% of Assets Under Management: PwC Report." PwC, October 10, 2022. Accessed April 29, 2023. https://www.pwc.com/gx/en/news-room/press-releases/2022/awm-revolution-2022-report.html.
30. Business Roundtable. "Business Roundtable Redefines the Purpose of a Corporation to Promote 'An Economy That Serves All Americans,'" August 19, 2019. Accessed April 29, 2023. https://www.businessroundtable.org/business-roundtable-redefines-the-purpose-of-a-corporation-to-promote-an-economy-that-serves-all-americans; Gelles, David, and David Yaffe-Bellany. "Shareholder Value Is No Longer Everything, Top C.E.O.s Say." *New York Times*, August 21, 2019. Accessed October 14, 2023. https://www.nytimes.com/2019/08/19/business/business-roundtable-ceos-corporations.html.
31. Carter, Zachary D. "The End of Friedmanomics." *New Republic*, June 17, 2021. Accessed April 29, 2023. https://newrepublic.com/article/162623/milton-friedman-legacy-biden-government-spending.
32. Cappelli, Peter. "How Financial Accounting Screws Up HR." *Harvard Business Review*, January 2023. Accessed April 29, 2023. https://hbr.org/2023/01/how-financial-accounting-screws-up-hr?utm_medium=email&utm_source=newsletter_perissue&utm_campaign=bestofissue_activesubs_nondigital&deliveryName=DM236533.
33. Fuller, Joseph, and Manjari Raman. "The Caring Company: How Employers Can Cut Costs and Boost Productivity by Helping Employees Manage Caregiving Needs." Harvard Business School, January 17, 2019.
34. Bloomberg Live, "Work Shifting 2.0: Redefining Normal," 1:02:00.
35. Morse, John J., and Jay W. Lorsch. "Beyond Theory Y." *Harvard Business Review*, May 1970. Accessed April 29, 2023. https://hbr.org/1970/05/beyond-theory-y.
36. Ton, *The Case for Good Jobs: How Great Companies Bring Dignity, Pay, and Meaning to Everyone's Jobs*, p. 111.
37. Schulte, Brigid. "Designing Equitable and Effective Workplaces for a 'Corona-Normal' Future of Work." New America, March 17, 2022. Accessed April 29, 2023. https://www.newamerica.org/better-life-lab/reports/designing-equitable-workplaces-for-a-post-pandemic-world-a-toolkit-for-digital-hybrid-essential-work/.
38. Wartzman, Rick. *Still Broke: Walmart's Remarkable Transformation and the Limits of Socially Conscious Capitalism*. New York: PublicAffairs, 2022, p. 223.
39. Ton, *The Case for Good Jobs: How Great Companies Bring Dignity, Pay, and Meaning to Everyone's Jobs*, p. 8.
40. O'Leary and Valdmanis, *Accountable: The End of Fiduciary Absolutism and the Rise of Citizen Capitalism*, p. 254.

Chapter 6: Workaholics in an Overworked World

1. *The Workaholics Anonymous Book of Recovery.* Menlo Park, CA: Workaholics Anonymous World Service Organization, 2009, p. 186.
2. Thompson, Derek. "The Religion of Workism Is Making Americans Miserable." *Atlantic,* February 24, 2019. Accessed April 22, 2023. https://www.theatlantic.com/ideas/archive/2019/02/religion-workism-making-americans-miserable/583441/.
3. Workaholics Anonymous. "About W.A." Accessed April 22, 2023. https://workaholics-anonymous.org/contact-us/about-w-a.
4. *Encyclopedia Britannica.* "Protestant Ethic," July 20, 1998. Accessed April 22, 2023. https://www.britannica.com/topic/Protestant-ethic.
5. Travis, Trysh. "Self-Help in America: A Project for Moral Perfection." *American Historian,* August 2017. Accessed April 22, 2023. http://www.oah.org/tah/issues/2017/august/self-help-in-america-a-project-for-moral-perfection/.
6. Clark, Malissa. "These Are the Four Drivers of Workaholism." *Fast Company,* February 20, 2018. Accessed April 22, 2023. https://www.fastcompany.com/40531406/there-are-four-types-of-workaholic-and-none-of-them-work.
7. Mackay, Jory. "You Don't Have to Work Long Hours to Be a Workaholic." *Fast Company,* May 29, 2019. Accessed April 22, 2023. https://www.fastcompany.com/90356014/you-dont-have-to-work-long-hours-to-be-a-workaholic#:~:text=The%20term%20%E2%80%9Cworkaholic%E2%80%9D%20was%20first,to%20alcoholism%20or%20substance%20abuse.
8. Robinson, Bryan. "National Workaholics Day Is July 5: Here's How You Can Celebrate." *Forbes,* July 1, 2019. Accessed April 22, 2023. https://www.forbes.com/sites/bryanrobinson/2019/07/01/how-you-can-celebrate-national-workaholics-day-on-july-5th-and-during-the-month-of-july/?sh=784844772475.
9. Doerfler, Marie Christine, and Phyllis Post Kammer. "Workaholism, Sex, and Sex Role Stereotyping Among Female Professionals." *Sex Roles,* May 1, 1986. https://doi.org/10.1007/bf00287455.
10. Statistics Canada, Government of Canada. "Workaholics' Lives Not Much Fun," January 9, 2009. Accessed April 22, 2023. https://www150.statcan.gc.ca/n1/pub/11-402-x/2008/0075/ceb0075_002-eng.htm.
11. Sussman, Steve, Nadra E. Lisha, and Mark D. Griffiths. "Prevalence of the Addictions: A Problem of the Majority or the Minority?" *Evaluation & the Health Professions* 34, no. 1 (March 1, 2011): 3–56. https://doi.org/10.1177/0163278710380124.
12. Schmall, Tyler. "Almost Half of Americans Consider Themselves 'Workaholics.'" *New York Post,* February 1, 2019. Accessed April 22, 2023. https://

nypost.com/2019/02/01/almost-half-of-americans-consider-themselves-workaholics/.

13. Clark, Malissa A., Jesse S. Michel, Ludmila Zhdanova, Shuang Y. Pui, and Boris B. Baltes. "All Work and No Play? A Meta-Analytic Examination of the Correlates and Outcomes of Workaholism." *Journal of Management* 42, no. 7 (November 1, 2016): 1836–73. https://doi.org/10.1177/0149206314522301.
14. Brummelhuis, Lieke Ten, and Nancy P. Rothbard. "How Being a Workaholic Differs from Working Long Hours—and Why That Matters for Your Health." *Harvard Business Review,* March 22, 2018. Accessed April 22, 2023. https://hbr.org/2018/03/how-being-a-workaholic-differs-from-working-long-hours-and-why-that-matters-for-your-health#:~:text=We%20found%20that%20workaholics%2C%20whether,than%20employees%20who%20merely%20worked.
15. Clark, "These Are the Four Drivers of Workaholism"; Clark, Malissa A., Rachel A. Smith, and Nicholas J. Haynes. "The Multidimensional Workaholism Scale: Linking the Conceptualization and Measurement of Workaholism." *Journal of Applied Psychology* 105, no. 11 (February 10, 2020): 1281–307. https://doi.org/10.1037/apl0000484.
16. Gillespie, Lane, and Tori Rubloff. "Bankrate's 2023 Annual Emergency Savings Report." Bankrate, February 23, 2023. Accessed April 22, 2023. https://www.bankrate.com/banking/savings/emergency-savings-report/.
17. Hanson, Melanie. "Student Loan Debt by Race." Education Data Initiative, January 16, 2023. Accessed April 22, 2023. https://educationdata.org/student-loan-debt-by-race.
18. Shamlian, Janet. "Millions of Americans Nearing Retirement Age with No Savings." CBS News, March 1, 2023. Accessed April 22, 2023. https://www.cbsnews.com/news/millions-of-americans-nearing-retirement-age-no-savings/.
19. U.S. Travel Association. "The Work Martyr's Cautionary Tale: How the Millennial Experience Will Define America's Vacation Culture," August 18, 2016. Accessed April 22, 2023. https://www.ustravel.org/research/work-martyr%E2%80%99s-cautionary-tale-how-millennial-experience-will-define-america%E2%80%99s-vacation.
20. Baluch, Anna. "Average PTO in the US & Other PTO Statistics (2023)." *Forbes,* March 30, 2023. Accessed August 8, 2023. https://www.forbes.com/advisor/business/pto-statistics/.
21. Truesdale, William. "How Long Should a Man's Vacation Be? President Taft Says Every One Should Have Three Months—What Big Employers of Labor and Men of Affairs Think on the Subject." *New York Times,* July 31, 1910. Accessed April 22, 2023. https://www.nytimes.com/1910/07/31/archives/how-long-should-a-mans-vacation-be-president-taft-says-every-one.html.
22. Moehrle, Thomas. "The Evolution of Compensation in a Changing Econ-

omy." Bureau of Labor Statistics, U.S. Department of Labor, January 30, 2003. Accessed April 22, 2023. https://www.bls.gov/opub/mlr/cwc/the-evolution-of-compensation-in-a-changing-economy.pdf.

23. Carroll, Aaron E. "The Real Reason the U.S. Has Employer-Sponsored Health Insurance." *New York Times*, September 5, 2017. Accessed April 16, 2023. https://www.nytimes.com/2017/09/05/upshot/the-real-reason-the-us-has-employer-sponsored-health-insurance.html.
24. International Labour Organization. "Convention C132-Holidays with Pay Convention (Revised), 1970 (No. 132)," 1970. Accessed October 14, 2023. https://www.ilo.org/dyn/normlex/en/f?p=NORMLEXPUB:12100:0::NO::P12100_ILO_CODE:C132.
25. Liu, Jennifer. "9 European Countries Where Workers Get More Than a Month of Paid Vacation." CNBC, August 18, 2023. Accessed October 22, 2023. https://www.cnbc.com/2023/08/18/9-european-countries-where-workers-get-more-than-a-month-of-vacation.html.
26. Hershfield, Hal E., and Cassie Mogilner Holmes. "What Should You Choose: Time or Money?" *New York Times*, September 9, 2016. Accessed October 14, 2023. https://www.nytimes.com/2016/09/11/opinion/sunday/what-should-you-choose-time-or-money.html.
27. Van Dam, Andrew. "The Mystery of the Disappearing Vacation Day." *Washington Post*, February 10, 2023. Accessed April 22, 2023. https://www.washingtonpost.com/business/2023/02/10/disappearing-vacation-days/.
28. Coser, Lewis A. *Greedy Institutions: Patterns of Undivided Commitment*. New York: Free Press, 1974.
29. Cha, Youngjoo, and Kim A. Weeden. "Overwork and the Slow Convergence in the Gender Gap in Wages." *American Sociological Review* 79, no. 3 (April 8, 2014): 457–84. https://doi.org/10.1177/0003122414528936.
30. Glauber, Rebecca. "Time-Intensive Occupations and the Motherhood Gap in Authority." *Community, Work & Family*, March 24, 2023, 1–26. https://doi.org/10.1080/13668803.2023.2187272.
31. Ansel, Bridget. "Why Do Americans Work 'Strange Hours'?" World Economic Forum, November 15, 2015. Accessed April 22, 2023. https://www.weforum.org/agenda/2015/11/why-do-americans-work-strange-hours/.
32. International Labor Organization. "Working Time and Work-Life Balance Around the World," 2022. Accessed April 22, 2023. https://www.ilo.org/global/publications/books/WCMS_864222/lan--en/index.htm.
33. Ferguson, Stephanie. "Understanding America's Labor Shortage." U.S. Chamber of Commerce, April 7, 2023. Accessed April 22, 2023. https://www.uschamber.com/workforce/understanding-americas-labor-shortage.
34. Davidovic, Ivana. "'Lying Flat': Why Some Chinese Are Putting Work Second." *BBC News*, February 16, 2022. Accessed April 22, 2023. https://www.bbc.com/news/business-60353916.

35. Kelly, Jack. "Reddit's Year in Review Reveals Antiwork and WallStreet-Bets as Top 10 Discussions." *Forbes*, December 8, 2021. Accessed April 22, 2023. https://www.forbes.com/sites/jackkelly/2021/12/08/reddits-year-in-review-reveals-antiwork-and-wallstreetbets-as-top-10-discussions/?sh=443b1595cf73.
36. Forsythe, Eliza, Lisa B. Kahn, Fabian Lange, and David Wiczer. "Where Have All the Workers Gone? Recalls, Retirements, and Reallocation in the COVID Recovery." National Bureau of Economic Research Working Paper Series, no. 30387 (August 1, 2022). https://doi.org/10.3386/w30387; Frost, Riordan. "Did More People Move During the Pandemic?" Joint Centers for Housing Studies of Harvard University, March 14, 2023. Accessed September 13, 2023. https://www.jchs.harvard.edu/research-areas/research-briefs/did-more-people-move-during-pandemic.
37. Weber, Lauren. "Burned Out, More Americans Are Turning to Part-Time Jobs." *Wall Street Journal*, February 25, 2023. Accessed April 22, 2023. https://www.wsj.com/articles/burned-out-more-americans-are-turning-to-part-time-jobs-e7ff4883.
38. Bach, Katie. "New Data Shows Long Covid Is Keeping as Many as 4 Million People out of Work." Brookings, August 24, 2022. Accessed April 22, 2023. https://brookings.edu/research/new-data-shows-long-covid-is-keeping-as-many-as-4-million-people-out-of-work/.
39. Gallup. "State of the Global Workplace 2022 Report," 2022. Accessed April 10, 2023. https://www.gallup.com/workplace/349484/state-of-the-global-workplace.aspx.
40. Gartner. "Gartner Forecasts 39% of Global Knowledge Workers Will Work Hybrid by the End of 2023," March 1, 2023. Accessed April 22, 2023. https://www.gartner.com/en/newsroom/press-releases/2023-03-01-gartner-forecasts-39-percent-of-global-knowledge-workers-will-work-hybrid-by-the-end-of-2023.
41. Faberman, R. Jason, Andreas Mueller, and Ahmet Z. Sahin. "Has the Willingness to Work Fallen During the Covid Pandemic?" National Bureau of Economic Research Working Paper Series, no. 29784 (February 1, 2022). https://doi.org/10.3386/w29784.
42. Vinopal, Courtney. "High-Earning Men Are Cutting Back on Their Working Hours." *Wall Street Journal*, January 26, 2023. Accessed April 22, 2023. https://www.wsj.com/articles/high-earning-men-are-cutting-back-on-their-working-hours-11674697563.
43. Gump, Brooks B., and Karen A. Matthews. "Are Vacations Good for Your Health? The 9-Year Mortality Experience After the Multiple Risk Factor Intervention Trial." *Psychosomatic Medicine* 62, no. 5 (September 1, 2000): 608–12. https://doi.org/10.1097/00006842-200009000-00003.
44. Chikani, Vatsal, Douglas J. Reding, Paul Gunderson, and Catherine A. McCarty. "Vacations Improve Mental Health Among Rural Women: The

Wisconsin Rural Women's Health Study." *WMJ: Official Publication of the State Medical Society of Wisconsin* 104, no. 6 (August 1, 2005): 20–23.

45. Schulte, Brigid. "Even Work-Life Balance Experts Are Awful at Balancing Work and Life." The Cut, March 28, 2017. Accessed August 30, 2023. https://www.thecut.com/2017/03/work-life-balance-experts-are-bad-at-balancing-work-and-life.html.
46. Schulte, "Even Work-Life Balance Experts Are Awful at Balancing Work and Life."
47. Schwitzgebel, Eric, and Joshua Rust. "The Moral Behavior of Ethics Professors: Relationships Among Self-Reported Behavior, Expressed Normative Attitude, and Directly Observed Behavior." *Philosophical Psychology* 27, no. 3 (April 14, 2014): 293–327. https://doi.org/10.1080/09515089.2012.727135.
48. Schulte, "Even Work-Life Balance Experts Are Awful at Balancing Work and Life."
49. Schulte, "Even Work-Life Balance Experts Are Awful at Balancing Work and Life."
50. Latkin, Carl A., and Amy R. Knowlton. "Social Network Assessments and Interventions for Health Behavior Change: A Critical Review." *Behavioral Medicine* 41, no. 3 (September 2, 2015): 90–97. https://doi.org/10.1080/08964289.2015.1034645.

Chapter 7: From Grief to Rage to Action: Fighting for a Decent Life in Japan's Karoshi Culture

1. Ministry of Labor, Institute of Labor Administration. "Labor Standards Act." International Labor Organization, June 9, 1995. Accessed September 21, 2023. https://www.ilo.org/dyn/travail/docs/2018/Labor%20Standards%20Act%20-%20www.cas.go.jp%20version.pdf.
2. Global Monitor. "Parents of Koroshi Victim Ask LDP: 'Will You Let WATANABE Stand?,'" 2013. Accessed August 6, 2023. https://www.globemonitor.org/node/1553.
3. Xun, Lu. *Essays*. San Francisco: China New Press, 1921. Quoted in N. Georgopoulos and Michael Heim, eds., *Being Human In The Ultimate. Studies in the Thought of John M. Anderson*. Atlanta: Rodopi, 1995.
4. Chen, Heather, Yoojung Seo, and Andrew Raine. "This Country Wanted a 69-Hour Workweek. Millennials and Generation Z Had Other Ideas." CNN, March 19, 2023. Accessed August 6, 2023. https://www.cnn.com/2023/03/18/asia/south-korea-longer-work-week-debate-intl-hnk/index.html.
5. Yang, Bairen, Jiaolong Shi, Q. J. Li, Laixin Xia, F. Zhang, Yan-Geng Yu, Ning Xiao, and D. R. Li. "The Concept, Status Quo and Forensic Pathology of Karoshi." *Journal of Forensic Medicine* 35, no. 4 (August 1, 2019): 455–58. https://doi.org/10.12116/j.issn.1004-5619.2019.04.015; Davidson, Helen. "Claims That Overwork Killed China Tech Worker Reignites '996' Debate."

Guardian, February 9, 2022. https://www.theguardian.com/world/2022/feb/09/claims-that-overwork-killed-china-tech-worker-reignites-996-debate; Kuo, Lily. "Weibo Users Applaud a Former Google China Executive's Call for Work-Life Balance." *Quartz*, July 21, 2022. Accessed August 6, 2023. https://qz.com/124313/chinese-workers-typically-get-zero-to-five-days-of-paid-vacation-a-year.

6. North, Scott, and Rika Morioka. "Hope Found in Lives Lost: Karoshi and the Pursuit of Worker Rights in Japan." *Contemporary Japan*, March 1, 2016. https://doi.org/10.1515/cj-2016-0004.
7. Subramanian, Sushma. "'Modern-Type Depression' Is Changing Japanese Work Culture." *Atlantic*, October 16, 2019. Accessed August 30, 2023. https://www.theatlantic.com/health/archive/2019/10/modern-type-depression-japan/600160/.
8. Japan Ministry of Health, Labour and Welfare. "The 2022 White Paper on Measures to Prevent Karoshi, Etc.," 2022. Accessed February 14, 2024. https://www.mhlw.go.jp/content/11200000/001065344.pdf.
9. Hunt, Elle. "Japan's Karoshi Culture Was a Warning. We Didn't Listen." *Wired UK*, June 2, 2021. Accessed August 6, 2023. https://www.wired.co.uk/article/karoshi-japan-overwork-culture.
10. Interview with Yoshimasa Obayashi at Hachioji Godo Law Office, facilitated by Chie Matsumoto, April 24, 2023.
11. Statista. "Suicide in Japan—Statistics & Facts," January 9, 2024. Accessed February 13, 2024. https://www.statista.com/topics/5259/suicide-in-japan/#topicOverview.
12. Ryall, Julian. "Can Japan Overhaul Its Unforgiving Office Culture as More Workers Die from Overwork?" *South China Morning Post*, November 3, 2023. Accessed February 13, 2024. https://www.scmp.com/week-asia/people/article/3240090/can-japan-overhaul-its-unforgiving-office-culture-more-workers-die-overwork; Otake, Tomoko. "Report on Overwork Highlights Japan's Work-Life Balance Issues." *Japan Times*, October 13, 2023. Accessed February 13, 2024. https://www.japantimes.co.jp/news/2023/10/13/japan/science-health/karoshi-report/.
13. Statista. "Japan: Work Related Suicides 2022," March 14, 2023. Accessed August 6, 2023. https://www.statista.com/statistics/622325/japan-work-related-suicides/.
14. Keegan, Matthew. "Which Is the World's Hardest-Working City?" *Guardian*, February 3, 2020. Accessed August 6, 2023. https://www.theguardian.com/cities/2019/sep/20/which-is-the-worlds-hardest-working-city; Kondo, Daisuke. "Death from Overwork in Japanese Society." *Economic Observer*, November 7, 2016; English translation: "In Japan, a Troubling Link Between Samurai Spirit and Workaholics." Worldcrunch, June 21, 2023. Accessed August 6, 2023. https://worldcrunch.com/business-finance/in-japan-a-troubling-link-between-samurai-spirit-and-workaholics.

15. Szczepanski, Kallie. "The Role of Bushido in Modern Japan." ThoughtCo, April 2, 2018. Accessed August 6, 2023. https://www.thoughtco.com/role-of-bushido-in-modern-japan-195569.
16. Editors of *Encyclopaedia Britannica*. "Seppuku | Definition, History, & Facts." *Encyclopaedia Britannica*, July 20, 1998. Accessed August 6, 2023. https://www.britannica.com/topic/seppuku.
17. McNeill, David. "Union City Blues." Foreign Correspondents' Club of Japan, May 2022. Accessed February 14, 2024. https://www.fccj.or.jp/number-1-shimbun-article/union-city-blues.
18. Hern, Alex. "Will Elon Musk's 120-Hour Week Stop Us Worshipping Workaholism?" *Guardian*, August 23, 2018. Accessed August 6, 2023. https://www.theguardian.com/technology/2018/aug/23/elon-musk-120-hour-working-week-tesla.
19. North, Scott. "Japan's Work Style Reform Consensus and Its Contradictions." Conference paper presented at the Society for the Advancement of Socio-Economics, New York, June 27–29, 2019. https://www.academia.edu/39982186/Japans_Work_Style_Reform_Consensus_and_Its_Contradictions_Scott_North_SASE_2019.
20. Ono, Hiroshi. "Why Do the Japanese Work Long Hours?" *Japan Labor Issues* 2, no. 5 (February–March 2018): 35–49. https://www.jil.go.jp/english/jli/documents/2018/005-03.pdf.
21. Nippon.com. "Japan's Productivity Ranks Lowest Among G7 Nations for 50 Straight Years," July 1, 2023. Accessed August 6, 2023. https://www.nippon.com/en/japan-data/h01196/; Organisation for Economic Co-operation and Development. "Labour Productivity Levels in the Total Economy." Data set, n.d. https://stats.oecd.org/Index.aspx?DataSetCode=LEVEL.
22. Paul, Kari. "Microsoft Japan Tested a Four-Day Work Week and Productivity Jumped by 40%." *Guardian*, November 8, 2019. Accessed August 6, 2023. https://www.theguardian.com/technology/2019/nov/04/microsoft-japan-four-day-work-week-productivity#:~:text=In%20addition%20to%20the%20increased,they%20liked%20the%20shorter%20week.
23. Kageyama, Yuri. "Digital Minister Aims to Wrest Japan out of Analog Doldrums." AP, September 20, 2022. Accessed February 19, 2024. https://apnews.com/article/technology-business-japan-government-and-politics-f36672d94aacc1e3565a0d989b9f5977.
24. Ono, Hiroshi. "Telework in a Land of Overwork: It's Not That Simple or Is It?" *American Behavioral Scientist*, January 13, 2022. https://doi.org/10.1177/00027642211066038; Ono, Hiroshi, and Takeshi Mori. "COVID-19 and Telework: An International Comparison." *Journal of Quantitative Description: Digital Media* 1 (April 26, 2021). https://doi.org/10.51685/jqd.2021.004.
25. Kopp, Rochelle. "Over Worked and Underpaid Japanese Employees Feel the Burden of Sabisu Zangyo." Japan Intercultural Consulting. Accessed August 6, 2023. https://japanintercultural.com/free-resources/articles/over

-worked-and-underpaid-japanese-employees-feel-the-burden-of-sabisu-zangyo/.

26. Morioka, Rika. "Anti-Karoshi Activism in a Corporate-Centered Society: Medical, Legal, and Housewife Activist Collaborations in Constructing Death from Overwork in Japan." PhD diss., University of California, San Diego, 2008.
27. Tamura, Yuko. "Are 'White' Companies Proving to Be Too Much of a Good Thing for Japan's Gen Z?" *Japan Times*, January 27, 2023. Accessed August 6, 2023. https://www.japantimes.co.jp/life/2023/01/27/language/white-companies-proving-much-good-thing-japans-gen-z/.
28. Sakamoto, Koji. "Companies That Deserve to Be Valued the Highest in Japan." Pacific Resource Exchange Center, October 13, 2020. Accessed August 6, 2023. https://www.prex-hrd.or.jp/en/prex_island/2388/.
29. World Bank Open Data. "Population Ages 65 and Above," 2022. Accessed September 21, 2023. https://data.worldbank.org/indicator/SP.POP.65UP.TO.ZS?most_recent_value_desc=true.
30. Yamaguchi, Mari. "Japan Birth Rate Hits Record Low amid Concerns over Shrinking and Aging Population." AP News, June 2, 2023. Accessed August 6, 2023. https://apnews.com/article/japan-birth-rate-record-low-population-aging-ade0c8a5bb52442f4365db1597530ee4.
31. Saito Jun. "Historical Background of the Japanese Restrictive Immigration Policy." Japan Center for Economic Research, July 15, 2022. Accessed August 6, 2023. https://www.jcer.or.jp/english/historical-background-of-the-japanese-restrictive-immigration-policy.
32. Nippon.com. "Japan Continues to Gray: Baby Boomers Reach 75," October 5, 2022. Accessed August 6, 2023. https://www.nippon.com/en/japan-data/h01446/#:~:text=Japan%20has%20by%20far%20the,820%2C000%20over%20the%20previous%20year.
33. Yeung, Jessie, and Junko Ogura. "It's 'Now or Never' to Reverse Japan's Population Crisis, Prime Minister Says." CNN, January 24, 2023. Accessed August 6, 2023. https://www.cnn.com/2023/01/23/asia/japan-kishida-birth-rate-population-intl-hnk/index.htm; Reynolds, Isabel, and Emi Urabe. "Japan Will 'Disappear' Without Action on Births, PM's Aide Says." Bloomberg.com, March 5, 2023. Accessed August 6, 2023. https://www.bloomberg.com/news/articles/2023-03-05/japan-will-disappear-without-action-on-births-pm-s-aide-says?cmpid=BBD030923_EQ&utm_medium=email&utm_source=newsletter&utm_term=230309&utm_campaign=equality.
34. Gender Equality Bureau Cabinet Office. "Women and Men in Japan 2020. Work-Life Balance," 2020. Accessed February 14, 2024. https://www.gender.go.jp/english_contents/pr_act/pub/pamphlet/women-and-men20/pdf/1-4.pdf.
35. Matsuo, Yohei, and Nami Matsuura. "Women's Working Hours Under-

score Gender Disparity in Japan." Nikkei Asia, January 20, 2022. Accessed August 6, 2023. https://asia.nikkei.com/Spotlight/Datawatch/Women-s-working-hours-underscore-gender-disparity-in-Japan.
36. Morinobu, Shigeki. "Making Work Pay for Japanese Women: Toward a Smarter Approach to Tax and Social Security Reform." Tokyo Foundation for Policy Research, May 30, 2023. Accessed February 20, 2024. https://www.tokyofoundation.org/research/detail.php?id=946.
37. Mesmer, Philippe. "Single Mothers in Japan Face Discrimination and Barriers to Support." *Le Monde*, June 23, 2023. Accessed August 6, 2023. https://www.lemonde.fr/en/international/article/2023/06/23/single-mothers-in-japan-face-discrimination-and-barriers-to-support_6036057_4.html.
38. *Japan Times*. "30% of Dads in Japan Seeking More Time for Housework and Child Care," June 16, 2023. Accessed August 6, 2023. https://www.japantimes.co.jp/news/2023/06/16/national/dads-child-care-time/.
39. Kyodo News+. "Japan Falls to Record-Low 125th in Global Gender Gap Ranking," June 21, 2023. Accessed August 6, 2023. https://english.kyodonews.net/news/2023/06/b041fdee1839-japan-falls-to-record-low-125th-in-global-gender-gap-ranking.html.
40. Bungate, Peter. "Japan's 105-Hour Workweek." Roads & Kingdoms, December 9, 2015. Accessed August 6, 2023. https://roadsandkingdoms.com/2015/japans-105-hour-workweek/; Weekender Editor. "Groundbreaking Japanese Business Leader Haruno Yoshida Passes Away at 55." *Tokyo Weekender*, July 9, 2019. Accessed August 6, 2023. https://www.tokyoweekender.com/japan-life/news-and-opinion/groundbreaking-japanese-business-leader-haruno-yoshida-passes-away-at-55/.
41. Reuters. "Watami Co Ltd 7522.T." Accessed August 6, 2023. https://www.reuters.com/markets/companies/7522.T/; Nikkei Asia. "Watami Co., Ltd.," 2023. Accessed August 6, 2023. https://asia.nikkei.com/Companies/Watami-Co.-Ltd.
42. Statista. "Watami's Net Sales FY 2013–2022," December 7, 2022. Accessed August 6, 2023. https://www.statista.com/statistics/1333100/watami-net-sales/.
43. *Asahi Shimbun*. "Japan Dead Last for Gender Parity Among Major Developed States," July 13, 2022. Accessed August 6, 2023. https://www.asahi.com/ajw/articles/14668828.
44. Miyamoto, Masao. *Straitjacket Society: An Insider's Irreverent View of Bureaucratic Japan*. New York: Kodansha International, 1994, p. 20.
45. Ono, Hiroshi. "Lifetime Employment in Japan: Concepts and Measurements," 2010. Accessed August 6, 2023. https://papers.ssrn.com/sol3/papers.cfm?abstract_id=1830736.
46. Molony, Barbara. "Japan's 1986 Equal Employment Opportunity Law and the Changing Discourse on Gender." *Signs* 20, no. 2 (January 1, 1995): 268–302. https://doi.org/10.1086/494975.

47. Inoue, Makiko, and Ben Dooley. "A Job for Life, or Not? A Class Divide Deepens in Japan." *New York Times*, May 18, 2021. Accessed August 6, 2023. https://www.nytimes.com/2020/11/27/business/japan-workers.html.
48. Sanger, David E. "Relaxing Takes Some Work as Weekends Come to Japan." *New York Times*, December 31, 1988. Accessed August 6, 2023. https://www.nytimes.com/1988/12/31/business/relaxing-takes-some-work-as-weekends-come-to-japan.html.
49. Timinsky, Samuel. "The Nation That Never Rests: Japan's Debate over Work-Life Balance and Work That Kills." *Asia-Pacific Journal: Japan Focus*, May 15, 2019. Accessed August 6, 2023. https://apjjf.org/2019/10/Timinsky.html.
50. Koshiro, Kazutoshi. "Lifetime Employment in Japan: Three Models of the Concept." Bureau of Labor Statistics, U.S. Department of Labor, August 1984. Accessed August 6, 2023. https://www.bls.gov/opub/mlr/1984/article/lifetime-employment-in-japan-three-models-of-the-concept.htm.
51. Barrett, Kelly. "Women in the Workplace: Sexual Discrimination in Japan." *Human Rights Brief* 11, no. 2 (2004): 5–8. https://digitalcommons.wcl.american.edu/hrbrief/vol11/iss2/2/.
52. Parkinson, Loraine. "Japan's Equal Employment Opportunity Law: An Alternative Approach to Social Change." *Columbia Law Review* 89, no. 3 (April 1, 1989): 604. https://doi.org/10.2307/1122868.
53. Molony, "Japan's 1986 Equal Employment Opportunity Law and the Changing Discourse on Gender."
54. Mun, Eunmi. "Why the Equal Employment Opportunity Law Failed in Japan." Work in Progress, August 10, 2016. Accessed August 6, 2023. https://workinprogress.oowsection.org/2016/08/10/why-the-equal-employment-opportunity-law-failed-in-japan/.
55. Robinson, Patricia A., Catherine Sibala, Kaname Ito, and Vicki L. Beyer. "The Deepening Divide in Japanese Employment: The Increasing Marginalization of Contract Workers as Explained by Path Dependence, Vested Interests, and Social Psychology." *Contemporary Japan* 34, no. 1 (January 2, 2022): 13–41. https://doi.org/10.1080/18692729.2022.2028229; Kyōko, Komatsu. "Persistent Gender Gaps in the Japanese Labor Market." Nippon.com, July 7, 2023. Accessed September 21, 2023. https://www.nippon.com/en/in-depth/d00863/.
56. Nakamura, Tomonori. "An Economy in Search of Stable Growth: Japan Since the Oil Crisis." *Journal of Japanese Studies* 6, no. 1 (January 1, 1980): 155. https://doi.org/10.2307/132003; Hunt, Elle. "Japan's Karoshi Culture Was a Warning. We Didn't Listen." *Wired UK*, June 2, 2021. Accessed August 6, 2023. https://www.wired.co.uk/article/karoshi-japan-overwork-culture.
57. Callen, Tim, and Jonathan Ostry. *Japan's Lost Decade: Policies for Economic Revival*. Washington, DC: International Monetary Fund, 2003.

Accessed August 6, 2023. https://www.imf.org/external/pubs/nft/2003/japan/index.htm#:~:text=The%20bubble%20in%20Japanese%20stock,the%201990s%20and%20early%202000s.

58. Ono, Yumiko. "In Japan, Layoffs Don't Stop Some Workers from Working." *Wall Street Journal*, July 5, 2001. Accessed August 6, 2023. https://www.wsj.com/articles/SB994277968704931826; Robinson et al., "The Deepening Divide in Japanese Employment: The Increasing Marginalization of Contract Workers as Explained by Path Dependence, Vested Interests, and Social Psychology."
59. North and Morioka, "Hope Found in Lives Lost: Karoshi and the Pursuit of Worker Rights in Japan."
60. Kopp, "Over Worked and Underpaid Japanese Employees Feel the Burden of Sabisu Zangyo."
61. Nikkei Asia. "Japan's Growing Part-Time Employment Weighs on Wages," March 24, 2023. Accessed September 21, 2023. https://asia.nikkei.com/Economy/Japan-s-growing-part-time-employment-weighs-on-wages.
62. Kotera, Shinya, and Jochen Schmittmann. *The Japanese Labor Market During the COVID-19 Pandemic*. Washington, DC: International Monetary Fund, 2022.
63. Inoue and Dooley, "A Job for Life, or Not? A Class Divide Deepens in Japan."
64. World Bank Open Data. "Part Time Employment, Female." Accessed September 21, 2023. https://data.worldbank.org/indicator/SL.TLF.PART.FE.ZS?locations=JP.
65. North and Morioka, "Hope Found in Lives Lost: Karoshi and the Pursuit of Worker Rights in Japan."
66. Tanaka, Emiko. "Do the Japanese Really Work Too Much? A Thorough Look at a Day in the Life of a Japanese Person!" Tsunagu Japan, May 25, 2020. Accessed August 6, 2023. https://www.tsunagujapan.com/day-in-the-life-of-a-japanese-person/.
67. Ryall, Julian. "Cases of Death from Overwork Soar in Japan." Deutsche Welle, April 5, 2016. Accessed August 6, 2023. https://www.dw.com/en/cases-of-death-from-overwork-soar-in-japan/a-19164258.
68. North and Morioka, "Hope Found in Lives Lost: Karoshi and the Pursuit of Worker Rights in Japan."
69. Iwasaki, Kenji, Masaya Takahashi, and Akinori Nakata. "Health Problems Due to Long Working Hours in Japan: Working Hours, Workers' Compensation (Karoshi), and Preventive Measures." *Industrial Health* 44, no. 4 (January 1, 2006): 537–40. https://doi.org/10.2486/indhealth.44.537.
70. Brasor, Philip. "Watami Under Scrutiny After Karōshi." *Japan Times*, June 17, 2012. Accessed August 6, 2023. https://www.japantimes.co.jp/news/2012/06/17/national/media-national/watami-under-scrutiny-after-karshi/.
71. Adelstein, Jake. "Exploitative Enterprises Continue to Menace Society."

Japan Times, February 6, 2016. Accessed August 6, 2023. https://www.japantimes.co.jp/news/2016/02/06/national/media-national/exploitative-enterprises-continue-menace-society/.

72. Liquid Bio TV. "Layers of Dishonesty: Data Problem of the Overwork Crisis in Japan," September 3, 2022. Accessed August 6, 2023. https://www.youtube.com/watch?v=J_HJgzqlqMo.
73. Schreiber, Mark. "Black Business Tales Cast Shadow on Candidate." *Japan Times*, July 13, 2013. Accessed August 6, 2023. https://www.japantimes.co.jp/news/2013/07/13/national/media-national/black-business-tales-cast-shadow-on-candidate/.
74. Brasor, "Watami Under Scrutiny After Karōshi."
75. Global Monitor, "Parents of Koroshi Victim Ask LDP: 'Will You Let WATANABE Stand?'"
76. North and Morioka, "Hope Found in Lives Lost: Karoshi and the Pursuit of Worker Rights in Japan."
77. Brasor, "Watami Under Scrutiny After Karōshi."
78. Brasor, "Watami Under Scrutiny After Karōshi."
79. Labornet Japan. "Defendant WATANABE Miki Failed to Keep His Promise; Absent from the First Hearing for Watami Karoshi Lawsuit," March 10, 2014. Accessed August 6, 2023. https://labornetjp.blogspot.com/2014/03/defendant-watanabe-miki-failed-to-keep.html.
80. Schreiber, "Black Business Tales Cast Shadow on Candidate."
81. Clark, Julia. "'Black Corporation' Watami Changes Name, Keeps Bad Reputation." JapanCRUSH, May 20, 2014. Accessed August 6, 2023. https://www.japancrush.com/2014/stories/black-corporation-watami-changes-name-keeps-bad-reputation.html.
82. Clark, "'Black Corporation' Watami Changes Name, Keeps Bad Reputation."
83. *Japan Times*. "Supreme Court Rules Dentsu Responsible for Man's Suicide," March 24, 2000. Accessed August 6, 2023. https://www.japantimes.co.jp/news/2000/03/25/national/supreme-court-rules-dentsu-responsible-for-mans-suicide/.
84. Knapp, Kiyoko Kamio. "Warriors Betrayed: How the 'Unwritten Law' Prevails in Japan." *Indiana International and Comparative Law Review* 6, no. 3 (January 3, 1996): 545–82. https://doi.org/10.18060/17669.
85. *BBC News*. "Dentsu's Overtime Fine Puts Spotlight on Japan's Work Culture," October 6, 2017. Accessed August 6, 2023. https://www.bbc.com/news/business-41521460.
86. North and Morioka, "Hope Found in Lives Lost: Karoshi and the Pursuit of Worker Rights in Japan."
87. North and Morioka, "Hope Found in Lives Lost: Karoshi and the Pursuit of Worker Rights in Japan."
88. Agence France-Presse. "Japan: One Fifth of Employees at Risk of Death from Overwork—Report." *Guardian*, October 8, 2016. Accessed August 6,

2023. https://www.theguardian.com/world/2016/oct/08/japan-one-fifth-of-employees-at-risk-of-death-from-overwork-report.

89. Labornet Japan, "Defendant WATANABE Miki Failed to Keep His Promise; Absent from the First Hearing for Watami Karoshi Lawsuit."
90. Business & Human Rights Resource Centre. "Japan: Pub Chain Watami Reaches Settlement over Case of Worker Suicide," December 10, 2015. Accessed August 6, 2023. https://www.business-humanrights.org/en/latest-news/japan-pub-chain-watami-reaches-settlement-over-case-of-worker-suicide/; *Mainichi*. "Pub Operator to Compensate Family of Employee Who Suicided Due to Overwork," December 9, 2015. Accessed August 6, 2023. https://mainichi.jp/english/articles/20151209/p2a/00m/0na/009000c.
91. Yahoo! "Japanese Pub Turns to Robots amid COVID-19," September 23, 2021. Accessed August 6, 2023. https://www.yahoo.com/lifestyle/japanese-pub-turns-robots-amid-093931790.html.
92. Kojima, Shinji, Scott North, and Charles Weathers. "Abe Shinzō's Campaign to Reform the Japanese Way of Work." *Asia-Pacific Journal: Japan Focus* 15, no. 21 (2017). https://apjjf.org/2017/23/Kojima.html.
93. Japan Ministry of Health, Labour and Welfare. "White Paper on Measures to Prevent Karoshi." 2017. Accessed February 14, 2024. https://fpcj.jp/wp/wp-content/uploads/2017/11/8f513ff4e9662ac515de9e646f63d8b5.pdf.
94. Suzuki, Takuya, and Kumiko Yasumoto. "Crisis Deepens in Japan's Short-Staffed Trucking Industry as Overtime Limits Loom." *Mainichi*, May 22, 2023. Accessed February 14, 2024. https://mainichi.jp/english/articles/20230519/p2a/00m/0na/019000c.
95. Osaki, Tomohiro. "Diet Enacts Key Labor Reform That Opposition Slams as Karōshi Promotion Bill." *Japan Times*, June 29, 2018. Accessed August 6, 2023. https://www.japantimes.co.jp/news/2018/06/29/national/politics-diplomacy/diet-enacts-key-labor-reform-opposition-slams-karoshi-promotion-bill/.
96. Baines, Wesley. "The Avenging Angels." Beliefnet. Accessed August 6, 2023. https://www.beliefnet.com/inspiration/angels/the-avenging-angels.aspx.
97. Ministry of Health, Labour and Welfare. "White Paper on Measures to Prevent Karoshi, Etc.," 2015. Accessed August 6, 2023. https://fpcj.jp/wp/wp-content/uploads/2017/11/8f513ff4e9662ac515de9e646f63d8b5.pdf.
98. Ministry of Health, Labour and Welfare, "The 2022 White Paper on Measures to Prevent Karoshi, Etc."
99. Osaki, Tomohiro. "Work Without Limits: Japan's Teachers Battle for Change." *Japan Times*, December 26, 2022.
100. Kyodo News+. "Average Working Hours of Teachers in Japan Longest in OECD Survey," June 20, 2019. Accessed August 6, 2023. https://english

.kyodonews.net/news/2019/06/2eef38da2630-average-working-hours-of-teachers-in-japan-longest-in-oecd-survey.html.

101. Takami, Tomohiro. "Current State of Working Hours and Overwork in Japan Part II: Why Do the Japanese Work Long Hours?" *Japan Labor Issues* 3, no. 18 (October 2019): 15–19. https://www.jil.go.jp/english/jli/documents/2019/018-04.pdf; Ministry of Health, Labour and Welfare, "White Paper on Measures to Prevent Karoshi, Etc."
102. *Japan Press Weekly*. "Convenience Store Worker Succeeds in Regaining His Job After Court Battle," October 4, 2013. Accessed August 6, 2023. https://www.japan-press.co.jp/s/news/?id=6518.
103. Royle, Tony, and Edson Urano. "A New Form of Union Organizing in Japan? Community Unions and the Case of the McDonald's 'McUnion.'" *Work, Employment & Society* 26, no. 4 (August 1, 2012): 606–22. https://doi.org/10.1177/0950017012445093.
104. Nippon.com. "Number of Suicides in Japan Rises in 2022," March 27, 2023. Accessed August 6, 2023. https://www.nippon.com/en/japan-data/h01624/; World Population Review. "Suicide Rate by Country 2023," 2023. Accessed August 6, 2023. https://worldpopulationreview.com/country-rankings/suicide-rate-by-country.
105. Kojima, North, and Weathers, "Abe Shinzō's Campaign to Reform the Japanese Way of Work."
106. Kojima, North, and Weathers, "Abe Shinzō's Campaign to Reform the Japanese Way of Work"; North, "Japan's Work Style Reform Consensus and Its Contradictions."
107. Dolan, David, and Makiko Yamazaki. "As Wages Go Up, Japanese Women Reckon with a Vast Pay Gap." Reuters, March 15, 2023. Accessed August 6, 2023. https://www.reuters.com/business/sustainable-business/wages-go-up-japanese-women-reckon-with-vast-pay-gap-2023-03-15/#:~:text=almost%20double%20the%20OECD%20average.
108. Rich, Motoko. "Shinzo Abe, Japan's Longest-Serving Prime Minister, Resigns Because of Illness." *New York Times*, December 24, 2020. Accessed August 6, 2023. https://www.nytimes.com/2020/08/28/world/asia/shinzo-abe-resign-japan.html.
109. Lin, Connie. "Japan Prime Minister Shinzo Abe's Legacy of 'Womenomics.'" *Fast Company*, July 8, 2022. Accessed August 6, 2023. https://www.fastcompany.com/90767744/japan-prime-minister-shinzo-abes-legacy-of-womenomics.
110. Fukai, Tomoki, Masato Ikeda, Daiji Kawaguchi, and Shintaro Yamaguchi. "COVID-19 and the Employment Gender Gap in Japan." *Journal of the Japanese and International Economies* 68 (June 1, 2023): 101256. https://doi.org/10.1016/j.jjie.2023.101256.
111. *Japan Times*. "Japan Hopes to Inspire More Men to Take Paternity Leave,"

June 22, 2023. Accessed August 6, 2023. https://www.japantimes.co.jp/news/2023/06/22/national/paternity-leave-birthrate/.

112. 21st Century Japan Politics and Society Initiative. "Special Event Recap: 10/27/2020 ABE Global 2020 on 'Work-Life Balance in the COVID Age,'" October 27, 2020. Accessed August 6, 2023. https://jpsi.indiana.edu/news-events/news/2020-10-27-recap-abe-global-2020.html; Tan, Josephine. "Japan Plans New Family Initiatives to Support Non-Regular Workers." HRM Asia, January 13, 2023. Accessed September 21, 2023. https://hrmasia.com/japan-plans-new-family-initiatives-to-support-non-regular-workers/; Nishikitani, Mariko, Mutsuhiro Nakao, Mariko Inoue, Shinobu Tsurugano, and Eiji Yano. "Associations Between Workers' Health and Working Conditions: Would the Physical and Mental Health of Nonregular Employees Improve If Their Income Was Adjusted?" *Medicines* 9, no. 7 (July 14, 2022): 40. https://doi.org/10.3390/medicines9070040.
113. Barrett, "Women in the Workplace: Sexual Discrimination in Japan."
114. Molony, "Japan's 1986 Equal Employment Opportunity Law and the Changing Discourse on Gender."
115. Osaki, "Diet Enacts Key Labor Reform That Opposition Slams as Karōshi Promotion Bill."
116. Bromley, Patricia, John Meyer, and Ruo Jia. "Entrepreneurship as Cultural Theme in Neoliberal Society." In Robert N. Eberhart, Michael Lounsbury, and Howard E. Aldrich, eds., *Entrepreneurialism and Society: New Theoretical Perspectives*. Leeds: Emerald Publishing, 2022.
117. De Sordi, José Osvaldo, André Rodrigues dos Santos, Marcia Carvalho de Azevedo, Carlos Francisco Bitencourt Jorge, and Marco Hashimoto. "Dark, Down, and Destructive Side of Entrepreneurship: Unveiling Negative Aspects of Unsuccessful Entrepreneurial Action." *International Journal of Management Education* 20, no. 3 (November 2022). Accessed February 17, 2024. https://www.sciencedirect.com/science/article/abs/pii/S1472811722000611.
118. Freeman, Michael A., Paige J. Staudenmaier, Mackenzie R. Zisser, and Lisa Abdilova Andresen. "The Prevalence and Co-occurrence of Psychiatric Conditions Among Entrepreneurs and Their Families." *Small Business Economics* 53 (August 19, 2019): 323–42. Accessed February 17, 2024. https://doi.org/10.1007/s11187-018-0059-8.
119. Adéchi, Jean-Pierre. "Why Do White Men Raise More VC Dollars Than Anyone Else?" Techstars, November 18, 2020. Accessed February 17, 2024. https://www.techstars.com/blog/pov/why-do-white-men-raise-more-vc-dollars-than-anyone-else.
120. Tolbert, Kathryn. "Japan's Voluntary Shut-Ins." *Washington Post*, May 29, 2002. Accessed August 6, 2023. https://www.washingtonpost.com/archive/politics/2002/05/29/japans-voluntary-shut-ins/81dbc9a7-6d08

-49f6-9711-65a108514746/; Ono, Yumiko. "Many Young Japanese Are Finding That a Job Is No Longer Guaranteed." *Wall Street Journal,* June 14, 1999. Accessed August 6, 2023. https://www.wsj.com/articles/SB929312894877846720.

121. Okamoto, Hiroshi. "'I Want to Die': Inside Japan's Gruelling Recruitment Season." *Financial Times,* December 30, 2020. Accessed August 6, 2023. https://www.ft.com/content/72cf350d-c7e0-4b83-ab93-0b0f9dbda4d1.
122. Ono, "Why Do the Japanese Work Long Hours?"
123. Demetriou, Danielle. "How the Japanese Are Putting an End to Extreme Work Weeks." BBC Worklife, February 25, 2022. Accessed August 6, 2023. https://www.bbc.com/worklife/article/20200114-how-the-japanese-are-putting-an-end-to-death-from-overwork.
124. Ono, "Telework in a Land of Overwork: It's Not That Simple or Is It?"
125. Kahan, Kim. "Fax Machines and CDs: 7 Things Still Being Used in Japan." *Tokyo Weekender,* February 24, 2023. Accessed August 6, 2023. https://www.tokyoweekender.com/japan-life/things-still-being-used-in-japan/.
126. Harding, Scharon. "Japan Government Accepts It's No Longer the '90s, Stops Requiring Floppy Disks." Ars Technica, January 30, 2024. Accessed February 19, 2024. https://arstechnica.com/gadgets/2024/01/floppy-disk-requirements-finally-axed-from-japan-government-regulations/#:~:text=Sony%2C%20the%20last%20floppy%20disk,%2C%20at%20times%2C%20to%20complications.
127. Ono, "Telework in a Land of Overwork: It's Not That Simple or Is It?"
128. Murakami, Sakura. "Haruno Yoshida, Leading Businesswoman and Adviser to Keidanren, Dies at 55." *Japan Times,* July 8, 2019. Accessed August 6, 2023. https://www.japantimes.co.jp/news/2019/07/08/business/haruno-yoshida-leading-businesswoman-adviser-keidanren-dies-55/.
129. Ueno, Hisako, and John Yoon. "How a Crisis in Trucking Could Change Life in Japan." *New York Times,* December 23, 2023. Accessed February 17, 2024. https://www.nytimes.com/2023/12/23/business/japan-truck-drivers-overtime-shortage.html.
130. Nippon.com. "Japan Has the Best Paternity Leave System, But Who's Using It?" July 25, 2019. Accessed February 20, 2024. https://www.nippon.com/en/japan-data/h00500/japan-has-the-best-paternity-leave-system-but-who%E2%80%99s-using-it.html.
131. Statista. "Ratio of Employees Taking Parental Leave in Japan from 1996 to 2002, by Gender," January 9, 2024. Accessed February 19, 2024. https://www.statista.com/statistics/1232867/japan-parental-leave-acquisition-rate-by-gender/.
132. Inoue, Yukana. "Children's Agency Chief Ayuko Kato Vows to Tackle Falling Birthrate." *Japan Times,* October 4, 2023. Accessed February 19,

2024. https://www.japantimes.co.jp/news/2023/10/04/japan/politics/kato-children-and-families-agency/.

Chapter 8: Short Work Hours for All in Iceland

1. Government of Iceland. "About Gender Equality." Accessed September 21, 2023. https://www.government.is/topics/human-rights-and-equality/equality/about-gender-equality/.
2. Maassen, Lena. "Mental Health in Iceland." Borgen Project, June 9, 2022. https://borgenproject.org/mental-health-in-iceland/.
3. Kobie, Nicole. "What Really Happened in Iceland's Four-Day Week Trial." *Wired UK*, July 12, 2021. Accessed April 24, 2023. https://www.wired.co.uk/article/iceland-four-day-work-week; Haraldsson, Guðmundur, and Jack Kellam. "Going Public: Iceland's Journey to a Shorter Working Week." Autonomy, July 4, 2021. Accessed April 24, 2023. https://autonomy.work/portfolio/icelandsww/.
4. Ferrant, Gaëlle, Luca Maria Pesando, and Keiko Nowacka. "Unpaid Care Work: The Missing Link in the Analysis of Gender Gaps in Labour Outcomes." OECD Development Center, December 2014. Accessed April 24, 2023. https://www.oecd.org/dev/development-gender/Unpaid_care_work.pdf.
5. Sanandaji, Nima. "The Nordic Glass Ceiling." Cato Institute, March 8, 2018. Accessed April 24, 2023. https://www.cato.org/policy-analysis/nordic-glass-ceiling.
6. Laker, Ben. "What Does the Four-Day Workweek Mean for the Future of Work?" *MIT Sloan Management Review*, May 16, 2022. Accessed April 24, 2023. https://sloanreview.mit.edu/article/what-does-the-four-day-workweek-mean-for-the-future-of-work/.
7. Joly, Josephine, and Luke Hurst. "Four-Day Week: Which Countries Have Embraced It and How's It Going So Far?" Euronews, February 23, 2023. Accessed April 24, 2023. https://www.euronews.com/next/2023/02/23/the-four-day-week-which-countries-have-embraced-it-and-how-s-it-going-so-far.
8. History.com. "Ford Factory Workers Get 40-Hour Week," November 13, 2009. Accessed April 24, 2023. https://www.history.com/this-day-in-history/ford-factory-workers-get-40-hour-week.
9. Scott, Robert, and David Cooper. "Almost Two-Thirds of People in the Labor Force Do Not Have a College Degree." Economic Policy Institute, March 30, 2016. Accessed April 24, 2023. https://www.epi.org/publication/almost-two-thirds-of-people-in-the-labor-force-do-not-have-a-college-degree/.
10. Tucker, Jasmine, and Kayla Patrick. "Low-Wage Jobs Are Women's Jobs: The Overrepresentation of Women in Low-Wage Work." National Women's

Law Center, August 2017. Accessed April 20, 2023. https://nwlc.org/wp-content/uploads/2017/08/Low-Wage-Jobs-are-Womens-Jobs.pdf.

11. Zundl, Elaine, Daniel Schneider, Kristen Harknett, and Evelyn Bellew. "Still Unstable: The Persistence of Schedule Uncertainty During the Pandemic—The Shift Project." Shift Project, January 2022. Accessed April 24, 2023. https://shift.hks.harvard.edu/still-unstable/.
12. Dunn, Megan. "Who Chooses Part-Time Work and Why?" Bureau of Labor Statistics, U.S. Department of Labor, March 2018. Accessed April 24, 2023. https://www.bls.gov/opub/mlr/2018/article/pdf/who-chooses-part-time-work-and-why.pdf.
13. Bahn, Kate, and Carmen Sanchez Cumming. "Factsheet: U.S. Occupational Segregation by Race, Ethnicity, and Gender." Equitable Growth, July 1, 2020. Accessed April 24, 2023. https://equitablegrowth.org/factsheet-u-s-occupational-segregation-by-race-ethnicity-and-gender/.
14. Miller, Claire Cain. "Pay Gap Is Because of Gender, Not Jobs." *New York Times*, April 23, 2014. Accessed April 24, 2023. https://www.nytimes.com/2014/04/24/upshot/the-pay-gap-is-because-of-gender-not-jobs.html.
15. Payscale. "2023 Gender Pay Gap Report." Accessed April 24, 2023. https://www.payscale.com/research-and-insights/gender-pay-gap/#module-11.
16. Whitmire, Richard. "Gender Gap." *Education Next* 10, no. 2 (2020). https://www.educationnext.org/gender-gap/.
17. Euronews. "Swedish Old Folks' Home Abandons Six-Hour Workday Experiment." Euronews, January 4, 2017. Accessed April 24, 2023. https://www.eurAnews.com/2017/01/04/swedish-old-folks-home-abandons-six-hour-workday-experiment.
18. Savage, Maddy. "The Truth About Sweden's Short Working Hours." *BBC News*, November 2, 2015. Accessed April 24, 2023. https://www.bbc.com/news/business-34677949.
19. French, Rachel, Linda H. Aiken, Kathleen E. Fitzpatrick Rosenbaum, and Karen B. Lasater. "Conditions of Nursing Practice in Hospitals and Nursing Homes Before COVID-19: Implications for Policy Action." *Journal of Nursing Regulation* 13, no. 1 (April 1, 2022): 45–53. https://doi.org/10.1016/S2155-8256(22)00033-3.
20. *Inequality for All*. Lionsgate, 2013.
21. Euronews, "Swedish Old Folks' Home Abandons Six-Hour Workday Experiment."
22. Hofverberg, Elin. "FALQs: The Icelandic Reduced Workweek Trial." Library of Congress, January 3, 2022. Accessed April 24, 2023. https://blogs.loc.gov/law/2022/01/falqs-the-icelandic-reduced-workweek-trial/.
23. Haraldsson and Kellam, "Going Public: Iceland's Journey to a Shorter Working Week."
24. Autonomy, "The Results Are In: The UK's Four-Day Week Pilot."
25. Villegas, Paulina, and Hannah Knowles. "Iceland Tested a 4-Day Workweek.

Employees Were Productive—and Happier, Researchers Say." *Washington Post*, July 7, 2021. Accessed April 24, 2023. https://www.washingtonpost.com/business/2021/07/06/iceland-four-day-work-week/.

26. Shi, Hongying, Tianyi Huang, Eva S. Schernhammer, Frank B. Hu, and Molin Wang. "Rotating Night Shift Work and Healthy Aging After 24 Years of Follow-Up in the Nurses' Health Study." *JAMA Network Open* 5, no. 5 (May 4, 2022): e2210450. https://doi.org/10.1001/jamanetworkopen.2022.10450.
27. Agence France-Presse. "Katrin Jakobsdottir, Iceland's Staunch Feminist PM, Begins Second Term." Voice of America, November 28, 2021. Accessed April 24, 2023. https://www.voanews.com/a/katrin-jakobsdottir-iceland-staunch-feminist-pm-begins-second-term/6331139.html.
28. Government of Iceland. "Indicators for Measuring Well-Being," September 2019. Accessed April 24, 2023. https://www.government.is/lisalib/getfile.aspx?itemid=fc981010-da09-11e9-944d-005056bc4d74.
29. Lyall, Sarah. "Iceland, Mired in Debt, Blames Britain for Woes." *New York Times*, November 1, 2008. Accessed April 24, 2023. https://www.nytimes.com/2008/11/02/world/europe/02iceland.html.
30. Einarsdóttir, Thorgerdur, and Gyda Margrét Pétursdóttir. "An Analysis of the Report of Althing's Special Investigation Commission from a Gender Perspective," September 2010. Accessed April 24, 2023. https://rm.coe.int/16806ccff4.
31. Sunderland, Ruth. "After the Crash, Iceland's Women Lead the Rescue." *Guardian*, February 21, 2009. Accessed April 24, 2023. https://www.theguardian.com/world/2009/feb/22/iceland-women.
32. Eimieho, Sylvia. "Facts About Women's Rights in Iceland." Borgen Project, April 4, 2022. Accessed April 24, 2023. https://borgenproject.org/womens-rights-in-iceland/.
33. McGee, Suzanne, and Heidi Moore. "Women's Rights and Their Money: A Timeline from Cleopatra to Lilly Ledbetter." *Guardian*, August 11, 2014. Accessed April 24, 2023. https://www.theguardian.com/money/us-money-blog/2014/aug/11/women-rights-money-timeline-history.
34. Global Nonviolent Action Database. "Icelandic Women Strike for Economic and Social Equality, 1975," 2009. Accessed April 24, 2023. https://nvdatabase.swarthmore.edu/content/icelandic-women-strike-economic-and-social-equality-1975.
35. *Guardian*. "The Day the Women Went on Strike," October 29, 2005. Accessed April 24, 2023. https://www.theguardian.com/world/2005/oct/18/gender.uk.
36. Government of Iceland. "Act on Equal Status and Equal Rights of Women and Men," 2008. Accessed April 24, 2023. https://www.government.is/library/04-Legislation/Act%20on%20equal%20status%20and%20equal%20rights%20of%20women%20and%20men%20no%2010%202008%20as%20amended%200101%202018%20final.pdf.

37. Organisation for Economic Co-operation and Development. "Indicator B2. How Do Early Childhood Education Systems Differ Around the World?" OECD iLibrary, 2020. Accessed April 24, 2023. https://www.oecd-ilibrary.org/sites/7e21871e-en/index.html?itemId=/content/component/7e21871e-en.
38. Care for Kids. "5 Reasons Why Child Care in Iceland Is Special," October 6, 2021. Accessed April 24, 2023. https://www.careforkids.co.nz/child-care-articles/article/662/5-reasons-why-child-care-in-iceland-is-special.
39. Child Care Aware of America. "Catalyzing Growth: Using Data to Change Child Care." Accessed April 24, 2023. https://www.childcareaware.org/catalyzing-growth-using-data-to-change-child-care/#ChildCareAffordability.
40. Malik, Rasheed. "Examining the Powerful Impact of Investments in Early Childhood for Children, Families, and Our Nation's Economy." Center for American Progress, August 10, 2022. Accessed September 21, 2023. https://www.americanprogress.org/article/examining-the-powerful-impact-of-investments-in-early-childhood-for-children-families-and-our-nations-economy/; Ajayi, Kehinde, Aziz Dao, Rebekka Grun, and Estelle Koussoubé. "What Happens When Early Childhood Development Meets Women's Economic Empowerment?" World Bank Blogs (blog), January 6, 2023. Accessed September 21, 2023. https://blogs.worldbank.org/developmenttalk/what-happens-when-early-childhood-development-meets-womens-economic-empowerment; First Five Years Fund. "Why It Matters." Accessed September 21, 2023. https://www.ffyf.org/why-it-matters/.
41. Koslowski, Alison, Sonja Blum, Ivana Dobrotić, Gayle Kaufman, and Peter Moss. "18th International Review of Leave Policies and Related Research 2022." International Network on Leave Policies and Research, August 2022. Accessed April 24, 2023. https://www.leavenetwork.org/fileadmin/user_upload/k_leavenetwork/annual_reviews/2022/Koslowski_et_al_Leave_Policies_2022.pdf.
42. Lenhart, Amanda, Haley Swenson, and Brigid Schulte. "Lifting the Barriers to Paid Family and Medical Leave for Men in the United States." New America, December 4, 2019. Accessed April 24, 2023. https://www.newamerica.org/better-life-lab/reports/lifting-barriers-paid-family-and-medical-leave-men-united-states/; Gíslason, Ingólfur V. "Fathers on Leave Alone in Iceland: Normal Paternal Behaviour?" In Life Course Research and Social Policies book series, vol. 6, 2016. https://doi.org/10.1007/978-3-319-42970-0_9; Chronholm, Anders. "Fathers' Experience of Shared Parental Leave in Sweden." *Recherches Sociologiques et Anthropologiques* 38, no. 2 (December 15, 2007): 9–25. https://doi.org/10.4000/rsa.456.
43. Yu, Wei-Hsin, and Yuko Hara. "Motherhood Penalties and Fatherhood Premiums: Effects of Parenthood on Earnings Growth Within and Across

Firms." *Demography* 58, no. 1 (February 1, 2021): 247–72. https://doi.org/10.1215/00703370-8917608.

44. Correll, Shelley J., Stephen Benard, and In Sung Paik. "Getting a Job: Is There a Motherhood Penalty?" *American Journal of Sociology* 112, no. 5 (March 1, 2007): 1297–339. https://doi.org/10.1086/511799.
45. Budig, Michelle J., and Paula England. "The Wage Penalty for Motherhood." *American Sociological Review* 66, no. 2 (April 1, 2001): 204. https://doi.org/10.2307/2657415.
46. Florian, Sandra. "Racial Variation in the Effect of Motherhood on Women's Employment: Temporary or Enduring Effect?" *Social Science Research* 73 (July 1, 2018): 80–91. https://doi.org/10.1016/j.ssresearch.2018.02.012.
47. Johnson, Jenna. "Paul Tudor Jones: In Macro Trading, Babies Are a 'Killer' to a Woman's Focus." *Washington Post*, May 23, 2013. Accessed April 24, 2023. https://www.washingtonpost.com/local/education/paul-tudor-jones-in-macro-trading-babies-are-a-killer-to-a-womans-focus/2013/05/23/1c0c6d4e-c3a6-11e2-9fe2-6ee52d0eb7c1_story.html.
48. Schulte, Brigid. "Providing Care Changes Men." New America, February 4, 2021. Accessed April 18, 2023. https://www.newamerica.org/better-life-lab/reports/providing-care-changes-men/introduction/.
49. Wagner, Ines. "How Iceland Is Closing the Gender Wage Gap." *Harvard Business Review*, January 8, 2021. Accessed April 24, 2023. https://hbr.org/2021/01/how-iceland-is-closing-the-gender-wage-gap.
50. Arnalds, Ásdís Aðalbjörg, Guðný Björk Eydal, and Ingólfur V. Gíslason. "Equal Rights to Paid Parental Leave and Caring Fathers—the Case of Iceland," *Stjórnmál og Stjórnsýsla* 9, no. 2 (December 15, 2013): 323. https://doi.org/10.13177/irpa.a.2013.9.2.4.
51. Indriðason, Hallgrímur. "Iceland's Record-Breaking Parental Leave 'Not Perfect.'" *Nordic Labour Journal*, September 19, 2022. http://www.nordiclabourjournal.org/nyheter/news-2022/article.2022-09-19.2091841182.
52. Petts, Richard J., Chris Knoester, and Qi Li. "Paid Paternity Leave-Taking in the United States." *Community, Work & Family* 23, no. 2 (May 7, 2018): 162–83. https://doi.org/10.1080/13668803.2018.1471589.
53. New America. "Men and Care in the United States," June 17, 2020. Accessed April 20, 2023. https://www.newamerica.org/better-life-lab/better-life-lab-collections/men-and-care-united-states/.
54. Snyder, Amanda Jacobson. "Majority of Democrats, Republicans Would Support Legislation to Ensure Paid Family Leave, Increased Child Care Funding." Morning Consult, August 1, 2021. Accessed April 24, 2023. https://morningconsult.com/2022/08/01/child-care-tax-credit-paid-family-leave-policies-survey/.
55. Mohdin, Aamna. "How Sweden's 'Daddy Quota' Parental Leave Helps with

Equal Parenting." *Quartz*, January 6, 2016. Accessed September 3, 2023. https://qz.com/587763/how-swedens-daddy-quota-parental-leave-helps-with-equal-parenting.

56. Indriðason, "Iceland's Record-Breaking Parental Leave 'Not Perfect.'"
57. Indriðason, "Iceland's Record-Breaking Parental Leave 'Not Perfect.'"
58. Arnalds, Eydal, and Gíslason, "Equal Rights to Paid Parental Leave and Caring Fathers—the Case of Iceland."
59. Schulte, Brigid. "The Case Against Maternity Leave." *Slate*, May 18, 2017. Accessed April 24, 2023. https://slate.com/human-interest/2017/05/the-case-against-maternity-leave.html.
60. Eurydice. "Initial Education for Teachers Working in Early Childhood and School Education," July 27, 2022. Accessed April 24, 2023. https://eurydice.eacea.ec.europa.eu/national-education-systems/iceland/initial-education-teachers-working-early-childhood-and-school.
61. McLean, Caitlin, Lea Austin, Marcy Whitebook, and Krista Olson. "Early Childhood Workforce Index 2020." Center for the Study of Child Care Employment, University of California, Berkeley, 2021. Accessed April 9, 2023. https://cscce.berkeley.edu/workforce-index-2020/the-early-educator-workforce/early-educator-pay-economic-insecurity-across-the-states/.

Epilogue

1. Matson, Erik W. "A Dialectical Reading of Adam Smith on Wealth and Happiness." *Journal of Economic Behavior and Organization* 184 (April 1, 2021): 826–36. https://doi.org/10.1016/j.jebo.2020.08.037.
2. David Graeber. "From Managerial Feudalism to the Revolt of the Caring Classes." Open Transcripts, December 27, 2019. Accessed August 28, 2023. http://opentranscripts.org/transcript/managerial-feudalism-revolt-caring-classes/.
3. Wellbeing Economy Alliance. "What Is a Wellbeing Economy?" Accessed August 26, 2023. https://weall.org/what-is-wellbeing-economy.
4. Sturgeon, Nicola. "Why Governments Should Prioritize Well-Being." TED Talk, July 2019. Accessed August 26, 2023. https://www.ted.com/talks/nicola_sturgeon_why_governments_should_prioritize_well_being?language=en.
5. Peck, Emily. "How Layoffs Can Have Negative Long-Term Consequences for Companies." *Axios*, March 3, 2023. Accessed April 16, 2023. https://www.axios.com/2023/03/03/how-layoffs-can-have-negative-long-term-consequences-for-companies; "How Layoffs Hurt Companies." Knowledge at Wharton, April 12, 2016. Accessed April 16, 2023.
6. Cleetus, Rachel. "Climate Change in 2022: Multiple Billion-Dollar Disasters and Unbearable Human Costs." The Equation, January 10, 2023. Accessed August 26, 2023. https://blog.ucsusa.org/rachel-cleetus/climate-change-2022-multiple-billion-dollar-disasters-unbearable-human-costs/.

7. Huggel, Christian, Laurens M. Bouwer, Sirkku Juhola, Reinhard Mechler, Veruska Muccione, Ben Orlove, and Ivo Wallimann-Helmer. "The Existential Risk Space of Climate Change." *Climatic Change* 174, no. 1–2 (September 1, 2022). https://doi.org/10.1007/s10584-022-03430-y.
8. Statista. "Child Poverty in OECD Countries 2020," March 24, 2023. Accessed April 24, 2023. https://www.statista.com/statistics/264424/child-poverty-in-oecd-countries/.
9. Tikkanen, Roosa, Munira Z. Gunja, Molly FitzGerald, and Laurie C. Zephyrin. "Maternal Mortality and Maternity Care in the United States Compared to 10 Other Developed Countries." Commonwealth Fund, November 18, 2020. Accessed April 24, 2023. https://www.commonwealthfund.org/publications/issue-briefs/2020/nov/maternal-mortality-maternity-care-us-compared-10-countries.
10. Kamal, Rabah, Julie Hudman, and Daniel McDermott. "What Do We Know About Infant Mortality in the U.S. and Comparable Countries?" Peterson-KFF Health System Tracker, October 18, 2019. Accessed April 24, 2023. https://www.healthsystemtracker.org/chart-collection/infant-mortality-u-s-compare-countries.
11. Thakrar, Ashish P., Alexandra D. Forrest, Mitchell Maltenfort, and Christopher B. Forrest. "Child Mortality in the US and 19 OECD Comparator Nations: A 50-Year Time-Trend Analysis." *Health Affairs* 37, no. 1 (January 8, 2018): 140–49. https://doi.org/10.1377/hlthaff.2017.0767.
12. Scottish Government. "Wellbeing Economy Monitor: December 2022 Update," December 6, 2022. Accessed August 26, 2023. https://www.gov.scot/publications/wellbeing-economy-monitor-december-2022-update/.
13. Scottish Government. "Scotland's Wellbeing—Delivering the National Outcomes," May 2019. Accessed August 26, 2023. https://nationalperformance.gov.scot/sites/default/files/documents/NPF_Scotland%27s_Wellbeing_May2019.pdf.
14. Robert F. Kennedy. "Remarks at the University of Kansas, March 18, 1968," John F. Kennedy Presidential Library and Museum. Accessed August 26, 2023. https://www.jfklibrary.org/learn/about-jfk/the-kennedy-family/robert-f-kennedy/robert-f-kennedy-speeches/remarks-at-the-university-of-kansas-march-18-1968.
15. UK and Scottish governments. "Devolution." Delivering for Scotland, July 17, 2023. Accessed August 26, 2023. https://www.deliveringforscotland.gov.uk/scotland-in-the-uk/devolution/.
16. Hayden, Anders, and Clay Dasilva. "The Wellbeing Economy: Possibilities and Limits in Bringing Sufficiency from the Margins into the Mainstream." *Frontiers in Sustainability* 3 (October 10, 2022). https://doi.org/10.3389/frsus.2022.966876.
17. Scottish Government. "Cabinet Secretary for Wellbeing Economy, Fair Work and Energy." Accessed October 14, 2023. https://www.gov.scot

/about/who-runs-government/cabinet-and-ministers/cabinet-secretary-for-wellbeing-economy-fair-work-and-energy/.

18. Hunter, Ross. "Stephen Kerr Slammed for 'Insulting Contribution' on Wellbeing Economy." *National*, March 22, 2023. Accessed August 26, 2023. https://www.thenational.scot/news/23405856.stephen-kerr-slammed-insulting-contribution-wellbeing-economy/.
19. Rayner, Frances. "200 Charities, Economists, Businesses, and Unions Call on FM to Turn Wellbeing Economy into Reality." *WEAll Scotland* (blog), July 31, 2023. Accessed August 26, 2023. https://www.weallscotland.org/post/200-charities-economists-businesses-and-unions-call-on-fm-to-turn-wellbeing-economy-into-reality.
20. Scottish Government. "New Leadership Group for Employee Ownership," August 27, 2018. Accessed August 26, 2023. https://www.gov.scot/news/new-leadership-group-for-employee-ownership/.
21. Scottish Government. "Community Wealth Building." Accessed August 26, 2023. https://www.gov.scot/policies/cities-regions/community-wealth-building/.
22. O'Hagan, Angela, and Suzanna Nesom. "Watching the Neighbours: Gender Budgeting in Scotland and Wales." *Public Money & Management* 43, no. 6 (February 21, 2023): 567–75. https://doi.org/10.1080/09540962.2023.2165275.
23. "The Fair Work Convention." Accessed August 26, 2023. https://www.fairworkconvention.scot/.
24. "Just Transition Commission." Accessed August 26, 2023. https://www.justtransition.scot/. https://www.justtransition.scot/.
25. Scottish Government. "Business Purpose Commission Report: Scottish Government Response," January 10, 2023. Accessed August 26, 2023. https://www.gov.scot/publications/business-purpose-commission-report-scottish-government-response/pages/5/.
26. Scottish Enterprise. "Co-Operative Development Scotland." Accessed August 26, 2023. https://www.scottish-enterprise.com/our-organisation/about-us/who-we-work-with/co-operative-development-scotland.
27. Scottish Enterprise. "Co-Operative Development Scotland."
28. Scottish Government. "Social Care." Accessed August 26, 2023. https://www.gov.scot/policies/social-care/; Scottish Government. "Frank's Law," September 7, 2017. Accessed September 13, 2023. https://www.gov.scot/news/franks-law/.
29. King's Fund. "A History of Social Care Funding Reform in England," May 4, 2023. Accessed August 26, 2023. https://www.kingsfund.org.uk/audio-video/short-history-social-care-funding.
30. Musa, Amanda. "The Cost of Senior Care Is Rising While Caregivers Are 'Drowning' Without Help." CNN, April 20, 2023. Accessed August 26, 2023. https://www.cnn.com/2023/04/20/health/senior-care-cost/index.html.

31. Johnson, Richard W., Karen E. Smith, and Barbara A. Butrica. "Lifetime Employment-Related Costs to Women of Providing Family Care." Urban Institute, February 2023. Accessed August 28, 2023. https://www.dol.gov/sites/dolgov/files/WB/Mothers-Families-Work/Lifetime-caregiving-costs_508.pdf.
32. Schamis, Martin. "How to Restructure Your Assets to Qualify for Medicaid." Kiplinger.com, November 7, 2021. Accessed October 14, 2023. https://www.kiplinger.com/personal-finance/insurance/health-insurance/603705/how-to-restructure-your-assets-to-qualify-for.
33. Scottish Government. "Early Learning and Childcare Expansion." Accessed August 26, 2023. https://www.gov.scot/policies/early-education-and-care/early-learning-and-childcare/.
34. Scottish Government. "Christie Commission on the Future Delivery of Public Services," June 25, 2018. Accessed August 26, 2023. https://www.gov.scot/publications/commission-future-delivery-public-services/pages/2/.
35. Scottish Government, "Christie Commission on the Future Delivery of Public Services."
36. Bureau of Labor Statistics, U.S. Department of Labor. "Home Health and Personal Care Aides: Occupational Outlook Handbook," September 8, 2022. Accessed August 26, 2023. https://www.bls.gov/ooh/healthcare/home-health-aides-and-personal-care-aides.htm#tab-6.
37. ILF Scotland. "Scottish Social Care Wage Update 2023," March 31, 2023. Accessed August 26, 2023. https://ilf.scot/news-post/social-care-wage-update-2023/.
38. Scottish Government. "Migration Advisory Committee Call for Evidence—Impact of Ending Freedom of Movement on the Adult Social Care Sector: Scottish Government Response," February 25, 2022. Accessed August 26, 2023. https://www.gov.scot/publications/scottish-government-response-migration-advisory-committee-call-evidence-impact-ending-freedom-movement-adult-social-care-sector/pages/6/.
39. Living Wage Scotland. "ENABLE Scotland." Accessed August 26, 2023. https://scottishlivingwage.org/employer_profiles/enable-scotland/.
40. Payroll Centre. "Scottish Care Workers to Get Living Wage for Overnight Hours," October 31, 2017. Accessed August 26, 2023. https://www.thepayrollcentre.co.uk/news/scottish-care-workers-to-get-living-wage-for-overnight-hours/.
41. Enable Cares. "PA Model." Accessed August 26, 2023. https://www.enable.org.uk/enable-cares/about-our-services/pa-model.
42. Enable Scotland. "ENABLE Scotland Annual Review 2021–2022," 2022. Accessed August 26, 2023. https://media.enable.org.uk/media/qzdda0ce/enablescotland-annual-review-2122.pdf.
43. Lero, Donna, Carolyn Pletsch, and Margo Hilbrecht. "Introduction to the

Special Issue on Disability and Work: Toward Re-Conceptualizing the 'Burden' of Disability." *Disability Studies Quarterly* 32, no. 3 (2012). https://dsq-sds.org/index.php/dsq/article/view/3275/3108.

44. *Slate*. "By All Means Worry About the Future of Work, but Don't Stress About Robots," March 22, 2022. Accessed August 26, 2023. https://slate.com/podcasts/better-life-lab/2022/03/the-future-of-work-doesnt-have-to-be-apocalyptic.
45. Autor, David, David Mindell, and Elisabeth Reynolds. "The Work of the Future: Building Better Jobs in an Age of Intelligent Machines." MIT Task Force on the Work of the Future, November 17, 2020. Accessed April 9, 2023. https://workofthefuture.mit.edu/research-post/the-work-of-the-future-building-better-jobs-in-an-age-of-intelligent-machines/.
46. Economic Research Service, U.S. Department of Agriculture. "AG and Food Sectors and the Economy." Accessed August 26, 2023. https://www.ers.usda.gov/data-products/ag-and-food-statistics-charting-the-essentials/ag-and-food-sectors-and-the-economy.
47. UBS Center. "David Autor—The Work of the Future: Shaping Technology and Institutions," December 2, 2019. Accessed August 26, 2023. https://www.youtube.com/watch?v=0FbFjCmZQRM.
48. Federal Reserve Bank of Minneapolis. "Interview with David Autor," September 7, 2016. Accessed August 26, 2023. https://www.minneapolisfed.org/article/2016/interview-with-david-autor.
49. Bouie, Jamelle. "Republicans Have a Twisted View of the Safety Net." *New York Times*, June 2, 2023. Accessed August 26, 2023. https://www.nytimes.com/2023/06/02/opinion/republicans-safety-net-medicaid.html. https://www.nytimes.com/2023/06/02/opinion/republicans-safety-net-medicaid.html.
50. Bregman, Rutger. "The Bizarre Tale of President Nixon and His Basic Income Bill." *The Correspondent*, May 17, 2016. Accessed August 26, 2023. https://thecorrespondent.com/4503/the-bizarre-tale-of-president-nixon-and-his-basic-income-bill/173117835-c34d6145.
51. Bregman, "The Bizarre Tale of President Nixon and His Basic Income Bill."
52. *Slate*. "Guaranteed Basic Income Is Surprisingly Economical," May 10, 2022. Accessed August 26, 2023. https://slate.com/podcasts/better-life-lab/2022/05/guaranteed-basic-income-was-effective-and-economical-for-stockton-california.
53. Mayors for a Guaranteed Income. "Mayors for a Guaranteed Income." Accessed August 26, 2023. https://www.mayorsforagi.org/.
54. Ekins, Emily. "What Americans Think About Poverty, Wealth, and Work." Cato Institute, September 24, 2019. Accessed August 26, 2023. https://www.cato.org/publications/survey-reports/what-americans-think-about-poverty-wealth-work.
55. Ekins, "What Americans Think About Poverty, Wealth, and Work."

56. Mitchell, Travis. "Finding Meaning in What One Does." Pew Research Center's Global Attitudes Project, March 22, 2022. Accessed August 26, 2023. https://www.pewresearch.org/global/2021/11/18/finding-meaning-in-what-one-does/.
57. Lufkin, Bryan. "Stephen Hawking's Advice for a Fulfilling Career." BBC, March 14, 2018. Accessed August 28, 2023. https://www.bbc.com/worklife/article/20180314-stephen-hawkings-advice-for-a-fulfilling-career.
58. Lips-Wiersma, Marjolein, Catherine Bailey, Adrian Madden, and Lani Morris. "Why We Don't Talk About Meaning at Work." *MIT Sloan Management Review*, June 7, 2022. Accessed August 28, 2023. https://sloanreview.mit.edu/article/why-we-dont-talk-about-meaning-at-work/.
59. Graeber, David. *Bullshit Jobs: A Theory*. New York: Simon & Schuster, 2018, p. 245.
60. Herber, Gerrie-Cor, Annemarie Ruijsbroek, Marc Koopmanschap, Karin I. Proper, Fons van der Lucht, Hendriek C. Boshuizen, Johan Polder, and Ellen Uiters. "Single Transitions and Persistence of Unemployment Are Associated with Poor Health Outcomes." *BMC Public Health* 19, no. 740 (June 13, 2019). https://doi.org/10.1186/s12889-019-7059-8.
61. Policy Institute at King's College London. "A World Without Work," December 2, 2020. Accessed August 28, 2023. https://www.youtube.com/watch?v=7fBflGVOcqk; Suskind, Daniel. "Work and Meaning in the Age of AI." Center for Regulation and Markets at Brookings, January 2, 2023. Accessed August 28, 2023. https://www.brookings.edu/wp-content/uploads/2023/01/Work-and-meaning-in-the-age-of-AI_Final.pdf.
62. Gao, George. "How Do Americans Stand Out from the Rest of the World?" Pew Research Center, March 12, 2015. Accessed August 28, 2023. https://www.pewresearch.org/short-reads/2015/03/12/how-do-americans-stand-out-from-the-rest-of-the-world/.
63. Ekins, "What Americans Think About Poverty, Wealth, and Work."
64. Hoyt, Crystal L., Jeni L. Burnette, Rachel Forsyth, Mitchell Parry, and Brenten H. DeShields. "Believing in the American Dream Sustains Negative Attitudes Toward Those in Poverty." *Social Psychology Quarterly* 84, no. 3 (July 3, 2021): 203–15. https://doi.org/10.1177/01902725211022319.
65. Balevic, Katie, and Kenneth Niemeyer. "Republicans Vote Unanimously to Ban Basic Income Programs in a State with One of the Highest Homelessness Rates." *Business Insider*, February 24, 2024. Accessed February 25, 2024. https://www.businessinsider.in/politics/world/news/republicans-vote-unanimously-to-ban-basic-income-programs-in-a-state-with-one-of-the-highest-homelessness-rates/articleshow/107974829.cms#:~:text=The%20Arizona%20House%20of%20Representatives,the%20Republican%20majority%20voted%20unanimously.
66. Celniker, Jared, Andrew Gregory, Hyunjin J. Koo, Paul K. Piff, Peter H.

Ditto, and Azim F. Shariff. "The Moralization of Effort." *Journal of Experimental Psychology: General* 152, no. 1 (January 1, 2023): 60–79. https://doi.org/10.1037/xge0001259.

67. Celniker et al., "The Moralization of Effort."
68. Shariff, Azim. "Does Working Hard Really Make You a Good Person?" TED Talk, May 11, 2023. https://ed.ted.com/lessons/does-working-hard-really-make-you-a-good-person-azim-shariff.
69. Tugend, Alina. "Is Following Your Work Passion Overrated?" *New York Times,* August 7, 2023. https://www.nytimes.com/2023/08/03/business/work-passion-overrated.html.
70. Library of Congress, The Aesop for Children. "The Ant and the Grasshopper." Accessed August 28, 2023. https://read.gov/aesop/001.html.
71. Popova, Maria. "The Ant, the Grasshopper, and the Antidote to the Cult of More: A Lovely Vintage Illustrated Poem About the Meaning and Measure of Enough." The Marginalian, July 29, 2023. https://www.themarginalian.org/2023/07/29/john-j-plenty-fiddler-dan/.
72. Popova, "The Ant, the Grasshopper, and the Antidote to the Cult of More: A Lovely Vintage Illustrated Poem About the Meaning and Measure of Enough."
73. Taylor, Astra. "Why Does Everyone Feel So Insecure All the Time?" *New York Times,* August 20, 2023. Accessed August 26, 2023. https://www.nytimes.com/2023/08/18/opinion/inequality-insecurity-economic-wealth.html; Waterworks of Money. "Waterworks of Money." Accessed August 26, 2023. https://www.waterworksofmoney.com/.
74. Desmond, Matthew. *Poverty, by America*. New York: Random House large print, Crown, 2023, pp. 154–55.
75. Hunnicutt, Benjamin Kline. *Free Time: The Forgotten American Dream*. Philadelphia: Temple University Press, 2013.

Appendix I: How to Change: Tools and Strategies to Make Work Better

1. Schulte, Brigid. "How Busyness Leads to Bad Decisions." BBC Worklife, December 2, 2019. Accessed September 3, 2023. https://www.bbc.com/worklife/article/20191202-how-time-scarcity-makes-us-focus-on-low-value-tasks.
2. Schulte, "How Busyness Leads to Bad Decisions."
3. Holland, Kelley. "Division of Labor: Same-Sex Couples Better at Sharing Chores." NBC News, June 4, 2015. Accessed September 3, 2023. https://www.nbcnews.com/business/consumer/division-labor-same-sex-couples-more-likely-share-chores-study-n369921.
4. Solan, Matthew. "The Secret to Happiness? Here's Some Advice from the Longest-Running Study on Happiness." Harvard Health, October 5, 2017. Accessed September 3, 2023. https://www.health.harvard.edu/blog/the-secret-to-happiness-heres-some-advice-from-the-longest-running-study-on-happiness-2017100512543.

5. Good Jobs Institute. "Help Companies Thrive by Creating Good Jobs." Accessed September 3, 2023. https://goodjobsinstitute.org/.
6. Woolley, Anita, and Thomas Malone. "Defend Your Research: What Makes a Team Smarter? More Women." *Harvard Business Review,* June 2011. Accessed September 3, 2023. https://hbr.org/2011/06/defend-your-research-what-makes-a-team-smarter-more-women; Bear, Julia B., and Anita Williams Woolley. "The Role of Gender in Team Collaboration and Performance." *Interdisciplinary Science Reviews* 36, no. 2 (June 1, 2011): 146–53. https://doi.org/10.1179/030801811x13013181961473. https://www.pnas.org/doi/10.1073/pnas.0403723101.
7. Slack. "New Research Reveals Trust Is the Key Driver of Productivity." Slack, July 26, 2023. Accessed September 3, 2023. https://slack.com/blog/news/future-of-work-research-summer-2023.
8. Schwartz, Barry. *Why We Work.* TED Books. New York: Simon & Schuster, 2015, pp. 24–30.
9. Cappelli, Peter. "How Financial Accounting Screws Up HR." *Harvard Business Review,* January 2023. Accessed September 3, 2023. https://hbr.org/2023/01/how-financial-accounting-screws-up-hr?utm_medium=email&utm_source=newsletter_perissue&utm_campaign=bestofissue_activesubs_nondigital&deliveryName=DM236533.
10. Fuller, Joseph, and Manjari Raman. "The Caring Company: How Employers Can Cut Costs and Boost Productivity by Helping Employees Manage Caregiving Needs." Harvard Business School, January 17, 2019. Accessed April 19, 2023. https://www.hbs.edu/managing-the-future-of-work/research/Pages/the-caring-company.aspx.
11. Praslova, Ludmila N. "The Radical Promise of Truly Flexible Work." *Harvard Business Review,* August 15, 2023. Accessed September 3, 2023. https://hbr.org/2023/08/the-radical-promise-of-truly-flexible-work.
12. Gillespie, Lane, and Tori Rubloff. "Survey: 89% of American Workforce Prefer 4-Day Workweeks, Remote Work or Hybrid Work." Bankrate, August 23, 2023. Accessed September 3, 2023. https://www.bankrate.com/personal-finance/hybrid-remote-and-4-day-workweek-survey/; Wood, Johnny. "Hybrid Working: Why There's a Widening Gap Between Leaders and Employees." World Economic Forum, December 20, 2022. Accessed September 3, 2023. https://www.weforum.org/agenda/2022/12/hybrid-working-remote-work-office-senior-leaders/.
13. Yu, Qiuping. "How to Design Predictable Scheduling Laws That Not Only Benefit Workers but Also Firms' Bottom Line?" Brookings, August 10, 2023. Accessed September 3, 2023. https://www.brookings.edu/articles/how-to-design-predictable-scheduling-laws-that-not-only-benefit-workers-but-also-firms-bottom-line/.
14. Suddath, Claire. "Return-to-Work RTO Push by Male CEOs Harms Working Mothers." Bloomberg.com, August 31, 2023. Accessed September

3, 2023. https://www.bloomberg.com/news/newsletters/2023-08-31/return-to-work-rto-push-by-male-ceos-harms-working-mothers?cmpid=BBD083123_EQ&utm_medium=email&utm_source=newsletter&utm_term=230831&utm_campaign=equality.
15. Acemoglu, Daron, Andrea Manera, and Pascual Restrepo. "Does the US Tax Code Favor Automation?" NBER Working Paper Series, no. 27052 (April 2020). https://doi.org/10.3386/w27052.
16. New America. "The Future of Wellbeing in an Automated World," May 27, 2022. Accessed September 3, 2023. https://www.newamerica.org/better-life-lab/podcasts/the-future-of-wellbeing-in-an-automated-world/.

Appendix II: The Problem with Work Stress and How to Solve It

1. Schwartz, Jeff, Tom Hodson, and Ian Winstrom Otten. "The Overwhelmed Employee." Deloitte Insights, March 8, 2014. Accessed April 30, 2023. https://www2.deloitte.com/us/en/insights/focus/human-capital-trends/2014/hc-trends-2014-overwhelmed-employee.html.
2. Goh, Joel, Jeffrey Pfeffer, and Stefanos A. Zenios. "The Relationship Between Workplace Stressors and Mortality and Health Costs in the United States." *Management Science* 62, no. 2 (February 1, 2016): 608–28. https://doi.org/10.1287/mnsc.2014.2115.
3. Virtanen, Marianna, Stephen Stansfeld, Rebecca Fuhrer, Jane E. Ferrie, and Mika Kivimäki. "Overtime Work as a Predictor of Major Depressive Episode: A 5-Year Follow-Up of the Whitehall II Study." *PLOS One* 7, no. 1 (January 25, 2012): e30719. https://doi.org/10.1371/journal.pone.0030719.
4. Virtanen, Marianna, Jane E. Ferrie, Archana Singh-Manoux, Martin J. Shipley, Jussi Vahtera, Michael Marmot, and Mika Kivimäki. "Overtime Work and Incident Coronary Heart Disease: The Whitehall II Prospective Cohort Study." *European Heart Journal* 31, no. 14 (July 1, 2010): 1737–44. https://doi.org/10.1093/eurheartj/ehq124.
5. World Health Organization. "Long Working Hours Increasing Deaths from Heart Disease and Stroke: WHO, ILO," May 17, 2021. Accessed April 30, 2023. https://www.who.int/news/item/17-05-2021-long-working-hours-increasing-deaths-from-heart-disease-and-stroke-who-ilo.
6. Goh, Joel, Jeffrey Pfeffer, and Stefanos A. Zenios. "Workplace Stressors & Health Outcomes: Health Policy for the Workplace." *Behavioral Science & Policy* 1, no. 1 (Spring 2015): 43–52. https://behavioralpolicy.org/article/workplace-stressors-health-outcomes/.
7. Boyd, Danielle. "Workplace Stress." American Institute of Stress, February 15, 2023. Accessed April 30, 2023. https://www.stress.org/workplace-stress.
8. Moen, Phyllis, Anne Kaduk, Ellen Ernst Kossek, Leslie B. Hammer, Orfeu M. Buxton, Erin O'Donnell, David M. Almeida, et al. "Is Work-Family

Conflict a Multilevel Stressor Linking Job Conditions to Mental Health? Evidence from the Work, Family and Health Network." In *Emerald Group Publishing Limited EBooks*, 177–217. Emerald (MCB UP), 2015. https://doi.org/10.1108/s0277-283320150000026014.

9. Work, Family & Health Network. "Work, Family & Health Network," 2023. Accessed April 30, 2023. https://workfamilyhealthnetwork.org/.
10. Healthy Work Campaign. "Healthy Work Stats and Infographs." Accessed April 30, 2023. https://www.healthywork.org/resources/statistics-infographs/.
11. Finnigan, Ryan, and Jo Mhairi Hale. "Working 9 to 5? Union Membership and Work Hours and Schedules." *Social Forces* 96, no. 4 (June 1, 2018): 1541–68. https://doi.org/10.1093/sf/sox101.
12. Blanchflower, David G., and Alex Bryson. "Now Unions Increase Job Satisfaction and Well-Being." National Bureau of Economic Research Series, no. 27720 (August 2020). https://doi.org/10.3386/w27720.
13. Patel, Rikinkumar S., Ramya Bachu, Archana Adikey, Meryem Malik, and Mansi Shah. "Factors Related to Physician Burnout and Its Consequences: A Review." *Behavioral Sciences* 8, no. 11 (October 25, 2018): 98. https://doi.org/10.3390/bs8110098.
14. Jehan, Shazia, Ferdinand Zizi, Seithikurippu R. Pandi-Perumal, Alyson K. Myers, Evan Auguste, Girardin Jean-Louis, and Samy I. McFarlane. "Shift Work and Sleep: Medical Implications and Management." *Sleep Medicine and Disorders: International Journal* 1, no. 2 (October 6, 2017): 36–42. https://doi.org/10.15406/smdij.2017.01.00008. https://www.ncbi.nlm.nih.gov/pmc/articles/PMC5836745/.
15. Choi, BongKyoo, Peter L. Schnall, Marnie Dobson, Javier Garcia-Rivas, HyoungRyoul Kim, Frank Zaldivar, Leslie Israel, and Dean Baker. "Very Long (> 48 Hours) Shifts and Cardiovascular Strain in Firefighters: A Theoretical Framework." *Annals of Occupational and Environmental Medicine* 26, no. 1 (March 6, 2014). https://doi.org/10.1186/2052-4374-26-5.
16. Harknett, Kristen, Daniel Schneider, and Véronique Irwin. "Improving Health and Economic Security by Reducing Work Schedule Uncertainty." *Proceedings of the National Academy of Sciences* 118, no. 42 (October 19, 2021). https://doi.org/10.1073/pnas.2107828118.
17. Aronsson, Gunnar, Töres Theorell, Tom Grape, Anne Hammarström, Christer Hogstedt, Ina Marteinsdottir, Ingmar Skoog, Lil Träskman-Bendz, and Charlotte Hall. "A Systematic Review Including Meta-Analysis of Work Environment and Burnout Symptoms." *BMC Public Health* 17, no. 1 (March 16, 2017). https://doi.org/10.1186/s12889-017-4153-7.
18. Landsbergis, Paul, Marnie Dobson, George W. Koutsouras, and Peter L. Schnall. "Job Strain and Ambulatory Blood Pressure: A Meta-Analysis and Systematic Review." *American Journal of Public Health* 103, no. 3 (February 6, 2013): e61–71. https://doi.org/10.2105/ajph.2012.301153.

19. Theorell, Töres, Katarina Jood, Lisbeth Slunga Järvholm, Eva Vingård, Joep Perk, Per Olof Östergren, and Charlotte Hall. "A Systematic Review of Studies in the Contributions of the Work Environment to Ischaemic Heart Disease Development." *European Journal of Public Health* 26, no. 3 (June 1, 2016): 470–77. https://doi.org/10.1093/eurpub/ckw025.
20. Theorell, Töres, Anne Hammarström, Gunnar Aronsson, Lil Träskman-Bendz, Tom Grape, Christer Hogstedt, Ina Marteinsdottir, Ingmar Skoog, and Charlotte Hall. "A Systematic Review Including Meta-Analysis of Work Environment and Depressive Symptoms." *BMC Public Health* 15, no. 1 (August 1, 2015). https://doi.org/10.1186/s12889-015-1954-4.
21. Theorell et al., "A Systematic Review Including Meta-Analysis of Work Environment and Depressive Symptoms."
22. Wigger, Erin. "Surface Acting and Deep Acting: Emotional Labor and Burnout in Firefighters." Unhealthy Work, May 27, 2011. Accessed April 30, 2023. https://unhealthywork.org/emotionallabor/emotional-labor/.
23. Healthy Work Campaign. "Healthy Work Survey—Individuals," January 6, 2022. Accessed April 30, 2023. https://www.healthywork.org/healthy-work-survey-individuals/.
24. Healthy Work Campaign. "Research." Accessed April 30, 2023. https://www.healthywork.org/resources/research/.
25. Ferrie, Jane E. "Is Job Insecurity Harmful to Health?" *Journal of the Royal Society of Medicine* 94, no. 2 (February 1, 2001): 71–76. https://doi.org/10.1177/014107680109400206.
26. Kivimäki, Mika, Jussi Vahtera, Jaana Pentti, and Jane E. Ferrie. "Factors Underlying the Effect of Organisational Downsizing on Health of Employees: Longitudinal Cohort Study." *BMJ* 320, no. 7240 (April 8, 2000): 971–75. https://doi.org/10.1136/bmj.320.7240.971.
27. Tugend, Alina. "Uncertainty About Jobs Has a Ripple Effect." *New York Times,* May 16, 2014. Accessed April 30, 2023. https://www.nytimes.com/2014/05/17/your-money/uncertainty-about-jobs-has-a-ripple-effect.html?ref=business&_r=2.
28. Ball, Kirstie S. "The Harms of Electronic Surveillance in the Workplace." PEN America, February 20, 2014. Accessed April 30, 2023. https://pen.org/the-harms-of-electronic-surveillance-in-the-workplace/.
29. Healthy Work Campaign, "Research."
30. Malinauskienė, Vilija, Palmira Leišytė, and Romualdas Malinauskas. "Psychosocial Job Characteristics, Social Support, and Sense of Coherence as Determinants of Mental Health Among Nurses." *Medicina-Lithuania* 45, no. 11 (January 1, 2009): 910. https://doi.org/10.3390/medicina45110117.
31. Odle-Dusseau, Heather N., Leslie B. Hammer, Tori L. Crain, and Todd Bodner. "The Influence of Family-Supportive Supervisor Training on Employee Job Performance and Attitudes: An Organizational Work–

Family Intervention." *Journal of Occupational Health Psychology* 21, no. 3 (July 1, 2016): 296–308. https://doi.org/10.1037/a0039961.

32. American Psychological Association. "Stress About Health Insurance Costs Reported by Majority of Americans, APA Stress in America™ Survey Reveals," January 24, 2018. Accessed April 30, 2023. https://www.apa.org/news/press/releases/2018/01/insurance-costs.
33. McWilliams, J. Michael. "Health Consequences of Uninsurance Among Adults in the United States: Recent Evidence and Implications." *Milbank Quarterly* 87, no. 2 (June 1, 2009): 443–94. https://doi.org/10.1111/j.1468-0009.2009.00564.x.
34. Carroll, Aaron E. "The Real Reason the U.S. Has Employer-Sponsored Health Insurance." *New York Times*, September 5, 2017. Accessed April 30, 2023. https://www.nytimes.com/2017/09/05/upshot/the-real-reason-the-us-has-employer-sponsored-health-insurance.html.
35. Merelli, Annalisa. "The Only Reason More Americans Haven't Quit Their Jobs Is Healthcare." *Quartz*, November 2, 2021. Accessed April 30, 2023. https://qz.com/2082849/one-in-three-americans-would-quit-if-it-wasnt-for-healthcare.
36. KFF. "2022 Employer Health Benefits Survey—Summary of Findings," October 22, 2022. Accessed April 30, 2023. https://www.kff.org/report-section/ehbs-2022-summary-of-findings/.
37. Gallo, William T., Hsun-Mei Teng, Tracy Falba, Stanislav V. Kasl, Harlan M. Krumholz, and Elizabeth H. Bradley. "The Impact of Late Career Job Loss on Myocardial Infarction and Stroke: A 10 Year Follow Up Using the Health and Retirement Survey." *Occupational and Environmental Medicine* 63, no. 10 (October 1, 2006): 683–87. https://doi.org/10.1136/oem.2006.026823.
38. Preidt, Robert. "After Job Loss, People Report More Health Issues." ABC News, May 9, 2009. Accessed April 30, 2023. https://abcnews.go.com/Health/Healthday/story?id=7540442&page=1.
39. Sullivan, Daniel C., and Till Von Wachter. "Job Displacement and Mortality: An Analysis Using Administrative Data." *Quarterly Journal of Economics* 124, no. 3 (August 1, 2009): 1265–306. https://doi.org/10.1162/qjec.2009.124.3.1265.
40. Ramchand, Rajeev, Lynsay Ayer, and Stephen O'Connor. "Unemployment, Behavioral Health, and Suicide." *Health Affairs*, April 7, 2022. Accessed April 30, 2023. https://doi.org/10.1377/hpb20220302.274862.
41. Laditka, James N., and Sarah B. Laditka. "Unemployment, Disability and Life Expectancy in the United States: A Life Course Study." *Disability and Health Journal* 9, no. 1 (January 1, 2016): 46–53. https://doi.org/10.1016/j.dhjo.2015.08.003.
42. De Witte, Melissa. "What Explains Recent Tech Layoffs, and Why Should We Be Worried?" Stanford News, December 5, 2022. Accessed April 30,

2023. https://news.stanford.edu/2022/12/05/explains-recent-tech-layoffs-worried/.

43. Knowledge at Wharton. "How Layoffs Hurt Companies," April 6, 2016. Accessed April 30, 2023. https://knowledge.wharton.upenn.edu/article/how-layoffs-cost-companies/.
44. Economic Policy Institute. "Reforming Unemployment Insurance: Stabilizing a System in Crisis and Laying the Foundation for Equity," June 2021. Accessed April 30, 2023. https://www.epi.org/publication/unemployment-insurance-reform/.
45. Kornfield, Meryl. "A City Gave People $500 a Month, No Strings Attached, to Fight Poverty. It Paid Off, Study Says." *Washington Post*, March 4, 2021. Accessed April 30, 2023. https://www.washingtonpost.com/nation/2021/03/03/stockton-universal-basic-income/.
46. Bregman, Rutger. "The Bizarre Tale of President Nixon and His Basic Income Bill." *The Correspondent*, May 17, 2016. Accessed April 30, 2023. https://thecorrespondent.com/4503/the-bizarre-tale-of-president-nixon-and-his-basic-income-bill/173117835-c34d6145.

ACKNOWLEDGMENTS

This book has been a decade-long labor of both labor and love, and simply would not exist without the help, belief, trust, and support of so many people from so many walks of life. It is, first, a book of ideas about how work, care, family, and home can be better, and I am grateful to the many writers, researchers, and thinkers whose books, papers, and articles line my bookshelves, are stuffed into my physical and virtual filing cabinets, and tower in stacks on my floor. Special thanks to Jan Lucassen and his *Story of Work*, which, in a particularly muddy reporting period, gave me the clarity I needed to keep going. It is also a book of stories of the people who are striving to bring many of those ideas to life. I am humbled by and grateful for the many people who've taken time out of their busy and often chaotic lives and entrusted me with theirs.

Gail Ross is an agent and a friend who, from our very first conversation over lunch, believed I was onto something, and then was willing to wait, and wait, and wait, until I could carve out the time to begin putting it all together. Thank you for your well-timed e-mail nudges over the years that gave me just enough push to persevere. Sarah Crichton, my beloved editor of *Overwhelmed*, I thank you for taking a chance on me again with *Over Work*. When the pandemic hit in March 2020 just as I sat down to write, you gave me the grace and time to keep reporting to see how this global phenomenon could reshape the future of work and care. And when your own care responsibilities required you to step back from work, thank you for the gift of Riva Hocherman. Riva, you are a dream editor and coconspirator and I am grateful for how you have made this book so much better than I could have imagined. I also have to credit Gail with the title—a reflection of how we were all feeling fried around the edges as the pandemic eased and ready for something new. Thanks to the editing, publicity, and marketing teams at Holt, including Clarissa Long, Amber Cherichetti, Alex Foster, and Hannah Campbell, for all their help in getting this book, its argument for why work must change, and its hopeful message that it can, out into the world. A thousand thanks to Madysen Luebke for terrifyingly thorough fact-checking and Allison Dunatchik for saving me hours of time formatting all the citations—and thanks to Elissa Strauss and Jerry Jacobs for the introductions.

I want to thank my colleagues and editors at both the *Washington Post*, where I began to report and write about these themes of work and care, and at New America, where, with the support of leaders like Anne-Marie Slaughter, Paul Butler, Mark Schmitt, Kevin Carey, Barry Howard, Cecilia Muñoz, Tara McGuinness, and Tyra Mariani, the Better Life Lab Advisory Council, and our funders and partners, I've had the opportunity over the years to dive in even further. I'm especially grateful to the Better Life Lab team, not only for their belief in and support for me and this book project but for their passion, dedication, and great work to further our mission of advancing work-family justice and gender equity and elevating the value of care. Haley Swenson, Alieza Durana, Elizabeth Weingarten, Jane Carr, Amanda Lenhart, Vicki Shabo, Rebecca Gale, Katherine Goldstein, Julia Craven, Jasmine Heyward, Keisha Dixon, Sade Bruce, Jahdziah St. Julien, Ai Binh Ho, Roselyn Miller, Mahogani Harper, Emily Hallgren, Leah Crowder, Stavroula Pabst, Marni Fritz, Maggie Hennessy, and Elizabeth Morehead, you have made the work worthwhile as well as joyful. Thanks, too, to my colleagues in the Family Economic Security and Wellbeing cluster, and the many advocates, activists, and scholars I have had the privilege to work with and learn from, especially my friends and colleagues at ideas42, Dan Connolly, Uyun Ung, Antonia Violante, and Matthew Darling. I want to give a special shout-out to David Schulman, podcast producer and friend, who has worked magic on my rambling interviews to make the Better Life Lab podcast a resonant exploration of how work shapes our lives and the art and science of living a full life. Thanks, too, to the podcast team at *Slate* over the years, including Steve Lickteig, Gabe Roth, and Alicia Montgomery.

I also want to thank the many editors I've worked with over the years as I reported and sorted out these ideas, including at the *Washington Monthly*, *Harvard Business Review*, *Financial Times*, *New York Times*, *Washington Post*, *Slate*, *Vox*, CNN, *Fast Company*, *New York* magazine, BBC, and the *Guardian*. I'm also grateful to the Solutions Journalism Network and their research-based approach to reporting on challenging issues, and the best advice I ever got, from Dan Heath at a conference ages ago: focus on the bright spots where change, no matter how small, is already underway. That's what gave me the idea to focus on change agents in this book, and also gave me the hope and inspiration I needed to continue looking beneath and challenging the seemingly intractable status quo. I'm so grateful to the many thinkers, researchers, scholars, advocates, and others whose names may not appear in the book, but whose work, time, thinking, and generous conversations over the years helped shape it, including Heejung Chung, Leah Ruppanner, Ellen Ernst Kossek, Liana Christin Landivar, Katie Milkman, Julia Hobsbawn, Kevin Delaney, Lynne Curran, Lynn Roseberry, Marissa Korbel, Jessica DeGroot of ThirdPath Institute, Jon Messenger with the ILO, Eileen McNeely of SHINE at Harvard, Michael Leiter, the researchers with NIOSH's Total Worker Health and the American Psychological Association's Work, Stress, and Health conference, Cynthia Calvert, Juliana Franco, Rebecca Pontikes, Elizabeth Gedmark at A Better Balance, and so many more.

This book belongs in the best sense to the workers, believers, evangelists, and change agents I spent time with. I owe enormous thanks to Kari McCracken, Kiarica Schields, Joe Liebman, Adia Harvey Wingfield, Dave Regan, Peter Schnall, Marnie Dobson, Jeff Pfeffer, Corey Feist, Erin Kelly, Leslie Hammer, and other WFHN researchers, Slack Future Forum's Brian Elliott and Sheela Subramanian, and the visionaries at Intel's now-defunct Freelance Nation—I hope sharing your story now will finally have been worth the wait. Thanks to my friend and mentor Joan Williams, and to Jessica Lee of the Center for WorkLife Law and all the connections they made for me to the people and attorneys fighting against caregiver discrimination, including Lindsey Smith. Thanks to Christy Johnson of Artemis Connection for her keen insights into work culture, and for connecting me to people like Natalie Orozco. Mark Attico, I am so grateful you answered my reporter call-out on Twitter/X about men and care. Your story continues to inspire me.

I want to thank Carrie Gleason, Rachel Deutsch, and Francisco Diez of the Center for Popular Democracy, who have done so much to educate me and have graciously connected me to workers willing to share their stories over the years. Thanks to SEIU 775 leaders in Washington State and Brittany Williams, who appeared on my pandemic-era Crisis Conversations podcast and, once the tape stopped rolling, mentioned how her mother, Danielle, had such a different experience as a home care worker because she lived in a right-to-work state. Brittany and Danielle have since become valued partners and advisers. Thanks to the amazing work of Danny Schneider and Kristen Harknett of the Shift Project, and their generosity in freely sharing their data and findings on chaotic scheduling in the hopes of making change, and to Sarita Gupta and José Garcia for sharing good jobs innovations. Special thanks to Adrian Ugalde, Ashley Worthen, Onie Patrick, Sam Hughes, and the hourly workers who've shared their struggles and their fight for something better. Onie, you brought me to tears when I was fact-checking the book with you and you said, "I finally feel seen." I'm grateful to Warren Valdmanis and Zeynep Ton and her amazing team at the Good Jobs Institute, including Sarah Kalloch and Amanda Silver, for sharing their work, time, and ideas.

I'm thankful for all I've learned from Christine, Jeff, Malissa Clark, and those struggling with workaholism. I wish us all strength and hope. Thanks, also, to Lonnie Golden, my go-to source for understanding the vagaries of labor history and law.

The opportunity to report about karoshi in Japan and the effort to push against entrenched overwork culture would not have been possible without the Social Science Research Council and the Abe Fellowship for Journalists. I owe a huge debt to Linda Grove, who brought some Japanese gender equality scholars to present their work to my team at New America and suggested that I should apply. Thanks to SSRC's Nicole Restrick Levit and Briyanna Brinson for their continued help, support, and friendship. Once in Japan, this chapter would never have been written without my brilliant translator and friend, Chie Matsumoto. Even when I was back in the States, she gamely helped arrange and translate interviews over Zoom so I could capture pandemic disruptions and make sure my reporting was up to date. Her passion for workers and pushing for a culture that enables people to live fully is infectious. I'm grateful to old friends who shared valuable insights, including Seigo Nishida, Paul

Linehan, and Yasuko Hirahara, as well as Makoto Iwahashi, Ryusuke Komura, Glen Wood, Helen Bentley, Tetsuya Ando, and many others. I am also grateful to Machiko Osawa, Setsuya Fukuda, Scott North, and Hiroshi Ono for patiently sharing their deep expertise on work culture, gender roles, and intricate labor policies. Thanks to the karoshi victims' family members, including Noriko Nakahara, Emiko Teranishi, and many others, who shared their time, pain, and determination to fight. Heartfelt thanks to Yuko and Tsuyoshi Mori, for revisiting the most agonizing episode of their lives to share their daughter Mina's story with me in the hopes it will spur those in power to change.

In Iceland, enormous thanks to Sonja Thorbergsdóttir, who knows just about everyone in the country, and who generously introduced me to them all, including Prime Minister Katrín Jakobsdóttir. To the PM—thank you for graciously meeting with me and serving me delicious coffee, even when I showed up rain soaked, lost, and late. I am so grateful to all those who opened their homes, cooked fabulous meals, and shared their stories, including Trausti Jónsson, Halldóra Gunnarsdóttir, Hreinn Hreinsson, and Arna Hrönn Aradóttir. Thanks to author Alex Pang for giving me the idea and for connecting me to Sonja in the first place, and to Kyle Lewis and the Autonomy team. In Scotland, I am indebted to Theresa Shearer, Richard Baker, and all the social care workers and their clients at Enable who generously spent time with me. Special thanks to Joyce and Catherine and her caregivers, and to John Summers. I'm grateful for the many conversations with Peter Kelly, Sarah Deas, Roz Foyer, Patricia Findlay, Noel Dolan, Nikki Slowey, Michael Cook, Andrew Wilson, Anna Ritchie Allan, Bonnie Clark, Stephen Boyd, Francis Stuart, Guy Daucey, Ian MacWhirter, Jane Miller, Hannah Tweed, Joe Cullinane, Kristy Innes, Emily Thomson, Eilidh Dickson, Carrie Exton of OECD, and for a day spent with MSP Paul McLellan. Thanks, too, to Amanda Janoo, Katherine Trebek, and Jimmy Paul of the Wellbeing Economy Alliance, and to my New Practice Lab at New America colleague Elizabeth Garlow for educating me and opening my eyes to a completely new way of thinking about the purpose of an economy—and helping me do the reporting that showed it in action.

I am so grateful for Jenny Heimberg, my dear friend and running/walking partner, who has spent many miles over the past ten years patiently listening to me wrestle with these ideas, manage my anxiety over not writing sooner, and struggle with my own workaholic tendencies, and who read every early chapter, some several times over, and offered invaluable perspective. Thank you for the gift of your magical oasis in Tennessee on the Clinch River, where I finally had the time and space to put it all down on paper. Thank you to Marcia Call, an unshakable friend and force of nature who read early drafts, helped me untangle awkward prose, and edited like a pro. Thanks to Mary Huber for her eagle eye. I am grateful to my wise and kind sister Mary Nelson, and soul sister, Meg Connelly, for their regular mental health check-ins. Thanks to my sister, Claire Schulte, and to my mom, Ruth Schulte, and my extended Wyoming family for their love and care. Thank you to my Del Rey community, who came together to support me and my family at a particularly difficult time, as I was recovering from shoulder surgery and trying to finish writing the book in a bulky sling. Thanks to the eeBoo puzzles and Spotify's Deep Focus playlist that kept me on track writing in pulses and breaks. I am blessed by my daughter, Tessa Bowman, who carefully read drafts and offered insights, encouragement, and suggestions, including sharing the Crystal Eastman essay that I love. Thanks to my son, Liam Bowman, for bringing me decaf almond milk lattes in the mornings, and for sharing his love of literature and good writing. To my husband, Tom Bowman, thank you for your love and understanding, for being my partner, for cooking me dinner every night, for pushing me to make my case, even when it made me cranky, and for giving me grace every time I turned down the offers to spend time together so I could toil in my office. Now, it's time to play.

INDEX

ABOUT THE AUTHOR

Brigid Schulte is the author of the bestselling *Overwhelmed: Work, Love, and Play When No One Has the Time* and an award-winning journalist formerly for the *Washington Post,* where she was part of a team that won a Pulitzer Prize. She is also the director of the Better Life Lab, the work-family justice and gender equity program at New America. She lives in Alexandria, Virginia, with her husband and two children.